AWAKENING AND INSIGHT

Buddhism first came to the West many centuries ago through the Greeks, who also influenced some of the culture and practices of Indian Buddhism. As Buddhism has spread beyond India it has always been affected by the indigenous traditions of its new homes. When Buddhism appeared in America and Europe in the 1950s and 1960s, it encountered contemporary psychology and psychotherapy, rather than religious traditions. Since the 1990s many efforts have been made by Westerners to analyse and integrate the similarities and differences between Buddhism and its therapeutic ancestors, particularly Jungian psychology.

Taking Japanese Zen Buddhism as its starting point, this volume is a collection of critiques, commentaries, and histories about a particular meeting of Buddhism and psychology. It is based on the Zen Buddhism and Psychotherapy conference that took place in Kyoto, Japan, in 1999, expanded by additional papers, and includes:

- New perspectives on Buddhism and psychology, East and West
- Cautions and insights about potential confusions
- Traditional ideas in a new light

It also features a new translation of the conversation between Shin'ichi Hisamatsu and Carl Jung, which took place in 1958.

Awakening and Insight expresses a meeting of minds, Japanese and Western, in a way that opens new questions about, and sheds new light on, our subjective lives. It will be of great interest to students, scholars and practitioners of psychotherapy, psychoanalysis, and analytical psychology, as well as anyone involved in Zen Buddhism.

Polly Young-Eisendrath is Clinical Associate Professor of Psychiatry at the University of Vermont Medical College and a psychologist and Jungian analyst practicing in central Vermont, USA.

Shoji Muramoto is Professor of Foreign Studies at Kobe City University in Kobe, Japan, and a psychologist.

Contributors: Christa W. Anbeek, Peter A. De Groot, James W. Heisig, Enko Else Heynekamp, Katherine V. Masis, Dale Mathers, Jan Middeldorf, Melvin E. Miller, Shoji Muramoto, Akira Onda, Moriya Okano, Richard K. Payne, Jeff Shore, Haya Tatsuo, Adeline van Waning, Polly Young-Eisendrath.

Awakening and Insight

Zen Buddhism and Psychotherapy

Edited by
Polly Young-Eisendrath
and Shoji Muramoto

First published 2002 by Brunner-Routledge
27 Church Road, Hove, East Sussex BN3 2FA

Simultaneously published in the USA and Canada
by Taylor & Francis Inc
29 West 35th Street, New York, NY 10001

Brunner-Routledge is an imprint of the Taylor & Francis Group

Typeset in Times by
M Rules
Printed and bound in Great Britain by
TJ International Ltd, Padstow, Cornwall

British Library Cataloguing in Publication Data
A catalogue record for this book is available from the British Library

Library of Congress Cataloging in Publication Data
Awakening and insight: Zen Buddhism and psychotherapy/edited by
Polly Young-Eisendrath and Shoji Muramoto.
    p. cm.
  Includes bibliographical references and index.
    1. Psychotherapy—Religious aspects—Buddhism
    2. Psychotherapy—Religious aspects—Zen Buddhism.
    3. Buddhism—Psychology. I. Young-Eisendrath, Polly, 1947–II.
  Muramoto, Shoji.
BQ4570.P76 A98 2002
294.3′375—dc21

                                                    2001043332

ISBN 0-415-21793-8 (hbk)
ISBN 0-415-21794-6 (pbk)

CONTENTS

CONTENTS

ACKNOWLEDGEMENTS

This book is mainly based on a Kyoto seminar on Zen Buddhism and Depth Psychology held in May 1999 and sponsored by the International Research Institute for Zen Buddhism, Hanazono University.

The following chapters have been published before and are reproduced here with permission from the publishers;

Chapter 1, 'Buddhism, religion and psychotherapy in the world today' by Shoji Muramoto was originally published in *Psychologia,* published by Kyoto University.

Chapter 2, 'A Buddhist model of the human self: working through the Jung–Hisamatsu discussion' by Jeff Shore – an earlier version of this paper, in Japanese, first appeared in *Kikan Bukkyou* [Quarterly Buddhism], volume 48, published by Hozokan Publishing Company.

Chapter 3, 'Jung, Christianity, and Buddhism' by James W. Heisig, from *Bulletin of the Nanzan Institute for Religion and Culture.*

Chapter 4, 'The transformation of human suffering: a perspective from psychotherapy and Buddhism' by Polly Young-Eisendrath – an earlier version of this paper appeared, in Japanese, in *Kikan Bukkyou* [Quarterly Buddhism], volume 48, published by Hozokan Publishing Company.

Chapter 7, 'The Jung–Hisamatsu conversation' translated from Aniela Jaffés's original German protocol by Shoji Muramoto in collaboration with Polly Young-Eisendrath and Jan Middeldorf from *C.G. Jung im Gespräch* edited by L. Fischli and Robert Hinshaw, first published by Daimon Verlag, Zürich, 1986.

Chapter 8, 'Jung and Buddhism' by Shoji Muramoto, from *Studies of the International Research Institute for Zen Buddhism*, volume 6, 1998, published by the International Research Institute for Zen Buddhism, Hanazono University.

Chapter 9, 'What is I?' by Hayao Kawai from *Buddhism and the Art of Psychotherapy*, published by Texas A & M University Press.

Chapter 12, ' Buddhism and psychotherapy in the West: Nishitani and dialectical behavior therapy' by Christa W. Anbeek and Peter A. De Groot from *Studies in Interreligious Dialogue*.

Chapter 14, 'The Consciouness-only School' by Moriya Okano originally appeared in *Toransu-pasonaru Shinrigaku Nyumon* [An Introduction to Transpersonal Psychology] edited by Yoshihiko Morotomi, published by Nippon Hyoron-sha.

Note

Our use of diacritical marks on non-English words varies from chapter to chapter. Largely, we have adopted a policy of not adding diacritical marks to non-English words or names because the text looks cleaner and this is not a technical book on Buddhism in which Sanskrit terms would be used precisely. Adding or eliminating diacritical marks in the process of editing can lead to error and misreading. For this reason we have also decided to let stand the uses of these marks among those authors who used them in the first place, but not to add them to other papers where the same terms were used.

CONTRIBUTORS

Christa W. Anbeek is Assistant Professor of Religious Studies at the Catholic Theological Faculty in Utrecht, the Netherlands. She also works as a chaplain at the Psychiatric Hospital 'Veldwijk' in Ermelo, the Netherlands.

Peter A. de Groot is a psychiatrist at the Psychiatric Hospital 'Veldwijk' in Ermelo, the Netherlands.

Tatsuo Haya is Professor at Aomori Public University, specializing in Indian philosophy and Buddhism, and is a member of the Japanese Association of Indian and Buddhist Studies.

James W. Heisig is a permanent research fellow of the Nanzan Institute for Religion and Culture in Nagoya, Japan, where he has been since 1978 and which he served as director of from 1991–2001. His most recent book is *Philosophers of Nothingness: An Essay on the Kyoto School.*

Enko Else Heynekamp is a psychotherapist, psychoanalyst and Buddhist nun who lives and practices in Amsterdam, the Netherlands.

Hayao Kawai, is a Professor Emeritus at Kyoto University, the president of the Japan Society of Certified Clinical Psychologists and the Director-General of the Agency of Cultural Affairs of Japan. He has written and edited more than fifty books, including five books in English, including *The Japanese Psyche: Major Motifs in the Fairy Tales of Japan* (1988), *The Buddhist Priest Myoe: A Life of Dreams* (1992) and *Buddhism and the Art of Psychotherapy* (1996).

Katherine V. Masis worked as a translator for twelve years and taught philosophy for six years at the Universidad de Costa Rica in San Jose, Costa Rica, after which she began a career in psychotherapy. After a thirteen-year Zen practice, she has recently turned to Vipassana meditation and lives in Portland, Oregon. Her current interests include research on Buddhism in Latin America and inquiries into Buddhist child-rearing practices.

Dale Mathers is a Jungian psychoanalyst and a psychiatrist in private practice in London. He is an Associate member of the Association of Jungian Analysts, formerly of the British Association of Psychotherapy. He trained at St George's Hospital, London, and is a member of the Buddhist Society of London. His book, *Meaning and Purpose in Analytical Psychology*, was published by Routledge in 2000.

Jan Middeldorf is an instructor and training and supervising analyst at the Colorado Center for Modern Psychoanalytic Studies. He also maintains a private practice in Albuquerque, New Mexico. Among his interests are the study of narcissism and the formulation of an integrative psychoanalytic viewpoint.

Melvin Miller is a psychologist and relational psychoanalyst. He is Professor of Psychology, Director of Psychological Services, and Director of Doctoral training at Norwich University in central Vermont. He has a private practice, is on the editorial board of several journals, the author of many professional papers and chapters, and the editor of several books, including most recently, *The Psychology of Mature Spirituality*, with Polly Young-Eisendrath (Routledge, 2000). He has a long-time interest in Buddhism and philosophy.

Shoji Muramoto is Professor of Foreign Studies at Kobe City University. He has written widely on Jungian, Reichian and existential psychologies. http://www5d.biglobe.ne.jp/~shojimur/

Mariya Okano is Director of the Samgraha Institute for Psychological and Spiritual Studies, and is also a part-time lecturer at three universities.

Akira Onda is Professor Emeritus of Tokyo University and Honorary President of the Japan Creativity Society. He has written many books on the psychology of creativity, and the relationship between Enlightenment in Zen and creativity.

Richard K. Payne is Dean of the Institute of Buddhist Studies at the Graduate Theological Union, Berkeley. He specializes in the ritual practices of the Japanese Esoteric Buddhist tradition, Shingon, particularly the fire ritual (goma). In addition to studying the historical transmission of the goma from pre-Buddhist India to Japan, he is working on developing a cognitive theory of ritual.

Jeff Shore is a Professor of Zen Buddhism at Hanazono University in Kyoto, Japan. Originally from Philadelphia, he moved to Kyoto in 1981 where he has since lived and trained in Rinzai Zen monasteries. He has translated, written and lectured extensively on Zen thought and recently completed an anthology in English of works by Shin'ichi Hisamatsu.

Adeline van Waning is a psychiatrist and Freudian psychoanalyst. She is on the staff of Netherlands Psychoanalytic Institute and is a consultant for Health Services for Refugees, both in Amsterdam. She is also has a private practice and is the author of many papers and chapters. She is also a practitioner of Zen Buddhism.

Polly Young-Eisdendrath is Clinical Associate Professor of Psychiatry at the University of Vermont Medical College in Burlington, Vermont. A psychologist and Jungian psychoanalyst, she practices in central Vermont. She is the author and editor of many articles, chapters, and books. The most recent are *Women and Desire* and *The Cambridge Companion to Jung*. She is also a long-time student of Zen Buddhism and a recent student of Vipassana.

INTRODUCTION

CONTINUING A CONVERSATION FROM EAST TO WEST

Buddhism and Psychotherapy

Polly Young-Eisendrath and Shoji Muramoto

This collection of papers came into being largely as a beginning attempt to engage in a dialogue between a group of Western psychotherapists – mostly psychoanalysts (the majority Jungian) – and teachers and scholars of Japanese Zen Buddhism. The Westerners made the trip to Japan because of their gratitude for, and informed curiosity about, Zen Buddhism. The Japanese participants were interested in hearing from Western psychotherapists about their involvement with Zen because the Japanese were impressed with the fact of such an involvement. The Western participants were largely long-time practitioners of Buddhism (mostly Zen) – familiar with both psychotherapy and meditation – whereas the Japanese participants practiced *either* Zen *or* psychotherapy. This hidden and sometimes provocative difference between Western and Japanese participants was unknown until the conference was underway, but it became obvious in many group discussions in which Westerners were eager to ask questions about Zen practice and meaning, but the Japanese respondents could not relate their answers to any aspect of psychotherapy because they were not familiar with it. Nor did they seem curious about it.

When the conference was originally conceived, as we say below, we envisioned it as a highly select group of friends and colleagues from America and Japan coming together in Kyoto, to discuss Zen and psychotherapy. We thought that our psychotherapeutic focus would be on Carl Jung's psychology because we, the conference planners, both have considerable expertise in analytical psychology (Young-Eisendrath is a Jungian analyst and both of us are authors of books on Jung and his psychology) and Jung's depth psychology is better known in Japan than Freud's.

As things evolved, however, the conference grew by word of mouth until it included more than ninety participants from six countries: Japan, America, England, Belgium, Holland and Germany. Represented among the Western participants were both Jungian and Freudian analysts, as well as other kinds of therapists and a few non-therapists. Among the Japanese were psychologists and academics with a variety of approaches to psychology and psychotherapy, as well as Zen monks and scholars of Buddhism. There were also a number of American Zen monks and teachers participating in various ways, even in the unenviable role of translator (Japanese to English). Most of these people were Americans who now live in Japan because of their connection to Zen.

The formal conference was preceded by a four-day silent retreat (in the manner of a Zen sesshin). The retreat was held at a 530-year-old Zen monastery in the coastal mountains of central Japan and was attended by eighteen of the Western participants, led by Paul Haller, an American Zen teacher from San Francisco Zen Center.

As we say below, the focus of our conference and of the papers was opening a conversation about some of the insights, methods, and biases that emerge from Westerners and Japanese in relation to the subjects of Buddhism and psychotherapy. We hoped for true dialogue, but it was difficult to achieve. Partly this was due to language and cultural differences, but partly it was due to the foreignness of this type of conference for Japan.

Originally we thought that our scope of cultural interest would be Japan and America in relation to Zen and psychotherapy. Because our Western presenters and participants included people from Europe and England, and because the Buddhist topics went well beyond the confines of Zen, our focus expanded, but did not deepen. The papers show that our presenters varied greatly in their acquaintance with Buddhism (some practice it as a religion; others are scholars of it; others use aspects of Buddhist practice – for example, meditation – without practicing it as a religion). Similarly, there is a lot of variance of acquaintance with psychotherapy, psychoanalysis, and psychology.

This diversity, as well as the uniqueness of the conference, meant finally that the presenters did not share much common ground, with the exception of the American presenters who tended to know each other through their professional contacts. Even this similarity among the Americans lent nothing helpful to the dialogue because we Americans had come with the distinct desire to learn from our Japanese colleagues, not to huddle among ourselves. The difficulties of trying to understand each other, through translators and confusion and lack of common ground, was frustrating, but not undermining. Instead, good will, enthusiasm, shared warmth – even feelings of intimacy in being together in such a ground-breaking conference – were palpable at every moment. There was enormous excitement in feeling the respect we had for one another, while acknowledging the shadows of World War II still hanging over such meetings.

The nature of this extraordinary conference has both positive and negative effects on this volume of papers. On the positive side, it is an opportunity for readers to become acquainted with Japanese authors, and Americans living in Japan, who have a perspective that is deeply influenced by Japanese views. On the negative side, the papers do not appear to be responding to each other or deepening a dialogue. Rather, each paper stands somewhat alone in its perspective. This is especially true of the papers coming from Japan.

With all of this in mind, we would caution our readers not to judge too quickly what is being expressed here. Westerners now have access to many books about Buddhism and psychotherapy. Some readers may feel that nothing said here is 'new' or 'original,' but that would be a very narrow judgment. We recommend that you think of yourself meeting our Japanese and Dutch authors, and those Americans who live in Japan, as though you were listening to someone speaking in a foreign country, a context different from your own. Read carefully, try to see what is implied between the lines (so to speak), and then think about your own perspective on the issues. In Japan it would be considered extremely impolite to have even an academic conflict in a public conference. People do not engage in open conflicts, even about ideas. Ideas are offered with respect and are considered on their own merit. Respondents ask questions that expand or apply the ideas presented.

In the West, we tend to believe that only new or original thinking brings us forward in our understanding. We tend to look for such insights in reading. But we may then overlook how we can deepen by seeing things from a new angle, in a new light, although at first it seems that what is said is known to us, or at least that we have read it before. Please try to join us then in feeling the spirit of the conference and the challenge of the presenters – the authors here – of treading new ground together for the first time.

In the following remarks, we two editors speak individually and then join together to say something about how the conference was planned and evolved. These comments are meant to situate this book in the context of our experiences at the conference. We make no claims that these papers are comprehensive, in terms of a dialogue between Zen and psychotherapy. Rather, we believe that they are a good example of a first attempt to meet on Japanese soil to discuss some of the important ideas Western psychotherapists may have borrowed from Japanese Zen, as well as the perspective of our Japanese colleagues on the influences coming their way from the West.

YOUNG-EISENDRATH

Buddhism was introduced to the West many centuries ago, as early as the fifth century BCE, even before Alexander the Great came to India, where his followers remained after his death. As Buddhism traveled from India to other countries and cultures, as is well known, it blended with the indigenous religious practices of its new homes. When it came to Europe and America in the 1950s and 1960s, the fertile soil in which its roots were planted had been nourished largely by psychology and psychotherapy, rather than religion. Especially since the beginning of the 1990s, many efforts have been made to advance the differentiation and integration of Buddhism and its therapeutic ancestors in the West, especially in America (e.g. Meckel and Moore 1992;

Epstein 1995; Rubin 1996; Molino 1998; Welwood 2000) . Most of these efforts have been led by the therapeutic endeavor, that is, by the ways in which psychotherapists think and act from a therapeutic stance towards the ideas of Buddhism.

In some ways, this collection continues the same conversation. In some important ways, though, it has its own distinctive features, as we have said. In 1958, Professor Shin'ichi Hisamatsu of the famous Kyoto School of Philosophy at Kyoto University made a journey from Japan to the West in his own attempt to understand how contemporary Zen Buddhism might apply to certain Western disciplines, psychoanalysis being one of those. Among his various destinations was Zurich, Switzerland. In May of 1958, Professor Hisamatsu met with psychiatrist and psychoanalyst Carl Jung to speak with him directly about Jung's theory of an archetypal Self and to explore the similarities and differences between psychoanalysis and Zen, especially in regard to the alleviation of human suffering. In many ways, Hisamatsu was a radical and revisionist thinker – as well as a long-time Zen teacher – and he wanted to find out whether or not psychotherapy, as practiced in the West, had as its goal something akin to the extinction of suffering held out as an ideal for Zen practitioners.

In this volume, we present a new and revised translation (Muramoto, pp. 109–121) of this notorious meeting. Dr Hisamatsu and Dr Jung attempted to have a conversation about the matters at hand, but in fact the differences in their languages (neither spoke the other's native language) and their cultures have left us with a great deal of confusion and guessing about their access to each other's ideas. In fact, we know that they did not have a 'dialogue' because dialogue requires give and take, an attempt to understand the other's perspective, and a willingness to ask questions with an open mind. These conditions were not present in their conversation. All the same, their meeting opens up some important issues for those of us now wrestling with the fertile, but confusing, entanglement of Buddhism and psychotherapy in the twenty-first century. Several papers here (e.g. Shore, Heisig, Muramoto, and Payne) address themselves to various themes in the Hisamatsu–Jung meeting.

MEETING IN JAPAN: YOUNG-EISENDRATH AND MURAMOTO

On 24 May 1999, more than fifty people from America, Europe and Japan – psychotherapists, scholars, American and Japanese Zen monks and nuns, Jungian and Freudian psychoanalysts, and students of psychology and Zen – gathered for an opening ceremony of a unique five-day conference on Zen Buddhism and psychotherapy at a famous Rinzai Zen monastery, Myoshin-ji in Kyoto. Eighteen participants had earlier attended a four-day retreat held at Rinsoin, a Soto Zen temple in the mountains of central Japan. Rinsoin is headed by Abbot Hoitsu Suzuki-roshi, son of the late Shunryu Suzuki-roshi who was the founder of San Francisco Zen Center. Bringing together both Rinzai and Soto influences, kept apart as different Zen sects (much as various Protestant sects are kept apart in the West) in Japan, this conference was treading new ground.

In Kyoto at Reiun-in Temple in Myoshin-ji Temple, our special opening ceremony included a tour of Shunko-in Temple, where Hisamatsu had lived. We heard many stories and memories of his wonderful influence on countless people, including large numbers of Westerners (Americans especially) who were taught by Professor Masao Abe, a major disciple of Hisamatsu.

When the entire conference finally gathered to hear and discuss the presentations by our speakers, we had more than ninety people attending various events from case conferences to formal papers. At each session, there were two presenters, one from Japan and the other from a Western country, followed by impassioned discussion. It was our honor that Professor Abe was among our speakers, offering his paper on the self in Jung and Zen which is not included here because it is easily available elsewhere (e.g. Meckel and Moore 1992; Molino 1998). In all, we had about seventy Japanese participants and twenty-five from the US, Great Britain, and various parts of Europe. English was the language of the conference that included tours of several Rinzai monasteries, zazen at Ryosen-an Temple in Daitoku-ji Temple, a meeting with Professor Kawai at the International Research Center for Japanese Studies, and a visit to Hanazono University which offers basic studies for those who want to be Rinzai Zen priests, and was the main sponsor of the conference. Our daily conference meetings were held at a hall run by an Anglican church in Kyoto. Even with our team of about four very competent translators, we had many funny, frustrating, and complicated moments of not-knowing. For example, what is the Japanese word for 'deconstruction'?

For Japanese participants, this conference was perhaps the first occasion at which they encountered a context in which Buddhism and psychology had been combined by Westerners, a challenge to both psychology and Buddhism in Japan. In this regard, a comment by Zen priest Taiun Matsunami (from Ryosen-an) was illuminating. He said that modern Japanese Zen monks, unlike earlier ones, have generally spent so many years and so much energy getting *inka,* the certification for becoming a roshi, that they have little contact with the outside world and are often poorly equipped to face their own and their students' problems. In other words, in Zen training there is today a distinct absence of psychological knowledge.

This volume includes most of the papers given at the Kyoto conference. Unfortunately, a stimulating presentation on nirvanic substance by Kiyoshi Kato, a psychiatrist who is also a disciple of Hisamatsu, was not able to be included here. Three papers (Masís, Payne, and Heynekamp) have been added from people who wished they could have attended, but were unable. One paper (Anbeek and de Groot) was not able to be included in the conference program, although the authors were participants. Nevertheless, the intent of this volume is to reproduce the excitement (without the confusion and frustration) of a conference that was meant to be a continuation of a conversation that began in 1958.

Perhaps more important, this was an occasion of the West coming to the East. Those of us from America and Europe were looking to our Japanese colleagues for guidance. We came as questioners and seekers. We came in uncertainty and concern about whether we (many of us long-time practitioners of Buddhism) had been correct in making the assumptions that we had been making in comparing and contrasting Buddhism and psychotherapy.

And yet, surprisingly or perhaps not, Taitsu Kono-roshi – President of Hanazono University and Director of its International Research Institute for Zen Buddhism (IRIZ) – welcomed us with the statement that Japanese Zen Buddhism had become 'devitalized' and added that it was his hope that 'psychoanalysts coming from America and Europe' might revitalize it. He hoped that we could open new ways of thinking and speaking that might interest Japanese lay people anew in the practice of Zen. We Western practitioners of depth psychologies were keen to hear from Japanese Zen teachers, especially from those monks and nuns who might be interested in the conversation between psychology and Buddhism.

The Conference on Zen Buddhism and Psychotherapy was initially just a glint in the eyes of the two editors of this volume. When we first became acquainted in 1984 (Dr Muramoto translated from English into Japanese a book on Jung's psychology for couples written by Dr Young-Eisendrath), we were startled, even amazed, at the similarities in our interests: Jung's psychology, feminism, Buddhism, hermeneutic philosophy, and the confluence of East–West. Although we did not meet in person until 1996, we became very good friends through reading each other's work and corresponding. In 1996, Young-Eisendrath traveled to Kyoto for a visit and presentations that were hosted by Muramoto. At that time, we began to think about a special conference for our own friends and colleagues. That vision expanded to a formal program with many events. Our hopes and expectations for the conference also expanded. This volume is the final product of those hopes and expectations.

The assumptions that Japanese writers and practitioners of Zen bring to their essays are often quite different from the assumptions of our Western contributors, whether or not the latter practice some form of Buddhism. Asian philosophy and culture never endured an intellectual upheaval like the Cartesian split of mind and body that brought the so-called Enlightenment to the West. The consequent achievements of scientific method and the less fortunate by-products of secular self-interest together laid the groundwork, in Europe and America, for the personal psychology of psychoanalysis and psychotherapy.

Our Japanese colleagues take for granted a different perspective, whether or not they embrace it, in which mind and body, self and family, individual and group, life and death are fused or blurred or integrated in a way that is unknown among contemporary educated people in Europe and America. Our Japanese colleagues do not experience these dualities as split apart, rent asunder. Many of the concepts offered to any serious student of Buddhism, such as the teachings of karma and rebirth, stir consternation and discomfort in an educated Westerner, but seem familiar and comfortable (even if one disagrees with them) for an educated Japanese. The Westerner has to stretch her or his perspective on self–world and life–death to appreciate, much less practice, many fundamental Buddhist teachings. Consequently, the Westerner may find it useful, even comforting, to recast them somewhat in terms that are familiar from the personal psychology of psychotherapy which also deals with levels of subjective life and suffering.

On the other hand, the Japanese person has to stretch her or his perspective on self–world and life–death to appreciate, much less practice, many psychotherapeutic teachings about the importance of personal knowledge and insight without self-condemnation or shame. These differences are deep and difficult. They should not be quickly pushed aside in any desire to achieve a premature consensus about Buddhism and psychotherapy, even for the sake of trying to make sense of a particular moment – or a paper published here.

These are the differences that we encountered in our meetings in Japan in which we tried to speak together, through complicated translations of often technical terms, about the nature of human suffering and its alleviation. Whether we were discussing case material (e.g. transference and countertransference), personality theory (e.g. *yogacara* or the psychology of complexes or ego), we often were uncertain about our 'understanding' each other. And yet, we tried hard to reach that common ground from which a true dialogue can be launched. Still, it is uncertain whether a Japanese psychotherapist 'works with the transference' in the way an American psychoanalytic therapist might be trained to do. It is uncertain whether an American Zen teacher means the same thing by 'karma,' in casting it as intentional action and personal responsibility, as a Japanese Zen teacher would. It is even uncertain whether any of us at the conference could speak fully to people of a different language and background about the term 'unconscious' or 'unconsciousness.' We tried. But we may not have meant the same thing by the words we used. At times, these kinds of obvious and hidden differences seemed more than a little daunting.

On the other hand, the good will and strong positive intentions, as well as the times we spent meditating together, embraced us all throughout our time together. On one level, we did not seem to care whether or not we understood our words because we were so happy to meet, and to share our common concerns in an atmosphere of great respect for each other, true intellectual discipline, and genuine open-mindedness. We did not bring with us the fear and prejudice that Jung and Hisamatsu must have had to endure in their meeting with each other. At least, it seemed this way to this participant-observer. Overall, there was an atmosphere of pervading love for the practices that we shared, and ultimately for ourselves in our willingness to encounter the difficulties of trying to understand what had not previously been explored between Japanese and Westerners, especially concerning the more complex concepts of Buddhism and depth psychology.

There is one final bit of information that needs to be noted. For a variety of cultural reasons, some of which were alluded to in Professor Kawai's presentation (an informal talk that is not reproduced here), Jung's psychology takes precedence over Freud's psychology in the national character of Japan and its people. As Professor Kawai explained it, when Japanese psychologists and psychiatrists began to become acquainted with the depth psychologies that were coming from Europe, they quickly felt more at home with Jung's work. Jung gave primacy to the mother–child relationship and central focus to the 'mother complex' in the adult, especially the adult male. This immediately resonated for Japanese men and women. The Japanese mother tends to be a dominant force in the family system, although she has had little power in decision-making and status in the culture at large. Freud's concept of an Oedipus complex did not immediately make sense to Japanese men, who generally did not know their fathers well and respected them from a distance. The idea of a young son competing with the father to possess the mother just didn't make sense. A young son simply felt that he *possessed* his mother! No problem. The problems that might develop from this psychological situation as the son reached adolescence and adulthood, wanting to develop a family and place in the world of his own, seemed better mapped through the Jungian ideas of Mother and Child complexes, than through the Freudian notions of unresolved Oedipal conflicts. There were many other ways that Jung's psychology seemed a better fit than Freud's, not the least of which was Jung's theory of the archetypal Self or a universal organizing principle of subjectivity. This idea fits well with various aspects of Buddhism, especially as it has been shaped and practiced in Rinzai and Soto sects of Zen.

As we mentioned above, the conference was originally planned as a Jung–Buddhism event, but expanded over the course of its development as various Freudian and object-relational and interpersonal psychoanalysts heard about the event, and asked if they could attend. Both Young-Eisendrath and Muramoto have strong interests in object relations and interpersonal theories and practices of psychoanalysis. Young-Eisendrath's commitment to using the 'developmental approach' (see Young-Eisendrath and Dawson 1998 for a comprehensive review of the three Jungian schools or approaches) means that she practices a form of object-relational or intersubjective analytical psychology. Muramoto has also taken a keen interest in these aspects of analytical psychology as they also connect with his interest in constructivism and hermeneutical philosophy. These have much in common with contemporary Zen Buddhism, especially regarding perception and reality.

8

Thus, the reader might notice that, in addition to Zen Buddhism 'taking the lead' in the papers presented here, Jung's analytical psychology also takes the lead. And yet, one will also see that our contributors include Freudian and interpersonal psychoanalysts, as well as practitioners of object-relational approaches. And one paper deals with a contemporary cognitive-behavioral method, Dialectical Behavior Therapy, that was designed to incorporate various Buddhist ideas and methods. Overall, a reader interested in almost any aspect of the conversation between Zen Buddhism and psychotherapy will find something here that will bring new insights and raise new questions. Naturally, those readers who may be approaching this volume from religious studies will also find that many questions have been opened, and critiques offered, concerning the ongoing conversation between Zen Buddhism and Western religions, especially Christianity, because that encounter reflects, and is reflected by, many of the interests of psychotherapists.

We believe that we have achieved the basic groundwork for developing a true dialogue in future conferences. Although this volume and the Kyoto conference represent perhaps only the 'toe in the water' of true dialogue, they have been marked by a true open-mindedness. Our desire to understand each other and our deep love for our practices have joined us in a common effort. We have attempted to examine aspects of psychology and psychotherapy that concern the unconscious and its manifestations in light of the practices of Zen Buddhism. We have attempted to reveal and refine what we know about the transformation of human suffering through the formal relationship of therapist and client, as well as the formal relationship of Zen teacher and student. What we offer here is offered in this spirit and with the desire to carry the dialogue forward.

MURAMOTO

There is a saying that Buddhism is transmitted eastward. Apart from some historical evidence that it has also travelled westward, the history of Buddhism largely testifies to the saying. This is not only to say that the religion that originated in India was finally transmitted, via China and Korea, to Japan – the farthest eastern country in Asia, but that Buddhism crossed over the Pacific Ocean and reached further and further into America. As a world religion, Buddhism has no national boundaries, no formal center (like Rome, Jerusalem or Mecca), and pursues its inherent and universal logic of enlightenment.

On the other hand, no religion is more able than Buddhism to adjust to, and assimilate, the prevailing ideologies of its adopted cultures. The Buddhism of each country where it is practiced is characteristic of that society and culture: Indian Buddhism was speculative and logical through its interactions with Hindu philosophy; Chinese Buddhism was practical under the influence of Taoism and Confucianism; and Japanese Buddhism is aesthetic and merged with nature worship under the influence of Shintoism. American (and, to some extent, European) Buddhism seems to have developed against the background of psychology, as William James predicted a century ago. So it is misleading to have a monolithic conception of Buddhism. Buddhism in any society and culture expresses a very local character without necessarily having an interest in, or knowledge of, Buddhism in another place.

America is a country where Buddhism travelled westward across the Atlantic Ocean, as well as eastward across the Pacific. These two may be merging with one another, although there is still a gulf between the form of Buddhism practiced by immigrants from Asian countries (who largely came to the West Coast of America) and American converts (see Seager 1999: 233). And now, partly as a result of so many Americans coming to Japan to study and practice Buddhism, the Japanese may be about to experience American Buddhism imbued with psychology, psychoanalysis, feminism, and democracy. The Japanese also need to know how their ancestors, mostly practitioners of Shin Buddhism, have struggled to adapt their religion to the values and lifestyle of America since the 1870s.

I was born, raised, and have mostly been living and working in Japan. Buddhism here has for a long time been spiritually devitalized. People often take it for granted that it is only concerned with tourism and funeral ceremonies, both of which allow the Buddhist temples to secure a stable income. So the Japanese often consider Buddhism to be a business that has nothing to do with spirituality although this assessment also needs critical examination.

And as Gross (1993: 12) points out, unlike other Asian Buddhist countries, Japan has never adopted the ordination of nuns, and the male priests usually get married, are permitted to drink alcohol, and may have a more secularized lifestyle than Buddhist nuns would be permitted to have. Feminist theology in the West is unlikely to find in Japanese Buddhism a counterpart that could be called feminist or to be able to pursue a feminist approach to Buddhist studies, with a few exceptions.

It is interesting to see how many everyday Japanese words derive from Buddhism. For example, the word *ishiki*, a term that is currently translated as 'consciousness' in psychology, is a transliteration of a Chinese word that refers to *mano-vijnana*, a Buddhist term for a thought-conciousness, the sixth of eight conciousnesses. Without a cultural heritage of an accumulated fourteen centuries of Buddhist influences, Japan would have found it very difficult to interpret terms from psychology and philosophy that were imported into Japan from Western civilization in the late nineteenth century.

Many Japanese words of Buddhist origin are nowadays used in a completely secular, and sometimes opposite, meaning. For example, *hotoke*, a Japanese translation of 'Buddha,' also refers to 'the dead' or 'a corpse.' *Mushin*, a transliteration of the Chinese word *wu-hsin*, referring to the state in which the mind has stopped functioning so as not to be attached to

10

anything, often translated as 'no-mind' in English, is sometimes now used to describe one's behavior of begging or asking for money or something precious. In other words, it is the manifestation of greed. *Gaman*, usually translated as 'patience' – a favorite virtue of Japan – originally carried the Buddhist meaning of arrogance or boasting. The dramatic mask from Noh Theatre called *hannya*, after a transliteration of *prajna* or wisdom in Buddhism, expresses the rage and fury of an extremely hurt woman. So while Buddhism has long been self-evident for us Japanese, something that is in the air, we are very likely to have misunderstood and misinterpreted large parts of it.

In this and other ways, Buddhism in Japan may be similar to Christianity in the West. Christianity has long failed to meet the spiritual needs of many of the people it serves by being reduced to a social institution. Despite the emergence of several Japanese religious geniuses such as Kukai (774–835 CE), Shinran (1173–1262) and Dogen (1200–53), Japanese Buddhism has also failed to remain vitally connected to a spiritual path. Japanese people would rarely look to Buddhism when they feel spiritually frustrated. But that does not mean that they would look to psychology or psychotherapy to find an answer either.

There have been some Japanese psychologists such as Enryo Inoue (1858–1919 mentioned by Onda in this volume), and some philosophers such as the philosophers of the Kyoto School, especially Kitaro Nishida, who expected Buddhism to rescue the Japanese people from their predicaments. Buddhism has largely failed to meet such expectations, and we must inquire into this failure. There is a wide gap between the traditional Buddhism of social institutions and customs in Japan and the practice and study of Buddhism as initiated under the influence of Western scholarship. Such scholarship has proceeded independent of Japanese customs and is rarely accessible to the ordinary people of Japan. In the 1930s, Buddhism was mobilized into a national ideology in a nationwide campaign to justify the war of Japan with the West, as well as the invasion into other Asian countries. The Buddhist doctrine of no-self then degenerated into selflessness and self-annihilation in service of the emperor as a deity who would insure the victory of Japan. At that time, Kiyoshi Miki (1897–1945) – one of Nishida's students – warned against the political abuse of Buddhism, and pointed out the necessity to develop disciplines such as Buddhist philosophy, Buddhist psychology, and Buddhist economics so that Buddhism might legitimately address diverse social needs.

Defeat in World War II forced Japan to rid itself of nationalist and militaristic elements, and to be exposed, especially in scholarship and educational influences, to the massive and overwhelming influence of American culture. As a result, the development of Buddhist studies in Japan, as advocated by Miki, has yet to be accomplished. Unlike the influence of Christianity in Germany, Buddhism in Japan has yet to examine itself critically, especially in regard to its involvement in nationalism and militarism.

Philosophy, especially religious philosophy of the Kyoto School, represented particularly by Keiji Nishitani – a student of Nishida – has been the main entry of post-war Japanese Buddhism, especially Zen, in a dialogue with the West. The main partners in this dialogue have been theologians and philosophers, not psychologists and psychotherapists. But, as King (quoted in Molino 1998: xii) points out, Nishitani, in *Religion and Nothingness*, fails to appreciate how the psychological tradition of Westerners would contribute to a strong interest of Western people in Buddhism. Contemporary Western depth psychology has already been incorporated into the social systems of the West, and now may offer some help in spiritual crises such as boredom, meaninglessness, and obsessions with relationships when they emerge in the lives of ordinary people. In general, Japanese religious philosophers have paid little attention to psychology, humanities, and social sciences.

To make matters worse, Japanese psychologists are rarely interested in philosophy or religion because the curriculum in Japan has so far not required university students to study philosophy or religion. There is no conception of 'Buddhist psychology' in a contemporary Japanese university.

The conference that was the basis of this book was perhaps the first occasion for many Japanese Zen practitioners and mental health professionals to be exposed to the flourishing tree that has developed in the West from the seeds sown about forty years ago by two Japanese philosophers and practitioners of Zen. D. T. Suzuki and Shin'ichi Hisamatsu began a dialogue with various psychoanalysts – most especially Erich Fromm and C. G. Jung – that has continued and born fruit. Now it is no exaggeration to say that Zen Buddhism, affected by and affecting psychotherapy, is also transmitted westward across the Pacific Ocean, revealing more and more of its global character, a key to spirituality in the twenty-first century.

References

Epstein, M. (1995) *Thoughts Without a Thinker: Psychotherapy from a Buddhist Perspective*, New York: Basic Books.

Gross, R. (1993) *Buddhism after Patriarchy: A Feminist History, Analysis and Reconstruction of Buddhism*, New York: SUNY Press.

Meckel, D. and Moore, R. (eds) (1992) *Self and Liberation: The Jung–Buddhism Dialogue*, New York: Paulist Press.

Molino, A. (ed.) (1998) *The Couch and the Tree: Dialogues in Psychoanalysis and Buddhism*, New York: North Point Press.

Rubin, J. (1996) *Psychotherapy and Buddhism: Toward an Integration*, New York: Plenum Press.

Seager, R. H. (1999) *Buddhism in America*, New York: Columbia University Press.

Welwood, J. (2000) *The Psychology of Awakening: Buddhism, Psychotherapy and the Path of Personal and Spiritual Transformation*, Boston: Shambala.

Young-Eisendrath, P. (1984) *Hags and Heroes: A Feminist Approach to Jungian Psychotherapy with Couples*, Toronto: Inner City.

Young-Eisendrath, P. and Dawson T. (1998) *The Cambridge Companion to Jung*, Cambridge: Cambridge University Press.

Part I

NEW PERSPECTIVES ON
BUDDHISM AND PSYCHOLOGY
EAST AND WEST

1

BUDDHISM, RELIGION AND PSYCHOTHERAPY IN THE WORLD TODAY

Shoji Muramoto

Buddhism and psychotherapy

When we speak of Buddhism and psychotherapy, it is usually taken for granted that Buddhism is one of the representative religions of the East, while psychotherapy is a technique for healing mental diseases based upon modern psychology as one of the sciences developed in the West. Most discussions about Buddhism and psychotherapy therefore presuppose, implicitly or explicitly, the following diagram:

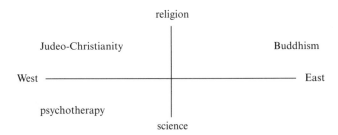

The axes of the East and the West and of religion and science intersect with each other. Judeo-Christianity and Buddhism are located respectively in the position of Western and Eastern religion, while psychotherapy is found in that of Western science. According to this diagram, both Judeo-Christianity and Buddhism are in the upper half, classified as religions, while both Judeo-Christianity and psychotherapy are in the left half belonging to the West. Because for Western people monotheism has been a historical factor without which they cannot conceive of Western culture, their discussions about Buddhism and psychotherapy refer, though not always overtly, to the connections that each has with Western religion. Westerners don't connect Buddhism and psychotherapy simply with each other. When they speak of psychotherapy, of Buddhism, or of their mutual relationship, one can usually

15

assume that some attitude toward Western religions is an underlying presupposition. In other words, their perspective on Buddhism and psychotherapy is more or less related to Western monotheism. On the one hand, this doubtless implies a limitation. Statements on Buddhism made by Westerners often are a mixture of knowledge gained through translations and general introductory works and their own projections on the basis of their religious experience. Buddhism then turns out to be merely the other side of Western religion as experienced by them. On the other hand, this also makes Westerners sensitive to the historical and socio-cultural limits of their statements about Buddhism. It causes a critical attitude, which is duly applied to the thinking of those living in cultures different from their own. That has nothing to do with whether they believe in their own religions or not. In my opinion, this is one of the factors historically responsible for the vigorous energy shown by Western culture.

The situation changes considerably when Japanese say something on the topic in question. Their context is different. Though it is a historical fact that Buddhism was transmitted from India by way of China and Korea, Japanese usually take it to be their traditional religion deeply connected to their native mind. Buddhism therefore, though to a lesser degree, corresponds to the function of Christianity in the West. Like the latter, Buddhism in the course of history has developed its own institutions, has itself been institutionalized. Many Japanese still experience Buddhism not so much as a way of authentic living taught by the Buddha, but as one of many institutions, part of the sociological processes of bureaucracy and functional rationality observed by Max Weber. In any case it seems remote from anything alive. This aspect does not seem to be fully appreciated by Westerners interested in Buddhism. Small wonder that they often feel disappointed when they finally come to Japan in order to experience Buddhism and find, very often, remnants of old-fashioned authoritarianism or, on the contrary, symptoms of modernization in Zen monasteries.

In Japan, psychotherapy is usually introduced without any reference to its historical and socio-cultural context as observed in the West. For the original psychotherapists, the relationship of their thinking to Western religion has always been of great concern. The question of how psychotherapy is related to traditional religion, for Japanese psychotherapists, refers to Buddhism more than to a Western creed. However, they hardly show any interest in traditional religions, be it of criticism or defense. Such an apparent indifference to Buddhism should not, however, be taken at face value. The interest in it may be latent and manifest itself only in the course of time. As a matter of fact, in recent years there has been a growing concern with traditional religion such as Buddhism and Shintoism among Japanese psychotherapists. This special issue is only one of many signs. Whereas Westerners, as pointed out above, develop a critical attitude towards their own religions, I wonder if the same thing can be said about statements on religion and psychotherapy by

16

Japanese psychotherapists. They consider Christianity and psychotherapy to be of Western origin, and what they say about them consists of their own projections upon them on the basis of an involvement in their own culture. But when they become aware of the historical and socio-cultural limits of their thoughts, their way of thinking may gradually become more critical.

Our discussion has so far been concerned with the horizontal axis of the East and the West crossing the vertical axis of religion and science in the diagram. We have taken its validity for granted. To be sure, the two lines and the four positions help us clarify some aspects of 'Buddhism and psychotherapy'. But does the diagram really express our concern to see the relationships among psychotherapy, and religions in the East and the West? Does it in fact help us unfold a train of thought? What is meant by each of the two axes and by their intersection? Using the diagram as a convenient scheme for explaining something is one thing. Trying to understand the meaning of the diagram is quite another. The latter is never self-evident. It turns out to be open to interpretations. The poles of each axis, the East and the West on the one hand, and religion and science on the other, can be thought of as opposite to and identical with each other. So are the two axes themselves. Let us reflect a bit upon the diagram. First we must say that it is in no way self-evident that Buddhism is an Eastern religion and psychotherapy a Western science. Such a statement has only been presupposed. The more deeply and widely one thinks, the more problematic is the character both of Buddhism and of psychotherapy.

Japanization of modern Western psychotherapy

Is psychotherapy really of the West? Indeed, almost all founders of modern psychotherapy such as Freud, Adler, Jung, Reich, and Rogers were born and brought up in the West. It is deeply rooted in Western culture. Something corresponding to psychotherapy can, however, be found everywhere in the world, so also in the East. To alleviate the suffering of the human soul and to search for its salvation lies in the nature of humanity. Could not Buddhism be called an Eastern form of psychotherapy? In Buddhist sutras and Zen texts, there are many passages with deep implications for Western psychotherapists. The dialogues recorded in them have evidently a psychotherapeutic significance. They could be examples of an Eastern version of psychotherapy. It is certainly interesting to compare them with conversations known from psychotherapeutic sessions today with regard to both form and contents. This leads beyond the concern of the present study. What I would like to propose here is that psychotherapy, as generally considered, is not necessarily of the West. In other words, I contend that Buddhism also has by nature psychotherapeutic elements.

Furthermore, modern Western psychotherapy, whether Freudian, Jungian, or other, is becoming more and more popular in Japan. Though there are still only a very few Japanese psychotherapists in private practice, the knowledge of clinical or depth psychology is widespread through the mass media. The number of those interested in psychotherapy and having experiences as therapists or as patients is definitely on the increase. We witness the emergence of a certain image of the human person intrinsically connected with the popularization of psychotherapy which American scholars have described as the 'other-directed person' (Riesman 1950), 'psychological man' (Rieff 1959), or 'protean man' (Lifton 1968). This phenomenon reflects to some extent the modernization of Japanese society in the sense of its Westernization. And as Berger has clearly shown (Berger, Berger and Kellner 1973), the modernization of a society is transferred to the consciousness of those who live in it. The consciousness of the Japanese is also in a process of modernization.

Yet, this aspect should be neither underestimated nor overestimated. On the one hand, there are only a few Japanese today, whether intellectuals or not, who follow the traditional way of life and are well versed in their own traditional culture. On the other hand, it cannot be simply said that the consciousness of the Japanese including psychotherapists has undergone modernization. Though various perspectives and forms of Western psychotherapy have been and are still being introduced to the Japanese one after another, it appears that there simultaneously is what may be called the Japanization of modern Western psychotherapy. This seems to me to be the fate of any foreign thought imported to Japan. In a sense, it is inevitable and even necessary that it unfold itself in a way adequate to the historically determined climate of Japan. The problem is that this Japanization is either simply ignored or justified without any serious confrontation with the original Western context from which modern psychotherapy emerged and developed. The Japanization of modern Western psychotherapy, irrespective of any differences of schools, shows, for example, in the lack of open discussions between a therapist and his client as well as between colleagues, be it in academic congresses or in therapeutic sessions, and in the relatively low appraisal of individualism leading to self-realization not only among clients but also among therapists. Bowing to social 'harmony,' the nature of which is seldom examined, Japanese often, consciously or unconsciously, give up what Freud recommends us to observe and respect as the basic rule of psychoanalysis: to put into words without any recourse to moral or social calculation whatever occurs to the mind. I often wonder whether psychoanalysis and Christianity were really brought to Japan despite their popularity.

Buddhism

Is Buddhism really of the West? Historically speaking, for us Japanese it is a religion that in the seventh century came not from the East but from the West. Buddhism originated in India, and was therefore transmitted from the West to Japan. Pali and Sanskrit, the original languages of Buddhist sutras and commentaries, are cognate with most Western languages. Nowadays there is a development of Buddhism in the West due in large measure to the efforts of Japanese Zen Buddhists such as Daisetsu T. Suzuki, Shin'ichi Hisamatsu and others. It is true enough that the understanding of most Westerners remains on a rather primitive level and is full of prejudices and misconceptions. At the same time, the phase of intensive introduction of Zen Buddhism to the West is gradually coming to an end. The so-called 'Zen boom' is certainly passing away. There is less and less 'Beat Zen' as one of the phenomena of the counter-culture, and instead there are more and more Western scholars who are no longer satisfied with translations or with introductions written in English, but find it very important to read Buddhist texts in their original languages. In addition, they strive to experience Buddhism directly in the Eastern countries where it has long been a central element of cultural tradition. They must be clearly distinguished from those Westerners who, unable or unwilling to confront themselves with their own Western tradition, frivolously escape to any different world. More than half a century ago, Jung already criticized such behavior severely. He said, 'The usual mistake of Western man when faced with this problem of grasping the ideas of the East is like that of the student in Faust. Misled by the devil, he contemptuously turns his back on science and, carried away by Eastern occultism, takes over yoga practices word for word and becomes a pitiable imitator . . . Thus he abandons the one sure foundation of the Western mind and loses himself in a mist of words and ideas that could never have originated in European brains and can never be profitably grafted upon them' (Jung 1929: par. 3). The new type of Western intellectuals interested in Buddhism seems wholly different from the type just described. Neither unable nor unwilling to accept Western tradition, their concern with Buddhism is not motivated by the denial of their own identity, but rather by the need for reinterpretation of themselves and their own culture. They are full of the critical spirit which has been cherished academically and religiously in the West, and can be directed both to the East and to the West.

Such a new development among Western intellectuals distinguishable from the earlier enthusiasm for Zen as a socio-pathological phenomenon can be observed, for example, in the contributions by the participants in the Kyoto Zen Symposium. They presuppose a certain breadth and depth that Buddhism has attained in America. Gomez, for example, suggests the model of a dialogue with tradition as an alternative according to which one does not have to seek or find a singular voice in it. For him the 'nature' of a religious system and practice is not necessarily an unchanging essence; rather, the historical reality of religion, like other human phenomena, suggests a much more complex model. He tries to combine two perspectives: that of a historian and that of a believer, and proposes to change first of all the assumption that emptiness (Sanskrit: *sunyata*) as a fundamental truth of Buddhism has to do with passivity and resignation. He proposes something like active emptiness. Firmly trained in the humanities, he alludes to the tasks which American Buddhists and scholars of Buddhism today find themselves confronted with, but at the same time gives relevance to Japanese Buddhists and scholars of Buddhism inasmuch as they, too, live in the contemporary world and have to play an important role therein (Gomez 1983). Maraldo poses the fundamental question 'What do we study when we study Zen?' After summarizing various ways of studying Zen, namely as a topic and a type, as a phenomenon and historical entity, he attempts to answer the question raised by himself, saying 'the Zen tradition proves . . . a turning point which challenges those fields to clarify their methods and presuppositions' (Maraldo 1983).

In the preface to his recent book, the former Zen monk Stephen Batchelor mentions a crisis in the present condition of Buddhist studies. Between Eastern teachers insisting upon absolute authority and Western academics studying Buddhism with scientific 'objectivity' he sees 'an abyss which, despite the occasional attempts to bridge it, appears as a disconcerting vacuum' (Batchelor 1983: 22).

The general crisis of contemporary Western culture is reflected here; thus he feels 'it necessary that Buddhist teachings speak to his contemporaries in a language that they can authentically hear.' He continues, 'The presentation of Buddhism in a culturally alien way of thinking often fails to totally communicate the teachings, thereby leaving us existentially untouched' (ibid.). His involvement with Buddhism is apparently inseparable from his keen awareness of the spiritual crisis of our days. Reading the works of existential theologians and philosophers such as Paul Tillich, Gabriel Marcel, John Macquarrie, and Martin Heidegger, he finds that they as Christians were trying to deal with precisely the same problem that he was facing as a Buddhist. And he states, 'Their writings not only gave me many ideas for a means to help resolve these conflicts, but also opened my eyes for the first time to the richness of the Judeo-Christian tradition.'

What is the East?

From the discussion so far we can see that it is never self-evident that Buddhism and psychotherapy belong to the East and the West respectively. Our situation talking about them is more complicated than we imagine. It has become quite possible to speak of Western Buddhism or Eastern psychotherapy. We must however go on to question even the terms, 'East' and 'West'.

We know well that the words 'left' and 'right' are in essence relative. An object to my left will be on my right, when I turn around. It is called left or right according to the direction of my attention. This is true of all the words denoting directions in space such as 'before' and 'behind', 'above' and 'beneath'. All of them are used only relatively.

On the contrary, the words 'east', 'west', 'north', and 'south' are not relative but absolute. Tokyo is to the east of Kyoto where I work, but does not become to the west of Kyoto even when I turn my back to Tokyo. It remains to the east of Kyoto so long as I work in Kyoto, whatever I may do here. Even when I go to Nagoya, Tokyo for me is in the east. But when I go to Chiba, Tokyo for me is in the west. 'For me' is not an exact expression because 'east' and 'west' don't depend upon my action but upon the place where I am. The latter itself is independent of me. I only happen to be in the place. In geography we use neither 'left' nor 'right' but 'east' and 'west'.

But when these words are written with capital letters as in 'the East' and 'the West', they become important basic concepts in history. East and West have never referred to any fixed geographical area. Areas called the East or the West have changed in the course of history. For Europeans, the East at first was only the region we today call Arabia or the Near East. With the campaigns of Alexander the Great, the area meant by the East was expanded to include India. Later China was discovered and called the East, until Japan became the Far East, i.e. the farthest country of the East.

The concept of the East is therefore relative to the expansion of the European consciousness in history. It is no wonder that we Japanese find it somewhat unnatural to call Persia or India, even China, countries of the East. When we use the word East we have already introjected, though in most cases unconsciously, the European viewpoint into ourselves. Our consciousness has been, in so doing, partly Westernized. It may therefore be a peculiarity of us Japanese to overemphasize the uniqueness of the so-called Eastern spirituality. Our preoccupation with it is perhaps only possible on the basis of the partial accommodation of the Japanese consciousness to the European historical perspective.

It has been hitherto taken for granted that the United States of America is the most representative country of the West. But when we seriously consider the fact that more and more Americans become interested in Buddhism and remember the Buddhist saying that Buddhism is always being transmitted to the East, it becomes less and less self-evident that America is a Western country. Isn't America already, geographically at least, to the east of Japan? And what about Japan? Our country is proud of the highest level of science and technology, and in international politics we are closely allied with the countries of the West. Is Japan really an Eastern country? And then what about the countries of the former Soviet Union? By giving only a little consideration to these questions we can see that the East and the West are historically defined entities; that the East and the West are therefore also quite relative.

To what does this awareness lead us? In other words, what would be more reliable than the East and the West? Perhaps a concept of the world, the universe, or the cosmos. Our age can be characterized by the growing consciousness of the world as a whole. Our historical era is in essence cosmological. Despite or because of the ubiquitous presence of severe collisions

21

we may be, as a matter of fact, suffering from our still slumbering awareness of the historical process in which we exist, willingly or not. We can say nowadays that the so-called encounter between the East and the West is taking place within Buddhism as well as within psychotherapy. No serious problem of the contemporary world, be it politics or philosophy, can be simply said to belong to either the East or the West, but must be recognized as a worldwide problem because it necessarily concerns all the people of the world. In the confrontation with any problem we already find ourselves permanently connected with all people in the world, most of whom we do not know personally at all.

Historically speaking, the notion of the world is not new but as old as the history of humankind, as it is part of our nature. Heidegger (1967) ontologically characterizes the fundamental condition of human as 'being-in-the-world' (*In-der-Welt-sein*). However, we must keep in mind that any Heideggerian concept is ontological, not ontic, that is, not to be naively transferred into the realm of facts historically studied. The notion of the cosmos played a decisively important role in the lives of the ancients. The meaning of human existence for them was unthinkable without a reference to the cosmos, because here the divine, supreme principle was believed to reside. It was in accordance with the cosmic principle that the ancients measured their own behavior and judged it as human or not human. Human was any act corresponding to the cosmic principle, and not human any one going against it. They believed in its universal validity in terms of their intuitive knowledge transmitted through the process of tradition. It was an unquestionable presupposition of their lives.

Modern view

Modern humanity cannot simply accept this assumption any longer. The notion of the cosmos or the world still remains, but it has greatly changed. There seems to be no other principle than a cold mechanism called the 'laws of nature'. Confirmed only by mathematical procedures, they provide us with the means of technological manipulation of all beings. The personified universe of the good old days does not show us a familiar face any longer. All that we can read in its indifferent countenance is meaninglessness. There appears to be no place where one could live in a way suitable to the word 'human being'. To illustrate this uncanny alteration of the subjectively felt meaning of the world, we need only mention nuclear weapons and genetic manipulation, for example. It is an irony that words referring to 'being-in-the-world' (or being-in-the-cosmos) such as 'cosmopolitan' were used much less when people believed in the divine cosmos than nowadays when it seems unrelated to us.

Interestingly, Jonas (1963) suggests a certain affinity between late antiquity and modernity. In late antiquity, the ancient belief in the supreme cosmic order was shaken to its foundation. This crisis provided the spiritual atmosphere in which the Gnostic religions flourished and Christianity emerged. While the Gnostics were strongly anticosmic, the Christians revered nature in terms of their belief in the supreme goodness of the Creator. But both had the tendency to question the cosmos as a whole, as well as their identity as cosmopolitans. Identity was found in a life transcending the cosmos, and unlike that of ancients. Jonas finds existentialism and nihilism, the spiritual expressions of our age, analogous to the Gnosticism of late antiquity. Both are, in his view, related to each other like lock and key (Jonas 1963; 1964). More recently he has thus turned to study the ethics required in our historical situation, with modern technology progressing in an uncanny way to an unforeseen, maybe apocalyptic, future (Jonas 1963; 1981; 1983; 1984). In his historical perspective he remains true to his early studies. The apparently natural existence of humankind is not self-evident. In late antiquity, human life was believed to be possible only through the invisible act of God. Our era, too, reveals the insufficiency of the humanistic viewpoint in its modern sense. What seems to be needed is a reconsideration of the perspective of late antiquity.

Everything in the cosmos now proves to be relative. Nothing is autonomous in itself. All things in the world betray their interdependence with each other. Metaphysics ceases to be an abstract system of thought and becomes an experiential reality. Not beings in the world but the world itself comes to be questioned. Any religion answering existentially to these ontological questions deserves to be called a world religion. Western religions are world religions not merely because they are spread worldwide but also because they reveal that all things, including the human, owe existence to the creative act of God. Awareness of the existence of oneself leads to a crisis in which one's being-in-the-world is fundamentally questioned. One's existence, however, is not simply denied. Instead, one faces the basic fact that one is responsible for one's relations to all humans and other beings through one's acts. At this point one may be ready to hear the calling of God, as in Christian belief. Even when the gospel was heard only in Israel, Christianity was thus a world religion because it saw the world as a whole in crisis, and appealed to all men in the world to save their souls.

This holds true also for Buddhism. Though developed in India and has been sustained mainly in Asian countries, it is undeniably a world religion. Unlike Western monotheism, it does not speak of the Creator of the world but rather proposes the emptiness of all our experiences. All is void of self (Sanskrit: *anatman*). The core of Buddhism is the radical experience of our being-in-the-world as crisis. For Buddhists nothing in this world can be relied on. Convinced of universal emptiness, they know that even this insight of emptiness can become an entity and thus an obstacle to enlightenment. What has attracted Westerners to Buddhism therefore seems not a trivial or frivolous curiosity, but a serious quest for authentic spiritual radicalism.

Western religions and Buddhism

It is far from my point to designate Judeo-Christian religion and Buddhism as Western and Eastern religions. The tendency to describe a certain world view in terms of its geographical background can be rightly called 'regionalist'. Implicitly ideological, it deprives world views of their universal contents. Yet it should be distinguished from the correct assumption that types of world view are limited historically and socioculturally. Buddhism and Western religions being world religions, one might say that the dialogue between the East and the West is a manifestation of the dialogue of the world with itself. The encounter between these religions is not so much an encounter between the East and the West, but a dialogue, or rather a monologue, of the world or the cosmos with itself. In other words, the self-realization of the world as a whole is taking place, despite the obvious plurality of the world religions.

What is a world religion? Not defined through its worldwide spread, it is elaborated by its conception of the world as a whole. But this wholeness of the world manifests itself especially in times of crisis. Then all things of the world display their interrelatedness, insubstantiality, and dependence on their metaphysical basis which makes the world appear as a whole. Such a definition of world religion, however, sounds rather abstract. Concretely speaking, what does it mean? Peter Meinhold (1978), a Protestant theologian, in this context claims that every concept of a world religion needs a certain world experience and a certain world interpretation. Specifying their special character in the twentieth century, he states that 'world religions' in the modern sense are 'those religions which are ready to confront themselves with the problem of their plurality and to bring it to a resolution corresponding to the conception of the world today and meeting it' (Meinhold 1978: 24). How is 'the world' understood today? Through modern means of communication it has come to be experienced more and more as a unit. With this experience of the unity of the world modern people have come to realize the connection of its parts, they have seen that there are no isolated problems in the world. Every problem proves to be, sooner or later, a world problem. According to Meinhold, 'world problems' appear in all parts of the world simultaneously and demand similar and unified solutions (ibid.: 23). World religions are therefore religions which see all problems in the world as world problems and occupy themselves deliberately with their solution. World problems thus come to be considered as the very area where religions show themselves as world religions.

But how and where do problems in the world reveal themselves as world problems? In other words, what makes the world appear as such? With these questions our discussion proceeds from the horizontal axis of the East and the West to the vertical axis of religion and science. It may be true that belief in its traditional sense provides for an experience of the world as such. But even pious people today admit that belief does not develop without serious experiences of one's existence in the world. Belief therefore presupposes some

24

facts pertaining to our lives. Religion is not something beyond our concern in and with the world. Science, on the other hand, means an empirical investigation of facts, including human existence, and thus is intrinsically related to religion. This is what the vertical axis crossing the horizontal in the above diagram refers to.

This conception of science, however, leads to a confrontation with scientism or positivism prevalent today. Scientism proposes that scientific investigation is nothing more than the accumulation of 'facts'. The question thus arises: what actually are 'facts'? They are not simply existing there, waiting for scientific investigation. Only a little phenomenological reflection reveals that they show themselves as facts because of the construction of, or at least the correlation with, what is usually called mind. Mind thus is a fundamental fact. It is psychology that reveals this truth.

This concept of psychology must be distinguished from psychologism, a form of reductionism that reduces all things to psychology. Without the awareness of this distinction every psychological statement would be misleading and absurd, the worst form of ideology. Jung is, indeed, right when he says: 'Every science is a function of the psyche, and all knowledge is rooted in it. The psyche is the greatest of all cosmic wonders' (Jung 1947/1954: par. 357). He obviously claims the primacy of psychology over all the other sciences, but psychology must be subjected to this same self-criticism.

Self-criticism is therefore a touchstone of psychology. A psychology not open to self-criticism would be a form of psychologism. One cannot be sure how far Jung's psychology is free from psychologism. He says, 'Whoever speaks of the reality of the soul or psyche is accused of "psychologism". Psychology is spoken of as if it were "only" psychology and nothing else' (Jung 1944: par. 9), but he does not seem to actually distinguish his psychology from psychologism.

Jung's psychology

Jung is not the first who expressed this psychological truth. Much earlier, Aristotle said in his *De Anima*, 'In a sense the psyche is all.' As Hillman's extensive works (Hillman 1972; 1975) clearly show, there is a long history of psychology in its primordial sense as well as its amnesia. It is not a mere accident that physicians of the soul rediscovered psychology as 'soul-making' and that the key-concept of the unconscious paved the way to religion which had been forgotten in the historical process of modernization. At a first glance, medical psychology seems to have nothing to do with religion. But at its depth it provides a new, though at the same time primordial, perspective on what should be the subject matter of religion. It is both a criticism and an approval of religion. It is in and through the soul that problems of the world reveal themselves as world problems. The psyche is in no way merely one of the parts of the world, but, to say it again with Aristotle, all the world.

In various passages Jung speaks of *esse in anima*, that is, 'being-in-the-soul'. He might be referring to Heidegger's key-concept of being-in-the-world. In any case, it is interesting to compare these concepts with each other. While the former is associated with the concept of introversion as a central attitude toward life, especially in the second half of life, the latter indicates the limitation of previous philosophies based upon subjectivism which fail to grasp man's unique mode of being, i.e. openness to the world. Being-in-the-soul and being-in-the-world then seem to be in opposition to each other.

Thinking further, however, especially in reference to the concrete problems confronting both patients and physicians in psychotherapy, it becomes clear that they are only different aspects of one and the same phenomenon of human existence.

I have already pointed out that psychology consists in self-reflection. Yet, it is not self-evident that the psyche reflects upon itself. Rather, it can usually be described as pre-reflective in the sense that it takes almost everything for granted. To use a Husserlian term, it represents the natural attitude which constitutes the world of everyday life.

What causes the psyche to reflect on itself, or what causes the psyche to experience itself in its own being, is some event in the world that questions its natural or pre-reflective attitude. It interrupts the natural stream of consciousness. This is what we usually call a problem. It affects the core of the person in question. All that the person has hitherto taken for granted suddenly proves to be uncertain. The world shows him or her a different face from before.

But it is when that person himself or herself asks why it is so and what it means that the functioning of his or her own psyche becomes apparent to him or her. Only then does the psyche come to reflect on itself. It has been, so to speak, in a state of slumber. It is the occurrence of a problem that awakens and activates it. Though experienced as if coming from the outside, it does, yet, not deny inwardness as one of the essential aspects of the psyche. The psyche knows that the problem which alarms it is the meaningful manifestation of its own dynamism. In principle, between the psyche and the world there is a dialectic or hermeneutically circulatory relationship. Every problem that occurs in the world can make the psyche self-reflective. And in this self-reflection the world as a whole becomes a problem.

Psychotherapy and religion

The subject matter of psychotherapy is usually described as personal problems. Its importance has been recognized only in the private sphere, not in the public. The more seriously one takes this 'trivial' affair, however, the more apparent it becomes that it is inseparably related to many things that at first appeared to have nothing to do with it. This fundamental fact of human life which psychotherapists have known on the basis of their experiences is certainly the point of encounter between psychotherapy and religion.

As a matter of course, a person in need of help is not so much concerned with the distinction between religion and psychotherapy as with the resolution of problems. Problems treated in psychotherapy are sexuality, the will to power, insecurity, loneliness, aggression, identity, self-realization, and so on. But they manifest themselves as a complex, and turn out to be universal in that they concern anyone independent of any religion or ideology. Many psychotherapists find that traditional religions still underestimate complexes while being, albeit unconsciously, preoccupied with them. The task of any religion today consists in the rediscovery of its self-identity between the two extremes of traditionalism and modernism. To take the problems discussed in psychotherapeutic sessions more seriously, in my opinion, would enable a religion to more adequately meet the need of our age, and only then would it deserve to be truly called a world religion. Furthermore, following Marcel, it is an essential function of religion to transform a problem into a mystery (Marcel 1940).

The dialogue and collaboration between psychotherapy and religion is not an easy task but needs to be accomplished. We already have an abundance of literature about it, but 'religion' there means in most cases Christianity. Nevertheless, the review of the relevant works, particularly of the three models of psychology and religion proposed by Peter Homans (1968) gives us a framework of reference for evaluation of the existing literature on Buddhism and psychotherapy.

The first model, according to Homans, is associated with the phrase 'psychology of religion', represented by William James. In this model, religion is the object of psychological investigation, deprived of its inherent teachings. The second is the pastoral psychology model, in which psychodynamic insight into personality development takes the place of the conversion experience as the focal point in the first model. The third, the theology–psychology model provides a careful and sophisticated interpretive integration of the proper place as well as the limits of psychology in the theological enterprise, and is exhibited by Freud and Tillich. Most works on the relationship between Buddhism and psychotherapy seem to correspond either to the first or to the third model. There are only very few considered to belong to the second.

It is noteworthy that among the many sects of Buddhism, Zen is the preferred object of study for psychology. It understands Zen, without any recourse to its self-understanding, only as an interesting psycho-physiological phenomenon, an artificially caused psychopathology, an effective training for psychophysical adjustment and so on. This is especially true of a series of so-called scientific studies of Zen performed in Japan from the late 1950s on, which I recently reviewed (Muramoto 1984). On the contrary, the attempts at psychological interpretations of Zen Buddhism by some Western psychologists (such as Jung 1939; Fromm 1960) are to be more appreciated because of their keen awareness of the spiritual crisis which their own culture faces and their clear formulations of the typical motives for the interest of Westerners in various forms of Eastern spirituality. These interpretations, however, remain on the level of assimilation. In other words, the interpretive framework used is taken for granted, and therefore awaits a deeper analysis.

Between Zen and psychology, as I pointed out elsewhere (Muramoto 1983), there are so far only a few meaningful dialogues because each of them has only insufficient knowledge of the other, yet believes, without any serious reflection upon its own possible prejudices, to know the other well. The primary concern in a dialogue is not to prove which party is the greater, but to let the truth reveal itself through the dialogue so that both parties gradually and mutually deepen their understanding of each other and confirm their common ground. A dialogue is no competition or conquest but an experiential process of the common participation in finding the truth, and demands the confession that everyone knows the truth a little but not in its totality. It is worthy of practice in our pluralistic world.

[First published in *Psychologia* 38 (1985): 101–14.]

References

Batchelor, S. (1983) *Alone with Others*, New York: Grove Press.
Berger, P., Berger, B., and Kellner, H. (1973) *The Homeless Mind: Modernization and Consciousness*, New York: Random House.
Fromm, E. (1960) *Zen Buddhism and Psychoanalysis*, New York: Harper & Brothers.
Gomez, L. O. (1983) 'Expectations and assertions: perspectives for growth and adaptation in Buddhism', *Zen Buddhism Today* 1: 28–48.
Heidegger, M. 1967 *Sein und Zeit*, Tübingen: Max Niemeyer Verlag.
Hillman, J. (1972) *The Myth of Analysis*, New York: Harper & Row.
Hillman, J. (1975) *Re-visioning Psychology*, New York: Harper & Row.
Homans, P. (1968) 'Toward a psychology of religion: by way of Freud and Tillich', in P. Homans (ed.), *The Dialogue between Theology and Psychology*, Chicago: The University of Chicago Press.
Jonas, H. (1963) *The Gnostic Religion*, Boston: Beacon Books.
Jonas, H. (1964) *Gnosis und spätantiker Geist*, Gottingen: Vandenhoeck & Ruprecht.
Jonas, H. (1981) *Machat oder Ohnmacht der Subjektivität?* Frankfurt am Main: Insel Verlag.
Jonas, H. (1983) *Das Prinzip Verantwortung*, Frankfurt am Main: Insel Verlag.
Jonas, H. (1984) 'Technik, Ethik und biogenetische Kunst', *Die pharmazeutische Industrie* 46: 685–93.
Jung, C. G. (1929) 'Commentary on *The Secret of the Golden Flower*', in *Collected Works*, vol. 13.
Jung, C. G. (1939) 'Foreword to Suzuki's *Introduction to Zen Buddhism*', in *Collected Works*, vol. 11.
Jung, C. G. (1944) 'Psychology and alchemy', in *Collected Works*, Vol. 12.
Jung, C. G. (1947/1954) 'On the nature of the psyche', in *Collected Works*, vol. 8.

Lifton, R. (1968) 'Protean man', *Partisan Review* 35(2): 13–27.

Maraldo, J. C. (1983) 'What do we study when we study Zen?', *Zen Buddhism Today* 1: 71–8.

Marcel, G. (1940) *Du refus à l'invocation*, Paris: Gallimard.

Meinhold, P. (1978) *Die Religionen der Gegenwart*, Freiburg im Breisgau: Herder.

Muramoto, S. (1983) 'On the relationship of psychology to Zen Buddhism (l)', *Studies in Zen Buddhism* 62: 72–98.

Muramoto, S. (1984) 'On the relationship of psychology to Zen Buddhism (2): *Psychologia* and Koji Sato', *Zengaku–Kenkyu (Studies in Zen Buddhism 63)*: 69–93.

Rieff, P. (1959) *Freud: The Mind of the Moralist*, New York: Viking Press.

Riesman, D. (1950) *The Lonely Crowd*, New Haven: Yale University Press.

2

A BUDDHIST MODEL OF THE HUMAN SELF

Working Through the Jung–Hisamatsu Discussion

Jeff Shore

Once Chuang Chou dreamt he was a butterfly, a butterfly flit-
ting and fluttering around, happy with himself and doing as he
pleased. He didn't know he was Chuang Chou. Suddenly he
woke up and there he was, solid and unmistakable Chuang
Chou. But he didn't know if he was Chuang Chou who had
dreamt he was a butterfly, or a butterfly dreaming he was
Chuang Chou. Between Chuang Chou and a butterfly there
must be *some* distinction! This is called the Transformation of
Things.

Chuang Tzu, chapter 2 (Watson 1968: 49)

Introduction

On 16 May 1958, Shin'ichi Hisamatsu (1889–1980) met with C. G. Jung at
Jung's home outside of Zurich. Hisamatsu, an outstanding Zen layman and
professor of Buddhism, was on his way back to Japan after lecturing on Zen
Buddhism and Zen culture at Harvard University the previous year. On his
one and only trip abroad, Hisamatsu was eager to meet and have discussions
with leading figures in the fields of religion, philosophy, and psychology. He
had had a number of discussions in Cambridge, Massachusetts, with the
Protestant theologian Paul Tillich. On 18 May, two days after Hisamatsu's
meeting with Jung, the German thinker Martin Heidegger led a colloquy
with Hisamatsu at Freiburg University.

The conversation with Jung was held in Japanese and Swiss German with
interpretation. Communication problems arose, naturally enough, in the
course of their conversation, and Jung did not consent to its publication.
After his passing in 1961, however, transcriptions of the discussion have been
repeatedly revised, translated, and published in English and in Japanese. This

was due to the profound and ground-breaking nature of the discussion, communication problems notwithstanding. I can think of no better way to address, from the Zen perspective, the fundamental issues raised in the present volume than in clarifying – in 'unpacking,' so to speak – what Hisamatsu was driving at in this discussion with Jung.

Toward the end of the conversation, Hisamatsu asks whether or not one can be liberated even from the collective unconscious, and Jung replies affirmatively. Shoji Muramoto suggests that this is 'the gravitational center of the entire conversation, comparable with a critical confrontation between a Zen Master and his disciple in Zen *mondo* (question and answer)' (Muramoto 1998: 48, note 8). I agree with Muramoto's assessment, but further suggest that throughout the entire discussion Hisamatsu is attempting to engage Jung in just this manner. In short, from beginning to end, Hisamatsu is not only showing or explaining what Zen Buddhism is; he is provoking, rousing Jung to awaken to it himself.

For example, immediately after the preliminary introductions Hisamatsu already jumps into the fray by stating that he is asking about the final goal or aim of psychoanalysis so that he can compare it with Zen Buddhism. Hisamatsu then queries Jung on the relation between conscious and unconscious: Which, he asks, is the 'true self'? He pointedly inquires into the nature of *dukkha* and whether or not it is the goal of therapy to free us from *dukkha* itself. (The Pali term *dukkha* expresses the first of the fourfold Noble Truths so central to Buddhism. It has been translated as 'suffering' but is perhaps better rendered as discontent or *dis-ease*; in the conversation with Jung, Hisamatsu used the common Japanese term *nayami*.) In spite of Jung's objections, Hisamatsu concludes by repeatedly stating that the true self has no form or substance whatever. He is clearly speaking to – and from – what he is speaking about: 'The true self is without form or substance. Thus it can never be bound by anything. Precisely this is the essence of religious liberation.'

Some of Hisamatsu's assertions and questions may strike the reader as radical Zen *mondo* at its best – or worst, depending on one's viewpoint. The mutual linguistic, cultural, and intellectual stumbling-blocks that arose during the conversation add to the effect, occasionally giving the discussion, especially the earliest English translation, a somewhat bizarre tone, described by one reviewer as sounding like *Alice in Wonderland* (see Muramoto 1998: 38–9).

Upon a careful reading, however, one may be struck by the fact that Hisamatsu's statements and questions constitute a dynamic, persuasive, and penetrating presentation of the fundamentals of Buddhism: that *dukkha* is inherent in life, and that there is, indeed, a liberation or awakening in which *dukkha* is eliminated at its root source. While we need to be wary of monolithic statements about Buddhism (and facile comparisons or contrasts with psychotherapy), I will try my best here to present Buddhism rather than sectarian or dogmatic Zen. When presenting a specifically Zen Buddhist position, I will state it as such.

JEFF SHORE

Working through

Masao Abe, in his article 'The self in Jung and Zen,' states: 'Although it is a relatively new scientific discipline, modern Western psychology shares with older Western spiritual traditions the affirmation of the existence of a self.' Thus, for Abe, despite Jung's long and deep interest in Eastern spiritual traditions, and his discussion with Hisamatsu, 'there is no suggestion of the realization of the No-self in Jung.' Jung, on his part, refused to allow the publication of the discussion, based on what he considered basic East–West differences – linguistic, philosophical, and psychological – that would take years to sort out (see Meckel and Moore 1992: 114–15).

Let us now 'work through,' in the sense of uncover, clarify, and make our own, what Hisamatsu was driving at in that ground-breaking encounter with Jung. In a word, my task here is to elucidate Buddhism's fundamental standpoint of 'No-self' in terms of 'formless self.'

Dukkha

The Pali term *dukkha* calls out for clarification in this context. Hisamatsu probes Jung about the possibility of psychotherapy liberating us from *dukkha* itself, at a stroke, 'in one fell swoop' (see Muramoto 1998: 44–5). Jung seems taken aback at the very possibility – or desirability – of such a thing. A bit later in the conversation, however, Jung agrees, at least in principle. But what is *dukkha*?

Dukkha can be described as the universal and constant discontent or *dis-ease* caused by blind desire or craving to have or to be something. One of the basic tenets of Buddhism is that not only is the desired object ultimately illusory, but so is the desiring self as subject. And yet, as long as craving continues, this complex of *dukkha* continues. In a word, the entire complex of self–world is *dukkha*. And it is truly *unbearable*: we can neither find, nor ourselves be, the ground or bearer of this, and thus we cannot stand or bear it.

Buddhism does not posit some substantial, underlying reality called *dukkha*. (Interpreters have sometimes made this mistake, thus branding Buddhism as pessimistic, gloomy, and without hope.) There is no substantial, underlying reality. The self, ignorant of this fact, is ceaselessly driven by restless desire and thus cannot avoid experiencing *dukkha*.

Nor can the self do anything to free itself from *dukkha*. We are unable to free ourselves from the constant threat of death even in the most intense living, unable to be free of illness even in our healthiest state, unable to extricate ourselves from pain even in our most pleasurable moments. In short, we are unable to free ourselves of negativity in all its forms, be it death, illness, error, evil, or sin. Hisamatsu often presented this ineluctable human situation as a fundamental koan: 'As I am – however I am – will not do. Now what do I do?'

32

Pleasures as such are not, of course, denied. Buddhism is neither pessimistic nor morbid. Rather, it points out the fact that even pleasures grasped and aversions avoided are part and parcel of *dukkha*. Being trapped within the dualistic matrix of pleasure–pain, good–evil, life–death, is itself *dukkha*. It is easy to see that we are in *dukkha* when we do not have or become what we desire, or when we cannot avoid what we are averse to. But are we really free from *dukkha* even when we *do* have or become what we desire? Don't we then fret over losing it, or doesn't the object of our desire lose its appeal once we possess it? In a word, we do not truly come to rest even when the desired end *is* attained or the aversion avoided. This is the universal truth of *dukkha*, the first Noble Truth of Buddhism.

Fundamentally subjective

But it is not enough just to be aware of *dukkha* or 'the existence of suffering.' Thus, Hisamatsu often speaks of the need to inquire into, to penetrate, *dukkha* in a manner that is 'fundamentally subjective.' *Fundamentally* subjective means that it is not merely arbitrary, individual, or personal in contrast to being 'objective.' This attitude can be discerned in Shakyamuni sitting under the bodhi tree. In the preface to his major study on *Eastern Nothingness*, Hisamatsu spells it out:

> Here my very being becomes an urgent problem. And yet I myself cannot become some objective data to be solved, for the problem is the totality of my own suffering existence. This living problem is no other than my own suffering existence. Like a doctor suffering from a fatal illness with which he might live or die: not something which can be examined objectively, it is his own illness which moment by moment draws nearer, threatening. The concreteness of this problem is realized when I suffer, just as the concrete fact of illness is realized when the doctor gets ill rather than when he deals with it as the object of his research.
>
> The problem that I have is my suffering. Because it is I myself that am suffering, it cannot be dealt with in an objective manner. Because I myself am suffering I try to free myself – to save myself – from suffering. I am none other than the problem that must be resolved. And since this existence is a problematic existence, it cannot be said to truly be existence. This problem resolved is true existence, in which I find myself settled.

This fundamentally subjective attitude is crucial in Buddhism. Any approach – whether practical or theoretical – will fall short if it remains merely object-oriented, assuming something to be grasped, understood, or attained by the subject. This is true whether the approach involves entering samadhi, passing koans, contemplating the Buddha in various forms, calming, or introspection. Through such Buddhist practices it is possible to attain a special state of mind, even to gain some insight. If the root-source of *dukkha* is not cut off, however, there is the danger of falling into a vicious cycle, an infinite regress, of merely going into and out of samadhi or other such states. Thus, Hisamatsu stressed the need to cut off the entire complex of *dukkha* once and for all. This can be done only in a fundamentally subjective manner.

Total and immediate

In his commentary on his conversation with Jung, Hisamatsu pointed out this danger in relation to psychotherapy by contrasting psychotherapy with 'deliverance from all suffering' through self-awakening to 'complete and final emancipation':

> Awakening to the *self* unbound by anything whatever, one is liberated from all illness at once. If each illness is treated individually as it arises, one recovers from one illness only to fall victim to another. We can never be free from illness that way. This in itself can be considered a most deep-seated illness. . . . I pointed this out as the vicious cycle of psychoanalytic therapy. It is the fatal shortcoming of psychoanalytic treatment. A truly thoroughgoing cure can only be achieved by severing the root of all illness.
>
> (cf. Meckel and Moore 1992: 117)

Zen Buddhist expressions such as 'One cut, all is cut' describe this complete and final, total and immediate awakening. 'Immediate' here does not mean temporally sudden or abrupt, but, literally, *un-mediated*: *dukkha* – the entire temporal–spatial complex of self–world – has collapsed. Awakening cannot be a gradual, step-by-step process; it is, naturally, total and immediate.

Thus, neither can it be approached through mere theory – nor through practice in the ordinary sense of the self trying to do something. This is likened to trying to free oneself while only becoming more tightly bound and entangled. In a very real sense the self cannot go toward or approach awakening; we can only decisively come from it, through self-awakening in which the root of *dukkha* has been severed once and for all.

From No-self to formless self

Severing the root of *dukkha* has a positive as well as a negative significance. The basic Buddhist teaching of 'No-self,' mentioned above, was given a more affirmative rendering in Mahayana Buddhism, and especially in Chinese Zen.

Hisamatsu preferred terms like 'true self,' 'original self,' and 'formless self' because one is not just breaking free from all conditioned forms, but rather realizing who I truly am – and that I am originally so.

The same holds true for 'dependent origination' or 'dependent co-arising' – the basic Buddhist teaching that all things and events, internal and external, mutually arise and cease while depending on conditions which are themselves interdependent. In Zen Buddhism, dependent co-arising was transformed into 'self-emancipated and independent' (*doku-datsu mu-e*). This is another key expression used often by Hisamatsu, based on two terms found in *The Record of Lin-chi* (Japanese: Rinzai, the leading Tang dynasty Zen master after whom Rinzai Zen is named). 'Self-emancipated' refers to being awakened by oneself; 'independent' means not dependent on anyone or anything. In short, 'self-emancipated and independent' not only declares that there is no substantial reality anywhere; it requires that one actually awaken to this by and as oneself. Further, one then works freely and autonomously as this living, active 'Nothingness' or 'Emptiness.'

In their discussion, Jung emphasized the importance of the unconscious. Hisamatsu countered by stressing the necessity to be liberated 'even from the collective unconscious, and from the bondage which derives from it' (cf. Meckel and Moore 1992: 111). Hisamatsu was not denying the relative value of psychotherapy for the troubled self; rather, he was directly pointing out the need to awaken to our formless, original self as the ultimate source of wholeness and health. As Hisamatsu has written in *Zen and Culture: The Formless Self and Its Creation*:

> In Buddhism this genuine subjectivity is intrinsically the complete and final emancipation, just as this emancipation is genuine subjectivity. Therefore, genuine subjectivity can work freely or be active without any hindrance. If it is not active, it could not be called complete and final emancipation. And if emancipation is lost when it is put into action, it is not genuine subjectivity. Buddhism's genuine subject works freely without losing its emancipation.

Indeed, for Hisamatsu it is not even limited to Buddhism:

> Speaking of this 'Buddhist subject,' it may sound like it is a particular subject in the specific religion known as Buddhism. . . . It is, however, the ultimate and true subject of humankind itself. It is called the Buddhist subject only because it has been decisively realized in Buddhism. But it is not limited to Buddhism; it is the universal subject of humankind.

Hisamatsu is not beating around the bush: Not only is this 'complete and final emancipation,' it is each and everyone's true self – whether we are aware of it or not. It is not limited to certain 'enlightened' individuals, nor to states of mind, consciousness, or the individual or collective unconscious. This is one of the reasons Zen Buddhism prefers the term 'no-mind.'

What does all this mean for the therapist or caregiver? *The Vimalakirti Sutra*, a Mahayana text held in high regard in Zen Buddhism, provides a decisive answer. In this sutra, when the great layman Vimalakirti is asked about his illness, he responds that as long as living beings are ill, his illness is prolonged. And when the illness of all living beings comes to an end, then his illness will also end. Just as loving parents share in the suffering of their child when ill, and feel relieved when their child recovers, so does the Bodhisattva (awakening being) suffer out of compassion for all beings. And where does this 'illness' come from? Vimalakirti states that a Bodhisattva's illness itself arises out of Great Compassion.

In a word, the formless self is free from all suffering even as it compassionately 'takes on' the suffering of all. As Hisamatsu emphasized in conversation with Jung (and hammered out in detail in his commentary on the *Vimalakirti Sutra*), awakening to this formless, original self, we are free from all suffering. As mentioned above, this is not limited to certain 'enlightened' individuals; thus, we naturally and freely take on the suffering of others to help them awaken and thus realize that they, too, are originally and fundamentally free from all suffering. Here is the heart of genuine 'Buddhist therapy.' I will return to this crucial point at the end.

The dreamer awakes: a Buddhist model of the human self

Many metaphors and images have been employed to clarify certain aspects of the Buddhist No-self or formless self. For example, the metaphor of ocean-wave is used in the sutras. The self-as-wave is attached to the form of itself and thus endlessly rises and falls, ignorant of its own nature, source, and end, never at rest until it realizes itself as none other than the vast ocean. This metaphor was also a favorite of Hisamatsu's; he mentioned it at the end of his conversation with Jung. When Jung passed away in 1961, Hisamatsu wrote the following (based on a translation by Hisamatsu and Richard DeMartino in the *FAS Society Journal*, Summer 1992):

The All-Bearing Empty Sea
On May 15 [*sic* – the date was 16 May], 1958, I visited Professor C. G. Jung at his home in Zurich, Switzerland, and talked with him about the 'collective unconscious' and Zen's 'no-mind.' Recently he passed away, leaving this koan unsolved. My respect for him and regret for his untimely death being so deep, I dedicate the following poem to his memory.

Boundless in expanse
bottomless in depth
the vast ocean:

Waves without number
large and small
from the beginningless beginning
appearing only to disappear
disappearing only to appear
endlessly, ceaselessly
rising and falling.

But who is it who knows

that ever fulfilled and undisturbed
the ocean originally bears
not the slightest trace of a wave

That formless
it is present *now* –
where there obtains
neither past, present, nor future,
And is present *here* –
where there obtains
neither east nor west
neither above nor below?

Bearing all yet grasping none
Grasping none yet bearing all

How wondrous –
this all-bearing ocean is none other than the empty sea!

In this poem Hisamatsu summarized, and clarified, the crux of his discussion with Jung.

But there is no need to rely on Hisamatsu. To tie together what has been said so far, I will draw out the implications of 'awakening' as a metaphor and present it as a living model of the human self – of our selves.

In the Pali canon, Shakyamuni is asked if he is a god (*deva*). No, he replies. Are you a spirit, then? No. A demon? No. Are you a human being? No. (Note that Shakyamuni even denies this category – at least as the questioner intended it.) What then are you? I am awake (*Buddha*) (see Kalupahana 1992: 122–3). Buddha means 'an awakened one.' Keep in mind that, the 'dream' or 'sleep' from which we awaken is the *dukkha* of life–death in its entirety, including our ordinary dreaming, sleeping, and waking states – conscious and the unconscious. Let us now consider what this metaphor really means.

Can I wake up in a dream? I can dream that I woke up – but I'm still in the dream. Within the dream there is nothing I can do to get out of the dream. I am the one dreaming, yet within the dream I become caught, entangled in the dream and cannot get out of it. This shows the universal and inescapable aspect of *dukkha*. Recall the crystal-clear, razor-sharp challenge to directly break free and wake up expressed by Hisamatsu's fundamental koan: As I am – however I am – will not do. Now what do I do?

Is suffering in a dream real? Within the dream it sure as hell is! *Dukkha* is real, seemingly the only reality, while I am dreaming. Once I wake up, however, where is *dukkha*?

What happens when I wake up? I awaken to the fact that the whole complex – for example, in a nightmare, the scary figure chasing me and myself scared – was all just a dream. Everything in the dream, including myself in the dream, was just a dream. The entire dream world was just a dream, including rivers and mountains, space–time, life–death, health–illness. Now awake, it is all gone without remainder.

Nothing remains? Nothing of the dream, and yet everything! The whole world and I myself are still here and yet, unlike in the dream, all is now unbound, unrestrained, formless-form. Everything is still here – really here for the first time in their original nature, wondrously transformed. Not one thing has been added, yet all is fundamentally transformed from the ground up.

What about 'myself'? Is the self that awakens the same as the self in the dream? Or is it different? The same, except for one tiny difference: Now it's awake. And that makes all the difference in the world. But I do not become another self; on the contrary, I become truly myself. Unencumbered by the entire dream complex, I 'come back' to my original, formless self. No more, no less.

When I wake up I realize who I really am and have always been, yet was somehow lost in a dream. Within the dream it could not be realized, although I may have had an intimation. In a sense the original self was not there in the dream (not awakened, realized, or actualized). And yet the original self is never totally absent. After all, who is dreaming?

This original self – now awake as the boundless, formless universe – is not some projected or objectified reality (like what appears in a dream). The original, formless self can in no way be measured or grasped by the standards of the dream-complex. Thus the difficulty – in a very real sense *impossibility* – for the self in the dream to waken. Only the awakened self truly knows the nature of the dream as dream, and now truly comes to, and knows, itself, the other, and the world directly and immediately.

How then do I wake up? Zen Buddhism stresses that, finally, there is no way to wake up short of waking up! This accounts for the paradoxical logic of Zen *mondo* or spiritual debates. To give one sterling example: Shih-t'ou

(700–90) was one of the great early Chinese masters. Once he was speaking to a group about the fact that this very mind is Buddha – awakened. (This was before the idea became fashionable in Zen circles.) A monk came forward and asked him, then what about emancipation, the Pure Land, and Nirvana? For the monk these were perhaps inevitable problem-questions that Shih-t'ou's statement had aroused. After all, aren't we supposed to practice diligently in order to get emancipated from all that binds us? Aren't we supposed to achieve the Pure Land, free of all defilement? Aren't we supposed to attain Nirvana and get out of the miserable cycle of samsara? How do we answer?

Here is how Shih-t'ou resolved the problem:

> What about emancipation?
> Who binds you?
> What about the Pure Land?
> Who defiles you?
> What about Nirvana?
> Who puts you in samsara?
> (see Miura and Sasaki 1966: 301)

To each question of the dreaming monk the master answered – simply by being awake. The master could see the monk's self-confusion; he could also 'see through' to the monk's formless self. Thus, the master's paradoxical – yet perfectly honest and straightforward – responses. He might just as well have said: 'I see no chains on you, brother!'

In Buddhism and in Zen a variety of provisional methods have been put forth. For example, the method of concentrated sitting in which one does not hold onto anything in the dream, nor even to the dream itself or the dreamer. One thus confirms that one is indeed awake by allowing the entire dream complex to fall away. Another method is shocking the dreamer awake when the conditions are ripe. But any method must break through the total dream complex from within, in a fundamentally subjective manner, and not just convert, modify, or diminish the 'dream state.'

As long as I continue to dream I can't truly practice. Only the awakened can truly practice. Genuine practice itself is by the awakened. And yet, this truly practicing one is never separate from you or me, here and now. Each and every one of us practices by being awake – we don't wake up by practicing.

Unlike dreaming, awakening is completely unattached and without form – even the form of itself. To what, then, do I awaken? To the dream? No, the dream is gone when one wakes. If I don't awaken to the dream, do I awaken to being awake? No. I awaken to there being nothing whatever to awaken to, nor any one to be awakened. Here there is no such thing as awakening – let alone anything to be called *dukkha* or a dream. This is 'self-emancipated and independent.'

In a sense, the dreamer cannot wake. Boundless reality awakens of itself, to itself, by itself. This is the end of *dukkha*, this is dependent co-arising awakening to itself as self-emancipated and independent.

Let us now return to the role of therapist or caregiver. When a person in a nightmare – metaphorically speaking – screams out for help, what do we do? A Buddha or Bodhisattva, that is, an awakened person, willingly enters another's dream to help them awaken. Therapeutically, it may be necessary to enter another's 'dream' to work with the contents of the dream, change a nightmare into a better dream, and so on. This, of course, can be extremely valuable.

But the person is still dreaming. A Buddha enters another's dream to help the other wake up. Sometimes, just being awake in the presence of another is enough; you don't necessarily have to do anything. Of course, you don't wake them up to your awakening; you help to wake them to their own awakening. One cannot – indeed, need not – awaken another. One can, however, help to spur and spark another. This is perfectly natural, for it is not something that some special person possesses but the awakening and true ground of all humankind.

Besides the *Vimalakirti Sutra*, mentioned above, another Mahayana sutra that Zen Buddhism holds in high esteem is the *Diamond Sutra*. This sutra makes clear that our task is none other than to save all beings. And yet, when all is said and done, there is no one to save – nor is there any one who saves. This is indeed the awakening of all humankind, the free functioning of the formless self in which one, who is neither other nor self, ceaselessly works to help awaken those still entangled in self and other. Here is the basis for a genuinely Buddhist therapy.

Sometimes when you try to wake someone up they respond, in their sleep, 'I'm awake, I'm awake.' One task of the Buddhist therapist can be to gently nudge them and remind them; 'No, you're still asleep. Wake up, wake up!'

Conclusion

Hisamatsu ended his commentary on the conversation with Jung by reminding us that even though Jung had initially denied the possibility of release from suffering once and for all,

> he later acknowledged Nirvana as complete and final emancipation, and agreed that we can be liberated even from the collective unconscious. This was a momentous statement for a psychoanalyst to make. If Professor Jung's statement is accurate, then a way from psychoanalysis to Zen Buddhism could indeed be opened. . . .
>
> (cf. Meckel and Moore: 118)

Just as a small child grows out of its sensory-centered world and awakens to the world of reason, so the rational person awakens to a world beyond mere senses or reason. This awakening is no regression to, nor a mere denial of, the senses or reason. The limits of the senses and reason have been broken through; now, the senses and reason come back into *full and unhindered play* – for they have been returned to, and thus themselves reveal, their original, formless ground.

Psychotherapy can be a genuinely Buddhist therapy if it actually reveals this formless self-awakening, rather than only dealing with the ordinary self's interminable integration of non-rational, unconscious elements. This crucial distinction should neither be exaggerated, nor be understated.

How does this actually play itself out in our daily lives? In the discussion, Jung spoke about how a healthy young man's anxiety over and fear of death differs from Jung's own as an old man. Here is how Hisamatsu, in another discussion, described composure unto death:

> Authentic composure is not lost even when you're turned head over heels. That's the way it is: Even in death you are composed. Not composure because you're resigned to die, but composure even unto death. Otherwise, it's not authentic.
>
> People sometimes say things like they are free from life and death, or there is no living and dying. But right now if you were on the brink of death and you were able to remain undisturbed, that's not freedom from life and death at all, though it's often misconstrued that way. If you were terminally ill, yet able to remain calm and unshaken in your last moments, wouldn't that be just a matter of your mental or psychological state?
>
> On the contrary, *death itself must be composed.* It's not a matter of remaining calm though you fear death: death itself is 'free from all fear' [as the *Heart Sutra* states]. Saying, 'I'm not afraid, I'm not afraid' – that's not real freedom from all fear. Truly be the formless self, and you are totally free of fear.
>
> (Hisamatsu 1998: 79, with revisions)

More concretely, in 1957, during Hisamatsu's visit to the United States, Albert Stunkard (Professor of Psychiatry at the University of Pennsylvania School of Medicine) brought a friend and medical student named Alan Balsam, who was dying of cancer, to meet Hisamatsu at his hotel in New York City. As soon as they met and sat facing each other, here is how Dr Stunkard recalls that encounter:

> There followed a long but comfortable pause. Then Professor Hisamatsu said, slowly, 'I understand that you are dying.'
>
> The direct, matter-of-fact quality of this statement, or question, stunned me. This was a time when doctors still shielded patients from information about their illnesses, particularly fatal illnesses, and we went to great pains to speak in euphemisms about death. I had never heard a physician talk to a patient about his death.

Before I had a chance to do more than register my surprise, Alan, looking intently at Hisamatsu, replied in firm voice, 'Yes.'

Another pause.

Then Professor Hisamatsu said, 'Does that frighten you?'

Still looking intently at Professor Hisamatsu, Alan again said 'Yes.'

Another long silence followed.

'What frightens you about it?' Professor Hisamatsu asked.

Again silence.

Alan began slowly but with an assurance that surprised me.

'For a long time I have wanted to come to terms with myself, what Christians might call knowing God.' After a pause, he added, 'Enlightenment.'

Professor Hisamatsu nodded encouragingly.

'I guess that I had always thought that I would have an infinite amount of time to get there. Now I know that I won't. And I'm afraid that I won't get there.'

'That is a good answer,' Professor Hisamatsu said quietly. The two continued to look at each other.

After another long period of quiet, Professor Hisamatsu began to speak. Exactly what he said in those days so long ago eludes me now. It had to do with the waves on the surface of the sea and the deep stillness under it. The stillness is always there, no matter how turbulent the waves. He spoke only briefly and then asked if we would like to have tea. . . .

(Stunkard 1998: 3–4)

How does this fit in with dealing with the individual problems and distress that people bring, for example, to psychotherapy? To those unfamiliar with Buddhism, it may seem narrow and inflexible, even cold and heartless, to focus only on the fundamental problem of *dukkha* and the fundamental solution that is Buddhism.

But is there better medicine for the fundamental suffering of each and everyone than that of directly revealing the one who is originally free of suffering? This is what Hisamatsu tried to impress upon Jung in their conversation – and upon Alan Balsam, for that matter. It can be the beginning of truly 'working through' (not only in the sense of uncovering, clarifying, and making our own, but also in the Freudian sense of overcoming) the particular problems that plague us all.

The fundamental problem that we are, and the particular problems and distress that we have, need to be clearly distinguished. They are not, however, completely separable but vitally conjoined and present in and as each of us. Thus, professional therapists and other caregivers can help to nudge and spur others awake in the very process of dealing with particular problems.

Not ignoring or denying the particular problem, but taking it to its very root; precisely here the root problem of *dukkha* can be solved once and for all. This, by the way, is what real koan practice is all about, what Vimalakirti is all about – and what Buddhism is all about.

Let me close by offering some other suggestive illustrations of this in practice, although Shih-t'ou's above-mentioned responses to the monk and Hisamatsu's encounter with Alan Balsam are worthy of much deeper reflection. Much could be said about each of these stories, but I will keep my comments to a minimum, and leave the interpretations to you.

A group of men were enjoying themselves in the woods when one of the women with them stole some of their valuables and ran away. Encountering Shakyamuni as they chase after the woman, Shakyamuni asks them, 'Which is better for you, that you should seek for a woman or that you should seek for the self?' (Horner 1971: 31–2). This may sound like Shakyamuni is unconcerned with the stolen items, or with the woman – he is only concerned with the men's fundamental problem. But is that really so?

The traditional parable of the mustard seed tells of a mother, distraught over the death of her only son, who carries him in her arms to Shakyamuni in hopes of obtaining medicine for him. Shakyamuni tells her to enter the city and get mustard seeds for medicine, but they must be from homes where no one has ever died. During her search, she hears the sorrows of many others when they explain to her why they cannot give her a mustard seed from their homes, for indeed many have died there. Her heart is eventually opened to the universal – not just objective – truth of impermanence. She then takes her dead child to the pyre and returns to Shakyamuni (see Burtt 1955: 43–6).

What do you see when looking in the eyes of another? I heard that once Mother Theresa was asked what she saw when she looked in the eyes of the filthy, diseased, and dying cradled in her shoulder. She replied, 'Christ in his distressing disguise.' While we should not gloss over the differences in this Christian 'metaphor,' I take it as an illuminating illustration of who the other truly is: A Buddha. Perhaps a Buddha who has not yet fully awakened to this fact. But a Buddha nonetheless.

Is this not what genuine Buddhist therapy comes down to?: Buddha encountering Buddha.

> While he is dreaming he does not know it is a dream, and in his dream he may even try to interpret a dream. Only after he wakes does he know it was a dream. And someday there will be a great awakening when we know that this is all a great dream. Yet the stupid believe they are awake, busily and brightly assuming they understand things, calling this man ruler, that one herdsman – how dense! Confucius and you are both dreaming! And when I say you are dreaming, I am dreaming, too.
>
> *Chuang Tzu,* chapter 2 (Watson 1968: 47–8)

References and further reading

An earlier version of this paper was presented in Japanese in *Kikan Bukkyō* (October 1999), Hōzōkan, Kyoto.

Unless noted, translations are by the present author.

Alcopley, L. (ed.) (1963) *Listening to Heidegger and Hisamatsu*, Kyoto: Bokubi Press. (Contains Japanese, German, and English versions of the Heidegger–Hisamatsu colloquy.)

Burtt, E. A. (ed.) (1955) *The Teachings of the Compassionate Buddha*, New York: New American Library.

DeMartino, R. (1970) 'The Human Situation and Zen Buddhism', in Erich Fromm, D. T. Suzuki and Richard DeMartino, *Zen Buddhism and Psychoanalysis*, New York: Harper & Row. (Predates the Jung–Hisamatsu discussion by nine months, having been presented at a conference in Cuernavaca, Mexico, in August of 1957.)

Hisamatsu, S. (1998) 'True sitting: a discussion with Hisamatsu Shin'ichi', *The Eastern Buddhist* 31(1): 72–84.

Hisamatsu, S. (1999) 'Talks on the *Vimalakirti Sutra*', Parts 5 and 6, *FAS Society Journal*: 15–27.

Hisamatsu, S. and Keiji Nishitani, et al. (1963) 'On the peace of mind', *Psychologia* 6: 117–24. (Translation of a discussion in Japanese on Hisamatsu's discussion with Jung.)

Horner, I. B. (trans.) (1971) *The Book of the Discipline*, Sacred Books of the Buddhists, 4, London: Luzac & Company.

Kalupahana, D. (1992) *A History of Buddhist Philosophy: Continuities and Discontinuities*, Honolulu: University of Hawaii Press.

Meckel, D. J. and R. L. Moore (eds) (1992) *Self and Liberation: The Jung/Buddhism Dialogue*, New York and Mahwah, NJ: Paulist Press. (Includes commentaries on the Jung–Hisamatsu conversation by Jung and Hisamatsu.)

Miura, I. and R. F. Sasaki (1966) *Zen Dust: The History of the Koan and Koan Study in Rinzai (Lin-chi) Zen*, New York: Harcourt, Brace & World.

Muramoto, S. (1998) 'The Jung–Hisamatsu Conversation', in Anthony Molino (ed.), *The Couch and the Tree: Dialogues in Psychoanalysis and Buddhism*, New York: North Point Press. (Includes an introduction detailing the publishing history of the conversation and a recently revised translation.)

Sasaki, R. F. (trans.) (1975) *The Record of Lin-chi [Rinzai]*, Kyoto: Institute for Zen Studies at Hanazono University.

Stunkard, A. (1998) 'A friendship', *FAS Society Journal*: 2–4.

Tillich, P. and S. Hisamatsu (1971–73) 'Dialogues East and West: conversations Between Dr Paul Tillich and Dr Hisamatsu Shin'ichi', in three parts, *Eastern Buddhist* 4(2): 89–107; 5(2): 107–28; 6(2): 87–114. (Includes extensive commentary by DeMartino, student of Hisamatsu and Tillich and one of the interpreters for the conversations.)

Watson, Burton (trans.) (1968) *The Complete Works of Chuang Tzu*, New York and London: Columbia University Press.

3

JUNG, CHRISTIANITY, AND BUDDHISM

James W. Heisig

Throughout the past generation of Christianity's encounter with Buddhism, the role played by Jungian psychology has been ancillary at best. True, Jung's ideas are cited with a certain regularity, but for some reason the systematic body of thought he left behind has not attracted Christians or Buddhists as a common forum for mutual criticism and enrichment. In this essay I would like to draw attention to what I see as an unnecessary closure in Jung's idea of the psyche and to suggest how its opening could nudge Christianity and Buddhism into closer contact with each other and with the shifts that have taken place in the general spirituality of our age.

The body of writings Jung left behind is at once forbidding and fascinating. The sheer volume of his output, which continues to grow as notes from his seminars and other unpublished material are added, makes it more and more unlikely that any but a small coterie of devoted specialists will take the time to become familiar with the whole. Even so, the academic background the specialist needs to read with understanding all but ensures that large blocks of his work will simply be skimmed over uncritically. For the same reason, general readers, in which group one must include the greater part of Jungian analysts, commentators, and critics, tend to dip into his writings according to their needs and to rely on secondary sources for general outlines of his thought. As a result, Jung's influence, while it reflects the breadth of his interests, tends to flow in most cases from no more than a small portion of his work.

Still, the captivating quality of Jung's work greatly outshines the impossible demands he places on his readers. The maps he drew of the psyche and the wealth of clinical and historical material he snares with his interpretative nets have a way of relativizing one's ordinary way of thinking about the experiences of life and of lending depth to his frequent asides about self-actualization, culture, and religion. And everywhere, between the lines, the unmistakable traces of personal experience work a subtle seduction on the reader. Simply put, Jung's ideas cannot be approached from books about Jung's ideas. One has first to enter into the atmosphere of his thought and breathe it in, resisting the gullibility or hasty skepticism that it is wont to prompt from the unprepared. He is not the only thinker of whom this can be said, of course, but the way his disciples and critics have abused his work makes it worth repeating at the outset of yet another appraisal of his ideas.

Jung and the Buddhist–Christian dialogue

Given Jung's own pioneering attempts to pry Christian tradition open to the truth of other religions and his considerable efforts to appropriate Eastern thinking into his understanding of the psyche, the neglect of his thought in interreligious dialogue is more than a little surprising. In addition to the many Christian thinkers who have acknowledged Jung's influence in their attempts to appropriate Buddhist ideas, there are any number of Buddhist thinkers who have picked up on his theory as a way to initiate contact between Buddhist teaching and the psychology of unconscious mind. The literature that reflects this is ample and widely translated. For all that, Jungian psychology as such has not been accepted as a rational foundation for sustained intellectual exchange among Christians and Buddhists.

Jung's exclusion from the dialogue

Nothing in Jung's writings or correspondence, published or otherwise, seems to offer a suitable explanation. Even a review of the brief dialogue Jung held with the Zen Master Hisamatsu Shin'ichi at Küsnacht in 1958 leaves us empty-handed. Jung himself was profoundly dissatisfied with the meeting; he found the transcript so full of errors of translation and misunderstandings that he expressly forbade its publication.[1] In the end one has the impression that the participants were unprepared to learn much from one another, or at least that their resistance to the expectations of the organizers kept them at a distance from one another. At the same time, one is left with the sense of a vast, uncharted sea for which Jung's thought would at one future date provide useful tools for navigation.

For his part, Jung welcomed the dialogue with the East in general and was flattered by the suggestion that his thought might serve as a bridge. Indeed, in a letter dated the same day as his meeting with Hisamatsu, he wrote, 'It has happened to me more than once that educated East Asians rediscovered the meaning of their philosophy or religion only through reading my books.'[2] At the same time, he never abandoned his early suspicions about Western Christians rushing East in search of what is right under their feet:

> Shall we be able to put on, like a new suit of clothes, ready-made symbols grown on foreign soil, saturated with foreign blood, spoken in a foreign tongue, nourished by a foreign culture, interwoven with foreign history, and so resemble a beggar who wraps himself in a kingly raiment, a king who disguises himself as a beggar? . . .

> We are, surely, the rightful heirs of Christian symbolism, but
> somehow we have squandered this heritage. We have let the house
> our fathers built fall into decay, and now we try to break into
> Oriental palaces that our fathers never knew.[3]

This was written in 1934, when his knowledge of the East was still rather
meager, the same year in which he turned down an invitation to go to China.[4]
In the following years, partly in preparation for a trip to India three years
later, he began to read more widely, as reflected in his writings and correspondence. Still, his misgivings about the escape to the East remained with
him to the end. The year before he died, Jung came across Arthur Koestler's
essays on 'Yoga unexpurgated' and 'The stink of Zen'[5] and found himself
largely sympathetic with their critique of Western ideas of the East. (In a
little-known aside in a letter confirming his opinion, he says of the author of
Zen in the Art of Archery, 'It is just pathetic to see a man like Herrigel acquiring the art of Zen archery, a non-essential if ever there was one, with the
utmost devotion . . .'.[6] Jung's comment should be read as a criticism not of
the Zen art, but of a man whom he knew to have been a confirmed Nazi distracting his conscience through Eastern religion.[7]) But that Jung should have
insisted on his own moorings in the Christian West hardly disqualifies his
thought from playing a role in the Buddhist–Christian encounter. If experience has taught us anything, it is that just such a sense of identity enhances
the possibility of authentic dialogue.

Though it has only been a generation since Jung's death, the level of education in religious studies in the Christian West and a corresponding
improvement in popular understanding have meant a more critical audience
for the kinds of generalizations depth psychology imposes on data outside its
field. That Jung's cloak as an authority on world religions should have frayed
in the process is hardly to be wondered at.

On the one hand, Western Christian participants in the dialogue with
Buddhism are too well informed of the great advances that have taken place
in Buddhist studies to consider Jung the authority on Buddhist ideas he may
once have been considered to be.[8] On the other, Buddhist thinkers entering
into dialogue are aware that Jung's reflections on Christian dogma are held
suspect by the majority of Christian theologians, and that his greater expertise in more esoteric and arcane currents of the Christian tradition is no
substitute for confrontation with the Christian mainstream. Given the important role that the Christian mystical tradition has played in the dialogue, this
amounts to no more than a short fall from a small pedestal; it is hardly
enough reason to erase the wider possibilities for its deepening the intellectual
encounter among the two religions. Whatever Jung's status as a representative
of Buddhist or Christian thought – in any event, even his diminished authority as a scholar of world religions leaves him standing head and shoulders
above most of those devoted to interreligious dialogue – surely the mysterious

inner world of the psyche as such still offers an important forum where religions can meet, leaving their dogmas at the door, and pursue together the elusive quest for a common humanity that transcends religious differences. And as psychologies of the unconscious go, surely Jung's remains as respectable and accessible to the modern mind as ever.

It is often said, not without a hint of distrust, that the driving force behind the encounter of Buddhism with Christianity has come from the Christian West. Even if this were true, there is little cause for shame in accepting the accusation. The enthusiasm for dialogue with Buddhism has been one of the major contributions of Christianity to the religious health of modern times, just as the repression of that enthusiasm has to be reckoned among the most pathological forces in Christian faith today. In my experience the initiative to dialogue is less a continuation of 'orientalism' than its critique. What is more, the sources of the inspiration are far more diverse than changes going on in the missionary ideal of Christianity. One has only to think of the many Christian scholars who have found a sure footing for their dialogue in Buddhist philosophies like that of the Kyoto school thinkers Nishida, Tanabe, and Nishitani, a body of thought that has prompted as many Japanese Buddhists to take the initiative in the encounter with Christianity. And there are other examples from the Buddhist world that come to mind when the focus of the dialogue shifts from doctrine to religious experience and social ethics.

Even so, this is only part of the picture. In the end, the most decisive spiritual force behind the search of Buddhist and Christian scholars for a common forum to discuss questions of religion and to reassess their self-understanding may belong to the general spiritual atmosphere of our age in which people feel less affinity for traditional religion than for the kind of thinking that Jung represented. Yet why should so timely, cross-cultural, and open-minded a venture as this have reduced the psychology of religion in general, and Jungian psychology in particular, to so incidental a role?

In asking the question and then dismissing the obvious answers, my aim is not to clear the air for a better diagnosis and then suggest a forum for Buddhist–Christian dialogue grounded on Jung's thought. I want rather to shift the question in order to suggest another way of bringing Jung into the dialogue.

A Jung–Buddhist–Christian dialogue

The intellectual dialogue between Buddhists and Christians today – excluding encounters limited to a mere exchange of information – has concentrated itself in two models which we may call the comparative and the ethical.

The *comparative model of dialogue* consists of a common, more or less neutral, forum into which each side can enter to discuss selected ideas from their respective traditions. In addition to the general rules of rational discussion, such a forum typically structures itself around a specific set of ideas that provide a common focus and language. In principle this super-structure can range from the generalized concepts, more or less explicit, that define a particular discipline (such as philosophy, anthropology, hermeneu-tics, comparative religions, psychology, or sociology) to the more specific concerns of particular currents or schools of thought (such as phenomenol-ogy, structuralism, Marxism, or psychoanalysis), and even to particular thinkers (such as Tillich, Radhakrishnan, Eliade, Whitehead, or the philoso-phers of the Kyoto school). The range of possibilities, only a few of them explored in practice, is as wide as the study of religion itself. As long as com-parative dialogue preserves this protean character, it protects itself from expropriation by the new breed of 'specialists' nipping at its heels like sheep-dogs trying to drive the flock into its own corrals.

The aim of the comparative dialogue is insight: an increased awareness of the variety of religious world views and values, a reawakening to things neglected or forgotten in one's own tradition, and eventually a reform of self-understanding in the light of what has been learned. It is a kind of exper-iment in mutual conversion whose success or failure depends not only on the academic level of the discussions, but also on the receptivity of the partici-pants to rethinking the conventions of their own belief.

The *ethical model of dialogue* brings Buddhists and Christians together by focusing their respective traditions on a common ethical concern. Though no less subject to the demands of reason, the ethical dialogue differs from the academic in taking its agenda from the injustices, oppressions, and environ-mental destruction at work in history. At times the agenda may take the more general form of the search for religious ideas to stimulate awareness or for-mulate principles. At times it may address a specific issue with a view to concerted action by the participants themselves. In either event, it looks beyond the metanoia of the academic to the world outside, to stimulate spe-cific moral sensitivities or even concrete praxis.

Given the choice of these two forms of intellectual dialogue and the absence of a social ethic,[9] Jungian psychology seems better suited to serve the aims of the academic model than those of the ethical. (Admittedly its thera-peutic techniques could also prove useful in forms of dialogue that concentrate on the practice of meditation.) There is another option, however: Jungian psychology can enter the dialogue as a third partner alongside Buddhism and Christianity.

At first glance, the suggestion may sound mischievous, or at least somewhat odd. For one thing, psychology is not religion; for another, the writings of a single individual can hardly be expected to stand shoulder to shoulder with major world religions. But what if there were issues that challenge the future evolution of depth psychology itself, issues that can be clearly formulated in the context of Jung's work and that at the same time challenge the future of Buddhism and Christianity? In other words, say that there are certain religious questions arising in our time which traditional religions like Buddhism and Christianity lack the doctrinal basis to reformulate or respond to; and say that these same questions demand a revision of psychological theory. In such circumstances, surely a psychology like Jung's, deeply committed to the importance of religion as it is, could be welcomed not as a common foundation for an ongoing dialogue, but as a kind of tugboat, to pull the Buddhist–Christian dialogue out of its harbor and into the open, uncharted sea.

Jung's original work began from a daring conviction that psychology had a great deal to learn from the data its theories had overlooked. Our aim in drawing his work into the dialogue is to emulate his courage, not his answers. The questions that I believe urge this *heuristic model of dialogue* on us, do not belong to the usual sorts of criticisms one hears Buddhists or Christians raising against Jung, nor to the criticisms Jung levels against them. They come from a religiosity of a different sort. A brief skepsis on his ideas of ego and Self can help specify what kinds of questions I have in mind.

A skepsis of ego and Self

Undiscovered Self, uneradicable ego

However much Jung insisted that ego-consciousness was only one part of the psyche, whose true center was the Self, in an important sense his psychology – both in theory and in practice – remained centered on the concrete individual as the subject of the first person singular. He always made it clear that his first duty as a therapist was to the individual. This was more than a statement about the therapeutic setting. It reflected his conviction about the 'profound unimportance' of general events of world history in comparison with the 'essential' life of the individual, which becomes more unreasonable, irresponsible, emotional, erratic, and unreliable the larger the group.[10] As a result, Jung took a dim view of group therapy. But more than that, he completely excluded the notion of collective consciousness from his map of the psyche. He was not unaware of theories of the social determination of knowledge, not to mention Freud's notion of the super-ego, but he could not use the term without immediately railing against the dangers of 'collectivism' and complaining of the 'almost unbridgeable gap' between collective consciousness and the collective unconscious.[11] It is one thing to argue that collectivity and consciousness are mutually exclusive. It is another to conclude that the shape that the public world of custom, law, social convention, and language give to individual consciousness is only important to the extent that it disrupts the work of consciousness, in which case the disruption is seen as a personal problem usually couched in symbolic form.[12] Apparently Jung did not see the difference.[13]

This sense of duty to the individual and distrust of the collective affected his thinking on the structure and teleology of the psyche. Consciousness by itself did not distinguish the human from the rest of the animal world, but the knowledge that one was conscious did. In the same way, it is not the mere fact of unconscious events in the mind that raised the collective unconscious above animal instinct, but conscious attention to these events. And the locus of this self-awareness, the one who did the knowing and the attending, was what Jung called the ego. It is therefore a mistake to think of the ego as an 'everyday' knowing subject and the Self as another 'truer' or 'deeper' knowing subject that takes over in proportion as the ego is dissolved. The peculiar economy of Jung's language, in which strict definition of terms so easily relaxes into metaphor, is partly to blame for the idea of one 'center' displacing another in the psyche. At the same time, since it was not merely an objective theoretical account of how the mind works but the *transformation* of the individual's self-knowledge that interested Jung, and since he saw this process of 'individuation' as a confrontation with the imagery thrown up from the unconscious mind, it was inevitable that symbolic representations of the process would not always coincide with more precise psychological theory. For Jung, as well as for those who pursue his ideas in therapeutic practice, the theory has always to retain a degree of flexibility in its application to individual subjects. Insofar as it claims to be a unified theory, however, one expects that it be self-consistent. What I am aruging here is that Jung's theory only hangs together *as theory* if centered on the idea of the conscious ego.

Jung nowhere denies that all self-awareness and self-identity require a conscious subject. In the normal, healthy mind this means a single, unified, ego. When some other complex usurps control from the ego, self-awareness and self-identity disintegrate. This is normal in sleep or fantasy or some other lowering of consciousness; it is indeed the very definition of an unconscious event. In the waking state it usually looks pathological. In this sense, there is nothing in principle to distinguish the working of the unconscious in the sane individual from the clinically insane. The difference is that the latter remains submerged in the unconscious while the former returns to the conscious ego. Jung's aim was never to displace the ego with some other complex, however deeply imbedded in the collective recesses of the mind, but always to expand the self-awareness of the ego. The *impulse* to this expansion may come from outside the ego, but from start to finish, the encounter with the unconscious has to be seen as the work of one and the same first-personal, individual subject. Indeed, the unconscious 'cannot be investigated at all without the interaction of the observing consciousness.'[14] On the contrary, 'it must be reckoned a psychic catastrophe when *the ego is assimilated by the Self.*'[15]

The idea of positing a Self as the goal of the process of individuation did not, then, aim at uprooting the ego and replacing it with an alternate center of subjectivity. The aim was rather a different *form* of subjectivity. When Jung talks of overcoming the ego and making room for the Self, he means exchanging one way of seeing subjectivity with another. Only in this sense can we speak of the Self as an *alter ego*.[16] In other words, Self has to be seen as a transformation of the everyday waking individual – the ego – from a normal, narrow-minded awareness of itself and its autonomy in consciousness to the realization that there are reaches of the mind out of its control but essential to its development. The aim was not less ego but a reformed ego, less self-sufficient, less centered on controlling perception and experience, more open to unknown and uncontrollable dimensions of mind. Only in this sense can it be called a change in the core of consciousness.

Like the carving on the wall of the oracle's cave at Delphi, *Know thyself*, the idea of the Self served to remind the subject that knowledge of life's mysteries begins in awareness of the presence of superior forces. The task of the ego is to discern the meaning of these forces, to broaden the reach of its consciousness. At the same time, like the carving on the opposite wall of the Delphi cave, *Nothing in excess*, the idea of the Self was a reminder never to presume that the unknown and uncontrollable workings of the mind can be reduced without remainder to categories of rational meaning, nor to allow the powers of the conscious ego to be swallowed up passively by the non-rational realm of the unconscious. The totality of the psyche is not unintelligible, but only *inexhaustibly* intelligible.[17] In a word, Jung's idea of the individuated Self comes down to this: an integration of conscious and unconscious forces achieved in ego-consciousness.

The monarchic psyche

The ontological status of ego and Self in Jung's writings is ambivalent at best, muddled at worst. Depending on the context, they are alluded to as energies, forces, functions, classes of phenomena, archetypes, or entities.[18] On the other hand, despite his strictures against metaphysical speculation, Jung often claimed that 'the psyche alone has immediate reality,' that it is an 'equivalent of the universe without,' 'a cosmic principle . . . coequal with the principle of physical being,' 'an objective reality,' a 'precondition of being,' and 'superlatively real.'[19] Whatever their status as distinct ingredients of mind – which question did not seem to detain Jung for very long – ego and Self participate in objective 'reality' in virtue of a kind of cooperative partnership in the enterprise of the psyche. Behind this grand idea lies a simple logical process wherein the idea of the Self is constructed as a negative image of the idea of the ego.

For Jung, the psyche is structured as a field of force on which the contrary but complementary forces of consciousness and the unconscious interact with each other. The hypothesis of a 'center' of consciousness in which 'contents' of consciousness are retrieved from perceptual memory and processed – the ego – does not of itself require the positing of an unconscious mind with contents of its own. But once it *is* posited (the history of its 'discovery' is indispensable for understanding the idea, but not for the point I am making here[20]), it needs a principle of organization of these non-conscious contents. For Freud, this principle was supplied by sexual libido; for Jung, by the archetypes. But since Jung assumed the unconscious to be a negative image of consciousness (a 'negative borderline concept' he called it, following Kant), he also needed a central agent in the unconscious to balance the ego of consciousness. In other words, unless he was to redefine consciousness as a field of energy without a core agent, Jung would have to hypothesize a central agent for the unconsciousness as well.

Now while the core agent of the unconscious would reflect that of the conscious ego as its negative image, it would have to do so in a distinctively unconscious manner. That is, it would have to perform a function that complemented but did not contradict the essential functions of the conscious ego, lest the whole idea of psychic totality be forfeited. The defining function of this agent would be to promote the integration of unconscious contents in the ego, the subject of knowledge for the psyche as a whole, and thus serve as the bearer of a *telos* for the psyche as a whole. It is in these complementary, mutually reflective functions of ego and Self that Jung realized most clearly the 'cosmic meaning of consciousness' as creator of objective culture: once the self-enclosed ego has awakened to its own illusory nature vis-à-vis the wider world of the unconscious, it is able to shake off the conventional view of the world and give objective reality to the Self in the world of space and time, to 'complete creation' by 'living out one's myth.'[21]

In broad strokes, this seems to me to be the rationale at work behind the scenes of Jung's distinction between ego and Self and of their ambivalent ontological status. Admittedly, absent the clinical data that Jung used to support his idea of the Self as well as the mythical and symbolic parallels he cites, the hypothesis of the Self looks more arbitrary than it should. At the same time, it brings into clearer relief certain tacit assumptions that those data tend to obscure. In particular, I would note three points.

First, however older and wiser the unconscious might be at its deepest strata, it is essentially a kind of consciousness, just not an *ego*-consciousness. We see this already from the two types of metaphor Jung used for the collective: as womb, matrix, or sea, the unconscious is the birthplace of the conscious ego; and as storehouse or mine its images and motifs hold in deposit centuries of experience that may once have been conscious to the ego. Theoretically as well, without a wide basis of commonality in basic mental functioning, there would be no way for unconscious 'contents' to be received in consciousness and processed by the ego into meaning.

Now if we accept the fact that the acquisition and exercise of consciousness is conditioned by the historical and cultural circumstances in which individual subjects come to birth, then there is no reason to suppose that the unconscious can sidestep these conditions and enter directly into consciousness in a pure form. Jung saw this in the case of the personal unconscious, which inflicts on consciousness a kind of scotoma that biases its perception of collective elements in the psyche. He assumed that once one had dissolved this subjective 'shadow,' the ego could enter the objective unconscious as an impartial spectator, which he found symbolized in the dream state as an *anima* or *animus* that leads the ego into this underworld. To question this assumption is not to question the fundamental stability of structure of the psyche across the centuries and therefore the possibility of innate, archetypal conditioning in the background. It merely introduces a permanent suspicion regarding apparent coincidences in symbolic form between the images met in the modern unconscious and those found in myths and religions of antiquity, and the conclusions that can be drawn from these coincidences.

Second, the idea of a solitary, 'atomic ego'[22] at the center of consciousness feeds into the assumption that the psyche as a whole is also structured around a single center that takes the form of an individuated ego or Self. Although each of the archetypes of the unconscious can be said to function as a kind of microcosm of the psyche as a whole, he never backed down from the conviction that one of these archetypes must be more central and more comprehensive, namely the archetype of the Self. The experience of the body, bound by a single skin and centered perceptually in the head, leads naturally enough to the idea of a single mind with a single center. Subjectivity, self-identity, self-reflection, memory, and so forth rest on this assumption and its continued reaffirmation by the uniqueness of the individual body. Accordingly, collectivity is restricted to participation in a common form. In the same way that the visible anatomical structure of the body with its perceptual apparatus is seen to have evolved and reproduced itself in more or less stable patterns, the invisible world of the mind can be assumed to have evolved into a stable structure reproduced in individual subjects.

Obviously Jung was guided by this assumption in his attempts to explore both the structure of the unconscious as well as its contents. In interpreting the imagery of the unconscious not only did he single out certain basic patterns of symbolic form – the archetypes – but he saw an underlying drama being worked out which culminated in the image of a single unifying archetype around which all other contents would revolve like planets around the sun. This archetype, the Self, he came to see, has as its 'psychic equivalent' the image of God: 'The symbols of divinity coincide with those of the Self: what, on the one side, appears as a psychological experience signifying psychic wholeness, expresses on the other side the idea of God.'[23] Changes in God imagery, whether within the psychic life of the individual or in general cultural history, run 'parallel with changes in human consciousness' and are required by it to such a degree that '*the destruction of the God-image is followed by the annulment of the human personality.*'[24]

Jung was careful not to make any claims in his public writings regarding which was first – the archetype of the Self or the image of God in the psyche – but he never faltered in the claim of a one-to-one correspondence.

This correspondence is in fact the keystone in Jung's monarchic psyche. The idea of a consciousness centered on the ego is offset by that of an unconscious centered on the archetype of the Self, and these opposites are embraced by a greater totality centered on the individuated ego or actualized Self. The first principle of order is therefore both center (which brings coherence to the psyche) and totality (which insures that nothing is omitted), and this lends itself readily to expression in monotheistic images of divinity. Jung says this in so many words in an interesting comment that opens his study on *Psychology and Alchemy*: 'The Self is not only the center, but also the whole circumference which embraces both conscious and unconscious; it is the center of this totality, just as the ego is the center of consciousness.'[25] In another context he cites the Gnostic saying, which frequently appears in alchemical literature, that 'God is an infinite circle (or sphere) whose center is everywhere and the circumference nowhere,'[26] without worrying that it challenges a statement made earlier in the paragraph identifying the God-image as the central point in the circle. In fact, nowhere in his study of myth, primal religions, or Eastern thought does Jung seriously entertain the idea that his archetype of the Self may be based more on a monotheistic preconception than on the actual data. That Jung identified the Self with symbols of God may be more than merely the humble submission to the facts that Jung would have us believe. In any case, the monarchic structure of the psyche and the monotheism of the Christian support the same tacit assumption.

A third assumption that corroborates the monarchic quality of the Jungian psyche is the idea that archetypal symbols of the collective unconscious tend to seek completion in their opposite (reflecting the tendency of conscious and unconscious mind towards wholeness), crystallizing in symbols of the Self that take the form of a union of opposites. As a logical form, the idea of relating polar opposites so that each maintains its identity without eliminating its other is one of the most primitive forms of abstraction, arguably grounded in basic experiences like the rising and setting of the sun or the interaction of the sexes. At least as far as a two-valued logic of affirmation and negation with its laws of contradiction and the excluded middle are concerned, there is no simpler way of avoiding a dualism, not to say a pluralism, of worlds. Little wonder that the pattern should appear with such frequency in ritual, myth, and other forms of symbolic activity representing the totality of the cosmos. Little wonder, too, that Jung should have adopted it as the matrix for his map of the psyche of the whole and found it mirrored microcosmically in the interplay among psychic contents.

To make this 'dynamic monism' work, all that was needed was to insure that such contents as reflected the elemental functions of the psyche be read as symbols, bracketing any literal reference to any outer reality, which would interfere with the purity of the form.[27] This Jung achieved by seeing the collectivity of an unconscious symbol as a measure of its truth, depth, and reliability. The symbolism of the Self as a totality arranged as a complex of opposites is not, therefore, a pure conclusion drawn from an objective presentation of the facts, but an a priori condition for interpreting the contents of the collective unconscious symbolically.

Questioning the frontiers of the inner life

Insofar as these assumptions are in fact at work in Jungian psychology, they suggest a much shorter tether to Western, Christian roots than is commonly associated with his thought. I hesitate to rush to the conclusion that slackening the ties to allow Jung's ideas more freedom to roam about Eastern and Buddhist ideas would produce a better, more universally applicable psychology. At the same time, I am persuaded that many of the criticisms that arise in stretching Jungian psychology to the outer limits of its relevance for the non-Christian West are equally relevant for Christianity and Buddhism, both of which know very well today what it is to be at the end of their rope and going around in circles, unable to reach the masses of modern men and women in search of spiritual meaning. What I would like to attempt in this concluding section is to point to a number of areas in the contemporary perception of the inner life where the influence of traditional Buddhism, traditional Christianity, and traditional Jungian psychology have been muted, but which offer the grounds for the sort of three-way heuristic dialogue suggested above.

With Jung's volumes scattered around me, and armed with the ordinary tools of logic and whatever common sense I have, I feel a certain sureness of foot tracing arguments to their sources and dodging conclusions that overreach their premises. When it comes to refreshing my view of the original experiences and events that this intellectual apparatus is supposed to have obscured, however, I find myself wobbling uncomfortably in the extreme. Add to this the fact that the context of these remarks is the Buddhist–Christian dialogue and I flush at the biases of my Western, Christian upbringing. In spite of myself, I will try to approach the heart of my thesis with as much objectivity as I can.

Higher consciousness, higher reality

For all the ambiguity of usage and the tacit assumptions that entangle the terms, the question of a true Self different from the everyday ego continues to provide an important meeting point in the dialogue between psychology and religion East and West. Without a shift in the question, however, the dialogue is likely to idle interminably on the differences between their respective cultural and philosophical approaches to subjectivity.[28] William James, with his uncanny knack for catching the heart of the matter with just the right phrase, can help to point the way.

In drawing up his conclusions to *The Varieties of Religious Experience*,

James notes that the idea of the naturally broken, divided self, is not of itself enough to account for religious faith. The individual enters into the presence of something 'more' – a relation of 'the germinal higher part of himself' to a wider reality:

> *He becomes conscious that this higher part is coterminous and contin-*
> *uous with a* MORE *of the same quality, which is operative in the universe*
> *outside of him* . . . Disregarding the over-beliefs and confining our-
> selves to what is common and generic, we have *in the fact that the*
> *conscious person is continuous with a wider self through which saving*
> *experiences come*, a positive content of religious experience which, it
> seems to me, *is literally and objectively true as far as it goes.*[29]

In our normal, everyday forms of consciousness, we suffer from what James calls a 'lifelong habit of inferiority to our full self.' Insofar as the self that encases the seed of a wider consciousness like a husk is seen as 'convention-ally healthy,' cracking it open to uncover the higher part leaves the individual exposed to neurosis; but then, as James reminds us and as Jung himself knew, this may well be the chief condition for receptivity to these higher realms.[30]

This idea of a wider self walled in by the habits of ego-consciousness but equipped with the facility to experience higher realities was more than a figure of speech for James. His abiding interest in spiritualistic phenomena and the paranormal was reflected in his attention to Theosophy, the New Thought Alliance, Christian Science and a host of other manifestations of the search for 'higher consciousness' that seemed to offer America's preoccu-pation with mental illness 'new ranges of life succeeding on our most despairing moments.'[31] For James, it seemed as if the country were in the grip of a spiritual revival of a different order from what was going on within the organized churches. 'These ideas are healthy minded and optimistic,' James pronounced, 'and it is quite obvious that a wave of religious activity, analo-gous in some respects to the spread of early Christianity, Buddhism, and Mohammedanism is passing over our American world.'[32] Always careful to keep the theoretical claims associated with this activity at arm's length from his own psychology, one cannot read James without feeling the slow boil of this enthusiasm just under the surface. This is particularly true of his idea of the 'wider self.'[33]

Reluctantly, because there are so many more doors he could open, I take leave of James here and return to the main line of my argument with the fol-lowing proposition: it was precisely at this idea of uncovering a *higher* self equipped to encounter *higher* realms of reality that Jung drew the line for his psychology of religion – a line he did not need to draw and we would do better to erase.

Jung's idea of actualizing the full powers of the psyche (individuation) was controlled in large part by the image of a journey of the ego out of consciousness and into the deep, dark recesses of the mind. The inhabitants of this realm are more often shadowy figures blending themselves in and out of each other under the soft light of the moon, transforming and changing shapes against a nocturnal landscape. Things that appear pitifully discrete and separate in the bright light of the sun are 'deepened' in the unpredictable, always slightly frightening, haze of the unconscious.[34] The stimulus to enter this inner world is also typically dark: despair, sin, failure, anxiety, finitude, nihilism, and self-devastation figure more prominently than bright, exhilarating, oceanic, climactic explosions of emotion that open up a vaster consciousness with a sense of 'grace abounding.'

At bottom, Jung's objection to the idea of higher consciousness as he saw it in Eastern thought was that it tried to eliminate too quickly the suffering ego without which the revelations of the unconscious have no meaning. Blotting out the distinction between subject and object looked to him like a simple swallowing up of ego in the unconscious – with the difference that for the Easterner 'the unconscious is above, with us it is below'[35] – which only anesthetized the subject from its suffering. Rather than lead to greater self-awareness, it amounted to a self-deception of having transcended the dark side of life (rather, I suppose, like Dickens's Mrs Gradgrind, who 'thinks there is a pain in her room somewhere' but 'is not sure whether she is the one who has got it or not'). For Jung 'I know that I suffer' is not only superior to 'I suffer' but also to 'I know suffering to be an illusion of the ego.'[36]

The upshot of Jung's position is that it begs the question of whether there is a 'wider self' – or 'selves' – capable of receiving a range of information inaccessible to the ego-centered psyche. The methodological decision to 'symbolize' accounts of states of mind associated with spiritualistic phenomena, shamanism, astrology, alchemy, cabalism, divination, and even extraterrestrial manifestations in order to extract their 'meaning' for the conscious ego casts aside the question of multiple centers or progressive stages of consciousness beyond the normal first-person, singular individual. It also relieved him of the obligation to pronounce judgment on their causes. Like James, Jung knew of experiences of 'uncovering' so overwhelming to the experiencer that one is no longer sure if it is tracts of consciousness or reality itself that is being uncovered.[37] He knew what it was to trust in the revelations of dreams; he consulted the *I Ching*, used the services of a dowser (successfully),[38] and had more than the normal share of paranormal experiences. But rather than pursue the question of what was real and what not, or whether there were such things as higher states of consciousness, or whether consciousness had multiple centers or not, or whether in the end one had to suffer the humiliation of not being able to answer these questions satisfactorily, he found it enough to concentrate on 'synchronicities' between events and their meaning for ego-consciousness. It was not the 'more' as such that concerned him so much as the symbolic meaning that could be mined from phenomena that seemed to transcend the reach of the conscious ego.[39] Despite the occasional speculation in his seminars and letters, in the end all questions about reality and existence could be swept under the rug of 'the unconscious' with the broom of scientific detachment.

Jung's refusal to distinguish God from the collective unconscious *qua* psychic phenomena begins to look less and less loyal to the facts. In commenting on the direct continuity of structure between ego-consciousness and the unconscious in Jung's map of the psyche, I suggested above that the model was basically monotheistic. This also helps explain why for Jung the 'more' naturally came to take the form of an absolute One – a collective unconscious to cover all non-ego conscious functions, an image of God to cover the reality uncovered. In claiming his map of the psyche for science and leaving to theology and metaphysics the question of the existence or non-existence of God, he excluded in principle the possibility of plurality in higher consciousness and higher reality.

What appeared to him a gesturing towards science and away from theology was in fact a severe constriction of thought. Behind the vast sweep of Jung's idea of an *unus mundus* whose microcosm was the Self, lay a much more limited view of the structure of reality that contains the 'immensity' of the one, absolute macrocosm. In describing the thought of William James, Henri Bergson notes that the needs of modern reason are fulfilled by imagining the world as *infinite*, in contrast to antiquity, which saw it as *finite*; James, on the other hand, saw it as *indefinite*, leaving reason less satisfied and diminished in importance but the totality of the human person 'immeasurably enhanced.'[40] In linking his theory to the finite classical world he met in ancient texts and symbols, Jung neither satisfies modern reason nor provides sufficient cause for it to suffer dissatisfaction.

Beyond the Buddhist–Christian world view

There is much in Jung's distinction between ego and Self that the Buddhist mind will find alien, just as much of the criticism of it will appear self-evident. Insofar as Jung stands accused of being deceived by coincidences of terminology and plying ideas without due concern for native context, the mere application of his concepts to more and more Buddhist material will not do.[41] The easiest response is to debit the differences to Western Christianity's loss and credit Buddhism and the East with having treated the whole question more exhaustively. A more demanding, but in the end no less evasive approach is to argue that the 'Eastern mind' is not a mere variation on a common human psychic structure but requires its own definition of consciousness.[42] To cast the matter aside with so simple a wave of the hand and gloss over the efforts that have been made to study the value of Jung's thought as a bridge from the Christian West to the Yogic, Hindu, Taoist, Tibetan, Mahayana, and Zen traditions of the East is likely to content only the most dogmatic of temperaments. Insofar as these questions belong to the history of ideas, a tougher, more patient approach, grounded in fidelity to the textual evidence, is in order. Its execution I leave to those more competent than I.

When it comes to a shift in the basic structure of world view that is held in common by the traditions under scrutiny, however, the historical sources alone do not suffice. If, as I believe to be the case, the world views of Buddhism and Christianity are cut of the same cloth as the finite classical cosmos of Jung's thought, and if that world view no longer forms the backdrop against which the spirituality of our times is taking shape, then the discussion of different ideas of Self and ego needs radical rethinking. Beliefs in higher reality and higher consciousness set against that background cannot be absorbed *tout court* into the available categories of traditional doctrine; either they are allowed to solicit new formulations or they replace them. What we see happening today – in both Christianity and Buddhism – is a tilt towards the latter, to which the interreligious dialogue may even be adding its weight. The openness to an *indefinite* view of the psyche and the cosmos, however menacing at first sight, may contribute to that immeasurable enhancement that James hoped for. In what remains I would like to give some idea of the extent of the requisite openness, free of any conjecture as to the conclusions to which it might conduce.

Since the middle of the nineteenth century, new teachings about the place of the human person in the natural cosmos have made their way from the Orient, from ancient Pharaonic Egypt, from medieval mysticism and alchemy, and from the perennial undercurrent of arcane doctrines that have accompanied Christianity and Judaism from centuries past, into the cultures of the West. At first these teachings spread among a small circle of philosophers and poets; from there they spread into spiritualist and esoteric movements, mainly at the fringes of psychology and religion. For at least a generation now, they have become part of the cultural mainstream. This shift from periphery to center is often misunderstood as a rise in the general level of superstition or interest in the perennial underground currents of organized religion. The difference is that these new teachings no longer define themselves primarily as a critique or filling out of established religion but as an alternative basis for religion. Even the scientific community shows a greater interest in these 'whisperings from beyond' as a possible object of research than it does in the classical doctrines of established religion.[43]

We are still too much a part of the story of what is happening to religious consciousness to assess its meaning. What seems clear, however, is that the cosmos and the place of human beings within it are not those of Christianity or Buddhism or Jung. It is as if the evolution of consciousness has come full circle. In its infancy, the mind mixed up feelings and fantasies with what it observed in the natural world. Self-awareness fashioned itself after the movements of birds of the air and the animals of the forest, of the sun, the moon, and the stars, by giving them human form. With the advance of civilization, the mind became aware of itself as the highest glory of the natural world, withdrawing into itself all but the most abstract projections of superior forces. The doctrines of the great religions followed other forms of the pursuit of true knowledge that this world view opened up. However differently the observed data were jumbled into explanation, the superiority of the observer to the observed was not in question. This anthropocentric bias is no longer self-evident today. Today the mind has taken a turn towards an organic interconnectedness among all things in the apparent attempt to restore something in self-awareness that had been lost in classical scientific method and religious orthodoxy.

When Jung saw flying saucers as symbolic of a *desire* for salvation from without, and belief in an afterlife as the symbolic anticipation of the *desire* for an ideal society,[44] he was thinking from the same basic posture as that which produced the Christian heaven or the Buddhist nirvana – just offering a different, more radically anthropocentric explanation of the phenomena. In refusing to entertain the possibility of any ontological reality at the other end of the raw mental intentionality, he nonetheless reaffirmed the supremacy of human consciousness looking out at the rest of the cosmos.

Today, when we look at the starry sky above, we see something different. We have seen images from light years beyond our own galaxy and trust the mathematical extrapolations that everything in the space between us and them is no more than a few grains of dust in a sandstorm. The possibility of intelligent life, even qualitatively superior intelligent life, beyond earth has moved from science fiction to reasonable hypothesis. Even as the wonderland of the brain begins to yield more and more of its secrets to scientific method, the bonds between mind and body have loosened to the point of serious research into psychosomatic healing, extracorporeal consciousness, and life-energies. Along with animal communication, manifestations of disembodied spirits, former lives, dead souls, telekinesis, and other parapsychological phenomena, extraterrestrial visitations, simultaneous universes, time-warps, and other paranatural phenomena are no longer merely fanatical trimmings of common sense. We are still a long way from having sorted out wild conjecture from reasonable hypothesis in the maelstrom of ideas. Meantime, it has become irrevocably clear that there are whole blocks of experience that do not fit received patterns and may require new paradigms of mind.

The dislodgings of ego-consciousness from the center of the mind, the mind from the center of the galaxy, and the galaxy from the center of the universe leave Christian and Buddhist orthodoxy without the compass that had guided the development of their teachings. It is not only that most traditional religious responses to these phenomena no longer make sense to the vast majority of the people who know them through personal experience; Buddhist and Christian scholars carry on in dialogue with the modern world, and with each other, as if these things were not even happening, as if they were no more than symptoms of a mass neurosis that will work itself out in time. Like that part of the scientific community stuck in a classical, mechanistic view of science, but for different reasons, they bide their time until the nuisance passes and things get back to 'normal.'

Meantime, the quest of spiritual experience continues to move ahead. The growing dependency of culture on scientific knowledge has not suppressed the counter-movement of a pervasive disillusionment with mechanistic explanations of the totality of the cosmos and human life within it. Of itself the critique of science does not, however, signal a revival of religion. On the contrary, to the extent that today's esoterica and search for new forms of spiritual experience confine themselves to the shadows of science, they promote a greater alienation of religion from the everyday world and strengthen the 'normal,' scientific-technological way of valuing the things of life.

Though not an old story, all of this is by now too familiar to belabor with still more generalizations. To the extent that the traditional Buddhist and Christian myths have fallen from grace, Jung has fallen along with them, repeating the sin he set out originally to avoid: excluding experiences or aspects of experience that contradict the accepted doctrine. For all that, Jung's psychology, by virtue of its foundation on the primacy of religious experience and a critique of dogmatic religion, may be of assistance to Buddhism and Christianity in confronting this common problem. What shape this confrontation will take, and at which point it will come to a head, is hard to predict.

If I may state my own suspicion in the matter: *Buddhism and Christianity need to stimulate each other to a recovery of elements in their respective traditions that have been exiled in the name of orthodoxy or sectarianism, but that can speak more directly to the experience and phenomena that have captured the religious imagination in our time.*

I think it unreasonable to expect that the dialogue create new doctrine – or new psychological theory, for that matter – but it can help to thaw what has been frozen in self-understanding so that it may once again flow into the living tradition. From my own experience of the dialogue in Japan, I see a clear precedent of this in the way that Japanese Buddhist interest in the Christian mystical tradition has stimulated a more serious appraisal of these men and women and their writings among Christian scholars engaged in the dialogue with Buddhism. What we have not seen in the dialogue, however, is the way the current resurrection of interest in the doctrines and practices of Shugendo, Kundalini and Tantric Yoga, Kalacakra Tantra, and so forth have begun to stimulate mainline Japanese Mahayana to reassess their historical distance from these traditions.[45]

One thinks, for example, of the idea that emotional and mental energies can be stored in the natural environment as a kind of non-conscious 'memory' and effect a kind of 'wisdom' outside of the human individual – an idea that has virtually no religious significance for Buddhism or Christianity (or Jungian psychology, for that matter, except as symbolic projections). If the idea of harmony with the forces of earth resonates at all in the teachings of these 'world' religions today, it is most likely as a faint echo of 'secular' spiritualities of the age, the same spiritualities that have helped to kindle criticism of the ruthless scarring and disfiguring of the planet we see all about us. In any case, it is this kind of groping around in the twilight regions of religious traditions that I have in mind by speaking of a heuristic model of dialogue.

As a rule Christian scholars engaged in the dialogue with Buddhism tend to take a more tolerant view of heresies in their own tradition than do scholars closer to the centers of orthodoxy. To many of these latter, the dialogue not only promotes relativism, it often feeds a negative view of official doctrine as a musty baroque castle inhabited by pedants and eccentrics, unsuited to house the spirit of our times. Although the majority of Buddhist scholars engaged in the dialogue with Christians may not feel in the same measure the sting of complaints by an orthodox establishment against their interest in 'perverted and wrongly adhered to' doctrines,[46] the dialogue does not seem to have stimulated among them a greater ecumenical attitude towards doctrines and practices of competing sects, let alone a review of their own discarded heresies. It is possible that a more concerted confrontation with the non-affiliated religiosity of our times could propel them in this direction. As St Paul says, 'There must be factions among you in order that those who are genuine among you may be recognized' (1 Cor. 11:19). Among the possibilities that the dialogue opens up is that of converting the factions among us all to factions within us each. On the possibility of just such a metanoia I rest my suggestion of a three-way dialogue with Buddhism, Christianity, and Jung's psychology.

Notes

1 The text was, however, reprinted in *Self and Liberation: The Jung–Buddhism Dialogue*, ed. Daniel J. Meckel and Robert L. Moore (New York: Paulist Press, 1992), together with the responses of Jung and Hisamatsu and a transcript of a roundtable discussion held in Kyoto afterwards to assess the encounter (103–27).

2 C. G. Jung, *Letters, vol. 2: 1951–1961* (London: Routledge & Kegan Paul, 1975), 438.

3 *CW* 9/1: 14–15. See also *Letters, vol. 2*, 247, where Jung advises a correspondent to do everything she can to get her son back to Europe from the monastery he had joined in India.

4 The proposal seems to have originated with Erwin Rousselle, then director of the China Institute in Frankfurt. See B. Hannah, *Jung: His Life and Work* (Wilmette: Chiron, 1974, 1997), 240.

5 These would appear later that year in Koestler's *The Lotus and the Robot.*

6 *Letters, vol. 2*, 602.

7 In 1961 Gershom Scholem wrote an open letter in response to Koestler's criticisms of Zen, informing him of the 'carefully hushed' secret that Herrigel joined the Nazi Party after the outbreak of the war. Although biographical notes prepared by his widow make no mention of the fact, Scholem learned of it in 1946 from a circle of former friends of Herrigel's who claimed that he had remained a convinced Nazi to the end. See *Encounter* 16(2) (1961): 96. A more fully documented account of this can be found in Yamada Shōji, 'The myth of Zen in the art of archery', *Japanese Journal of Religious Studies* 28, 1–2 (Spring 2001).

8 See J. J. Clarke, *Jung and Eastern Thought: A Dialogue with the Orient* (London: Routledge, 1994), part 3. Although a number of broadsides and sideswipes are mixed indiscriminately with more serious appraisals, it is a good catalogue of Buddhist criticisms of Jungian thought. More complete bibliographical information can be found in John Borelli, 'C. G. Jung and Eastern religious traditions: an annotated bibliography', in Harold Coward, *Jung and Eastern Thought* (Albany: SUNY Press, 1985), 191–212.

9 I have taken up this question at some length in 'Yungu shinrigaku to kōteki jiko' [Jungian psychology and the public self], *Nanzan Shūkyōbunka Kenkyūjo Kenkyūshohō* 9 (1999). Elsewhere I have argued, in a contrast of James with Jung, that the idea of the 'primacy of religious experience' does not of itself require a bracketing of general ethical questions of the age nor the exclusion of the moral dimension from the evaluation of the 'truth' of a theory. 'The myth of the primacy of religious experience: towards a restoration of the moral dimension', *Academia* (Nanzan University) 64 (1998): 25–45.

10 *CW* 10: 149; 18: 571.

11 The longest passage I know in his works appears in *CW* 8: 217–22.

12 We see this reflected in a late letter in which he admitted that the problem of ethics 'cannot be caught in any formula, twist and turn it as I may; for what we are dealing with here is the will of God. . . . Therefore I cannot reason about ethics. I feel it unethical because it is a presumption', *Letters, vol. 2*, 379–80.

13 Barbara Hannah recalls Jung saying that he was aware how much his focus on the individual had moved him to the fringe of collectivity, rendering his approach too 'one-sided', *Jung*, 290. And in a late interview, he is reported to have said that 'it is absolutely necessary that you study man also in his social and general environments', R. I. Evans, *Jung on Elementary Psychology: A Discussion between C. G. Jung and Richard I. Evans* (London: Routledge & Kegan Paul, 1976), 151, 221–2.

14 *CW* 11: 469.

15 *CW* 9/2: 24. Emphasis in original.

16 This is why Jung was able to speak in his own case of 'an extension of the ego or consciousness achieved in old age.' See *Erinnerungen, Träume, Gedanken* (Zurich: Buchclub Ex Libris, 1961), 229. The English translation mistranslates the passage, omitting the reference to the ego. See *Memories, Dreams, Reflections* (New York: Pantheon, 1961), 225.

17 It is important to distinguish the non-rational here from the simply irrational. Jung was adamant in principle, though perhaps not always successful in practice, that sloppy logic or unclarity of thought were an impediment to confrontation with the unconscious. See my essay, 'The mystique of the nonrational and a new spirituality', in David Ray Griffin (ed), *Archetypal Process: Self and Divine in Whitehead, Jung, and Hillman* (Evanston: Northwestern University Press, 1989), 167–201, 209–13. Recently the director of the French translation of Jung's works, Michael Cazenave, has published a remarkable work showing how Jung's resistance to the rationalizing ego was not a mere negative critique of the limits of the mind to comprehend reality but a positive attempt to give oneself over to the mystery of images as nature's invitation to the mind to transcend itself. *Jung: L'experience intérieure* (Éditions du Rocher, 1997).

18 Elsewhere I have argued that Freud and Jung confirmed *de facto* a reification of the ego which they had inherited from modern philosophy and which has also passed over into Buddhist appropriations of the distinction between ego and Self. 'The quest of the true Self: Jung's rediscovery of a modern invention', *Journal of Religion* 77(2) (1997): 252–67; see also 'Shin no jiko no tankyū' [The quest of the true self], *Shūkyōgakukaihō* 6 (1991): 32–50.

19 *CW* 8: 384, 347; 4: 332; 10: 271.

20 The classic text here remains Henri Ellenberger's *The Discovery of the Unconscious: The History and Evolution of Dynamic Psychiatry* (London: Allen Lane Penguin, 1970).

21 *Memories, Dreams, Reflections*, 256, 324–5.

22 As far as I remember, Jung uses this phrase only once, but in a context intended to distinguish his position from the non-dualistic position of Eastern thought. *CW* 11: 505.

23 *CW* 10: 339.

24 *CW* 9/2: 194, 109. Emphasis in the original. In other contexts, Jung objects that 'there is no evidence that the unconscious contents are related to an unconscious center analogous to the ego' (*CW* 11: 485; see also 17: 190).

25 *CW* 12: 41.

26 *CW* 9/1: 325. See also 13: 336–7; 11: 155. The saying is traced back to the *Liber Hermetis* (fourteenth century) or *Liber Termegisti* (1315), Cod. Paris. 6319 and Cod. Vat. 3060.

27 In this connection Jung has been accused of expurgating from his edition of the Chinese *Secret of the Golden Flower* an image that suggests yogic sexual practices in order to preserve the purely symbolic-philosophic interpretation of the text. See Kenneth Rexroth's Preface to A. E. Waite (ed.), *The Works of Thomas Vaughan, Mystic and Alchemist* (New Hyde Park: University Books, 1968). For his part, Jung felt he was paying a tribute to Eastern thought in seeing them as 'symbolical psychologists, to whom no greater wrong could be done than to take them literally' (*CW* 13: 50).

28 An example of this impasse from a Buddhist perspective can be seen in Masao Abe's attempt to differentiate Jung's idea of the Self from the Buddhist, 'The Self in Jung and Zen', in Meckel and Moore, *Self and Liberation*, 128–40.

29 *The Varieties of Religious Experience: A Study in Human Nature* (New York: Modern Library, 1902), 498–9, 505. Emphasis in original.

30 *Varieties*, 26.

31 *A Pluralistic Universe* (Cambridge, MA: Harvard University Press, 1977), 138.

32 'The energies of men', in *Essays in Religion and Morality* (Cambridge, MA: Harvard University Press, 1982), 143.

33 In elaborating his theory of the conscious subject, for instance, he is sympathetic to the suggestion of multiple selves developed by Pierre Janet (with whom Jung had also studied for a brief period). *The Principles of Psychology* (Cambridge, MA: Harvard University Press, 1981), vol. 1, ch. 10.

34 I have patched together phrases Jung himself uses to contrast the relational Eros of the unconscious with the discriminating Logos of consciousness. *CW* 14: 179.

35 'Psychological commentary on the Kundalini Yoga: Part 1', *Spring* (1975): 12–13.

36 See *Letters, vol. 2*, 248.

37 'A suggestion about mysticism', in *Essays in Philosophy* (Cambridge, MA: Harvard University Press, 1978), 157–65. Henri Bergson wrote to James in 1931 that whenever he would come close to this kind of 'uncovering' he felt something dangerous 'stretching and swelling in me' that he interrupted out of fear, but to his later regret. See Ralph Barton Perry, *The Thought and Character of William James* (New York: Harper Torchbooks, 1948), 350.

38 In 1931, to locate a freshwater spring on his property. See Hannah, *Jung*, 154.

39 On this point, see my 'Chōestsuteki kinō no chōetsu: Yungu shisō ni okeru shūkyōteki kinō-honnō to tōzai shoukyō mondai o megutte' [Transcending the transcendent function: instinct and religious function in Jung and religion East and West], *Pushiké* 6 (1987): 88–102.

40 *The Creative Mind* (New York: Philosophical Library, 1946), 250–1.

41 Although I have learned a great deal from the work that Miyuki Mokuzen has

done, I find his brand of Buddhism too far removed from the texts and cultural questions. See, for example, the work he co-authored with J. Marvin Spiegelman, *Buddhism and Jungian Psychology* (Phoenix: Falcon Press, 1987).

42 On this question, see my 'Self-healing: the dilemma of Japanese depth psychology', *Academia* (Nanzan University) 49 (1989): 1–24.

43 A popular account of this history can be found in Jacob Needleman, *A Sense of the Cosmos: The Encounter of Modern Science and Ancient Truth* (New York: Arkana, 1988). For a more elaborately documented telling, see the volume (he edited) by Antoine Faivre, *Modern Esoteric Spirituality* (Crossroad: New York, 1992).

44 *CW* 10: 328, 526.

45 For a good sample of research into these questions, see the special issue of the *Japanese Journal of Religious Studies* on 'The New Age in Japan', ed. by Haga Manabu and Robert J. Kisala, 22(3–4) (1995).

46 See Takeda Ryūsei, 'Mutual transformation of Pure Land Buddhism and Christianity', *Bulletin of the Nanzan Institute for Religion and Culture* 22 (1998): 68–90.

4

THE TRANSFORMATION OF HUMAN SUFFERING

A perspective from psychotherapy and Buddhism

Polly Young-Eisendrath

In my view, there are two main objectives that are shared by Buddhism and long-term analytic psychotherapy: the gain of a perspective and skill that alleviate personal suffering in everyday life, and an increase of compassion for self and others. Although my training as a psychoanalyst is Jungian, I have for many years been associated with institutions and settings that were mainly Freudian, object-relational and/or intersubjective. In the following paper, I mean to speak to the goals of psychotherapy and Buddhism in ways that are common to all analytic approaches to psychotherapy.

Clarifying the ways in which Buddhism and psychotherapy are both similar and different in their goals and methods should assist the practitioners of both in addressing the concerns of people who seek help for their suffering. Tracing the boundaries and domain of subjective distress – specifically *dukkha* as it is described in Buddhism – may also assist us in making scientific investigations of certain well-established methods and processes of the transformation of human suffering.

Throughout my development as a psychologist and psychoanalyst, I have been sustained and renewed through my own practice and study of Buddhism – as a student first of Zen and now of Vipassana. I became a Zen Buddhist in a formal ceremony in 1971, nine years before I received my Ph.D. in psychology in 1980, fifteen years before I received my diploma as a Jungian analyst. Recently, I have attempted to refine some of the concepts of analytic psychotherapy and psychoanalysis (e.g. Young-Eisendrath 1996; 1997a; 1997b; 2000; 2001), drawing on my experiences in, and understanding of, a Buddhist approach to the transformation of suffering. Buddhism and feminism, the latter especially in regard to the effects of gender stereotypes and inequality, have assisted me in my work as an analytical psychotherapist over the past twenty years. Feminism has made me alert to the ways in which both Buddhism and psychoanalysis, like other institutionalized traditions, can oppress and oppose women and others, through intentional or unintentional hierarchies and biases. Buddhism has helped me appreciate the importance of concentration, equanimity, and compassion in psychoanalytic work. Without Buddhism and feminism, I could not practice psychotherapy and psychoanalysis as I do. These two other practices have allowed me to see how human suffering, rooted in ignorance, can teach us compassion when we understand the meaning of our own suffering.

In my work as a Jungian psychoanalyst and psychotherapist, I have many opportunities – in both individual and couples therapy – to engage in the struggles of human suffering, and as many opportunities to test my compassion. In the following, I attempt to reflect on my own current encounter with the problem of suffering in my field of work. Prominent for me is the North American fear of even the topic of suffering. An American dread of suffering, based on ignorance about what suffering teaches and how it can be transformed, has recently led to more and more physicalistic and materialist explanations of our pain and adversity. Instead of recognizing the role of subjective distress – the ways in which disappointment, anguish, fear, envy, pride, and hostility, for instance, contribute to our suffering – the American anti-suffering campaign now addresses people at the level of neurotransmitters, organ transplants, genetic engineering and biological determinism. This cultural movement has already had massive ill-effects on the practice of psychiatry and psychotherapy over the past two decades in the United States, as I shall illustrate.

Particularly significant for me is the medical context that has come to surround the practice of psychotherapy. This context demands that therapeutic interventions be brief, and assumes that long-term psychodynamic psychotherapy is of little benefit, especially for those people who have severe psychological difficulties. Only medication, electroconvulsive treatment, and/or brief behavioral interventions are promoted as truly effective. This cultural mood in America is especially the product of the decade of the 1990s and the dominance of the pharmaceutical industry in medical practices.

This mood is now expressed as a demand that human miseries be treated as quickly as possible. So-called 'managed care' and other stripped-down services for the ill and emotionally troubled have derailed both psychodynamic and humanistic therapeutic movements. In the twenty years prior to these influences, psychodynamic and humanistic psychologies had begun to encourage Americans to look into their suffering with a kind of interest that leads, inevitably I believe, to spiritual yearnings in the effort to resolve suffering for oneself and others. Psychodynamic and humanistic therapies have now lost their ability to persuade the public, to acquire any substantial funding for systematic research, and to be fully included in most medical settings. In our current cultural *zeitgeist*, a new form of scientific materialism – biological determinism – has taken hold of the public imagination.

In this same period of time that this has been unfolding, Buddhism has become a major religious and cultural movement in North America in a way that no one could have easily anticipated in the early 1970s. As a result, Buddhism (especially in its popular Western forms of Zen, Vipassana, and Tibetan Buddhism) has, perhaps surprisingly, opened up the possibility of a renewed appreciation of psychodynamic practices of psychotherapy. Because Buddhism presents a spiritual argument for the transformation (not the medication) of suffering, as well as specific and systematic methods of analyzing subjective distress, it now assists me in being able to address audiences about the principles and uses of analytic psychotherapy. Buddhism has much to offer psychotherapists, and those who seek help from them. Buddhism has myriad time-tested approaches to understanding and transforming human misery. Psychotherapy also has something to offer Buddhism, especially in our study of personal unconscious emotional habit patterns or 'psychological complexes,' as I shall try to show. At this unique moment in history we in America can witness the powerful influx of ancient Asian teachings into our society where our own psychological sciences are being eroded by biological determinism and the economics of managed care.

The spiritual problem of the end of the century

Carl Jung more than once said that science is the 'spiritual adventure of our age' (e.g. 1992/1939: 50). Science, with its skeptical and objective methods, allowed us to see that many powers we had projected into an animistic world were, in fact, our own. Jung described this as 'the last step out of humanity's childhood, out of a world where mind-created figures populated a metaphysical heaven and hell' (1992/1939: 49). Science did not transcend metaphysics, however. It created its own metaphysics with widespread cultural consequences. For example, (1) science has awarded the names of 'matter' and 'energy' to the ultimate principles of existence and (2) this has led to radically different modern beliefs about human life – as for example the 'scientific' conclusion that afterlife does not exist. Whether or not individuals actually understand this new metaphysics, we are all constantly influenced by it. For instance, the ways in which science has permitted humankind to explore and manipulate our phenomenal world (including our own bodies) leads us to speak of 'miracles of science' that have largely replaced the miracles of religion in educated societies. Renowned geneticist and zoologist Lewontin of Harvard University says the following about how we have elevated scientific beliefs:

> Not only the methods and institutions of science are said to be above ordinary human relations but . . . the product of science is claimed to be a kind of universal truth. The secrets of nature are unlocked. Once the truth about nature is revealed, one must accept the facts of life.
>
> (1991: 8–9)

Lewontin goes on to discuss Darwin's theory of evolution as a case in point. I would like to address this briefly as a prime example of a particular spiritual problem that marked the end of the twentieth century.

Much of our reasoning about human life and other beings on this planet now rests on the theory of natural selection. Most educated people believe (at least vaguely) in the scientific principle that the living organisms on earth have evolved over billions of years from other organisms that were unlike them, and are now mostly extinct. When this story is told of humanity, it wholly eliminates the role of personal meaning and human intentions in the development of societies and the lives of individuals. The 'master molecule' of the gene, falsely endowed with an autonomous power, is most often used to explain personal desires, intentions, and actions. The term 'gene' or 'adaptation' has replaced intention, purpose, and meaning in most psychological accounts of the ways in which people thrive or fail to thrive in their everyday lives. All of our struggles – such as finding a mate or becoming a compassionate person – can now be recast in terms of their supposed 'advantages' of leaving the greatest number of offspring.

When people seek psychotherapeutic or other kinds of psychosocial help, they now come with vague theories of biological determinism such as 'I am depressed because I inherited depression from my mother's family' or 'I have an addiction because my genetic history is loaded for substance abuse' or 'I have attention deficit disorder because of my genetic background' and so on. These people often continue to feel hopeless even after they have taken the appropriate medications, and comforted themselves with the company of their ancestors, because they do not understand why they suffer. Of course, this can be addressed through effective psychotherapy, but for those who never consider psychotherapy, and most people do not, these vague organic explanations only block any desire to understand the personal motives and meanings that lead to much or most of human suffering through our emotional habit patterns.

The belief that our own intentions and attitudes can change our actions, thoughts, and moods is now considered outmoded in many training programs for psychiatrists and psychologists in the US. Many of the psychiatric residents that I have supervised in the past five years have no idea of how to talk with a patient about motivations and intentions, whether conscious or unconscious. These residents learn only how to diagnose symptoms and determine appropriate medications, and to conduct brief symptom-oriented counseling. Moreover, the suffering people who come to the offices of these newer psychiatrists are asked to believe that they will be cured by some form of biological intervention, not through a change of awareness or attitude.

A great deal of harm has already occurred as a result of embracing biological determinism as a fundamental explanation of human suffering. This is not to say that we should disregard the important advances that genetics and biochemistry have provided, both in understanding ourselves and in medicating serious psychiatric conditions. And yet we need to become acutely aware of the consequences of embracing a widespread ideology of biological determinism.

Unique among religions, Buddhism has developed systematic methods for investigating the roots of suffering and other psychological responses in ways that are valid and reliable. The methods of Buddhism are objective and empirical and do not contradict the metaphysics of science. Buddhism also possesses an extensive psychology of unconscious processes, as the paper by Okano in this volume illustrates. Buddhism and depth psychology stand side by side in helping us to diagnose and treat the spiritual problem that emerged wholecloth in the final decade of the twentieth century: secular self-interest reinforced by the metaphysics of scientific materialism. Biblical scholar Miles (1999) describes the problem this way:

> Enlightened self-interest seems to hold as a necessary postulate that the world is real and the world's goods really worth acquiring. A stock portfolio, a law degree, a flat stomach, an art museum membership card, a foreign vacation, a sex life, a baby – the list is long, and each item on it seems to have generated an advertising campaign, a market strategy, an expert adviser. *Materialism* is too narrow a word for the army of cultural imperatives that both preserve and besiege the . . . self . . .
>
> (1999: x)

Buddhism teaches that our suffering arises from the illusion that the individual self is enduring and needs to be protected. The schools of depth psychology warn of our tendencies to repeat experiences of fear and gratification through our psychological complexes and repetition compulsions. Defending ourselves against events and feelings that we evaluate as negative makes us desire only those things we believe to be in our favor – and to abhor what we believe is not. These conditions naturally lead to overwhelming experiences of despair, anxiety, and envy, as well as compulsions and addictions. All of these ordinary forms of human suffering are now further complicated by a metaphysics of vague notions of biological determinism.

Biological determinism is clearly no help with the burden or boredom of a demanding self. It cannot answer questions about subjective meaning, nor address the compulsions that arise from personal insecurity, without reducing them to organic processes.

If you explain suffering only in organic terms, then you exclude the possibility that you can change your life through changing your mind. If you further believe that the world's goods are worth acquiring, you will eventually face the fact that individual and collective resources are depleted. What I have sketched out is the outline of a unique problem of our period of time: human suffering without interest in its origins or knowledge about its causes.

Dukkha

The First Noble Truth taught by the Buddha is often translated into English as 'Life is suffering.' I find myself in agreement with those translators who prefer the terms 'discontent' or 'anguish' to suffering as a definition of *dukkha*. The First Noble Truth then becomes 'Human life is filled with discontent' or 'Our lives are mired in anguish.' The Sanskrit word *dukkha* refers to a vast range of phenomena from the inevitable aspects of illness, decline, and death to the ordinary discontent of everyday life. And yet the word itself conveys a specific metaphor that sheds light on what it means to be a human being.

Dukkha refers literally to a state of being off-center or out of balance, like a wheel riding off its axle or a bone riding out of its socket. This off-centeredness is most often experienced as negativity and restlessness. Most of us tend to notice *dukkha* more acutely at times of adversity such as loss, illness, or difficulties in intimacy or parenting that confront us with our limited control over the circumstances of our lives. But *dukkha* occurs countless times in an ordinary day.

Contemporary psychological research on 'flow experience' (engaged, unselfconscious activity that eliminates the experience of a separate self) gives some interesting scientific evidence of the First Noble Truth. After years of researching the character of flow experience in everyday life, the psychologist Csikszentmihalyi (1993) says,

> when attention is not occupied by a specific task, like a job or a conversation, thoughts begin to wander in random circles. But in this case 'random' does not mean that there is an equal chance of having happy and sad thoughts. [T]he majority of thoughts that come to the mind when we are not concentrating are likely to be depressing.
>
> (1993: 35)

This human hyper-alertness to negativity, as described in the research of Csikszentmihalyi and his colleagues, appears to have promoted a desire for constant 'improvement' that may have been beneficial to our species in some aspects in our early adaptation in that we were able to spread over many kinds of landscapes and conditions, quickly overtaking many other species. But this widespread human dominance of the planet has now created a threat to our survival as we are exhausting the environmental resources we need for our own life supports.

How therapy transforms *dukkha* and awakens compassion

Much of our suffering originates with our sense of separateness and fear, through our evaluations of ourselves and others. Our psychological complexes, ego and otherwise, form our basic habits of mind that develop first in our early relationships, eventually becoming the trigger points or reactive cues for our personal emotional patterns of reaction and defense. These complexes are major aspects of what Buddhism calls *karma*: consequences of our conscious and unconscious intentions expressed through our actions. As Buddhist scholar Dharmasiri (1989) has said,

> Although a bad thought may seem to disappear . . . it does not completely disappear but goes . . . to the unconscious and starts forming a complex around the original nucleus . . . [T]he complex becomes charged with more and more power as it grows bigger . . . This is the maturation of karma. When the complex is fully matured, at some point it explodes into the fruition of karma.
>
> (1989: 37)

Such complexes, derived from universal emotional conditions of being human, are driving forces in generating and re-generating images of self and others, through distortions and delusions of fear and desire, dominance and submission, and power and weakness. From a Jungian perspective, psychological complexes develop universally through archetypes or innate predispositions. *Archetypes* are innate tendencies in humans to form coherent emotionally charged images in states of arousal. The perceptual and emotional systems of human beings everywhere are organized by archetypes around which we form our emotional habit patterns, at first in adapting to the emotional and interpersonal demands of the conditions we are born into. Later, in adult life, these complexes are played out with others, in our families and worklife, as though our emotional meanings were reality. Negative experiences from our childhood are especially powerful. For example, if a child was treated aggressively and unfairly by a parent or older sibling, as an adult that child will have a strong tendency to recreate both the roles of victim and aggressor, sometimes identifying with one and projecting the other, and other times reversing that.

Not only the complexes of the unconscious, but also the ego complex of conscious awareness can throw us off balance through defensive emotional patterning. The ego complex forms around the core of an archetype of self, the universal human tendency to form a coherent image of being an individual embodied subject who exists over time. The experience of individual subjectivity first comes into conscious awareness between the ages of 18 months and two years in normal development. No wonder the 'terrible twos' are known as the 'me me me' period! Once the ego complex is formed, the self-conscious emotions such as jealousy, shame, pride, self-pity, embarrassment, envy, and guilt – as well as fears and desires – can trigger defenses of the ego. Then we experience ourselves as separated and isolated from others and the world around, the pervasive root of subject–object duality.

Jung believed that modernity engendered a revolutionary self-consciousness in human development: a new awareness that allowed for self-investigation and accountability that gave birth to psychoanalysis among other things. He regarded this development as a mixed blessing because excessive self-consciousness can result in the alienation of the ego from the rest of the personality. All of the complexes of the personality – including those that are typically unconscious such as Mother, Father, and Child – have a certain degree of autonomy or intentions of their own. Excessive self-consciousness of the ego can lead us to the denial of other complexes and their motives, believing that our actions are guided only by our conscious intentions.

Because humans all have universal features of emotion and embodiment, Jung postulated a *collective unconscious* – a shared common ground of unconscious experiences – in which individuality is embedded. When someone projects an unconscious complex into another, it is thus likely that the other has had emotional and conceptual experiences for receiving and identifying with that projection. Projection of alien states into others is an unintentional invitation to another to enact those states. In intimate and hierarchical relationships, people often project and enact each other's darker feelings and images, making for a great deal of pain and confusion in human relationships.

In a successful long-term psychotherapy or analysis, the two people – therapist and patient – come to witness directly how and why this happens. Investigating the projections of the patient, the therapist and patient together will see how the patient has needed to place aspects of her or his motives or feelings or ideals in others. Patient and therapist need each other to make this kind of study, and through witnessing what has taken place between them, they come to feel a deep gratitude for their unique work together, a gratitude that transcends even the insights gained.

Through the specific meeting of these two people, each discovers in the context of their relationship how the self-centered self-conscious subject mistakes the world and others to be separate, passive, external, and permanent. In place of this separateness, the therapeutic partners come to see and experience their mutual, fluid self–other constructions that are rooted in the emotions and desires of the moment. Both people – especially the patient because the therapy is focussed on her or him – see clearly how the ego complex constructs others and the environment to be reflections of its own wishes and needs. The technical terms for these mistaken projections and perceptions are 'transference' and 'countertransference.' Transference means the experience of one person that another is a particular way, or feels a particular way, that the first has unknowingly imposed from her or his internal state of pressure, feeling, or image. One person *transfers* a whole context or story, or a particular feeling state, to another and believes that it originates with the other. Countertransference is simply the reaction of the second person to the transference of the first, especially in the feeling states and images of the second person. As these are witnessed and interpreted within the safe bounds of effective psychotherapy, the two individuals begin to awaken to greater compassion and wisdom through their knowledge of how suffering is created. In the process of such an awakening, the two people of the therapeutic dyad feel deeply grateful for their interdependence in this process.

Aspects of interdependence in Zen and Jung

In one example of how this interdependence can be traced in psychotherapy, Kopf (1998) compares Jung's account of the transferential phenomena of therapy with the account of *katto* (vines) from Zen Master Dogen's analysis of the master–disciple relationship in the chapter of *Katto Shobogenzo*. Dogen exhorts the Zen student to attain the face of the teacher, and vice versa, while averring that the interwovenness of master and disciple still includes the individuality of each. 'The self attains the other' and 'the other attains the self' while the self never abandons itself to the psyche of the other. Self and other are not one, and they are not two (summarized in Kopf 1998: 282–3). If it is possible for the self to attain the other without dissolving its individuality, argues Dogen, then the traditional concept of a separate self does not apply to our subjectivity. Dogen maintains that self and other are ultimately interdependent; the self does not exist prior to, or outside of, the other; we only have the possibility of experiencing self or other through relationship.

Both Zen discipleship and long-term psychotherapy demonstrate this interdependence to the practitioners when the relationship is effective. Psychotherapy was designed specifically to respond to personal pain and suffering, not to spiritual questions *per se*, while Buddhism offers a theory and many methods to respond spiritually to universal aspects of human suffering, not personal suffering with its unique familial and emotional patterns. I will give a brief example of the ways in which interdependence underpins each of these, including a short commentary on how compassion develops in such circumstances.

The core process of transformation in the long-term psychodynamic therapeutic relationship includes encountering difficult feelings, desires, and impulses, and investigating their origins and meanings with the therapist. Some of this takes place in the transference of sexual, aggressive, or other frightening feelings experienced as being caused by, or reactive to, the therapist. The effective therapist provides a gentle matter-of-fact attention (often called 'bare attention' or 'neutrality') that encourages the patient to explore such states, even though both patient and therapist may be somewhat self-conscious or uncomfortable. Both patient and therapist *are* initially ambivalent about such stressful encounters involving the transference, but in the course of therapy they come to feel deeply grateful, even freely creative, in their ability to explore together the patient's most difficult feelings and impulses within the transference, as well as in regard to other people in the patient's life.

Long-term psychotherapy achieves the transformation of suffering by leaving certain kinds of things unsaid – for example, most if not all of the therapist's hostile, erotic, aggressive, or hateful feelings towards the patient – while putting other things into words. The therapist's interpretation of unconscious meaning is one of the methods of achieving insight into the patient's troubling emotional habits. The therapist will use words, phrases, sentences, and gestures to communicate emotional meanings for what may have been unknown or hidden from the patient's awareness, but has been repeatedly implied or unknowingly expressed to the therapist. For instance, the patient may have frequently said to the therapist, 'I believe you are critical and judgmental of me' just when the patient is unconsciously feeling that way towards the therapist. The response to this type of projection of affect may be anything from a silent noting by the therapist that she or he does not in fact feel this way to saying openly something like 'Perhaps you are feeling this way about me at the moment?' or something similar. Over the development of a successful long-term treatment, such inquiry becomes quite ordinary. It is an opening to explore a whole context or narrative surrounding the patient's feelings (or occasionally the therapist's feelings) that will inevitably connect to the patient's troubling habits of mind (assumptions and emotional dynamics) that are at the root of a lot of her or his suffering.

Other therapeutic interpretations may respond to a patient's reports of daily life, silences, gestures, claims to truth, postures, and night-dreams. A therapist's ability to be truly helpful in making interpretations, that are not humiliating or belittling of the patient, depends on the therapist's training, expertise, self-awareness, and confidence in relying on the therapeutic relationship for the discovery of meaning. Within this relationship, patient and therapist are also two ordinary human beings who are working together to try to bring about the alleviation of suffering in at least one (the patient), and more profoundly in both. The patient has hired the therapist to do a job that the therapist has been trained to do. The therapist, like any other trained professional, will be more or less able to perform satisfactorily on a particular occasion, relevant to the therapist's state of mind and many other factors. The periodic expressed acknowledgment of such limitation is a requirement for any therapist to be effective. Sometimes the therapist feels confused, afraid, reactive, and ignorant about the task of the transformation of suffering. Acknowledging these limitations allows interpretations and other interventions, such as empathy, to be made with an openness and questioning, a kind of uncertainty or not-knowing. Within the effective therapeutic relationship the therapist will convey the sense that she or he also suffers and may not always know the way of transformation. This realistic acknowledgment of constraint on 'expert authority' will counterbalance the powerful forces of transference, and also invite the patient to be more open and unashamed in exploring her or his human foibles. Yet this kind of realism must be handled skillfully so that the patient has plenty of opportunities to experience the therapist as an authority figure and a trusted expert – conditions that are necessary for transference and trust.

In everyday life, we are constantly immersed in transferences and projections in our ordinary human relationships. Only in the therapeutic relationship do we encounter the special condition of being able to study the creation of such suffering in the moment. The requirements for effective psychotherapy – ethical conduct and non-retaliation on the part of the therapist, certain ground-rules for meetings and payment, the relative anonymity of the therapist and so on – nourish possibilities for self-understanding and the development of compassion for self and others.

Eventually the patient discovers what Jung (1969/1916) has called the 'transcendent function': an ability to contain tensions, conflicts, and other opposite pulls without prematurely deciding that they are 'good' or 'bad' or mean this or that (see, for example, Horne 1998). This function allows the patient to keep an open mind in the face of momentary impulses, feelings, pressures, and so on. Eventually the patient finds that the skill of the transcendent function can be used in many life situations in which the patient had previously reacted through old destructive emotional habits. The interdependence (of patient and therapist) in the discovery of meaning through the therapeutic relationship, and the skill of the transcendent function, together eventually allow the patient to 'suffer with' self and others. Suffering-with is the essence of 'com-passion' (literally, suffering-with) in its ability to witness pain, trouble, difficulty, and adversity with a sincere desire and ability to help. True help, and not pity or sympathy or sugar-coating, requires a matter-of-fact toleration of the demands of pain and suffering without becoming hopeless. This is the path that patient and therapist follow in the course of an effective long-term psychotherapy.

Buddhist methods, in contrast to therapy's focus on personal relational and identity themes, are designed to alleviate suffering and increase compassion in terms of broader universal themes. In all of its methods, Buddhism focusses attention on craving, aversion, and ignorance as experienced particularly through creating, sustaining, and defending the illusion of a separate, stable, independent self. All methods for transforming our delusions of separateness rely on both theory and experience in Buddhism. A teacher's job is especially to guide the process of awakening to the reality of interdependence and compassion through methods that have already been mastered by the teacher.

The Buddhist student–teacher relationship is transformative from the outset because it carries a belief in the teacher's perfected spiritual state (enlightenment, liberation, satori, etc.). The student initially sees this particular teacher as spiritually advanced, and wants to attain this for herself or himself, and so decides to follow the teacher's instructions. In Zen, a teacher who has been sanctioned to teach by her/his teacher *has* theoretically equalled or surpassed the teacher. So there is a reality to the student's belief that the teacher is well beyond the student in spiritual attainment. And yet, true and deep spiritual attainment should not set a teacher apart from others; the most spiritually adept teachers are often known for being very ordinary people. Paradoxically, then, a spiritual master in Zen (called a 'roshi') is both an especially enlightened or realized person and an ordinary person.

Such a teacher speaks from an authority that the psychotherapist or psychoanalyst lacks. Whereas the effective psychotherapist may still be almost as neurotic as the patient – although able to use insight, the transcendent function, and compassion to continuously transform neurotic habits – the Zen teacher is certainly not as ignorant of the nature of spiritual reality as the student is. In short, the realized Zen teacher is fundamentally unequal, spiritually speaking, with her or his student at the beginning of the transformation process.

This difference in status effectively eliminates the sense that the two are, on some level, just two human beings struggling together to discover meaning. The developed teacher has mastered her or his mind and not merely the knowledge of Buddhism and its methods. Many roshis would say that they definitely know what is best for their students without the kind of uncertainty that an effective therapist feels and expresses. In order for teacher and student to 'intertwine' in the way that Kopf (1998) describes, the student must learn the ways and means to her or his own True Nature or Mind. By the end of this process – if the process fully evolves between a particular teacher and student – the student will have assimilated her or his spiritual nature that was originally projected onto the teacher.

In Zen, the actions of the teacher in the process may be harsh and seem hostile, as well as openly caring and compassionate. These extremes are aspects of Zen teaching and not considered a personal matter. The student's reactions to such expressions by the teacher are not interpreted as they are in psychotherapy, and yet they will stir rather extreme transference feelings and fantasies in the student. The dependence and trust that are necessary in the effective Zen teacher–student relationship guarantee that there will be struggles with dependence–independence, trust–betrayal, and engulfment–abandonment between student and teacher. These often repeat or react to the student's parental or other familial patterns. The student feels vulnerable, dependent, and deeply concerned about the teacher in a situation that is unpredictable in regard to the extremes of the teacher's responses. Without the benefit of personal insights into specific personal habit patterns, the student must stop behaving and feeling like an omnipotent or victimized child. This happens, when it does, through the student mastering the reliable spiritual practices offered by the dedicated teacher.

At the point that the student awakens to the reality of Buddha Mind or True Nature, the student and teacher are one, although they remain two individuals. This intertwining is very different from the therapist–patient relationship of working through the projections of transference in the discovery of meaning. For the therapist–patient dyad, appreciation of inter-dependence emerges especially from the sense of being 'only human' in the context of difficult feeling states encountered, and successfully understood and digested, during therapeutic sessions. In the case of Zen teacher–student, the experience of interdependence arises in the student's awakening to the reality of impermanence and interdependence through eradicating the delusions of a separate self.

Conclusion

Through the transformation of our suffering in long-term psychotherapy and Buddhism, we learn that apparently negative experiences open our hearts. We cease experiencing self and others as wholly separate, permanent, stable, and independent. And we no longer experience ourselves simply as passive victims of circumstances we did not create.

Through the methods of psychotherapy and Buddhism we encounter the paradigm of our subjective world: the basis for our meanings and perceptions. Gradually we come to see that as we shift our subjective perceptions, the perceived also changes. Subject and object are joined in the ground of our perceptions. When we conceive of the human self as wholly interdependent and impermanent, as a function rather than a thing, then we appreciate more deeply the freedom that we have in this world. It is the freedom of opening ourselves to our constraints and limitations, and exploring these into the roots of our suffering. Our suffering has a purpose: it gives rise to our deepest compassion when it is transformed. This is a discipline that cannot be captured by any form of biological determinism and must be explored on its own terms – personally, spiritually, and scientifically – in the new millennium.

References

Csikszentmihalyi, M. (1993) *The Evolving Self: A Psychology for the Third Millennium*, New York: HarperCollins.

Dharmasiri, G. (1989) *Buddhist Ethics*, Antioch, CA: Golden Leaves.

Horne, M. (1998) 'How does the transcendent function?', *The San Francisco Jung Institute Library Journal* 17: 21–41.

Jung, C. G. (1969/1916) 'The transcendent function', in *The Collected Works of C. G. Jung*, vol. 8, trans. R. F. C. Hull, Princeton, NJ: Princeton University Press.

Jung, C. G. (1992/1939) 'Psychological commentary on *The Tibetan Book of Great Liberation*', in D. Meckel and R. Moore (eds), *Self and Liberation: The Jung–Buddhism Dialogue*, New York: Paulist Press.

Kopf, G. (1998) 'In the face of the other: psychic interwovenness in Dogen and Jung', in A. Molino (ed.), *The Couch and the Tree: Dialogues in Psychoanalysis and Buddhism*, New York: North Point Press, 276–89.

Lewontin, R. (1991) *Biology as Ideology: The Doctrine of DNA*, New York: HarperCollins.

Miles, J. (1999) 'Foreword', in J. F. Revel and M. Ricard, *The Monk and the Philosopher: A Father and Son Discuss the Meaning of Life*, New York: Schocken Books.

Young-Eisendrath, P. (1996) *The Resilient Spirit: Transforming Suffering into Insight, Compassion and Renewal*, Reading, MA: Addison-Wesley.

Young-Eisendrath, P. (1997a) 'The self in analysis', *Journal of Analytical Psychology* 42: 157–66.

Young-Eisendrath, P. (1997b) 'Jungian constructivism and the value of uncertainty', *Journal of Analytical Psychology* 42: 637–52.

Young-Eisendrath, P. (2000) 'Self and transcendence: a postmodern approach to analytical psychology in practice', *Psychoanalytic Dialogues* 10(3): 427–41.

Young-Eisendrath, P. (2001) 'When the fruit ripens: alleviating suffering and increasing compassion as goals of clinical psychoanalysis', *Psychoanalytic Quarterly* LXX: 265–85.

5

ZEN AND PSYCHOTHERAPY

From neutrality, through relationship, to the emptying place

Melvin E. Miller

I come to this topic humbly and reverently. Although no stranger to Zen, I confess to being no expert on either Zen theory or Zen practice. These truths notwithstanding, I am quite interested in Zen and other forms of Buddhist thought, and I am deeply committed to exploring the interface between Buddhism and psychotherapy. Thus, I approach these conceptual challenges not only with humility, but with an eagerness, an excitement, and the wish to offer a fresh angle on the ubiquitous and controversial notion of therapeutic neutrality and related concepts – ones that, to my mind, comprise essential components of the bridge between psychotherapy and Buddhist thought.

I have been a clinical psychologist for 28 years or more. Psychoanalysis and psychoanalytically informed psychotherapy provide the theoretical foundation for my work. I have been trained in the more contemporary traditions of psychoanalysis (object relations theory, self-psychology, interpersonal–relational theory, etc.). Despite my preference for the more contemporary approaches to psychoanalytic theory, I readily acknowledge being influenced by Freud and others who operate from the more classical theoretical perspectives.

In this light, I propose that therapeutic neutrality is one of the most fundamental and essential principles of the psychotherapeutic work. Freud and others since (e.g. Alonso 1996; Fosshage 1998; Gill 1979; Hoffer 1985) have described a way of sitting with patients that not only helps redress psychopathology and attenuate symptoms, but also often brings out the very best in patient potential. I present these thoughts about therapeutic neutrality – not strictly in the Freudian sense, but with a twist or two – with certain alterations and modifications. These modifications, I trust, will find both sympathy and support among Buddhists and the general psychoanalytic community.

Freud on neutrality

Let us begin with Freud and remind ourselves of his stance on neutrality (and the analyst's disposition or stance toward the patient) as it appears in this oft-quoted passage from his 'Recommendations to physicians practicing psycho-analysis'. Freud describes the fundamental technique of psycho-analysis thusly:

> It consists simply in not directing one's notice to anything in particular and in maintaining the same 'evenly-suspended attention' [evenly-hovering attention] in the face of all that one hears. . . . For as soon as anyone deliberately concentrates his attention to a certain degree, he begins to select from the material before him; one point will be fixed in the mind with particular clearness and some other will be correspondingly disregarded, and in making this selection he will be following his expectations or inclinations. This, however, is precisely what must not be done. In making the selection, if he follows his expectations he is in danger of never finding anything but what he already knows; and if he follows his inclinations he will certainly falsify what he may perceive.
>
> (Freud 1912/1989: 357)

Although this passage from Freud is cited frequently, it appears that there is no uniformly accepted interpretation of these remarks. For some, Freud's instructions infer a cold, surgeon-like demeanor toward the patient and the work, and for others, Freud's words invite the possibility of an empathic, caring, and accepting stance which promotes a warm, working relationship (Alonso 1996; Fosshage 1994; Hoffman 1998). The range of interpretations and responses to Freud's words notwithstanding, this passage remains a hermeneutic challenge;[1] a precise, definitive sense of his meaning remains elusive – with all subsequent interpreters arriving at meanings most consistent with their own theoretical and clinical predispositions.

Freud's instructions are simple and direct. His clarity and brevity stand in sharp distinction to the volumes that have been written about this passage. Today I want to add my own interpretive twists as well. Initially, though, I will remain close to what I assume to be Freud's original meaning. In this light, I believe that readers, regardless of theoretical persuasion (albeit Zen in particular), will be struck by a familiar quality resonating in Freud's instructions. His advice appears remarkably similar to what one is asked to do in a meditative practice. Let's think further about this similarity.

Dogen on Zazengi

Dogen and others (Senzaki and McCandless 1953) have offered instructions on sitting/meditation, or zazen. Here is an abbreviated version of how zazen is to be practiced – from Dogen's principles of zazen ('Zazengi'):

> Cast aside all involvement and cease all affairs. . . . Cease all movements of the conscious mind, the gauging of all thoughts and views. Have no designs on becoming a Buddha. . . . [Detailed instructions on hand, leg, and bodily positions omitted here]. . . . Think of not thinking. How do you think of not-thinking? Without thinking? This is the essential art of zazen.
>
> The zazen I speak of is not learning meditation. . . . It is the presence of things as they are.
>
> (From Dogen [1200–53], in Kasulis 1981: 70–1)

S. Suzuki (1970), a direct spiritual descendant of Dogen, echoes this point when he invites students to 'forget about all your preconceived ideas' (p. 110) and 'see and feel things as they are without any effort' (p. 128). Kasulis (1981) elaborates further on zazen and the phenomenon of 'experiencing things as they are' as he discusses the incontrovertible importance of arriving at (returning to) a pre-reflective state of awareness:

> What we experience prereflectively is screened out by the presuppositions of our reflectively constructed worldview. Experience therefore *turns against* its own drive toward unification, simplicity, and directness; it lives an internal lie. The reflective experience cuts itself off from its prereflective roots.
>
> This internal conflict can be suddenly resolved . . . when one comes face to face with the actual nature of prereflective experience. Zazen is the primary way of doing this. . .
>
> (p. 101, emphasis added)

The similarities existing between Freud's stance on neutrality and the attitude – the state of mind – of one engaged in zazen are strikingly similar. What are we to make of this?

Zen and psychoanalysis: contrast and integration

I humbly suggest that these two disciplines foster similar kinds of awareness – up to a point. That is, what an in-depth analysis induces in patients (and in analysts) is not markedly different from that which occurs in meditation. Moreover, I propose that these 'awarenesses of prereflective experience' and the calmness and wholeness which result (Suzuki 1970:

128), arise through similar kinds of 'neutrality.' Neutrality is essential to both disciplines. Now once I say this, I realize that I could be inviting some degree of controversy with proponents of both the Zen and psychoanalytic camps.

I can imagine those in the Zen camp retorting with 'No way, how can you propose that Freud – the avowed anti-religious theorist and atheist (and his cohorts) – are up to something similar to what we do.' Likewise, I can hear the Freudians countering with something like: 'We are undeniably different; we are offering a mode of healing neurosis – not a path to enlightenment and certainly not a religious path.'

I also get into a little bit of trouble with myself, with my own theoretical position and hard-won analytic tenets, as I proffer this view. Can these seemingly different perspectives, with ostensibly disparate technologies and goals, ever be truly reconciled? I think they can be. I propose they can, in large measure, be integrated and synthesized. Most assuredly they can be reconciled with respect to the complex issues of neutrality, 'evenly hovering attention,' being in the moment in this pre-reflective state, sitting without thinking. With regard to this state of non-judging, accepting awareness, I would suggest that both Zen and psychoanalysis foster a particular kind of stance, a special kind of relationship to data, to objects of experience, and – in general – a special kind of orientation toward the 'other.' It is a stance that attempts to permit the other to exist in its purity and autonomy. It attempts to permit the other 'to be' in its own right. This position eschews any attempt to influence the other, while it promotes being in the moment with the other. This position, it should be noted, is not dissimilar to that which is embodied in Heidegger's notion of *Dasein* (Nishitani 1982) and that found in the writings of some of the early phenomenologists (Merleau-Ponty 1962).

I am not alone in making such comparisons. Karen Horney, an early psychoanalyst, feminist thinker, and theorist (who was initially sympathetic to classical Freudian theory), became captivated by Zen ideas through her relationship with her friend, D.T. Suzuki. Horney met Suzuki in the later years of her career – first being introduced to him in the winter of 1950–51. Suzuki and Horney struck up a warm, although short-lived, friendship that lasted until Horney's death in 1952. During this brief period, Horney learned much about Zen and immediately began to incorporate Zen notions and principles into a series of lectures she presented through the American Institute for Psychoanalysis. These lectures were offered in the Fall of 1952, following Horney's return from extended travels in Japan, and are included in her posthumous *Final Lectures* (Horney 1987).

The similarities between Zen and psychoanalysis were immediately obvious to Horney. For example, she admired the Zen quality of being 'wholeheartedly in the moment,' and likened it to analytic neutrality. Horney espoused this phenomenon both as a therapeutic goal for the patient – *and* as an essential dispositional stance of the therapist (Westkott 1997: 83). Horney often compared her advice for the therapist with both Freud's aforementioned instructions on 'evenly hovering attention' and Zen sitting instructions (Horney 1987: 21). From Horney's *Final Lectures*:

> That attention should be wholehearted may seem banal, trite, and self-evident. Yet in the sense that I mean wholehearted attention, I think it rather difficult to attain. . . . This is a faculty for which . . . [Zen practitioners] . . . have a much deeper feeling than we do. Wholeheartedness of attention means being there altogether in the service of the patient, yet with a kind of self-forgetfulness . . . self-forget, but be there with all your feelings. . . .The best advice I can give is that [we should let] everything come up, emerge, and at the proper time, be observed.
>
> (pp. 19–21)

This passage shows that Horney adhered to a fairly strict interpretation of neutrality – sticking close to what she believes Freud intended. But she also compared what seasoned Zen practitioners seem to do with apparent ease (sitting wholeheartedly in the moment) with that state of mind (stance) to which analytic therapists should aspire – a neutral, non-judging, present-tense, fully attentive presence with the patient.

Horney believed that Freud did not intend a cold, scientific kind of objectivity. Moreover, she believed that an indifferent, objective stance was neither possible nor desirable. She maintained that the analyst should attempt to achieve more of an 'unlimited, nonjudgmental receptivity' (1987: 20) – the kind of genuine acceptance of ordinary experience of which she frequently heard Suzuki lecture. Westkott, a contemporary authority on Horney, explained her stance this way: 'Whatever words she may have chosen to describe it, . . . Horney was attempting to teach her students how to bring to the therapeutic setting the meditative attitude of mindfulness and receptivity . . . [a] nonjudgmental openness to feeling . . .' (Westkott 1997: 84).

Now, it is at this point that Horney begins to depart from the well-beaten path. I think I will accompany her. Traditional analysts would likely assert that Freud espoused neutrality so that the patient will 'free associate' and the transference will develop unimpeded. Analysts typically argue that we should not attempt to influence the patient in any other way. These are significant objectives and worthy of emphasis; their import should not be understated. However, it is at this juncture that Horney took a detour that I believe is pivotal. Horney believed that this 'attitude of wholehearted attentiveness' has a profound impact upon the inner life, inner structures, or core structure of the patient. She believed that the patient profoundly and deeply experiences (feels and is influenced by) this neutral, meditative posture of the therapist. The patient experiences this neutral, containing, caring presence as an invitation to be and to become – and often as encouragement for further psychological development. Furthermore, it appears that she believed the 'meditative posture [of the therapist toward patient] invites the emergence of the real self' (Westkott 1997: 84).

Mark Epstein (1995), a contemporary analyst and synthesizer of Zen and psychoanalytic theory, echoed Horney's view in his popular volume *Thoughts without a Thinker*. From Epstein:

> When a therapist can sit with a patient without an agenda, without trying to force an experience, without thinking that she knows what is going to happen or who this person is, then the therapist is infusing the therapy with the lessons of meditation. The patient can feel such a posture.
>
> (Epstein 1995: 187)

Epstein's theme is similar to Horney's and other Western analysts interested in Zen (e.g. DeMartino 1991; Rubin 1996), that this 'new' way of thinking about neutrality – this open stance to experience, this wholeheartedness of attitude which fosters an openness to pre-reflective experience – has a *transformative* quality and power to it, especially as it is experienced and felt by the patient. A neutral, non-judging, yet caring attitude or posture toward the other is now understood to have a kind of transformative quality for whoever participates in such a process – be it the bestower or the recipient – be it a Zen practitioner, therapist/analyst, or patient.

From a one-person field to a two-person (relational) psychology

In focusing upon the transformative power that comes into play when one is held within the context of a neutral yet caring relationship, Horney anticipated those contemporary analytic theorists who postulate the necessity of conceptualizing a two-person or relational model of psychotherapy (e.g. Gill 1983; Hoffman 1998; Jacoby 1984; Mitchell 1997) – a model of therapeutic involvement that recognizes the mutual influence of therapist on patient and vice versa. Moreover, it could be argued that Horney anticipated the intersubjective theorists (Stolorow, Atwood, and Brandchaft 1994) as she reflected upon the impact that this kind of therapeutic relatedness has – both consciously and unconsciously – upon both members of the therapeutic dyad. However, Horney did not go far enough in this direction; I would like to go a little further down this road.

Analytic theorists such as Winnicott, Kohut, Lichtenberg, Hoffman, Fosshage, and Mitchell have guaranteed that the importance of mutual interrelatedness in the therapeutic process has not been neglected in the contemporary perspective. These theorists have forayed deeply into the realm of a two-person psychology. In doing so, they have elaborated upon the dynamics of psychoanalytic treatment from the nuanced perspective of a two-person field (combining the intrapsychic material of both patient and analyst – and the interaction of the two). They describe and champion the interconnectedness of two subjectivities – two minds. They seem to understand this interconnectedness, the depth of it, and the degree to which it involves both a conscious connection and, at the same time, a deep, unconscious connection – one to the other. The contemporary emphasis upon the role of projective identification and its use in the analytic hour is one of the many benefits of working with the patient from the perspective of this two-person relational matrix.

In writing of this profound interrelationship, these authors echo Jung's (1969) conceptualization of the 'mutual unconscious' and the 'non-individual psyche' (pp. 169–76) – a mutual mind space in which the sharing of certain unconscious contents is commonplace. Jung (1969) had been formulating a two-person matrix or two-person field long before the interpersonal–intersubjective theorists emerged onto the scene. (See *CW* 16.) Jung spoke of a 'common ground' in which there is the 'transference of unconscious material from the self to a separate other . . . transpiring in a psychic dimension which transcends the boundaries and limitations of the individual' (Kopf 1998: 279). In fact, Jung (1969) went so far as to say that if the doctor or analyst does not change as a result of the psychotherapy, there is no therapy at all. Jacoby (1984) and Perry (1997) extended Jung's contribution to this ever-evolving conversation as they focused on, among other topics, the vicissitudes of countertransference within this interactional field.

Kopf (1998) compares Jung's position on this 'common ground' concept – and the sharing of unconscious material – with similar ideas espoused by the Zen Master Dogen in an engaging article entitled: 'In the face of the other: psychic interwovenness in Dogen and Jung'. Here we find that such a conception of 'psychic interwovenness' is not new; it dates at least as far back as the thirteenth century (*c.* 1200–53). Dogen speaks of the 'psychic interwovenness' that occurs between the Zen master and Zen disciple. Kopf (1998) explains Dogen's position on this essential psychic interwovenness by first citing Dogen's exhortation to the Zen practitioner: 'You should know that there is "You attaining me," "I am attaining you," "attaining me and you," and "attaining you and me"' (p. 282).

Here we find Dogen speaking of a kind of psychic interrelationship that is very similar to that offered by the contemporary two-person field theorists. Dogen describes a 'non-individual psyche which transcends the boundaries of the individual self' (p. 283) as he probes the depths and levels of intimacy and connectedness that come to exist between Zen master and disciple. One almost gets the sense that Dogen, in these writings, suggests that something akin to projective identification exists between master and disciple. As an aside, though, it should be noted that despite this level of intimacy and mutual sharing of unconscious content between master and disciple, Dogen is clear that neither party is to lose his/her individual self or character in the master–disciple relationship. To Dogen, although the demarcation between self and other blurs, self and other are not entirely one.[2]

As psychoanalytic theorists and Zen masters focus on this interconnection (and its transformative power) and how it is further enhanced by the right demeanor and right attitude of sitting with the other – be it in the therapeutic milieu or in meditation – they echo one of Horney's central points: that the individual feels this attentive stance (the warmth of the caring neutrality), and is moved and transformed by it. These theorists seem to understand the profound ways in which the person is affected by the relationship – while taking Horney beyond herself into the interrelational aspect of shared experience. Finally, and this is a central point in synthesizing psychoanalysis and Zen, these theorists realize that being in the presence of this non-judging other – in this containing space (in this psychological matrix of patient–analyst; of master–disciple) – not only enhances the growth of the individual in some kind of reparative, developmental sense, but also augments the organization of self-structure while furthering the individual's 'capacity to be alone' – and his or her subsequent ability to experience aspects of non-self (a central notion in Zen).

The capacity to be alone

D. W. Winnicott is one of the earlier, pivotal, contemporary theorists who has studied this two-person psychological field from a combined psychoanalytic, object-relations, and developmental perspective. Winnicott (1958) proposes that the psychological development of the child is initiated or 'jump-started' through the mother–child dyad. First the child must be *held* – both physically and psychologically – by the mother. The mother–child relational matrix must first be established. The child must be mirrored, cared for, loved (intimately related to) so that this new, dyadic psychological entity (the mother–child psychological matrix) will arise. This is the essential foundation for psychological development. Eventually, the child can begin to transition into being able to be alone – alone, by herself – once this sense of containment (and at-one-ment) with the mother has been firmly established. The child and mother had initially shared one, collective psychological matrix. Eventually, the child moves into a transitional space (held in the dyad yet outside the dyad) – slowly achieving the capacity for separateness, slowly developing the 'capacity to be alone' (Winnicott 1958: 29). Again, this capacity to be alone by oneself, Winnicott reminds us, is first established through the experience of being alone in the presence of someone else – the warm, caring other. Winnicott elaborates further on how this 'capacity to be alone' is an essential, foundational starting point for further developmental gains that transpire throughout the lifespan. Ogden (1986) elegantly expands the developmental unfolding of this process in an apt paraphrase of Winnicott: 'The child must [then] have the opportunity to play in the presence of the absent mother, and in the absence of the present mother' (p. 182). The achievement of this capacity is a precursor to the subsequent developmental tasks of separation and individuation.

It has been argued that these are the kinds of developmental and interpersonal (and intra/interpsychic) dynamics that begin to take place in good frame psychotherapy or psychoanalysis. Such a perspective on analytic 'cure' has been furthered by many contemporary theorists, but, in particular, by a group of psychoanalytic thinkers termed the 'deficiency-compensation' theorists (Stark 1996: 238). Self-psychologists such as Basch, Kohut, Lichtenberg, and Wolf would be included in this group. In short, these theorists contend that, in the course of therapy, the early developmental deficits are rectified by the healthy, reparative (caringly neutral) relationship that develops between patient and analyst – in much the same way that a young child with good-enough nurturing begins to develop those early, necessary structures and a solid sense of self. Feeling contained in this kind of therapy strategically positions the patient to get back on track developmentally – to be able to be with self without anxiety – to examine one's present thoughts and early developmental influences. Again, the 'capacity to be alone' seems to be an essential point of departure for moving ahead – both in a developmental context and in psychotherapy.

This capacity for being alone, I would suggest, also seems to be requisite for a sitting practice. One might argue that a sitter (a Zen student) will have to have progressed far enough along the developmental continuum – as a result of 'good-enough' early (and perhaps current) relationships – to be in a position to begin, and sustain, a meditative practice. One has to be contained enough and contented enough by self (with self) to sit and to risk the experience of non-self or loss of self.

The emptying place

In sum, I submit that both psychotherapy and Zen practice can work together in a synergistic way to further the psychological and spiritual development of the person. Both psychotherapy and Zen heal and transform lives because of the transformative power of a caring sort of neutrality. Both practices assume the existence of at least one good-enough parent imago in the mix – someone who is sitting in a neutral place with the patient (the meditator) without any expectations for the patient or meditator to do anything in particular – perhaps wanting nothing more for the student than his or her ongoing individuation, unfolding of self. In such a scenario, the therapist or teacher is sitting with the learner in a way that the learner knows she is cared for – that someone has her best interest in mind – that someone has her personal–psychological–spiritual transformation in mind, although not pushing for this either. The therapist/teacher will primarily (and simply) *be with* the student – in the moment. In the case of psychoanalysis, the analysand is held by the parent substitute in the form of the therapist, and in Zen, by the master and by the sangha (the meditative community).

Thus, it is the establishment of this essential, foundational base – solidified through a good-enough relationship and enhanced through therapy and/or a sitting practice – that promotes the ability to be alone, and further contributes to the individual's ability to experience nothingness, emptiness (Van Dusen 1998), and the loss of self so often addressed in Buddhist writings. Perhaps it is the sense of 'at-one-ness' experienced from the personal history of being held (by mother/father, therapist, teacher/master, and sangha) that will also enable the individual to have both the courage and the ability to better conceptualize and experience *sunyata* – the fundamental Buddhist doctrine of emptiness. Furthermore, I submit that the sense of at-one-ment – achieved through being held in this psycho-spiritual relational dynamic – will insure that the student will not become lost in some ill-conceived notion of emptiness, nor 'tormented [as is the "uninstructed worldling"[3]] when something permanent within oneself is not found' (Abe 1998: 184), nor lost in the ceaseless emptying movement of Sunyata (Abe 1990: 28), but will instead, in the words of Suzuki, enable this 'vast emptiness [to be] traversed' (Suzuki 1964: 44).

In short, I believe we have found that the 'journey of 1000 miles' begins with neutrality.

Acknowledgements

I would like to thank John J. McKenna, Loren H. Miller, Alan N. West, and Polly Young-Eisendrath for their helpful comments and suggestions on earlier versions of this manuscript.

Notes

1 For a further elaboration on hermeneutics, see Miller 1996. In this essay, I discuss the hermeneutic interpretation of text from the perspective of Gadamer, Dilthey, and others.
2 Kawai (1996) in his Fay Lecture Series discusses, in this context, the unique problem that arises in the Japanese culture with respect to the lack of separation of subject and object (self and other). Both the Japanese language and culture, according to Kawai, tend to keep the distinction between subject and object rather vague. Thus, on one hand, both parties are better prepared to move into (and experience) the two-person relational field, e.g. 'oneness [is] at the base of all togetherness' (p. 121); both parties are . . . 'floating in the evolving relationship' (p. 122). On the other hand, a complete merging of self and other (re: Dogen's warning) frequently becomes a matter of concern.
3 Masao Abe (1998: 184) anticipated that the Buddhist concept of 'no-self' would be both 'strange and frightening' to some. In this same essay, Abe relates the story of the bhikkhu's encounter with the Buddha where the Buddha says: 'O bhikkhus, this idea that I may not be, I may not have, is frightening to the uninstructed worldling' (p. 184). Of course, as Abe reminds us, this awareness did not impede the Buddha from widely preaching the notion of no self.

References

Abe, M. (1990) 'Kenotic god and dynamic sunyata', in J. B. Cobb and C. Ives (eds) *The Emptying God: A Buddhist–Jewish–Christian Conversation*, Maryknoll, NY: Orbis Books, 3–65.

Abe, M. (1998) 'The self in Jung and Zen', in Λ. Molino (ed.) *The Couch and the Tree: Dialogues in Psychoanalysis and Buddhism*, New York: North Point Press, 276–89.

Alonso, A. (1996) 'Toward a new understanding of neutrality', in L. Lifson (ed.), *Understanding Therapeutic Action: Psychodynamic Concepts of Cure*, Hillsdale, NJ: Analytic Press, 3–19.

DeMartino, R. J. (1991) 'Karen Horney, Daisetz T. Suzuki, and Zen Buddhism', *American Journal of Psychoanalysis* 51: 267–83.

Epstein, M. (1995) *Thoughts without a Thinker: Psychotherapy from a Buddhist Perspective*, New York: Basic Books.

Fosshage, J. (1994) 'Toward reconceptualizing transference: theoretical and clinical considerations', *International Journal of Psychoanalysis* 75(2): 265–80.

Fosshage, J. (1998) 'Countertransference as the analyst's experience of the analysand: influence of listening perspectives', *Psychoanalytic Psychology* 12(3): 375–91.

Freud, S. (1912/1989) 'Recommendations to physicians practicing psycho-analysis', in P. Gay (ed.), *The Freud Reader*, New York: Norton, 356–63.

Gill, M. M. (1979) 'The analysis of the transference', *Journal of the American Psychoanalytic Association* 27: 263–88.

Gill, M. M. (1983) 'The distinction between the interpersonal paradigm and the degree of the therapist's involvement', *Contemporary Psychoanalysis* 19: 200–37.

Hoffer, A. (1985) 'Toward a redefinition of psychoanalytic neutrality', *Journal of the American Psychoanalytic Association* 33: 771–95.

Hoffman, I. Z. (1998) *Ritual and Spontaneity in the Psychoanalytic Process: A Dialectical-Constructivist View*, Hillsdale, NJ: Analytic Press.

Horney, K. (1987) *Final Lectures*, ed. by D. Ingram, New York: Norton.

Jacoby, M. (1984) *The Analytic Encounter: Transference and Human Relationship*, Toronto: Inner City Books.

Jung, C. G. (1969) 'The practice of psychotherapy', in H. Mead, M. Fordham, G. Adler, and W. McGuire (eds), and R.F.C. Hull (trans.), *Collected Works*, Vol. 16 (Bollingen Series, vol. 20), Princeton, NJ: Princeton University Press.

Kasulis, T. P. (1981) *Zen Action: Zen Person*, Honolulu: University of Hawaii Press.

Kawai, H. (1996) *Buddhism and the Art of Psychotherapy*, College Station, TX: Texas A & M University Press.

Kopf, G. (1998) 'In the face of the other: psychic interwovenness in Dogen and Jung', in A. Molino (ed.), *The Couch and the Tree: Dialogues in Psychoanalysis and Buddhism*, New York: North Point Press, 276–89.

Merleau-Ponty, M. (1962) *Phenomenology of Perception*, trans. C. Smith, London: Routledge & Kegan Paul.

Miller, M. E. (1996) 'Ethics and understanding through relationship: I and thou in dialogue', in R. Josselson (ed.), *Ethics and Process in the Narrative Study of Lives*, Thousand Oaks, CA: Sage, 129–47.

Mitchell, S. (1997) *Influence and Autonomy in Psychoanalysis*, Hillsdale, NJ: Analytic Press.

Nishitani, K. (1982) *Religion and Nothingness*, trans. J. VanBragt, Berkeley, CA: University of California Press.

Ogden, T. H. (1986) *The Matrix of the Mind: Object Relations and the Psychoanalytic Dialogue*, Northvale, NJ: Jason Aronson.

Perry, C. (1997) 'Introduction: Jung and the post-Jungians', in P. Young-Eisendrath and T. Dawson (eds), *The Cambridge Companion to Jung*, Cambridge: Cambridge University Press, 141–63.

Rubin, J. B. (1996) *Psychotherapy and Buddhism: Toward an Integration*, New York: Plenum Press.

Senzaki, N., and McCandless, R. S. (1953) *Buddhism and Zen*, New York: Philosophical Library.

Stark, M. (1996) 'From structural conflict to relational conflict: a contemporary model of therapeutic action', in L. Lifson (ed.), *Understanding Therapeutic Action: Psychodynamic Concepts of Cure*, Hillsdale, NJ: Analytic Press, 237–52.

Stolorow, R. D., Atwood, G. E., and Brandchaft, B. (eds) (1994) *The Intersubjective Approach*, Northvale, NJ: Jason Aronson.

Suzuki, D. T. (1964) *An Introduction to Zen Buddhism*, New York, Grove Press.

Suzuki, S. (1970) *Zen Mind, Beginner's Mind*, New York: Weatherhill.

Van Dusen, W. (1998) 'Wu Wei, no-mind and the fertile void in psychotherapy', in A. Molino (ed.), *The Couch and the Tree: Dialogues in Psychoanalysis and Buddhism*, New York: North Point Press, 52–7.

Westkott, M. (1997) 'Karen Horney's encounter with Zen', in J. L. Jacobs and D. Capps (eds), *Religion, Society, and Psychoanalysis: Readings in Contemporary Theory*, Boulder, CO: Westview Press, 71–89.

Winnicott, D. W. (1958) 'The capacity to be alone', in *The Maturational Processes and the Facilitating Environment*, New York: International Universities Press, 29–36.

6

A MINDFUL SELF AND BEYOND

Sharing in the ongoing dialogue of Buddhism and psychoanalysis

Adeline van Waning

> Psychoanalytical-mystical openness to the unknown overlap.
> Analytic workers, not religious in the literal sense, may be
> touched by intimations of something sacred in the work.
> (Michael Eigen, in *The Psychoanalytic Mystic*, p. 11)

Introduction

Buddhism is a spiritual approach, developed 2500 years ago and aimed at enlightenment; psychoanalysis is a general psychology and a form of therapy, having its roots in the nineteenth century, and aimed at understanding and remedying psychological problems. While many distinguishing aspects can be named, we can also be aware of similarities in Buddhist psychology and psychoanalysis. Both psychoanalysis and Buddhism concern themselves with dissatisfaction, human suffering, and its alleviation; both offer a kind of 'diagnosis' and a 'treatment plan'. They both take place within an important personal emotional relationship: the relationship of therapist–client, and the relationship of teacher–student. They emphasize the importance of comparable experiential processes: in analysis evenly hovering attention and free association, in Buddhism the method of meditation. The obstacles in these processes are recognized and have an important function in the transformation-process: defence and resistance in psychoanalysis and what are called 'hindrances' in Buddhism.

Both can be named 'uncovering' approaches, aimed at insight into our nature and way of thinking and feeling. There are some 'technical' aspects that are characteristic for psychoanalysis (and less for other psychotherapy approaches) that can be linked with Buddhism. We may say that both approaches seem to share a relatively 'neutral', though compassionate stance of the therapist and teacher, who are attentive and may be noticing and naming, but are not giving direct advice (this may be more true for psychoanalysis than for Buddhism). The client and meditator is expected to observe what is there, without censorship. There is a certain 'abstinence' in the way that the therapist or teacher is not intentionally gratifying, but functions as a guide or midwife in the person's own process. We can also say that, in the beginning of the process, a certain benign 'split in the ego' is favored: one can experience in what way and what one experiences, while experiencing. The existential responsibility in this process is in the client and meditator, not the authority figure.

But there are many differences and certainly misunderstandings too. Freud wrote about meditation in terms of 'oceanic feelings', an experience of unlimited unity with the universe, aimed at 'the recovery of infinite narcissism' and return to the breast or the womb (Freud 1930). By making this erroneous judgment, a (negative) misunderstanding was created and continued for decades. Still, psychotherapists in the West have always had an interest in Eastern psychology and spirituality; Maslow and Watts are examples. Also depth-psychologists from the Jungian tradition showed an interest: for instance Jung himself (1964), Moacanin (1986), Meckel and Moore (1992), and Young-Eisendrath (1996). The same goes for psychoanalysts such as Fromm (1960), Horney (DeMartino 1991), Epstein (1995, 1998), Coltart (1996) and Molino (1998).

In this paper I would like to go into one aspect of profound difference between these two traditions, namely in the way that self and subjectivity are conceived and approached. A case example illustrates a way of integrating Buddhist insights into the 'working through' process in psychoanalytic treatment. I will also address two forms of Buddhist practice, mindfulness and koan practice. I hope to make clear that both fundamental approaches offer precious gifts to the client and the psychotherapist.

Self and subjectivity

The thirteenth-century Zen master Dogen says: 'To study Buddhism is to study the self. To study the self is to forget the self. To forget the self is to be one with others' (Epstein 1995: 20). The perception of this self is of great importance for both psychoanalysis and Buddhism. Psychoanalysis and Buddhism both examine the concept and experiencing of subjectivity, and emphasize the necessity of transformation of the self in order to develop fully. However, psychoanalytic and Buddhist ways of conceiving the self and its development differ widely.

The following story gives us a sense of the Buddhist approach:

> You are walking in the forest beside the old master, and come near a brook. He touches your shoulder, and you know he wants you to sit down. He shakes his head and points to a piece of cork which floats by. It is burned, half of it is black. 'That is your personality,' the master says, 'with everything that happens, every change of circumstance,

*every conflict, every defeat or victory, a small bit of it crumbles away.'
You look at the cork. You see pieces of it come loose and disappear.
'The cork is getting smaller and smaller,' you say, nervously. The calm
voice of the master is very close: 'until there is nothing left'. He looks
at you with a kind smile. There is this fragile old man who wants to
teach you something . . . You will lose your name, your body, your personality. Your fear lessens. If it has to happen, it will happen. Nothing
will be left. And you will no longer be there.*

(based on: Van de Wetering 1975: 21–2)

'Selflessness' in this sense can be seen as an insight and a liberation of the
burden of attachments to name, body, and personality, leading to a freer
way of being in the world. But the perception of this 'selflessness' in a
Western sense is often frightening. We can think, for example, of experiences
of therapy clients who indicate that they have 'no self', no personality or
identity, who have the feeling that all they are is a reaction, a response to
others. As a particular client said, about a cork as well: 'I feel like a cork floating in the ocean, I'm only going with the waves and the stream, I have no
individuality.'

*In this way, I think of a client, Ella, who always describes herself in
comparison with others; she does not know who she is. Yes, she's 'kind
of nice' and she gets on with her father better than her sister, and she
is more shy than her brother, and she gets jealous quickly. Ella is beginning to recognize that the members of her family are never addressed as
individual personalities. In conversations within the family they always
talked, as it were, 'through others'. 'I would like to become a person of
my own, a true me,' she states.*

We might say that Ella experiences her suffering in terms of a missing function in her personality: the ability to sustain the experience of being an
individual subject.

A Buddhist and a psychoanalytic perspective

In the *Buddhist perspective*, major psychological problems result from our
attachment to the image of the self as fixed and independent: fixed as
opposed to transitory, impermanent, changeable; and independent, separate,
as opposed to connected and dependent on everybody and everything. We
have no anchorage outside of this personal identity, which is always moving,
always changing. Under these circumstances images about the past are
'adapted' to how we feel at the moment, and images of the future are inspired
by present wishes and fears. As to the idea of being independent, in the West
we speak of a developmental process of separation–individuation. In other

95

cultures, among them those where Buddhism developed, one could better speak of separation-integration into the family or group. In a multicultural approach to subjectivity we recognize that personal identity always depends on a context. Multicultural society comments on the idea of a Western separate self in a cultural sense; Buddhism does the same in a radical way in an existential, spiritual sense.

Connection and unity do not exclude the perception of subjectivity; subjectivity is not bound to separation–individuation. In Buddhism, for example, a form of non-self-centered subjectivity is cultivated, which is characterized by clear, open attention, and tuning in to the other as well as to oneself.

The Buddha did not say, 'You don't exist,' but rather, 'You have no self.' His point was not to deny or reject the self, but to recognize the self-representation as *representation*, as a concept without existence of its own. The Zen master helps the student to gain the invigorating and broadening experience of no-self. Tenzin Gyatso, the Dalai Lama, explains it this way: the point of selflessness, of talking about no-self, is not that something that existed in the past no longer exists, but that this kind of self never existed at all. It is necessary to recognize the non-existence of something that has never existed but was only imagined. This may lead to an experience which may, at first, be painful rather than oceanic.

In the *psychoanalytical perspective*, 'self' is seen, in general, as a central organizer in the psychological universe of every human being, from which our identity and its accompanying 'otherness' emerge. We talk about consistency, coherence and continuity in the experiencing of the self, about 'true self' and 'false self'. In this view one suffers a great problem when lacking self-coherence or self-esteem. When viewing many serious afflictions (e.g. autism, psychoses, borderline and narcissistic problems) we speak of disorders, stagnation, or regression in the shaping of a cohesive, integrated self-image, as in the case of Ella. In current therapies the emphasis is on the question of how to make people feel better about themselves, rather than how to deal with internal conflicts. We now talk about the 'narcissistic dilemma': the sense of estrangement, or 'falseness' in the sense of not being real, linked with either idealizing or devaluing others or oneself, with self-exaltation or self-contempt as poles of this false self-image.

Self can be seen as the representation of a function of coherence, continuity, agency and relationship that allows us to perceive ourselves as a single, integrated, subjective embodiment.

In psychoanalysis, we use, one could say, 'self' as a help-construction in our endeavour to understand the person in being, suffering, enjoying, hoping, learning, and development. Developmentally, we understand the self as a function which is grounded in embodiment and the experiences of self-reflexivity that are typical of humans.

The analyst Nina Coltart puts her cheerful comment on this in the form of a limerick (1996: 139):

A Buddhist once said: 'To deny
That this I is an I is a lie;
For if it is not,
I should like to know what
Is the thing that says: "I am not I"'.

The problem is that, while we make a representation of an ever-changing function, we imagine this representation as a fixed 'thing'. We tend to create a fixed self in the same way we create objects. Varela, Thompson, and Rosch argue that 'this grasping after an inner ground is itself a moment in a larger pattern of grasping that includes our clinging to an outer ground in the form of an idea of a pregiven and independent world. In other words, our grasping after a ground, whether inner or outer, is the deep source of frustration and anxiety' (Varela et al. 1991: 143).

Integration

How might a possible integration of Buddhist insights and approaches concerning 'self-perception' into psychotherapy be of help? Long ago, Buddhism developed a technique for healing the problems that go with the fact that human beings make an image of themselves and get attached to it, a technique for healing problems connected with the narcissistic attachment to a fixed self-image of human beings. This is something Western psychology has only relatively recently started to focus on.

Before going further, I want to relate the following case example:

> *A client, John, relates an incident in which a friend, Rose, was very angry*
> *with him. She reproached him for not complying with her request that he*
> *go with her to a meeting which was important to her, saying that he had*
> *let her down terribly. Rose felt that this said something about him, that*
> *he was just not interested, and that he was no good. Her fierce reproaches*
> *gave John something of a shock. At first he winced at the thought that he*
> *really had been very thoughtless; and it also touched upon a sensitive*
> *spot: Am I really like that? He then started to wonder whether he con-*
> *sidered her reproaches justified under these circumstances – and then he*
> *became increasingly angry: he thought her reproaches were exaggerated*
> *and out of proportion. Actually he was furious: What did she think? He*
> *felt hurt, not only because of what she had said about the situation, but*
> *more about the way she made this into 'that he was like this'. No, he was*
> *not like this! He felt hurt; and at the same time he didn't want to be so*
> *touched by it; he didn't want to take it seriously.*

Her image of him and his self-image sound and felt fixed and stable. She says he is like this, and he thinks he is like that. Buddhists recommend 'keeping anger in check', which means to feel it and recognize it, but not to assume that the anger is a fact *in itself*. It was right that John had fully experienced his anger, and was able to stay with it. It was also right not to leave that feeling of fear that went with the hurt. Could it perhaps be true, what she had said about him? And then, true or not true, he felt the panic, for a short while: was he going to lose the friend? Naturally, John and I also looked at whether these feelings might possibly say something about the feelings that played a role in the therapeutic relationship, his transference to me. What did they mean to him, the feelings of abandonment, of anger that arose with Rose; might he feel that I didn't accept him, was he angry with me, was he afraid I was angry with him or criticizing him? And what were my (counter)transferential feelings in this?

Letting go of identification

'Working through' experiences in a Buddhist and in a psychoanalytic sense allows us to observe the workings of what is called the I. This goes beyond what we commonly name 'insight', and is focused both on content and on process, on the ways of working of the mind. In most therapies we will discuss with clients, in some ongoing way, how they deal with themselves, with feelings of superiority and inferiority in relationships with other people. We will talk about dissatisfactions with life, about how to make life meaningful.

I will name some general points here where in my opinion a Buddhist approach can enrich the commonly understood 'working through' process, and I will try to make a connection to John's experiences.

It is essential that, given the problems that the client presents, client and therapist look together at what the client is repeating, in such a way that he or she can really feel, experience it. We look at patterns of repetition in the resistance against fully being with it, which so often have to do with fears, linked to self-esteem: the feeling of having missed so much, of not being able to do without.

> *John knew of his sensitivity in many situations in actual life, and he made a connection to the reality of his mother's illness when he was three years old, which meant that at times he had been left in the care of relatives, not knowing how long it would last. She died when he was five. Anxiety about abandonment (as he was young, interpreted by him in ways such that this might be a punishment for things he had done wrong) and a reactive entitlement for attention made him vulnerable. His first reaction to the reproaches of his friend was one of guilty submission.*

It is important that the client truly feels his demand for reparation, and the fear of the pain and hollowness which lie behind it (and are fended off), against which he may try to defend himself with all possible means.

John's feeling of entitlement confused his precise attention to what was going on at the very moment in the interaction with his friend. To tolerate his despair at not being seen as he thought he deserved was hard. Often, before, he had had an inclination to enact and act out, or to make a fight in comparable circumstances.

Can the client 'live' this hollowness intensely? Going through it can be very painful and frightening.

John now really tried to be with his despair with 'bare attention' and without judgment; he tried to contain and to tolerate his emotions, in a way that had aspects of intrapsychic 'desensitization'.

It is important that the client recognizes the repetition (often, hurt self-esteem), the resistance (reactive self-importance or self-contempt), and that which is fended off (pain, emptiness, fear, depression) as *something of himself*, and that he feels how he identifies with these positions.

For John this meant being with his hurt feelings, with his anger and defensive feelings of grandiosity and with his anxiety for being insignificant, nobody, nowhere. Also it meant for him recognizing that his early biography, as sad as it was, served a function still now to continue feeling let down and feeling entitled to demand reparation; that in some, at first unconscious, way he cherished his early trauma.

It is fundamental that the client can then *let go of this identification*, to *dis-identify*. This will result in there being room for more openness, equanimity and energy.

And for John this letting go brought an ability to better be and experience in the here and now, aware of his feelings in the present situation instead of these feelings so much being colored by the past. In that way he needed no longer to live the extremes of self-contempt and self-importance as if he were just that; as if they formed his identity, as if he had a fixed identity. Instead, now he could more realistically explore the different aspects in his passing feelings, tolerate and accept the ambivalence and ambiguity in the situation.

It seems often more attractive to distract, to cover up and wait for better times, than to go through pain and hollowness and survive. Often something else happens, namely that the client has to fend off this recognizing something as being of himself, that he wants to externalize and project onto others. For John this might mean that he would just blame Rose. Often, letting go and dis-identifying will not be fulfilled, meaning that the client remains linked with his fixed identifications, unconsciously. John might continue to live the hurt, entitled child; and with every enacted conflict where he felt let down, his entitlement would grow and he might end up a bitter man.

Being with our acute, intense feelings seems very hard; often we avoid them in a phobic way.

Psychoanalytical (re)construction of the way something may have happened and has been experienced in the past can give meaning, and thus make it easier to let it go; but sometimes just such a construction, as a new piece of identity, can lead to holding on to it. It was right for John that he could feel all the emotions that have been described as his, and also see that they were temporary, passing by, and that he is more than his emotions. After John had cried in despair, while he recognized his identification with the angry let-down boy, his acceptance of the pain and anger freed the energy contained in them, which then he could use for constructive activities. It was also good for him to feel that his friend's criticism (and possibly mine, and possibly his to me) were passing and could not really touch him.

To be able to recognize all this, with non-judging attention, is similar to the perceptual abilities cultivated in 'mindfulness'. In what follows I will go into what has been called the special gift of Buddhism to the world: mindfulness meditation.

Mindfulness

In all Buddhist approaches, attention is given to the right meditative concentration and to non-judging mindful awareness of what comes floating up. Often observance of the breathing is taken as the base from where to start and where gently to return, when being distracted. As concentration grows and gradually we get less easily distracted, we have more attention for the coming and going of the 'objects of the mind', such as thoughts, memories, worries, wishes, physical sensations. Thus, we develop a refined, inclusive, non-selective, non-judging awareness in the moment, a 'such-ness' not related to anything else. This leads to more penetrating insights into emotional and physical processes, into 'self-awareness' and reality and, thus, to the development of empathy and commitment. Mindfulness helps us to recognize fear and resistance and to mitigate unconscious and punitive self-criticism. The dynamics of this criticism are aptly described by Kris (1990). Mindfulness also reduces the tendency to act on impulse and habit. Mindfulness illuminates, accepts, and transforms.

Epstein (1990) describes what happens in concentration and mindfulness meditation in psychoanalytical terms. The traditional psychoanalytical explanation of meditation as blending with an internalized image of a lost state of perfection, with 'oceanic' emotions, could be seen as the blending of the I and the I-ideal. In the beginning, when doing the concentration exercise, a person may have such expansive or pleasant feelings.

But 'mindfulness' meditation is an attention strategy which will lead to insights and experiences that can be totally different. At first, 'mindfulness' meditation means, just like free association and free-floating attention, a therapeutic splitting in the I, where the I observes itself. This results in the reinforcement of the ability of the observing I to notice changes from moment to moment. One could say that 'mindfulness' means *the development of the synthetic ability of the I within the I*: synthesis at still more complex levels of differentiation and 'objectification' of reality. Mindfulness can be seen as a developmental tool towards a mindful self and beyond.

What does mindfulness meditation mean to the therapist, to me?

The importance of Freud's recommendations about 'evenly hovering attention' (1912) is widely recognized for verbal, expressive therapies. At the same time, it is remarkable that so little attention was given to the pragmatic question, 'How can it be developed and cultivated?' People have written mainly about what one had to avoid in order to make this kind of attention possible (e.g. censure, expectations beforehand, too much reflection); Bion (1970) commented upon the necessity for an analyst to leave behind 'memory, desire and understanding'.

Precisely here, Buddhist psychology has a lot to offer: a systematic training of perception, attention, and awareness. Freud suggested *what* we should do; the meditative tradition shows *how* non-selective and non-restrictive attention can be learned. One can probably only appreciate the value of this once one has experienced it. Concentration-meditation creates the conditions for listening with evenly hovering attention, mindfulness meditation helps to implement, cultivate, and refine this. Why not introduce the practice of mindfulness meditation in the training of psychoanalysts and psychotherapists?

Helping clients develop an attitude of mindfulness can have very beneficial effects. In the case of Ella this has meant that she has started to do formal mindfulness meditation in a group. Her words: 'What for me is so important is that I always have it with me, it gives me a safe feeling. And it means that I have a choice, it gives some control because I can do something and I'm with it.' Ella in fact states that she feels more a 'person of her own', a seemingly paradoxical effect, because it helps to disidentify with a fixed identity! She experiences this space for being her true self.

A client can be asked to investigate a symptom or complaint with mindfulness, as a seemingly paradoxical question, while in one way we 'choose' the symptom for expressing our suffering, and in another way we want to get rid of it. One can 'sit' every day with a question, for example 'Why do I drink alcohol?' on every out-breath; an answer will come and often can be formulated as a new question. For instance, if the answer is 'To protect against loneliness' one can ask, 'What makes me so lonely?' (Kief 1999). The practice can help us to develop a steady motivation for deeper penetration into our questions and problems and support in desensitization of concomitant anxieties.

Mindfulness supports living in the present, and sharpens perception and consciousness. The practice has been taken up as a universal approach, and been included in psychotherapy, and in stress and pain management programs with significant positive effects (see Kabat-Zinn 1990; Kabat-Zinn et al. 1992).

Beyond the separate self

Mindfulness can be seen as an attention strategy that can help us non-judgmentally to investigate our doings, thinking, and feeling, in order to get better insight into the ways we represent our fluctuating selves, and can help us towards transformation beyond this self. Koan practice from Zen Buddhism takes us radically beyond this self. A koan, often presented as a story, sometimes a metaphor, is a question that may sound 'non-rational', even paradoxical to our ears. 'What is the sound of one hand clapping?' Koan practice thwarts the desire for meaning and demands a new kind of encounter with the problem or question. In formal practice, a Zen student must manifest, actualize, or embody a response, not simply give a verbal answer. This kind of practice demands a new kind of attentive concentration and mindfulness. A koan is a strategy to break through the dualism of the mind, and pass by the self–other dichotomy that tends to keep us defensively fixed and identified with our separate self.

'Sitting with a koan' in meditation can help to let go of ordinary thinking and to exercise a form of attention which for a therapist can be very helpful in the therapeutic relationship. Sometimes a psychoanalytical interpretation, developed from the intersubjective interaction between therapist and client, may have aspects of a liberating breakthrough for the client; suddenly there is an opening, exactly because the I was able to let go and give room to the creativity and intuition of a non-conscious stream of thought, from which we can name a non-discriminative, non-discursive, 'lateral' thinking; a knowing which has been lifted to a wider form of consciousness and awareness. The solution to a koan may be seen as the lived manifestation of a transcendence beyond dualistic self where there is no need for discrepancies of experiencing an attached and an unattached self, because you are who you are, because it is the way it is.

Polly Young-Eisendrath gives an impressive example of her application of what is called the 'fundamental koan' in her treatments: 'When it is impossible to do anything, what do you do?' This koan is about the value of tolerating insecurities, about room for ambiguity, open-endedness, for potentially new things for both client and therapist, instead of the illusion that the therapist knows, in which solutions are sought, or support and advice are given (Young-Eisendrath 1997).

To get back to John: he and Rose turned out to be good 'teachers' to one another, resulting in a closer and closer relationship, and eventually marriage. After one year they had a son, named John Jr., of whom father John was extremely fond. At one time in our treatment John called me in the afternoon, crying and completely upset, to tell me of the tragedy that his two-year-old son had been hit in a traffic accident and died instantly. John came to see me immediately. There we sat, with his immense unspeakable grief. We both felt so powerless. What could I do except be with him, present and aware, mostly without words. Understanding his being the father, the husband, his self-reproach, his identification with being the little boy, himself the abandoned child – and not understanding.

Where pain and suffering of the client can be so profound, it is important that the therapist remains open-minded and knows that she or he doesn't know; and when it is impossible to do anything, one must do something with that.

Brazier cites the title of Carl Rogers' book *On Becoming a Person* as a modern koan. One could say: If I am not a person, what am I? Can I become fully the person that I can be? Rogers wanted us to take up this question afresh as a means to help us become the most we can possibly be. The answer cannot be in words, it can just show, and be manifested. As Brazier states, solving a koan means changing our way of being, and this generally means giving up some ideas rather than producing new ones (Brazier 1995).

Conclusion

Within certain critical arenas as I have presented, psychoanalysis and Buddhist psychology can provide each other with important insights and approaches. Psychoanalysis helps us to suffer less from unconscious conflicts, confusions, and fixed attitudes; Buddhism helps us to be more awake and aware in the here and now, and to be open to the spiritual dimension which is present in everything. As therapists and clients who practice Buddhism we become more open to the 'sacred' in the psychoanalytic work, as phrased by Eigen, the sacred in the transformations that awareness can facilitate, transformations into the mindful self and beyond.

What might psychoanalysis have to offer to Buddhism and what can psychoanalysis learn from Buddhism? One of the things psychoanalysis may have to offer is an extensive development of theories about forms of defense and resistance, and of the therapeutic intersubjective interaction, of (counter)transference and enactment. With the example of John, in his letting go of fixed self-identifications, we got a glimpse of what Buddhist psychology can offer psychoanalysis. Psychoanalysis can learn more about psychological health, maturation, and transformation. The most direct, essential contribution of Buddhism to psychoanalysts and psychotherapists is, in my view, the attention, concentration, awareness in the challenge of being 'awake' and unprejudiced right 'here' for both the other and yourself.

References

Bion, W. (1970) *Attention and Interpretation*, New York: Basic Books.

Brazier, D. (1995) *Zen Therapy: Transcending the Sorrows of the Human Mind*, New York: John Wiley.

Coltart, N. (1996) 'Buddhism and psychoanalysis revisited', in *The Baby and the Bathwater*, London: Karnac Books, pp. 125–39.

DeMartino, R. J. (1991) 'Karen Horney, Daisetz T. Suzuki and Zen Buddhism', *American Journal of Psychoanalysis* 51: 267–83.

Eigen, M. (1998) *The Psychoanalytic Mystic*, London: Free Associations.

Epstein, M. (1990) 'Beyond the oceanic feeling: psychoanalytic study of Buddhist meditation', *International Review of Psycho-Analysis* 17: 159–66.

Epstein, M. (1995) *Thoughts Without a Thinker: Psychotherapy from a Buddhist Perspective*, New York: Basic Books.

Epstein, M. (1998) *Going to Pieces without Falling Apart: A Buddhist Perspective on Wholeness, Lessons from Meditation and Psychotherapy*, New York: Broadway Books.

Freud, S. (1912) 'Recommendations to physicians practicing Psycho-analysis', *Standard Edition* 12 (1924), pp. 109–20.

Freud, S. (1930) 'Civilization and its discontents', *Standard Edition* 21 (1961), pp. 57–145.

Fromm, E. (1960) 'Psychoanalysis and Zen Buddhism', in E. Fromm, D. T. Suzuki and R. DeMartino, *Zen Buddhism and Psychoanalysis*, New York: Harper & Row, pp. 77–141.

Jung, C. G. (1964) *Man and His Symbols*, London: Aldus Books.

Kabat-Zinn, J. (1990) *Full Catastrophe Living: Using the Wisdom of your Body and Mind to Face Stress, Pain and Illness: The Program of the Stress Reduction Clinic at the University of Massachusetts Medical Center*, New York: Delta/Bantam Doubleday Dell.

Kabat-Zinn, J., Massion, A. O., Kristeller, J., Gay Peterson, L., Fletcher, K. E., Pbert, L, Lenderking, W. R., Santorelli, S. (1992) 'Effectiveness of a meditation-based stress reduction program in the treatment of anxiety disorders', *American Journal of Psychiatry* 147: 936–43.

Kief, H. (1999) 'Mediteren en ons functioneren', *Bres* (October–November): 13–21.

Kris, A. O. (1990) 'Helping patients by analysing selfcriticism', *Journal of the American Psychoanalytical Association* 38: 605–36.

Meckel, D. J., and Moore, R. L. (eds) (1992) *Self and Liberation: The Jung/Buddhism Dialogue*, Mahwah, NJ: Paulist Press.

Moacanin, R. (1986) *Jung's Psychology and Tibetan Buddhism: Western and Eastern Paths to the Heart*, Boston: Wisdom Publications.

Molino, A. (1998) *The Couch and the Tree: Dialogues in Psychoanalysis and Buddhism*, New York: North Point Press.

Rubin, J. B. (1996) *Psychotherapy and Buddhism: Toward an Integration*, New York and London: Plenum Press.

Van de Wetering, J. W. (1975) *A Glimpse of Nothingness: Experiences in an American Zen Community*, Boston, MA: Houghton Mifflin.

Varela, F., Thompson, E., and Rosch, E. (1991) *The Embodied Mind*, Cambridge, MA: MIT Press.

Young-Eisendrath, P. (1996) *The Gifts of Suffering: Finding Insight, Compassion and Renewal*, Reading, MA: Addison-Wesley.

Young-Eisendrath, P. (1997) 'The fundamental Koan and the value of uncertainty in psychotherapy', *FAS Bulletin*: 124–8.

Part II

CAUTIONS AND INSIGHTS ABOUT POTENTIAL CONFUSIONS

7

THE JUNG–HISAMATSU
CONVERSATION

Translated from Aniela Jaffé's original German Protocol by
Shoji Muramoto in collaboration with
Polly Young-Eisendrath and Jan Middeldorf

Translator's Introduction

Shin'ichi Hisamatsu (1889–1980), a member of the Kyoto School and disciple of Kitaro Nishida, was a leading Zen philosopher of modern Japan. In
1958, as part of his comparative research into Eastern and Western religion
and philosophy, he lectured extensively throughout the United States. On his
way back to Japan, he visited with a number of prominent European thinkers
for a series of conversations on Zen and Western thought. Among his inter-
locutors was C. G. Jung. Their conversation took place at Jung's home in
Küsnacht, Switzerland, on 16 May 1958. Also present were interpreter Koichi
Tsujimura, a student of Martin Heidegger's, and Aniela Jaffé, Jung's private
secretary, who later compiled his autobiography.

How the dialogue unfolded is basically unknown; as of this writing, only
Tsujimura is still alive. The only available documentation is Jaffé's transcribed
protocol, derived from her shorthand notes of the meeting, and Tsujimura's
Japanese translation of the German protocol. It is safe to assume that Jung
and Hisamatsu spoke their own languages, and that Tsujimura and Jaffé
functioned as translator and transcriber, respectively. Distortions resulting
from mistranslation and errors in recording were likely to have occurred
throughout the dialogue, of which no tape recording is known to exist. We do
not know, furthermore, whether and to what extent both Jaffé, originally, and
Tsujimura, later, edited the transcribed German text. What we do know, however, is that a copy of the German transcription was sent to Hisamatsu and
translated by Tsujimura. This Japanese translation was first published in July
1959 by *FAS*, the journal for the Zen-inspired FAS Society, founded by
Hisamatsu in 1944. (According to the Society's newsletter, 'the acronym refers
to the three inseparable dimensions of our existence: self, world and history.') Ten years later, in 1969, with the publication of *Eastern Nothingness*,
vol. 1 of *The Collected Works of Shin'ichi Hisamatsu*, the same Japanese

version appeared under the title 'The Unconscious and *Wu-Hsin*,' together with an introduction by Tsujimura and commentary by Hisamatsu.

Koji Sato, professor of educational psychology at Kyoto University, later asked Jung's permission to publish a protocol of the text in *Psychologia*, an English-language journal that he edited. But Jung refused. In a letter to Sachi Toyomura, who had translated Tsujimura's Japanese version into English, Jung explained the reasons for his refusal. The letter was later published in volume 3 of *Psychologia* (1960), and is now available in a book edited by Daniel J. Meckel and Robert L. Moore, *Self and, Liberation: The Jung/Buddhism Dialogue* (Paulist Press, 1992). Among his reasons for opposing this 'most delicate and correspondingly dangerous procedure,' Jung mainly cites inevitable and profound gaps in his and Hisamatsu's understanding of each other's traditions.

In 1968, seven years after Jung's death and one year before the inclusion of the Japanese version in *Eastern Nothingness*, Sachi Toyomura's English translation was finally published in volume II of *Psychologia*. The translation was accompanied by a statement by Sato, who claimed that Jaffé's gift of the German protocol to Hisamatsu could be interpreted as an expression of permission for Hisamatsu to publish it. More than twenty years later, Jaffé told me that Sato had misunderstood her intentions altogether, as she had sent the protocol to Hisamatsu only as a 'memento' (*Erinnerung*) of his encounter with Jung.

As I have already suggested, the English translation published in *Psychologia* was not directly from the German text, but from Tsujimura's Japanese translation. Nor was it revised by any native speaker of English. Four years later, in 1972, in reviewing the dialogue for *Psychologia*, Noma Haimes wrote: 'Partly on account of a strange translation, the dialogue sounds like *Alice in Wonderland*.' As Jung's letter to Toyomura suggests, he himself must have read the English translation – the quality of which may have played into his decision not to allow its publication. Now, however, even as Meckel and Moore, in republishing Toyomura's translation, have also clearly revised its English, the problem remains that the lone extant English version of the Jung–Hisamatsu dialogue is, at best, a retranslation of a Japanese translation of the original German protocol.

In the mid-1980s, I had the good fortune of meeting several times in Europe with Aniela Jaffé, to discuss the matter of the protocol and translation. On 3 January 1985, following our first meeting and more than twenty-five years after the historic encounter between the two men, she wrote to me as follows:

> When I reflected on our very interesting dialogue, a problem occurred to me, and I want to talk about it. I suppose that Prof. Hisamatsu and Prof. Jung spoke with each other in English (though I don't exactly remember). But if that were the case, I could certainly

not have taken such a detailed protocol. For I could only take short-hand in German. It is possible that I had taken notes in German in my notebook. But is it conceivable that Prof. Hisamatsu later elaborated on the text, especially his own comments?

Even if both scholars had spoken German, it would hardly have been possible for me to complete such a detailed protocol, especially of the scholarly exchanges. Therefore, someone had to add to the text. This would be acceptable only if Hisamatsu were to have done so. If you should find the original of the 'protocol' in the Jung Archive [where I had been directed by Jaffé to find the original German text – S.M.] I would be delighted to be able to consult it.

It should be noted that Jaffé seemed to forget that Tsujimura had been present as a translator. The protocol, as a result, became all the more important. I later obtained permission from Lorenz Jung to make a copy of the document, the use of which was allowed at the time only for reasons of 'personal study and research.' Upon securing the material, I immediately met with Jaffé again, and went over the document with her, comparing her transcription with the odd English text at our disposal. In further research I have since performed and published in Japan, I counted and commented on approximately fifty discrepancies between the two texts. (See my entry in *Annual Report* from the Institute for Zen Studies, vol. 19, 1993.) In the meantime, permission was finally obtained to publish a translation of the German protocol I had prepared in the course of my research. The following, therefore, is the first English translation to be published of Jaffé's original German transcription of the 1958 conversation between Shin'ichi Hisamatsu and Carl Gustav Jung.

16 May 1958

SHIN'ICHI HISAMATSU: In the United States I witnessed the great spread of psychoanalysis and talked about it with many scholars. I am very glad to speak today with the founder of psychoanalysis. I would like to hear your thoughts on the state of psychoanalysis today.[1]

CARL G. JUNG: I would prefer to know your view first, so that I may understand the nature of the question. Eastern language is very different from Western conceptual language. In India, I had many conversations with philosophers and came to realize that I always need to clarify the question first; so as to know what my Eastern partner is thinking. If I assume that I know what he thinks, everything will be misconstrued.

SH: As I am no specialist in psychoanalysis, I would first like to understand its essential position, in order to then compare it with Zen.

CGJ: That is possible, but you must bear in mind that Zen is a philosophy and that I am a psychologist.

SH: In a sense, one might say that Zen is a philosophy, but it is very different from ordinary philosophy, which depends on human intellectual activity. One might therefore say that Zen is no philosophy. Zen is a philosophy and at the same time a religion, but no ordinary religion. It is 'religion and philosophy.'

CGJ: I must pose these questions in order to hear what you think, so that I can then direct my questions accordingly. You want to know what I think psychologically of the task that Zen poses for us. The task is in both cases – Zen and psychology – the same. Zen is concerned with how we deal with *wu-hsin*, no-mind.

SH: To date there have been many interpretations of *wu-hsin*.

CGJ: I mean the unconscious by it.

SH: It is, therefore, absolutely necessary to find a true and strict definition for the term from the standpoint of Zen. This is extremely important. I would like to hear your thoughts on the matter.[2]

CGJ: It is the unknown that affects me psychologically, the unknown that disturbs or influences me, whether positively or negatively. Thus I notice that it exists, but I don't know what it is.

SH: Is this 'unknown' something different from the unconscious? From the collective unconscious?

CGJ: The unknown disturbs or influences me in certain forms. Otherwise I could not speak of it. Sometimes I sense that a personal memory is bothering me, or exerting an influence on me; other times I have dreams, ideas, or fantasies that do not have a personal origin. Their source is not the subjective; rather they have a universal quality. For example, the image I have of my father is a personal image. But when this image possesses a religious quality, it is no longer solely connected to the personal realm.

SH: Is the non-personal unconscious a fundamental unconscious? In other words, is the non-personal unconscious what you call the collective unconscious? Is this the most fundamental? Or perhaps just relatively more fundamental?[3]

CGJ: The personal unconscious develops in the course of life, for example through experiences, the memory of which I repress. The other, the collective, is something instinctually innate and universally human. My collective unconscious is the same as yours, even though you were born in Japan and I here in Europe. SH: Does the collective unconscious involve something common to all persons or something that is beyond the personal?

CGJ: One can only say that the collective unconscious is the commonality of all instinctive reactions found among all human beings. The possibility of our speaking with each other intellectually rests on our sharing a common foundation. Otherwise, we would be so different as to understand nothing.

SH: Fairy tales speak of various sufferings and joys. Do these all emerge from the collective unconscious?

112

CGJ: If, for example, you study a very primitive person with limited consciousness or, let's say, if you study a child – a child who cannot yet even say 'I' – you find that the child is still in the general mental state of all children, or of all people before they achieve consciousness. Consciousness has developed through the course of history; it is a common experience. Ontogeny repeats phylogeny.[4] In the child, consciousness develops out of a collective unconscious state. Emotional life, worries, joys, sufferings, hate, love, these are already present before consciousness proper develops. You see this in animals as well. It is connected with the essence of the unconscious. There are instinctive excitements observable in animals which are connected with the essence of the unconscious. Perhaps one could say that these are *klesas* – namely, properties or symptoms of the unconscious.

SH: From our viewpoint, *klesas* belong to the sphere of consciousness.

CGJ: Of course, consciousness is necessary, otherwise we could not establish that such things exist. But the question for us is: is it consciousness that creates the *klesas*? The answer is no; consciousness is their victim. Before consciousness, passions already exist. One cannot ask a raging animal whether it is raging. The animal is totally at the mercy of its rage.

SH: *Klesas* are usually thought to belong to consciousness, but how is this sphere of consciousness related to the unconscious?

CGJ: How is the unconscious related to consciousness? I really have no definite answer. But for us they are related: we see from experience that consciousness develops out of the unconscious. We can observe this in children, in primitive people and so on. And I see it as a physician. If I have to treat a person in the grip of the unconscious, the unconscious is like a landscape at night, when nothing of the mountains and lakes and woods is visible. Then, if a fire starts someplace, you can suddenly see all that's there – the lakes, the woods, and so on. That is consciousness.

SH: Which then is our real self, our real, our putative 'I': the unconscious or consciousness?[5]

CGJ: Consciousness refers to itself as 'I.' The self is no mere 'I.' The self is the whole personality – you as a totality – consisting of consciousness and the unconscious. This is the whole, or the self, but I know only consciousness; the unconscious remains unknown to me.

SH: In your view, the self is a totality. This prompts the following question: Is I-consciousness different from self-consciousness?

CGJ: In ordinary usage, one says self-consciousness, but that only means I-consciousness, psychologically speaking. The self is unknown because it indeed designates the whole of the person, both conscious and unconscious. The conscious person you are is known to you, but the unconscious person you are is unknown to you. The human self is beyond description, because it is only one-third, or perhaps two-thirds, in the realm of experience, and that part belongs to the 'I.' That which is known, however, does not encompass the self. The vernacular expression 'self-consciousness' translates psychologically as I-consciousness. The self is much more than the 'I.'

SH: So the self is unknown?

CGJ: Perhaps only half of it is known, and that is the 'I,' the half of the self.

SH: Is the way the self is unknown the same as the way that the unconscious is unknown?

CGJ: It is practically the same. I do not know what is within the unconscious, I am not conscious of it.

SH: Is what we call 'I' in ordinary life the same 'I' that experiences so many different emotions? The ordinary 'I' belongs to the sphere of consciousness. How is it related to the original unknown self? What place does the 'I' have in the whole personality?

CGJ: The 'I' is like a light in the darkness of night.

SH: In illness, a patient experiences many deep sufferings, and therapy perhaps consists of liberating the suffering patient from them. He is brought to a state of non-suffering. If this liberation is the nature of psychotherapy, how is therapy related to the fundamental unconscious?

CGJ: If the illness is caused by things that are unconscious, then there is the possibility of healing by making these causes conscious. The causes do not always have to lie in the unconscious, however. There are cases in which the symptoms point to psychic causes. For example, there was a man who lost his consciousness, so to speak, and became only half conscious. It was as if he had lost his good judgment. The reason for this was that the child to whom his wife had given birth was not his own child. While he was not conscious of this fact, it had nonetheless darkened his consciousness. He then chased after an old love of his, but this was only because he was always living in unawareness. He was unconscious of what was causing his suffering, and the therapy consisted in telling him that his wife had been unfaithful.

SH: What will become of this man when he has clearly recognized that the child is not his own? It could be that after learning the truth he becomes afflicted with another suffering. Does psychotherapy consist of making conscious the causes of suffering?

CGJ: In his case, yes, but not always. For example, there are other cases in which the causes are well known, in which a person already knows that a bad relationship with his father or mother is the cause of his suffering. Anybody can know as much. What everybody cannot know is the kind of consequences for the patient's character that result from the relationship. Nor do they know what kind of attitude he is now to have toward these consequences. Most patients say repeatedly, 'Father and mother are to blame for my illness,' but the real question is: How can I treat the patient so that he becomes able to cope with his experience? While the father's and the mother's responsibility may be a causal factor, when all is said and done, therapy hinges on the final question: What kind of meaning does my life have?

114

SH: Ordinary life has many kinds of suffering. Psychotherapy consists of liberation from suffering. What sort of changes in the sphere of the unconscious correspond to this liberation?

CGJ: This is the question of conscious attitude. In states of psychological suffering, it is important how I myself relate to a certain state, what kind of attitude I have. Let's say I am unhappy or sad because of something that's happened. If I think, 'How horrible that something like this has happened,' and cannot accept it, then I'll only suffer more. Each day has its own troubles, and the sun cannot always shine. Sometimes it rains or snows. If a person is able to adopt the attitude that both good and bad are part of life, that person will suffer less. With an objective attitude, he or she can find a way to be released from morbid neurotic suffering. If he or she can say 'yes' to the suffering and accept it, the pain is suddenly diminished.

SH: A universal suffering is the fear of death. How can this suffering be treated by psychotherapy?

CGJ: There is no general rule or method, but only individual cases. People fear death for many different reasons. The course of therapy depends upon the reasons for this death anxiety. My anxiety of death is quite different from anxiety in a young, healthy man. Why does he fear death? There may be no apparent reason and yet he fears it. So the situations are quite different. Therefore, there is no general course of therapy. We must always consider the individual case. Why is an old man anxious about death? Why is a young man anxious about death? The two must be dealt with quite differently.

SH: I only mention the fear of death as an example, because death is unavoidable. But people suffer in many, many ways. We must almost always live in suffering. I want to ask you whether or not it is possible, within the framework of psychotherapy, for a person to disengage from all these various sufferings in one fell swoop.

CGJ: Are you asking whether there exists a method by which suffering is healed?

SH: Yes. Is there no generally valid remedy for it?

CGJ: Are you asking whether there is a method through which one could spare a person suffering?

SH: Yes. Can psychotherapy liberate us from suffering in one fell swoop?

CGJ: Liberate us from suffering? One tries to reduce suffering, yet some suffering is always present. There would be nothing beautiful if the beautiful were not in contrast with ugliness or suffering. The German philosopher Schopenhauer once said: 'Happiness is the cessation of suffering.' We need suffering. Otherwise, life would no longer be interesting. Psychotherapy must not disturb the problem of suffering too much in people. Otherwise, people would become dissatisfied.

SH: Suffering is, in a sense, necessary for life. You are right. Nevertheless, we have a genuine wish to be liberated from it.

CGJ: Of course, if there is too much of it! The physician strives to reduce suffering, not to put an end to it.

SH: In the case of physical illness, the physician tries to release the patient from it and to eliminate sickness from the human world. Is this not also true of mental illness?

CGJ: Of course!

SH: The great messengers of religious truth – Christ, for example[6] – have said that all humans suffer a common lot: the suffering of death, or of original sin. Their intention was to liberate humans from this fundamental suffering. Is it possible to think that such a great liberation could be realized in psychotherapy?

CGJ: This is not inconceivable, if you regard the problem not as a personal illness, but as an impersonal manifestation of evil. The concern of psychotherapy is in many cases to make patients conscious, through insight, of the nidana chain, of the unnecessary suffering fostered by lust, desire, and passion. Passion ties us up, but through insight we are made free. The goal in psychotherapy is exactly the same as in Buddhism.

SH: The essential issue in this liberation is: How does one reach a fundamental self, one that is no longer captivated by the ten thousand things? How to get there, that is the problem. Is it necessary to liberate oneself from the collective unconscious as well, or from the conditions it imposes on us?

CGJ: If someone is caught in the ten thousand things, it is because that person is also caught in the collective unconscious. A person is liberated only when freed from both. One person may be driven more by the unconscious and another by things. One has to take the person to the point where he is free from the compulsion to either run after things or be driven by the unconscious. What is needed for both compulsions is basically the same: *nirdvandva*.[7]

SH: From what you have said about the collective unconscious, might I infer that one can be liberated from it?

CGJ: Yes![8]

SH: What we in Buddhism, and especially in Zen, usually call the 'common self' corresponds exactly to what you call the 'collective unconscious.' Only through liberation from the collective unconscious, namely, the common self, the authentic self emerge.[9]

CGJ: This self of which you speak corresponds, for example, to the *klesas* in the *Yoga Sutra*. My concept of self corresponds, however, to the notions of *atman* or *pursha*. This personal *atman* corresponds to the self insofar as it is at the same time the suprapersonal *atman*. In other words, 'my self' is at the same time 'the self'. In my language, the self is the counterpart to the 'I.' What you call the self is what I would call the 'I.' What I call the self is the whole, the *atman*.

SH: The authentic self corresponds to the *atman*. In the common

116

understanding *atman* still retains a faint trace of substance, but that is not yet what I call the true self. The true self has neither substance nor form.[10]

CGJ: So when I compare the self with *atman*, my comparison is an obviously incorrect one. They are incommensurable because the Eastern way of thinking is different from my way of thinking. I can say that the self both exists and does not exist, because I really can say nothing about it. It is greater than the 'I.' The 'I' can only say: This is the way it seems to me. If one were to say that atman either has or does not have substance, I can only acknowledge what the person says – for I do not know what the true *atman* really is. I only know what people say about it. I can only say of it: 'It is so' and, at the same time, 'It is not so.'

SH: Unlike the ordinary *atman*, the true self of Zen has neither form nor substance. It has no form, mental or physical.

CGJ: I cannot know what I don't know. I cannot be conscious of whether the self has attributes or not, because I am unconscious of the self. The whole human person is both conscious and unconscious. I only know that I may possess a certain set of attributes. What you say [concerning the ordinary *atman* and the true self of Zen – S.M.] is possible, but I don't know if that's really the case. I can, of course, make assertions. I can state metaphysical matters until I am blue in the face but, fundamentally, I don't know.[11]

SH: The true self is without form and substance, and is therefore never bound by the ten thousand things. That is the essence of religious liberation. This is also the religious character of Zen, with its insight into the value of transcending the passions and becoming the formless self.[12] That is why I said at the beginning of our conversation that Zen is both philosophy and religion.[13]

Professor Hisamatsu thanks Dr Jung for having found, together with him, the connection between the unconscious and what we have called 'the true self.'[14] He says that the connection has become very clear to him. He then proceeds to explain the true self further by using the metaphor of waves on water.[15]

Notes

1 Jaffé's note: C. C. Jung's psychology is called analytical psychology, to distinguish it from Freud's psychoanalysis.

2 Hisamatsu does not use the Chinese word *wu-hsin*, but rather its Japanese phonetic transcription, *mu-shin*. *Hsin*, meaning the mind or heart, is a Chinese word that decisively characterizes the whole of Chinese Buddhism including Zen. *Wu*, denoting nothingness, is not to be taken as a logical negation like in the Western sense, so *wu-hsin* is not necessarily the negation of *hsin*. In some Zen texts they are identical with each other, and, moreover, *hsin* is even equated with the Buddha. So Chinese Buddhism may be the philosophy of the mind, or a radical psychology. *Wu-hsin* appears already in a title of a Zen text as a collection of sayings by Bodhi Dharma, the first patriarch of Chinese Zen Buddhism: *Wu-hsin-lun*, 'A Discourse on No-Mind.' Like many other Buddhist terms, the word has settled

into the Japanese language, albeit with some variation in meaning. In the Japanese version of the protocol, Jung's statement that he means the unconscious by *wu-hsin* is given as a note by Jaffé.

3 The word 'fundamental' (*ursprünglich* in Jaffé's protocol) is my translation of both *komponteki* and *kongenteki* in the Japanese translation – terms which might be more exactly rendered 'original' or 'radical' because *kom* or *kon* refers to root. What Hisamatsu means to refer to is something metaphysical, and not genetically primal–though he would deny metaphysics in the Western sense. His meaning may be close to the German prefix *ur-*, as in Goethe's concepts of *Urpflanz*, *Urphanomen* and so on, because it is at once both metaphysical and accessible to experience. It is with some reservation, then, that I adopt the English term 'fundamental' instead of 'original.' It is essential in this context to keep in mind Hisamatsu's lack of familiarity with depth psychology. He speaks of 'the fundamental unconscious' in his own Zen sense of *wu-hsin* – and not in any psychological sense. Thus, even if the term 'fundamental' were replaced by words like 'original' or 'primal,' it is only the translator who grapples with such nuances of meaning and sophistication. Hisamatsu only uses the word 'unconscious' in this dialogue with Jung; otherwise, he, like D. T. Suzuki, would never speak of it. In the Japanese text, in fact, the word 'unconscious' is given in quotes, perhaps to suggest Hisamatsu's particular use and understanding of it.

4 Jung here refers to Ernst Heckel's famous biological thesis. The earlier English version of the conversation, based upon the Japanese translation, reveals that the Japanese translator was unaware of this. In that earlier version, 'ontogeny' and 'phylogeny' were respectively mistranslated as 'the development of the individual' and 'the development of psyche in history.'

5 Since the days of Strachey's translation of Freud, the German term *das Ich* is usually rendered 'the ego' in the psychological literature. But throughout the conversation, both Hisamatsu and Jung seem to refer to an everyday – rather than a technical – understanding of the term, along the lines of what Bruno Bettelheim, in his book *Freud and Man's Soul*, takes to be Freud's own original intent. Therefore, I consistently use 'I' instead of 'the ego' as the translation of *das Ich*. I am grateful to Jan Middeldorf for his insistence on this point.

6 The Buddha is mentioned along with Christ in Tsujimura's translation.

7 Sanskrit word meaning 'freedom from opposites,' but different from *nirvana*. *Nirdvandva* refers to an idea in which dualism is presupposed and at the same time overcome. It is no wonder that Jung adopted this word, as it fits well with his mode of thinking which is expressed, for example, in his key concept of the 'transcendent function' – namely, an attitude or a capacity to sustain the tension of opposites, from which a reconciling symbol can then emerge from the depths of the mind. The word *nirvana*, on the contrary, originally meaning 'the extinction of fire,' suggests an absolute transcendence or denial of dualism to nothingness – reflecting a mode of thinking which is foreign to Jung.

Upon reading the German protocol for the first time, I asked Jaffé whether the word *nirdvandva* was not a typing error for *nirvana*. Firmly saying 'No,' she opened to page 377 of vol. 11 of Jung's *Collected Works* (in the original German version of the *Gesammelte Werke*) and pointed to paragraph 435. The word *nirdvandva* was in fact there. However, in the editor's note to the expanded edition of vol. 1 of Shin'ichi Hisamatsu's *Collected Works*, published in 1996, Gishin Tokiwa writes that translator Tsujimura clearly heard Jung speak of *nirvana*, and not *nirdvandva*. According to Tsujimura, he had translated the typewritten protocol he'd received from Jung himself, thus making unlikely, if not impossible, any translation errors of this sort. Tokiwa goes on to claim that there is no difference between *nirdvandva* and *nirvana*. Personally, I think the difference between the two Sanskrit words is not to be overlooked, especially where the dialogue between Zen and psychology is concerned. The importance of the term *nirdandva* for Jung is clear from the fact that he used it already several times in *Psychological Types*, a work written more than thirty years before the conversation with Hisamatsu.

8 Hisamatsu's immediately preceding question is, in my opinion, the gravitational center of the entire conversation, comparable with a critical confrontation between a Zen master and his disciple in Zen mondo (question and answer). We are told, in fact, in Hisamatsu's commentary to the Japanese version of the translation appearing in vol. 1 of his *Complete Works* that both he and Tsujimura found Jung's 'Yes!' very unexpected. Unfortunately, however, we don't know what kind of 'yes' it was. Was Jung's reply a heartily felt affirmation, an expression of exasperation, or a 'yes' which was somehow forced from his mind, perhaps even against his will, by Hisamatsu's penetrating and somewhat intrusive questioning? Personally, I believe the latter was the case, and suspect that this was one of the reasons why Jung refused to have the conversation published in *Psychologia*.

9 Tsujimura's Japanese version includes this clarification of what is meant by the 'authentic self': 'That is the true self, or *doku-datsu mu-e*: namely, the self that is alone, independent, and detached.' The source of *doku-datsu mu-e* is *The Record of Lin-chi*, where not *doku-datsu mu-e* but the expressions *doku-datsu* and *fu-e*, not *mu-e*, appear separately. *Mu* implies a negation, while *e* means 'dependence.' *Doku* and *datsu* mean respectively 'alone' and 'detached.' Lin-chi (–867) is reported to have said: 'The Buddha is born from *mu-e*.' After a famous provocation of killing the Buddha and the Zen patriarchs, he scolds his disciples: 'You don't see yet from where a person emerges who is *doku-datsu*.' Hisamatsu seems to have coined the expression *doku-datsu mu-e* by combining *doku-datsu* and *mu-e*.

On the matter of 'authentic self,' the German *das eigentliche Selbst* cited in the protocol is perhaps Tsujimura's translation of Hisamatsu's term *honrai-no-jiko*. *Eigentliche* clearly suggests that Tsujimura – a student of Martin Heidegger – interprets *honrai-no-jiko* in the Heideggerian sense. Heidegger's concept of *Eigentlichkeit*, derived from his *Being and Time*, is usually translated *honrai-sei* into Japanese. The philosophers of the Kyoto School are generally sympathetic to Heidegger, whom Hisamatsu also met. (Their conversation, in fact, is recorded in vol. 1 of Hisamatsu's *Collected Works*. It is altogether free of the many tensions evidenced in Hisamatsu's conversation with Jung.) Because *Eigentlichkeit* is translated as 'authenticity' in English versions of *Being and Time*, I have opted to translate *das eigentliche Selbst* as 'the authentic self.'

10 To refer to something ultimate, or metaphysical, Hisamatsu uses in the Japanese version three different adjectival phrases: *honrai-no*, *shinjitsu-no* (or *shin-no*) and *kongenteki*, which I have rendered respectively as 'authentic,' 'true' and 'fundamental.' Though originally Chinese terms, they have been used by modern Japanese philosophers to translate Western philosophical terms into Japanese. Hisamatsu seems to use the three adjectives without any clear differentiation among them in his terminology. Thus, while Hisamatsu elsewhere speaks of 'the fundamental unconscious' in the Zen sense of *wu-hsin* (see note 3), we have reason to suspect that his use of terms like 'authentic' or 'true' refers to this same basic understanding.

Still, in this very passage Hisamatsu clearly states that 'the authentic self that corresponds to the *atman* is not yet what I call the true self'! I realize that such a statement seems in flagrant contradiction to the claim that 'true,' 'authentic', and 'fundamental' are all equivalent adjectives for Hisamatsu. In a sense, this passage reveals an inconsistency in the philosopher's use and understanding of the words 'the true self.' It may be due to a logical dilemma intrinsic to Buddhist philosophy of which Hisamatsu was likely to be deeply aware, to the point of coining the concept of the 'formless self.'

This discourse of self may sound contradictory to the Buddhist, especially Indian Buddhist basic tenet of non-self. But it can be regarded as the development of a philosophy elaborated in Chinese Buddhism, especially stimulated by the text *Ta-ch'eng-ch'i-hsin-lun*, *A Treatise of the Mahayana Awakening Faith* (see note 15), according to which *ti, xiang* and *yong* meaning 'substance', 'forms', and 'function' respectively, are fundamentally one and the same. So in *Ch'uan-hsin-fa-yao*, *The Essence of the Mind Dharma Transmission*, His-yün (–850), Lin-chi's master, says that the mind is nothing but no-mind.

Finally, it is interesting to note that, in the Japanese text, this same passage reads: 'The authentic self, insofar as semantics is concerned, corresponds to the *atman*.' Hisamatsu was aware of how difficult, if not impossible, it is to explain the meaning of the true self with the Indian concept of *atman*. He never identified the authentic self with *atman* in the Hindu sense. In my view, he borrowed the Hindu concept to explain his own concept to Jung, who did not share the same spiritual background but seemed to have some knowledge of Upanishad philosophy. Such a confusion is common between people from different cultures trying to reach a common understanding.

11 Jung's final two comments evidence his harsh criticism of Hisamatsu's conviction, which, in its resistance to any psychological investigation, resembles those Jung observed throughout his life in clergy and believers. Basically, we can see Jung opposing his psychological viewpoint to Hisamatsu's ontology.

In this light, a freer translation of Jung's response might read: 'Professor Hisamatsu, we must distinguish between your understanding of the true self of Zen – as one possible archetypal image of the self – and the archetype of the self as such. You may well know the self in your sense – be it fundamental, true or formless – but while I am sorry that I do not, neither of us can know the self as such.'

Jung's opening statement here is also quite perplexing, and warrants close attention. Perhaps tautological in expressing his agnostic stance, the phrase 'I cannot know what I don't know' seems to turn Jung's own understanding of the unconscious upside-down.

It is not characteristically Jungian, or true, that one cannot know what one does not know. In the course of a lifetime, one can indeed come to know what one ignores at any given time. Conversely, it is Jung's unequivocal contention that only the unconscious is destined to remain forever unknown – despite one's efforts to know it. Thus, a phrase like 'I don't know what I cannot know' somehow sounds more natural and consistent in a Jungian context than the cited 'I cannot know what I don't know.' We can perhaps assume that Jung's odd remark reflects an implicit refusal to further debate Hisamatsu's religious and philosophical convictions.

12 Hisamatsu's phrase 'with its insight into the value of transcending the passions' is not present in the Japanese text. It was perhaps edited out by Hisamatsu himself or by Tsujimura. In addition, the next phrase, 'and becoming the formless self,' is somewhat different in the Japanese text, where it reads: 'In short, becoming the formless self is the nature of Zen.'

On the matter of the formless self (*muso-no-jiko*, in Japanese): As a Buddhist, Hisamatsu does not regard the self as a metaphysical entity. This does not mean, however, that he advocates nihilism. He presents a concept of the self that is not metaphysical in the Western sense but, in a sense intrinsic to Buddhist philosophy, formless. It is the Mahayana understanding of the self as *bodhi* (awakening) that underscores, in fact, Hisamatsu's religion or philosophy of awakening. But while Hisamatsu's central idea is basic to the very origins of Buddhism, his idea of the formless self and other similar expressions (such as the fundamental, authentic, or true self) mark – through his assimilation of Western philosophy – his unique contribution to the development of modern Buddhism.

13 Hisamatsu's remark 'Zen is both philosophy and religion' actually reads 'Zen is both philosophy and psychology' in the German protocol. While this likely reflects an error in typing, the substitution offers an interesting example of what Freud considered 'the psychopathology of everyday life'!

14 I am not sure whom the 'we' here refers to. Two answers are possible. One is, of course, both Hisamatsu and Jung. Another is Hisamatsu himself, together with those who share his position.

15 The metaphor of waves on water is originally found in the *Lankavatara Sutra,* a sutra supposedly preached by the Buddha on Adam's Peak in Ceylon. It later became the source for the text *Ta-ch'eng-ch'I-hsin-lun,* 'The Mahayana Faith Awakening,' whose original Sanskrit version by Asvagosha was lost but later recast through two Chinese versions by Paramartha and by Siksananda. To illustrate the metaphor, I offer the following excerpt, taken from Hisamatsu's own essay 'The Characteristics of Oriental Nothingness': 'Waves are produced by the water but are never separated from the water. When they cease to be waves, they return to the water – their original source . . . While the water in the wave is one with the wave and not two, the water does not come into being and disappear, increase or decrease, according to the coming into being and disappearing of the wave. Although the water as wave comes into being and disappears, the water as water does not come into being and disappear. Thus even when changing into a thousand or ten thousand waves, the water as water is itself constant and unchanging. The Mind of "all is created by Alone-Mind" is like this water. The assertions of the Sixth Patriarch, Hui-neng, "Self-Nature, in its origin constant and without commotion, produces the ten thousand things," and "All things are never separated from Self-Nature," express just this creative feature of Mind.' (Translated by Richard DeMartino, in collaboration with Jikal Fujiyoshi and Masao Abe.) See *Philosophical Studies of Japan* (1960).

8

JUNG AND BUDDHISM

Shoji Muramoto

Jungian psychology and the historical Jung

Carl Gustav Jung (1875–1961) is one of the few Western psychologists who most early recognized and appreciated the psychological nature and value of an Eastern religion, Buddhism. The seeds he sowed in Western soil more than half a century ago were growing up as two trends from the late 1980s to the 1990s: the emergence of Buddhist Jungian analysts (Spiegelman and Mokusen 1985; Young-Eisendrath 1996; Odajnyk 1998) and the development of a discipline that is concerned with the comparison of Jung's analytical psychology and Buddhism (Coward 1985; Meckel and Moore 1992; Clarke 1994).

Remembering his own studies of alchemy in his autobiography, Jung says: 'it became clear to me that without history there can be no psychology, and certainly no psychology of the unconscious' (Jaffé 1965: 205–6). History was for Jung the search for his precedents and the experience of solidarity amidst loneliness in the confrontation with the unconscious, as well as an interpretive framework in assessing contemporary phenomena, clinical or social. History arouses a passion for and the question of origin, and at the same time teaches us to see things calmly and broadly while our contemporaries are fanatic in presenting their own distinct vision.

Why don't we apply this historical stance exemplified by Jung himself to his own psychology? Since Jung's death in 1961, his followers have searched for the logic inherent in his psychology in a way that may not have occurred to Jung himself. And, the emergence of Buddhist Jungians is one of the results. While this development of analytical psychology is to be validated because of the relative autonomy of any system from its alleged creator, it is necessary to trace back the history of Jung's encounter with Buddhism.

The present essay is concerned with the historical Jung in his relationship to Buddhism. In what historical, ideological, and personal context did he come to know this Eastern religion? What was the basic motif in his encounter with Buddhism? What were his reactions? What aspects of Buddhism made him enthusiastic, and what aspects reserved? Did his view of

Buddhism remain the same or change in the course of his life? What are Jung's contributions to Buddhism? These are the questions with which I want to deal here.

The historical and spiritual background of Jung's encounter with Buddhism

It is simply wrong to believe that Buddhism was only recently introduced to the West. As Rick Fields (1986) impressively shows, the history of the relationship of the West to Buddhism is much longer than we imagine. The Greeks who, led by Alexander the Great, had come to India and remained there after his retreat and death (323 BC) became the first Western Buddhists. Without them the school of Gandharan art would not have come to its full flower in North India from the first to the fifth century, and the practice of sculpting the Buddha's statues would not have been finally transmitted to Japan. King Ashoka in third-century BC India sent missionaries westwards to preach the Buddha-Dharma. In his seminars, Jung himself mentions that in the second century BC there were Buddhist monasteries in Persia, suggesting that through Persia, Buddhist ideas crept into the foundation of Christianity (McGuire 1984: 606; Jarrett 1989: 41).

Instead of recounting further evidence for the long history of the relationship between the West and Buddhism, let us jump to the immediate historical and personal context in which Jung came to know Buddhism. Most important for understanding his relationship to Buddhism is that he, born as a son of a Protestant pastor, suffered both alienation and isolation in the Christian community, represented by his father and the Preiswerk family on his mother's side. In *Memories, Dreams, Reflections* (Jaffé 1965) Jung reports how as a child he was initiated into a mystery of a phallic god in a fascinating, but tremendous dream and then secretly developed his own private ritual and theology.

His first memory of his own encounter with the Eastern spiritual world is that of his mother reading aloud to him out of an old illustrated book containing pictures of Hindu gods, which offered him an inexhaustible source of interest (Jaffé 1965: 17). This memory suggests that the new Orientalist enthusiasm for the Indian spiritual world, which had begun among German Romantics like Schlegel and Schelling in the late eighteenth century, also reached a country pastor's family in Switzerland.

Jung's father disappointed him very much by failing to teach him the Christian dogma of the Trinity. This disappointment, however, did not drive him to abandon Christianity, but to quest for either a substitute for it or a perspective which seemed to give him a more satisfactory interpretation of it. In this sense, Jung could not or would not completely liberate himself from his religion. As Peter Homans (1979) points out, Christianity was rather the matrix from which his psychological system emerged.

123

Goethe's *Faust*

The adolescent Jung who had been spiritually frustrated and hungry was greatly relieved by Goethe's *Faust*, which his mother had advised him to read. Though having no direct connection with Buddhism, it certainly provided him with an alternative spirituality. Later in the foreword to Daisetsu T. Suzuki's book *Introduction to Zen Buddhism*, Jung counts *Faust* as one of the few counterparts to Zen in the West (Jung 1978d: 155). And it is the work Jung quotes most in his writings. The adolescent Jung was especially attracted to Faust's words: 'Oh, two souls live in my bosom,' which were later to be elaborated by him and his followers as the theory of the ego–self axis.

'Faust and Buddhism' is too big a theme to deal with here. Suffice it to point out several affinities between them which are relevant to Jungian psychology as well. First, both are concerned with the contradiction of limitlessness and limitedness of the human ego's desire. Second, both admit as little divine intervention as possible and, on the contrary, trust human action as much as possible. Third, both see all things as transient and symbolic.

Schopenhauer

As a late adolescent suffering from a split in his personality into No. 1 and No. 2, Jung was absorbed in reading and felt healed to some degree by Schopenhauer's book *The World as Will and Representation*. We are nowadays struck by the similarities between Schopenhauer and Jung in views of the unconscious, archetypes, and dreams (Jarrett 1999). Schopenhauer, the admirer of Goethe, was the first Western philosopher who intensively studied Buddhism and incorporated it into his philosophical system. And Jung obtained through Schopenhauer some knowledge of Buddhism, especially Mahayana Buddhism.

Jung especially felt confirmed by Schopenhauer's pessimistic remark that there is something fundamentally wrong with this world created by God. For him Schopenhauer was the first philosopher who openly spoke of the inevitability of suffering, confusions, desires, and evils in the world, the first Noble Truth in Buddhism.

But Jung was not satisfied with Schopenhauer's idea that the intellect offers the blind will a mirror to lead it to its self-denial. He wondered how the will could see its real state. Even if it could, how could its conversion take place? Does the will not see only images it wants to see? What was the intellect? After all, Jung adopted Kantian philosophy, which made him realize that Schopenhauer had failed to grasp the Kantian concept of a thing-in-itself that cannot be empirically known. This disappointment with Schopenhauer, however, remained a tension in Jung's mind and seems to have given him an impetus for the later development of his psychological theory and technique of active imagination. Schopenhauer is a key figure in understanding Jung's relation to Buddhism.

Schopenhauer's mirror is not a symbol for the modern Western form of knowledge in which the subject and the object are divided. To explain the meaning of the mirror, Schopenhauer quotes from the *Upanishads tat twam asi*, which means: 'This is you' (1987: 499). So what the mirror reveals is nothing but the reflection of the will: the mirror refers to the self-awareness of the will.

Jung's disappointment in Schopenhauer suggests that he was caught in the Western dichotomy of intellect versus will. By contrast, they are one and the same in Buddhism. More psychologically and spiritually speaking, feeling amounts to healing. There is a tremendous difference between Jung's understanding of Schopenhauer's intellect and *Prajnaparamita*, Supreme Wisdom, in Mahayana Buddhism. Mark Epstein, a psychiatrist who has described a Buddhist perspective on psychotherapy, draws our attention to the fact that in the Buddhist hell, the most miserable of the six realms of existence, the Bodhisattva appears holding a mirror in his or her hand, suggesting that healing only takes place through the self-awareness of emotions (Epstein 1995: 22). This exactly corresponds to Schopenhauer's notion of a mirror in which the will reflects itself to attain its self-denial, Nirvana.

Schopenhauer does not identify the self-denial of the will with suicide. On the contrary, he condemns suicide as the self-affirmation of the will. The will here is to be understood metaphysically as something that subjects us to the principle of individuation (*principium individuationis*). The self-denial of the will is nothing but the freedom from the principle of individuation as egoism. To express the goal of his therapy, on the other hand, Jung later borrowed the term *individuation* from Schopenhauer. Noteworthy, however, is the huge difference in its meaning between Schopenhauer and Jung.

According to Schopenhauer, the self-denial of the will is nothing but the realization (*Erkenntnis*) of another's suffering. He says, 'Pure love consists in compassion (*Mitleid*)' (Schopenhauer 1987: 526). *Mitleid* is the German translation of *karuna* from the Sanskrit of Mahayana Buddhism. Similarly, *Erkenntnis* revealed through *Mitleid* is the German translation of *prajna*. In Mahayana Buddhism *karuna* and *prajna* are inseparable from each other. The basic message of *Parsifal*, the last work of Richard Wagner, who was deeply involved in Schopenhauer's philosophy, is 'knowing through compassion' (*Durch Mitleid wissend*). This clearly expresses the teaching of Mahayana Buddhism (App 1997: 13).

The search for a religious–psychological perspective

In the so-called Zofingia Lectures during his student days and his dissertation on occultism, Jung, having recourse to Kant and Schopenhauer, tried to construct his own psychological perspective for dealing with religious phenomena including spiritualism (Charet 1993). He regarded religion as something psychological. Psychology seemed to enable him to cross the boundary between Christianity and other religions as well as that between religion and science. But as is evident from Jung's words in his letter to Freud on 11 February 1910: 'Religion must be only replaced by religion.' To Freud's great embarrassment, Jung expected psychoanalysis to become a substitute for Christianity. In other words, he wanted to find something that would be both religious and psychological. And it is in this respect that Jung later appreciated Buddhism more explicitly. For him it was 'the religion of pure reason' (McGuire 1984: 475) and 'a most systematic education toward the utmost consciousness' (Jarrett 1989: 1333), though he remained reserved on the viability of its prescription.

Buddhism in transformations and symbols of libido

Transformations and Symbols of Libido (Jung 1912/1991), a work that made decisive Jung's break with Freud and became a turning point in the development of his thought, reveals Jung's ongoing and deepening understanding of Schopenhauer's ideas. He points out that libido is not confined to the sexual, but manifests itself in many ways, like the will in Schopenhauer (ibid.: 130). Did Jung not find an answer to the question how the blind will could be converted to its self-denial in the idea of the sacrifice of libido, the title of the final chapter of the book? Here he seems to be overcoming the Kantian subject–object dichotomy. Libido is not passively symbolized, but actively becomes symbols through its own self-sacrifice. Does this transformation of libido not echo the self-denial of the will in Schopenhauer?

Interestingly enough, Jung's references to Buddhism in this work show that he was especially interested in its symbolism. The tree under which the Buddha was enlightened, for example, was for him the symbol of Mother, and so his meditation under it was the introversion of libido as the return to Mother's uterus that is its origin (ibid.: 332).

Septum Sermones ad Mortuos

In search of a spiritual orientation during the time that followed his break with Freud in 1912, Jung needed to find historical representations of his own recent inner experiences that he called a confrontation with the unconscious. Gnosticism became such a representation. According to his autobiography, he studied it from 1916 until 1926.

His 1916 writing *Septum Sermones ad Mortuos* is, in his own words, what Philemon (Jung's alter ego in this text) might have said (Jaffé 1965: 190). Aniela Jaffé, the compiler of the autobiography, notes that, drawn to Gnostic thinking in paradoxes, Jung identified himself with the Gnostic writer Basilides (early second century AD) and took over some of the latter's terminology (ibid.: 378).

Perhaps Jung had also been acquainted with Gnosticism earlier than 1916, maybe through Schopenhauer's references to it in his main work.

Noteworthy is 'Alexandria, the East touches the West' in the title of this quasi-Gnostic writing. There is historical evidence for a connection between Alexandria and India (Fields 1986: 17–18). Conze (1975) points out similarities between Gnosis and Buddhism. Although Kennedy argued in 1902 that the 'negative theology' of Basilides in Alexandria was 'Buddhist Gnosticism,' de Lube denied a link between Gnosticism and Buddhism.

Pleroma or Creatura?

Septem Sermones ad Mortuos makes us suspect that Jung was familiar with some basic Buddhist ideas. In the name of Basilides, he opens his sermons with these words: 'I begin with nothingness. Nothingness is the same as fullness. In infinity full is no better than empty. Nothingness is both empty and full. As well you might say ye say anything else of nothingness, as for instance, white it is, or black, or again, it is not, or it is. A thing that is infinite and eternal hath no qualities, since it hath all qualities. The nothingness or fullness we name the PLEROMA' (Jaffé 1965: 379).

In fact, Moacanin (1992: 279) notes that *Septum Sermones ad Mortuos* echoes the words of the *Heart Sutra*, 'form is emptiness, emptiness is form,' and the *Lankavatara Sutra*, that 'space is form, and . . . as space penetrates into form, form is space.' Jung's statement that in Pleroma both thinking and being cease because the eternal and infinite possess no qualities corresponds to *fukashigi* or *hishiryotei* in Buddhism, which means the 'unthinkable.' So Jung's Pleroma seems to be very close to *sunyata*.

Like the *Heart Sutra, Septum Sermones ad Mortuos* abounds in paradoxes. Moacanin emphasizes that polarity and its integration link *Vajrayana* in Tibetan Buddhism with Jung's concept of the transcendent function. His argument is, however, not beyond dispute. For, even if Pleroma seems akin to *sunyata*, Jung does not regard it as the ultimate principle of human existence. The dissolution into Pleroma is for him the denial of Creatura which consists of distinctiveness. Jung firmly stands on the side of Creatura, not of Pleroma.

Jung names the natural tendency of Creatura to distinctiveness as *principium individuationis* which is to be later elaborated as a goal of Jungian psychotherapy. Now this term is originally a concept in scholastic philosophy that denotes the principle of matter, and Jung knew it through Schopenhauer's main work. Unlike Jung, however, Schopenhauer uses it to mean something to be overcome and resolved. Individuation is nothing but the self-affirmation of the blind will, attachment to the self which must be given up through the self-denial of the will. Schopenhauer is clearly closer to understanding Buddhism and Gnosticism than is Jung in this regard.

For Jung, the individuality of Creatura should not be resolved into

Pleroma. On the contrary, it is the very principle of human development. By contrast, Schopenhauer sees in the principle of individuation the philosophical foundation of egoism. It is far from being the goal of human life. It was only the process and the result of becoming bound by time and space, driven by the blind will.

Jung, however, had no intention of openly advocating egoism, and so he had to demonstrate how he and Schopenhauer differ on the principle of individuation. This may be the reason why Jung later developed the idea of the self in distinction from the ego and this is hinted at in the concept of self-sacrifice of the libido in *Transformations and Symbols of Libido*.

Gnosis in *Psychological Types*

Jung was attracted to the religion of Gnosis because it seemed to compensate the one-sidedness of Christianity. While Christianity seemed to Jung to demand the sacrifice of one's intellect in preference to the practical requirement of faith, Gnosis satisfied both intellect and faith. Its three types of humans – *pneumatikoi*, *psychikoi*, and *hylikoi* – respectively corresponded to thinking, feeling, and sensation in Jung's theory of four functions of the mind set out in *Psychological Types* (Jung 1976: 11). The Gnostic movement was interpreted as the emergence of elements repressed by Christianity (Jung 1976: 20). Jung sees in it 'man's unconscious psychology in full flower,' and 'a belief in the efficacy of individual revelation and individual knowledge,' and 'the beginning of the path that led to the intuitions of German mysticism' (Jung 1976: 241–2).

The prototypes for many basic concepts in Jungian psychology are, indeed, to be found in Gnosticism. As Coward (1985: 13) aptly points out, Eastern thought and medieval alchemy form a missing link between Gnosticism and modern psychology, in Jung's theories. We must, however, not overlook the fact that Jung failed to grasp essential features of Gnosticism and misinterpreted or reinterpreted it. Segal contrasts Gnosticism and Jung: 'What for Jung is only a means to an end – return to the unconscious – is for Gnosticism equivalent to the end itself. What for Jung is the end – the integration of the unconscious with ego consciousness – is for Gnosticism the present predicament: the association of divinity with matter. Conversely, what for Gnosticism is the end – the severance of the link between divinity and matter – is the Jungian predicament: the dissociation of the unconscious from ego consciousness' (Segal 1992: 25–6). This twist in Jung's assimilation of Gnosticism was also to be reflected in his approach to Buddhism.

Buddhism in *Psychological Types*

In *Psychological Types*, Jung acknowledges Schopenhauer for his contributions to Oriental studies and characterizes his own system as essentially Buddhist, a reaction to the West as represented by Schiller (Jung 1976: 136).

This contrast of the East and the West is further developed in his scheme of introversion and extraversion. Jung counts Tibetan Buddhism as an example of a one-sided development of consciousness (ibid.: 137) and mentions that in Buddhism everything is dissolved into consciousness (ibid.: 247). In the same vein, he characterizes Christianity, Buddhism, and German writers like Spitteler and Goethe as devoted to God, the self, and the soul (symbolized by the Feminine) respectively (ibid.: par. 375). In this sense, Jung seems to regard Buddhism as one-sided and lacking balance.

On the other hand, Jung points out that the East from ancient times has developed a psychological view of salvation based on the process of mediating opposites, and especially values Buddhism for its 'redemptive middle way of magical efficacy which is attainable by means of a conscious attitude' (Ibid.: 326). Here he clearly links the Buddhist Middle Way with his own concept of a transcendent function that spontaneously produces a symbol of reconciling opposites. Thus, in *Psychological Types*, Jung considers Buddhism as one-sided, namely as representing introversion in the extreme, and also values it as synthesizing the opposites, a position that reveals his ambivalent attitude toward Eastern thought.

Dvandva or opposites: from Indian thought to Chinese thought

The study of Gnosticism opened Jung's eyes to the theoretical problem of opposites, but *Psychological Types* reveals that his ideas further developed by way of Indian thought. In a section titled 'The Brahmanic conception of the problem of opposites' he draws readers' attention to the Sanskrit term *dvandva* for pairs of opposites in strife, particularly man and woman, the creation of which, in Indian thought, is believed to lead to the emergence of the world. Jung interprets that *dvandva* is brought about through the splitting of psychic energy at the level of the unconscious.

When Jung visited India in 1938, he argued that *nirdvandva*, which means overcoming pairs of opposites, is impossible in human life because perfect liberation amounts to death. The same view is also expressed in his autobiography: 'The Indian's goal is not moral perfection, but the condition of *nirdvandva*. He wishes to free himself from nature; in keeping with this aim, he seeks in meditation the condition of imagelessness and emptiness. I, on the other hand, wish to persist in the state of lively contemplation of nature and of the psychic images. I want to be freed neither from human beings, nor from myself, nor from nature; for all these appear to me the greatest of miracle. Nature, the psyche, and life appear to me like divinity unfolded – and what more could I wish for? To me the supreme meaning of Being can consist only in the fact that it *is*, not that it is not or is no longer' (Jaffé 1965: 276).

Jung seems in this way to be attracted more to Chinese thought than to

Indian thought because the former, unlike the latter, is principally concerned with the balance of opposites, not their abolition, and therefore sees in every disaster the loss of balance. His therapeutic effort consisted in the restoration of the lost balance in the mind. In Jung's view, it is loss of balance that is happening in the West.

The self as the conjunction of opposites

Psychological Types raised the question of how opposites are reconciled. As Jung himself says in his autobiography, this question immediately led him to the Chinese concept of Tao. The encounter with Wilhelm and his German translation of *The Secret of the Golden Flower* became decisive for the development of Jung's later theory. Recalling the publication of *The Secret of the Golden Flower* in his psychological commentary in 1929, he says: 'It was only after I had reached the central point in my thinking and in my researches, namely the concept of the *self*, that I once more found the way back to the world'(Jaffé 1965: 208). Jung does not see the self beyond opposites, but sees the self as a conjunction or reconciliation of opposites and points out that this is expressed in mandala symbols in both the East and the West.

Jung is not concerned with the reconciliation of human beings with God, but that of opposites within the image of God, a very important point in Coward's book (1985: 20). What Jung sought in Eastern thought was not another theology, but a framework for reconciling opposing images of God. In the East, divine images seemed to Jung to be basically understood as psychic images. Therefore, the encounter with Eastern thought was for him the psychologization of theology. That is why he contrasts the West and the East respectively as presenting extraversion and introversion. This difference was also understood as the conflict of religion and science.

Jung's deep appreciation of Buddhism should be understood in relation to the Jungian concept of the self. When he was invited by the British Government of India, he had an opportunity of directly experiencing Buddhism in the temple of Sanchi. He was deeply moved to see its structure where the path leads into a clockwise circumambulation around the stupa, and statues of the Buddha stood at the four cardinal points, and to hear the prayer of *Om mani padme hum* followed by the stroke of the gong. There is no doubt that he experienced there the reality of what he called 'self' in his theory. He knew, however, that this was the experience of something not new but familiar, though its significance had previously been unconscious. So his experience of Buddhism in India was the confirmation of what he had known.

The concept of the self provided Jung with a psychological framework for contrasting and connecting the two world religions from a unifying perspective. For him both the Buddha and the Christ were an embodiment of the self, though in an altogether different sense. 'Both stood for an overcoming of the world: Buddha out of rational insight; Christ as a foredoomed sacrifice' (Jaffé 1965: 279). Yet, inasmuch as the two religions are given the possible status of revelations of the self, we might well raise a question whether Jung's psychology itself is not functioning as a religion. In other words, how is the autonomy of each religion acknowledged within his system as partners in a dialogue?

Psychological commentaries on Eastern spiritual texts

In almost all his psychological essays on Buddhism, as well as other Eastern spiritualities (Jung 1978a; 1978b; 1978c; 1978d), Jung expresses several characteristic concerns. He first emphasizes the difference in mentality between the East and the West, and, as a consequence, warns Western readers not to blindly imitate Eastern spiritual practices. He rather advises them to firmly stand on Western soil. Then, he advocates something apparently contradictory, namely, he stresses how much Eastern spiritualities deserve to be studied. For they seemed to him to suggest a way out of the predicament in which Western people found themselves: the conflict of religion and science, the one-sided development of consciousness, and the destructive emergence of the unconscious as a consequence, the loss of balance and so on.

Jung's interest in the East had nothing to do with Orientalism as escapism that is often suspected to hide Western imperialism, but was rather motivated by the need for self-exploration. For Jung, the East was a mirror in which the West could find wisdom for its much-needed self-awareness. Clarke (1994) rightly places Jung in the long tradition of dialogue with the East as a means to self-examination.

A conversation with Shin'ichi Hisamatsu

In 1958, three years before his death, Jung was visited by Shin'ichi Hisamatsu (1889–1980), a Japanese Zen philosopher who was on his way back to Japan after lectures in America. The protocol of their conversation is the subject of Chapter 7 in this volume. Historically speaking, the late 1950s were the time that saw the first worldwide increase of an interest in Zen Buddhism. For example, in 1957 D. T. Suzuki, Fromm and DeMartino (1958) held a symposium on Zen Buddhism and psychoanalysis in Cuernavaca, Mexico. In the same year, Sato began to publish *Psychologia*, an English journal from Kyoto University providing a medium for the international exchange of ideas about psychology East and West. Hisamatsu's lectures in America and the conversation with Jung took place in this historical context.

From the dialogical viewpoint, this conversation would be assessed as a failure because it failed to meet the most important condition for dialogue: each party's readiness to open his heart to the partner's view and to make his standpoint relative in search for a common ground. Neither Jung nor Hisamatsu was willing to free the other from his stereotypes. Hisamatsu, showing little interest in the difference in the character of psychology between Freud and Jung, wrongly called the latter the founder of psychoanalysis, and only wanted to know whether or not the psychologist believed that his psychology could and would transcend its alleged limitation. Sensing that the Zen philosopher regarded him as a mere psychologist, Jung returned to the characteristically agnostic stance he would take whenever he faced someone with firm religious beliefs. The two men's reactions after the conversation were very different. Hisamatsu, on one hand, was satisfied with it because he had succeeded in finally forcing Jung to say something beyond the assumed limitation of psychoanalysis, which was akin to Hisamatsu's own philosophy. Jung, on the other, was not content with the conversation because he felt misunderstood and so did not give Sato permission to publish the conversation in *Psychologia*. He ascribed the failure to the difference in language and ways of thinking between the East and the West, as he had done before, and proposed that each party be involved in the other's practice, a plan which he was too old to materialize and in which Hisamatsu is supposed to have been hardly interested.

This conversation, however, was a challenge to both Hisamatsu and Jung. For Hisamatsu, it was to be an invitation to modify his stereotype of psychology as a superficial treatment of mental problems without any spiritual element. For Jung, the encounter with Hisamatsu provided him with an opportunity of facing and reexamining the basic premise of his psychology, a problem he had always struggled with throughout his life.

The question on liberation from the collective unconscious

After a series of Hisamatsu's somewhat aggressive primary questions like whether psychotherapy could liberate us from suffering in one fell swoop, and Jung's hesitations to answer them directly, the conversation reaches the climax with Hisamatsu's question whether one can be liberated from the collective unconscious and Jung's positive reply (Muramoto 1998: 46). Given Jung's usual views and his later refusal of the publication of the conversation, I suspect that Jung's 'Yes' needs to be examined.

I would now ask Jung whether one could be liberated from the ego, rather than the 'collective unconscious.' For, despite the hermeneutic function of the collective unconscious, Hisamatsu seemed actually to mean by this Jungian term nothing but the ego's creations. I believe that Jung's answer to my question would be ambiguous. On the one hand, he would say that the ego is only one of the complexes, suggesting that it is something formed and therefore able to be resolved. On the other hand, he would point out that the establishment of the ego is the prerequisite for individuation, either in analytic therapy or in real life. In the 1932 lecture 'Psychotherapy or the clergy', he goes on to say: 'I must even help the patient to prevail in his egoism' and even speaks of 'sacred egoism' (Jung 1984: 209). Therefore, we can say that he would not give a final answer.

Jung's potential contribution to Buddhism seems to consist of what he was forced to discard by Hisamatsu: the concept of the collective unconscious. To Hisamatsu's question I would say 'No' in defense of Jung. But I don't mean one cannot be liberated from egoism. I propose to mean by the collective unconscious a hermeneutic structure of human existence, the fact that humans already and always find themselves in a situation with a structure and history in which they understand or misunderstand each other, and are understood or misunderstood by each other, searching for the meaning of their own and their neighbors' human existence.

Indeed, as Hisamatsu points out, even when one disease is cured, another disease appears. This sequence of cure and disease, however, may mean a series of modifications in our experiencing being-in-the-world. It is not necessarily a vicious cycle but may be a creative hermeneutic circle when observed and treated seriously. Otherwise we would not be able to realize how we are in this structured and structuring world. One cannot get out of this structure itself so long as one lives. In fact, Huineng, the sixth patriarch of Chinese Zen Buddhism, is reported to have warned us in *The Platform Sutra,* 'Don't try to get rid of anything, without thinking of hundreds of things. If the stream of thoughts stops at any moment, then you will be born in another world, which means you will die. Don't try to cut the connection of beings and thoughts.'

The collective unconscious seems to be not so much something to be liberated from, but something to be acknowledged. It always manifests itself in particular concrete images, social relations, gender differentiation, and cosmology, which Buddhism often tends to underestimate, erroneously appealing to the doctrine of Emptiness, Absolute Nothingness or the Formless Self. The Jung–Hisamatsu conversation may have revitalized a pivotal recurring tension inherent in Buddhist metaphysics between unity and diversity in the tension between Zen and depth psychology.

References

App, U. (1997) *Richard Wagner und der Buddhismus*, Zurich: Museum Rietberg.

Charet, F. X. (1993) *Spiritualism and the Foundations of C. G. Jung's Psychology*, Albany: SUNY Press.

Clarke, J. J. (1994) *Jung and Eastern Thought: A Dialogue with the Orient*, London: Routledge.

Conze, E. (1975) 'Buddhism and Gnosis', in *Further Buddhist Studies: Selected Essays*, Oxford: Bruno Cassirer.

Coward, H. (1985) *Jung and Eastern Thought*, Albany: SUNY Press.

Epstein, M. (1995) *Thoughts Without a Thinker: Psychotherapy from a Buddhist Perspective*, New York: Basic Books.

Fields, R. (1986) *How the Swans Came to the Lake: A Narrative History of Buddhism in America*, revised and updated edition, Boston and London: Shambhala.

Homans, P. (1979) *Jung in Context: Modernity and the Making of a Psychology*, Chicago: University of Chicago Press.

Jaffé, A. (1965) *Memories, Dreams, Reflections*, New York: Vintage Books.

Jarrett, J. L. (ed.) (1989) *Nietzsche's 'Zarathustra': Notes of the Seminar given in 1934–1939*, given by C. G. Jung, London: Routledge.

Jarrett, J. L. (1999) 'Schopenhauer and Jung', in P. Bishop (ed.), *Jung in Contexts*, London and New York: Routledge.

Jung, C. G. (1976) *Psychological Types*, Princeton: Princeton University Press.

Jung, C. G. (1978a) 'Commentary on *The Secret of the Golden Flower*', in C. G. Jung, *Psychology and East*, Princeton: Princeton University Press.

Jung, C. G. (1978b) 'Psychological Commentary on *The Tibetan Book of the Dead*', in C. G. Jung, *Psychology and East*, Princeton: Princeton University Press.

Jung, C. G. (1978c) 'Psychological Commentary on *The Tibetan Book of the Great Liberation*', in C. G. Jung, *Psychology and East*, Princeton: Princeton University Press.

Jung, C. G. (1978d) 'Foreword to Suzuki' s *Introduction to Zen Buddhism*', in C. G. Jung, *Psychology and East and West*, Princeton: Princeton University Press.

Jung, C. G. (1984) 'Psychotherapy or the clergy', in C. G. Jung, *Psychology and Western Religion*, Princeton: Princeton University Press.

Jung, C. G. (1991) *Wandlungen und Symbole der Libido*, Deutscher Taschenbuch Verlag.

McGuire, W. (ed.) (1984) *Dream Analysis: Notes of the Seminar Given in 1928–1930 by C.G. Jung*, Princeton: Princeton University Press.

Meckel, D. J. and Moore, R. L. (eds) (1992) *Self and Liberation: The Jung–Buddhism Dialogue*, New York: Paulist Press.

Moacanin, R. (1992) 'Tantric Buddhism and Jung: connections, similarities, differences', in *Self and Liberation*, ed. D. J. Meckel and R.L. Moore, New York: Paulist Press (1992).

Muramoto, S. (1998) 'The Jung-Hisamatsu conversation: a translation from Aniela Jaffé's original German protocol', in A. Molino (ed.), *The Couch and the Tree: Dialogues in Psychoanalysis and Buddhism*, New York: North Point Press.

Odajnyk, V. W. (1998) 'Zen Meditation as a way of individuation and healing', in A. Molino (ed.), *The Couch and the Tree: Dialogues in Psychoanalysis and Buddhism*, New York: North Point Press.

Schopenhauer, A. (1987) *Die Welt als Wille und Vorstellung*, Band 1 und Band 2, Stuttgart: Reclam.

Segal, R. E. (1992) *The Gnostic Jung*, Princeton: Princeton University Press.

Spiegelman, M., and Mokusen, M. (1985) *Buddhism and Jungian Psychology*, Phoenix: Falcon Press.

Suzuki, D. T., Fromm, E. and de Martino, R. (1958) *Zen Buddhism and Psychoanalysis*, New York: Harper & Row.

Yanagida, S. (1978) *Zen no Goroku* [*Zen Texts*], Tokyo: Chuokoron-shuppansha.

Young-Eisendrath, P. (1996) *The Gifts of Suffering*, New York: Addison Wesley Longman.

9

WHAT IS I?

Reflections from Buddhism and psychotherapy

Hayao Kawai

We ordinarily use the word 'I' as if what it designates were completely self-evident. The Japanese and the English usages and their meanings of the word do differ somewhat, but in both languages, 'I' is used without much reflection, without seeing that it is a complex matter. Yet, if you start thinking about I, the more you think, the more you find its existence becoming incomprehensible. I heard the following Buddhist story in my childhood, unforgettably.

A certain traveler happened to stay overnight in a lonely hut. In the middle of the night, a goblin came in, lugging a corpse. Almost immediately another goblin came and argued that the corpse was his. They couldn't agree at all and finally asked the traveler for his judgment. 'It belongs to the first goblin,' he suggested. Exploding with anger, the second goblin ripped out the traveler's arm. Seeing that, the first one pulled an arm off the corpse and put it onto the traveler's body. The second goblin, infuriated, jerked another arm off the traveler. Again it was replaced with the corpse's other arm by the first goblin. They kept this up for awhile, and by the time the bodies of the traveler and the corpse had gotten completely exchanged, the two goblins were finally exhausted. So they stopped fighting and ate half the corpse each. With that, they left. The shocked traveler, seeing that what apparently had been his body had been eaten by the goblins, became confused as to whether the one now alive was really himself or not.

To my young mind, this was quite an awesome and at the same time humorous story, so I never let myself forget it. However, I could only remember this much of it, and not the conclusion, no matter how hard I tried. Eventually, I had to find a person who still owned the book, and I was able to read it. According to that book, the conclusion is as follows:

Being terribly upset, the traveler went to talk with a monk. 'Not having your body, that's nothing new,' the monk commented. 'The I of a human being is a composite of various elements. It's only temporarily formed into one thing.

Foolish people, captured by this I, suffer a great deal. Once you know what real I is, your suffering will disappear at once' (Takakura 1929: 161–5).

With words of such deep significance even when I read it now, no wonder this ending didn't stick in a child's mind. Whether or not you agree with this Buddhist conclusion, you still will sense how difficult it is to grasp and to understand what this existence, this I, is.

Ego and I

When I have thought of *I*, I have been influenced by the Western way of thinking. When I was young, in thinking about something or studying, we relied only on the Western method. It never crossed our minds to consider the Buddhist approach to such matters. It may sound strange to Westerners, but this is the way it generally is for Japanese.

During my student years, I read Freud with great interest. As I studied little by little, I found that the original German word, which in English is translated as *ego*, originally was written in Freud's publications as *ich*. I was surprised. Freud describes *ich* and *es* – that is, *I* and *it* (always translated as ego and id) – as separate elements of oneself. If I and it are separable in such a way is it possible, for example, that while *I* speak in the US, *it* is sleeping at my house in Japan? Ordinarily speaking, it never happens that way. *I* and *it* are always together and the existence which includes both we call 'I.'

Yet with Freud, I as a whole was divided into two. It is worth remembering here that Freud deliberately denominated half of the whole, the *ich*, or 'ego.' This *Ich* of Freud's probably is the same as the I of the modern individual and the I of Descartes' 'I think; therefore I am.' Freud's contribution is that he clarified ego as always threatened by the id, even though he used *Ich* to refer to only a part of the mind. By this we realize how much he valued that part. Therefore, even though pointing out the importance of the id, his oft-quoted phrase, 'Where id was, there ego shall be' (Freud 1964: 80), indicates clearly that the main focus was on *ich*, on ego. In Europe in Freud's time, it was to be expected that such a powerful 'I' would build modern European culture and extend it over the whole world. It is truly amazing that, in such an environment, Jung, from early in his career, asserted the significance of *Selbst* (Self) as opposed to Freud's *ich*. When Freud's work was translated into English, his *ich* and *es* were given the Latin equivalents 'ego' and 'id'. The merit of this usage was that it became possible, when we human beings think about our own minds, to objectify a great deal. By doing so, we are able to analyze the human mind. Analysis enables us to know the dynamism and structure of the human mind. Various schools of depth psychology have emerged as a result. The understanding of neurosis also has been advanced. All this occurred as psychotherapy developed.

At the same time, this selection of terms for translation created various problems. The Freudian psychoanalyst Bruno Bettelheim (1983) initially criticized the use of Latin words as bringing psychoanalysis too close to the medical model, giving the impression that analysts were observing the patient's mind objectively. As a result, psychoanalysis became broadly accepted in the United States. Only recently have the problematical aspects of this orientation become noticeable. People seemed to forget that psycho-analysis had begun with *ich*, self-analysis, and too much emphasis was placed on trying to manipulate the patient. Such self-analysis is not a matter of applying the laws of natural science. Unfortunately, the use of terms such as ego and id caused people to mistake this psychology for a branch of natural science.

Would it be better to use 'I' to express all of me, instead of distinguishing between ego and id, or between Jung's ego and unconscious? It might be more correct but less effective in terms of thinking about problems of the human mind. Thinking about the human mind and about existence is very difficult. It is effective to think of the mind as divided, but that is not the real-ity. It may be more correct to think of it as a whole, but you cannot go anywhere with that definition, as it is difficult to discuss the structure of the psyche if everything is 'I.' Nonetheless, you can say that thinking of ego and *I* as identical reflects very clearly the mode of modern Western thought. In contrast to this, then, I shall consider the questions: How do Japanese think? How do Buddhists think?

I am a Kannon

The following story shows the medieval Japanese view of 'I.' This story, from a collection of Buddhist fables called *Konjaku Monogatari* (Yamada et al. 1951a) edited in the twelfth century AD, is one of my favorites. First I would like to comment briefly on Buddhist tales in that era. After Buddhism was transmitted to Japan in the sixth century it spread quickly. Among the general population, however, it was not well understood, as its doctrines, rules, and rituals were totally unfamiliar. Instead, Buddhism was received to the extent that it fused with Shinto, the indigenous animistic religion, and gradually it came to permeate daily life. Buddhist monks, by explaining the sutras and teaching the doctrines, on the one hand, and by telling many illustrative sto-ries, on the other, transmitted the values of Buddhism. These stories recounted true episodes and also legends containing Buddhist teachings. Many of these, collected in the Middle Ages, have been preserved. Reading them, I have felt that the nature of Buddhism which the Japanese accepted was more readily grasped in these stories than in the sutras per se. I was glad to learn that William LaFleur (1983), Professor of Japanese studies at the University of Pennsylvania, also holds this view. This story is called 'Wato Kannon in Shinano, taking the tonsure':

A man living in a village with a medicinal hot spring had a dream in which someone said, 'Tomorrow about 2 p.m. Kannon [Kuan Yin], the Bodhisattva of Compassion, will arrive in this hot spring.' He was surprised and asked what appearance the Kannon would have. Someone said, 'A samurai of about forty years, on horseback,' and went on describing his appearance in detail. Then the man woke up. He told everybody in the village. They cleaned the area and then gathered at the spring to welcome the Bodhisattva. Two o'clock passed. About four o'clock in the afternoon, a samurai exactly matching the description appeared. Everyone prostrated themselves before him. The samurai, perplexed, asked, 'What's going on?' A monk told him about the dream oracle. The samurai explained that he had fallen from his horse and injured himself and that was why he had come to the hot spring. But the villagers kept praying. The samurai said, 'Then, I must be Kannon,' and he took the tonsure on the spot. It is said that, following this, he went up to Mount Hiei, near Kyoto, and became a disciple of the priest Kakucho.

(Yamada et al. 1951c: 87–9)

The most impressive aspect of the story for me is that the samurai believes 'I must be Kannon,' on the basis of a stranger's dream. Abandoning his forty-year life as a warrior, he is convinced that 'I am Kannon' and becomes a priest. If I take Descartes' maxim, 'I think, therefore I am,' and express this situation, it becomes 'Someone dreamed of me, therefore I exist.' One might well think that this is just nonsense, but Jungians might remember the dream that Jung described from his later years:

I was on a hiking trip. I was walking along a little road through a hilly landscape; the sun was shining and I had a wide view in all directions. Then I came to a small wayside chapel. The door was ajar, and I went in. To my surprise there was no image of the Virgin on the altar, and no crucifix either, but only a wonderful flower arrangement. But then I saw that on the floor in front of the altar, facing me, sat a yogi in lotus position, in deep meditation. When I looked at him more closely, I realized that he had my face. I stared in profound fright, and awoke with the thought: 'Aha, so he is the one who is meditating me. He has a dream, and I am it.' I knew that when he awakened, I would no longer be.

(Jung 1963: 323)

Upon reading this, you see that Jung also used another dream to answer the question, 'What am I?' The yogi dreams, and Jung is supported by the yogi's dreaming. Therefore, the sentence, 'Someone dreamed me, therefore I am,' seems to fit.

There is, of course, a clear difference between Jung's case and that of the samurai in medieval Japan. In Jung's case, the yogi is a character in his own dream, and, as Jung related, 'he had my face.' In his comment, Jung states, 'It is a parable.' In contrast, for the samurai in that era, the dream was someone else's; and he, the character who had been dreamed of, accepted the content as literal reality. Jung commented on his own dream as follows:

> The aim of [this dream] is to effect a reversal of the relationship between ego-consciousness and the unconscious, and to represent the unconscious as the generator of the empirical personality. This reversal suggests that, in the opinion of the 'other side,' our unconscious existence is a real one and our conscious world a kind of illusion, an apparent reality constructed for a specific purpose, like a dream which seems a reality as long as we are in it. It is clear that this state of affairs resembles very closely the oriental conception of Maya.
>
> (Jung 1963: 323)

Here, Jung recognizes his own dream experience as being similar to 'the Oriental' view. Considering these aspects, I get the impression that Jung's *I* existed astride both Japan's Middle Ages and the modern Occident. When you think about what *I* is, in the contemporary West, ego is equal to *I*. Jung, who questioned the equation, began at the ego and descended to the depths of the mind. In contrast, the medieval Japanese *I* did not discriminate itself from others and accepted an existence which fused self and other. But modern Japanese, including myself, are trying to find *I* as more individual and are rising toward the light of discrimination. I met the Occident in the field of analytical psychology. Jung's psychology is quite deep and expansive, so, in order to accept it, Westerners have tried to understand it in relation to ego. In contrast, I have observed that Japanese or Asians in general have tried to understand it in relation to Being itself before the division of self and other.

I in the dream

It is well worth considering the active *I* in dreams when we think about the nature of *I*. Obviously, this includes not only *I* in my own dream but also myself in another's dream. Therefore, I am aware of my dream, and also, as a therapist, I am attentive to the appearance of myself in my analysands' dreams. The latter give insight into various points of 'what I am.' Here is one example. Near the termination of therapy a school-phobic high school student dreamed as follows:

> I come to Sensei's [therapist's] house, but there is no response, so I go around to the back. In the backyard, people are sitting in a half circle. They look like stone Jizo (the guardian deity of children). In

the front row there are children, and behind them are adults. Looking more carefully, I see that there are people sitting the same way in the living room. In the center, Sensei is lying down. (The half circle of people gives the strong impression of being half in the light and half in darkness.) I yell loudly from the back, 'I am here,' or 'I got here on time,' but no response. Soon Sensei stands up and tries to say something, but no sound comes out. Everybody pushes him back and makes him lie down. The whole scene looked like a picture of the Buddha's Pari Nirvana (i.e. his passing away while entering Nirvana).

This client thought of this last scene as the death of his therapist, so he hesitated in telling me about it, thinking that it might indicate bad fortune, but finally he told me. Actually, I have 'died' several times in clients' dreams. In almost all of them, this was dreamed near the termination point of therapy. As a Jungian analyst, of course, one does not think of a dream as 'bad fortune.' In the therapeutic process, the experience of 'death and rebirth' manifests itself to the client as well as to the therapist in dreams. This dream occurred close to termination and thus indicated transformation not only of the image of the therapist, but also of the therapist himself – of me, in this case. That is, it meant that some transformation already had taken place, or was going to take place, within me.

The significance of the initial dream has often been pointed out. You can also say that termination dreams have special significance. The above dream indicates that the therapist has finished his role and is leaving. This client and I then discussed this. He too felt that the therapy had nearly reached the end. At this point, we both felt that it was quite interesting that, although both of us were completely indifferent to Buddhism, the significant Buddhist image, the Buddha's Pari Nirvana (final Nirvana), appeared. At that time, I did not give any more thought to the dream. I focused on the idea that the dream indicated a change in his image of the therapist. But when I look back on it now, I believe that the dream was referring to my reality as well. I feel that this dream was indicating how much weight Buddhism exerts on the way I conduct psychotherapy even though at that time I was not ready consciously to accept the fact. I saw the dream's half-light and half-dark field of people surrounding the central figure in terms of the client's work on his 'Shadow' problem. Now I see that it may have indicated my own half-conscious state of mind as regards Buddhism. In my own dreams, my *I* does things that would be completely out of character for the *I* in the awake state. In one's dream, sometimes the *I* becomes not oneself, but another or an animal, a plant, or even an inorganic being. Here is an old story from a dream in which the *I* becomes an animal:

There was a man who hunted birds with falcons. He lived with his wife and three children and kept many falcons and dogs for hunting.

He was getting quite old, and one night he was sick but not able to fall asleep. Finally, near dawn, he fell asleep and had a dream. He and his family were pheasants living happily in the meadow. Suddenly hunters, with falcons diving and dogs charging, started after them. Right there in front of his eyes, his wife and three children were murdered in cold blood by the falcons. When he saw he would be next, he woke up.

He began to think about all the many pheasants he had killed. Those pheasants must have felt as sad as he felt in the dream. So he let all of his falcons and dogs loose. In tears, he told this dream to his wife and children. Immediately he renounced the world and took the tonsure (ordination as a monk).

(Yamada et al. 1951b: 77–80)

I have summarized the story for you, but the original contains a lively and detailed description of how frightened the hunter/pheasant became, witnessing his wife and children being murdered in front of him. This shows how well he had experienced the sadness of pheasants in the dream.

The notable characteristic of this story is that, in the dream, the dreamer became a being other than human and by that gained empathy toward pheasants. Then this experience in the dream became the generator of his behavior in the waking state. This type of thing happens in varying degrees in my practice of analysis at the present time. The cases of becoming an animal in dreams are rare, but they do exist in Japan. There may be fewer in Europe and America.

You sometimes see yourself doing something impossible in a dream – for example, you see yourself falling from a high place. In a dream you might clearly experience your 'double.' In a dream, you might see another you. The phenomenon of the 'double' was long considered abnormal. Goethe and the French poet Alfred de Musset experienced it. But, in a dream, although it is not uncommon, it is not considered pathological. This phenomenon is interesting in terms of learning about *I*, so I decided to collect cases and present an essay on it. Then I had my own dream of my 'double.' A short one, it had strong impact:

> I was walking down the hallway next to a psychiatric hospital. Then, I saw myself clearly there, wearing an ochre-colored sweater (one which, in fact, I wear often), sitting as though waiting for an appointment. I passed by. Then I had a feeling of surprise: This must be a dream of a double! I awoke thinking that the one who was walking was wearing a navy blue sweater.

To do 'research' on dreams of the double sounds somewhat like looking on from outside. But to dream such a dream myself and, in addition, to see that the 'other me' obviously was waiting to be examined as a patient – these aspects struck my heart strongly. The one walking down the hallway was there in a 'therapist' role. The half of my self was a 'patient.' Both of them came together there.

Adolph Guggenbuhl-Craig (1971) discusses the healer archetype in his book *Power in the Helping Professions*. Any archetype includes opposite elements, e.g. therapist/patient, healer/wounded. Thus Guggenbuhl-Craig affirms that this opposition exists in the healer archetype. If a therapist simply defines herself or himself as a 'healthy person without ailment,' this archetype gets split and the therapist becomes just a therapist and the patient just a patient. Sadly the patient then loses the opportunity of healing the self through the functioning of the healer archetype. In order to prevent such a splitting of the archetype, the therapist first has to recognize the patient that exists within herself or himself. Therefore, meeting myself as a patient in that dream was meaningful to me in carrying on my work as a psychotherapist.

Having little awareness of 'the patient,' I actually became a patient in my own dream. Experiencing the encounter of the therapist-self with the patient-self was significant in reinforcing my consciousness of our fundamental coexistence. To 'Who am I?,' I can answer, 'I am a psychotherapist.' But the answer to the question 'What is I?' must be, 'I am a psychotherapist and at the same time a patient.' Isn't it wonderful that a dream can actually make one feel this!

The world of Hua-yen

I am a therapist as well as a patient. Recalling the dreams I have presented so far, I can also say that I am an animal as well as Kannon. In a psychotherapy session, quite often I feel myself sitting like a rock or a patient or Kannon, rather than as a 'therapist.' These other ways seem to have better results. So I easily become this or that. Then, if I were asked afresh, 'What is I?' what could I say?

While I was preoccupied with the above ideas, I encountered the world of the *Garland Sutra*. It is very difficult to read this sutra. So, I just keep reading, half-sleeping and skimming, on and on. But, when I enter that world in such a manner even without comprehending each meaning and relationship, I get the feeling that I am enveloped in light. I am immersed in the feeling. Sometimes you see amazing words, but if you are absent-minded, you will just pass on, continuing to read as if they are nothing special. For example: 'Every act is empty; no reality; ordinary people think it is real; all things, no self-nature, all, completely equal to nothingness.'

As I explained above, 'no self-nature' is important among the teachings in the *Garland Sutra*. Until now I have been persistent in asking, 'What is I?' According to the *Garland Sutra*, my essence, my unique nature, is nothing, non-existent. So this question makes no sense. This is quite a radical idea. As

I continued reading the sutra, I felt, 'This is really something! What am I going to do?' It was so vague and impossible to grasp. Although I could not think that 'my unique nature' does not exist, it started to give me the feeling that my nature is but a drop of water in the ocean. Luckily, I found an essay in English on the *Garland Sutra* by the Japanese philosopher Toshihiko Izutsu (1980: 384–5). Thanks to him, I shall explain briefly the principal idea of this sutra.

This sutra calls the world of ordinary life 'the Dharmic World of Phenomena.' Its condition is such as we ordinarily experience two separate things, A and B. A has its own particular characteristics, as does B; A and B thus are clearly distinguished from one another, and there is no question of confusing the two. If the boundaries between phenomena are removed, however, we see the world differently. This dissolution of boundaries is characteristic not only of Hua-yen, but also of Buddhism in general and other Eastern philosophies. 'The minute and infinite differences of actual existence instantly disappear in a vast space of nondiscrimination' (Izutsu 1989: 18). This world of Hua-yen is called 'the Dharmic World of Principle.'

Here, the differences between objects disappear, and so self-nature is negated. This state Zen Buddhism calls 'nothingness' or 'emptiness'; the *Garland Sutra* uses the term 'absolute emptiness.' Everything lacks or is without a distinct self. Such terms as 'nothingness' and 'emptiness' do not signify an empty world of no things, but rather a world that contains infinite possibilities for 'being.' Emptiness in the Dharmic World of Principle is pregnant with the dual meaning of nothingness and being. According to Izutsu, in order to have such 'emptying' of existence, the same process of emptying existence has to happen on the side of the consciousness of the subject which is viewing it. In short, it is necessary to empty our ordinary consciousness, our 'discriminating mind,' always wanting to see the differences. 'It is the prerequisite. Emptying consciousness is the precondition for emptying existence' (Izutsu 1989: 26). The world of the Principle, which is itself absolutely emptied and hence infinitely potential, self-divides into innumerable phenomenal forms, the world we call 'reality.' The Principle manifests itself into phenomena. This kind of manifestation of the Emptiness Principle is predicated in Hua-yen philosophy as 'the Arising of True nature.' The most important point of the arising is complete manifestation. That is, the Principle, as Emptiness, always manifests itself completely in its appearance as form. Each and every thing which can be said to belong to our world of experience manifests this principle wholly and without exception. Even a small flower – a flower in a field, a single speck of dust floating in the air – manifest this creative energy totally. This world of phenomena embodies various kinds of discrimination. Each and every thing can be seen separately. But once a person fully experiences this Emptiness before or beneath discrimination, one can see the world entirely non-discriminately. Everything exists in the principle: 'All things manifest in the Arising of True Nature.' Izutsu comments:

> The Principle permeates phenomena without the slightest hindrance and is thus none other than the phenomena themselves. Conversely, phenomena manifest the Principle without the least obstruction and are thus none other than the Principle itself. The Principle and phenomena are tracelessly interfused and mutually interpenetrating. This relationship between Principle and phenomena is termed in Hua-yen philosophy, 'the Mutual Interpenetration of Principle and Phenomena.'
>
> (Izutsu 1989: 41)

Having presented the important concepts in Hua-yen philosophy of the Dharmic World of Phenomena, the Dharmic World of Principle, and the Dharmic World of Mutual Interpenetration of Principle and Phenomena, I shall now introduce a final formulation, by which the development of Hua-yen's theory of existence reaches its innermost core. It can be termed 'the Mutual Interpenetration of Phenomena and Phenomena.'

Interdependent origination

I have mentioned that the Principle always manifests itself completely in its appearance in form. Each of these forms is a different existence. The Principle is their utter non-discrimination, i.e. there are separate things, A, B, C, and these are all 'non-self-nature.' How is this possible? Hua-yen answers in two ways. In preparation, I shall introduce the idea of 'ontological nexus' in Hua-yen philosophy. Suppose there are the phenomena A, B, and C, and each of them is itself without any self-nature, yet they all are related. The existence of A as 'A' is determined by its relation to B and C and all other phenomena. Everything is related to everything; nothing can be considered apart from its relatedness to the whole. As any thing moves in time or space, all things will change in relationship to it. Although A is without self-nature, still it is A because of its relationship to everything else. In short, the inner structure of A includes everything else in hidden or 'powerless' form. And by such relationship, A is A, not B or C.

The entire universe supports the existence of any single thing, and absolutely nothing exists as an individual particular by itself alone. All things continually and simultaneously manifest themselves together as a whole. The philosophy of Hua-yen calls this ontological reality 'Interdependent Origination.'

The Arising of True Nature and Interdependent Origination are fundamental to all basic Buddhist teachings. The Indian Buddhist philosopher Nagarjuna said, 'Whoever sees Interdependent Origination can see

Emptiness.' As no individual can exist in itself alone, it exists by support of everything other than itself. Through everything, one invisible principle exists: in short, the Mutual Interpenetration of Phenomena and Phenomena.

The way of thought of Interdependent Origination has a nature completely different from the conceptual mode of Aristotle, which explains phenomena by the relationship of cause and effect. Although modern science, utilizing the cause-and-effect point of view regarding phenomena, has proven extremely effective, we need to reflect upon the modern problems that stem from our habit of viewing all human phenomena in a cause-and-effect mode. It seems quite worthwhile to look at these problems from the standpoint of Interdependent Origination. Jung's concept of synchronicity belongs to the thought pattern of Interdependent Origination.

One other idea, an ontology of Master and Servant, is needed in order to explain the Dharmic World of Mutual Interpenetration of Phenomena and Phenomena. Suppose that there are entities A, B, and C, each differing from the other. Each in turn is constituted by an infinite number of the same ontological elements, a, b, c, d, e, f, g, . . . , even though A, B, and C differ. If we use semantic thinking, the signifier is always everything (a, b, c . . .), whereas the significants differ, like A, B, C. In order to explain this enigma, Hua-yen employs the aspects 'powerful' and 'powerless.' 'Powerful' designates the presence of a positive, manifest, self-asserting, and controlling element; 'powerless' denotes the opposite: passive, seclusive, self-negating, and subservient. Among the infinite elements, one of them – a, l, or x, perhaps – becomes powerful, while the rest of them are understood to be powerless. As A, L, or X, they are recognized in the daily world as different things. At any one moment, the powerful element is not necessarily the only one; and it changes in relation to the whole and over time.

As explained above, A, B, and C will be recognized as different from each other, but that is due to the relationships of the constituting elements, both powerful and powerless. When you pay complete attention to the constituting elements, all entities are embraced in profound samadhi. This is the Mutual Interpenetration of Phenomena and Phenomena. In our daily life, only the 'powerful' element manifests, so we human beings cannot resist focusing on differences; that means not noticing the 'powerless' elements, though they are essential to the depth-structure of A, for instance, and support its manifestation. With this bit of familiarity with the idea of the Interpenetration of Phenomena and Phenomena, when we reconsider I, we can deepen our understanding.

Level of consciousness

When you apply this understanding of Hua-yen, I then is basically empty; so my self-nature, my true quality, doesn't exist in itself. And also, I am not only other humans. I am similarly animals, plants, and all other things organic and inorganic. In order to experience the emptiness of existence, the conscious side of the subject must become empty. This relates deeply to the nature of human consciousness. In terms of thinking about I, my consciousness becomes focal. From early times, Buddhists were interested in human consciousness. They have practiced meditation as their methods of training, and they have engaged in careful self-observation on changes in consciousness during meditation.

This sort of work is practiced not only by Buddhists. Other paths, such as Taoism and Shamanism, have similar practices. Indeed, they are common to every religion in the East and South-east Asia.

In daily consciousness, it is important to see the differences in things. By doing so, you can discriminate usefully. Through finer and more accurate discrimination, science develops. Natural science requires increasing refinement of ordinary consciousness. With the development of natural science and technology we humans became capable of manipulating our environment in nearly any way our hearts desire.

Buddhism has refined its way of consciousness in a different direction. It has moved in the direction of negating the use of consciousness for discrimination between things. In an image, I might say 'gradually lowering' the level of consciousness or gradually annihilating discrimination. When you lower it to an extreme degree – that is, when consciousness becomes emptied – the world manifested is that presented in the *Garland Sutra*, as we have seen. You might say that the lowered level of consciousness means the 'unconscious.' But, as Jung noted, 'the characteristic of the unconscious is not being able to be conscious.' Therefore, the so-called 'unconscious,' as long as you can talk about it, actually is conscious. The modern West has thought ego so important that it identifies ego with 'I.' So, as an Asian, I guess that, in regard to this 'lower' consciousness, it was impossible to say 'conscious,' since the modern Western ego does not comprehend this aspect. Thus this 'lower' consciousness can't help but be called the 'unconscious.'

There is a most important point to be kept in mind regarding this descent of the level of annihilating discrimination. It does not necessarily imply a lowering of the power of conscious judgment, concentration, observation, etc. In the modern West, this has not been understood. Because the West emphasized the ego so much, all lowering of the level of consciousness was considered 'abnormal' or 'pathological.' Carl Jung is the person who made the greatest effort to correct such an idea. From the beginning, he pointed out that regression not only has a pathological side, but also has a constructive and creative role. His experience of 'Confrontation with the unconscious,' described in his autobiography, is indeed such an example of the descent of the level of consciousness with the full faculties of judgment, concentration, and observation intact. Active imagination, which he developed, was considered to be one of the powerful methods of constructively lowering the level of consciousness.

Jung has separated the personal unconscious and the collective unconscious as strata deep in the mind. They represent, if expressed in the Buddhist way, the gradual deepening of the level of consciousness. Jung made no mention of a level of Emptiness. However, Jung's statement, 'The psyche is the world pivot' (Jung 1960: 217) may be taken as representing in Western terms the level of the ultimate state of non-discrimination or emptiness. I think the reason such a big gap has emerged between Eastern and Jungian terminology for such consciousness is that Jung was protecting his position as a psychologist while still trying to relate to this Emptiness. Moreover, Jung's work, fundamentally, consisted of caring for the ego. I recall Jung's frequent reminder that he does not speak about God himself but, rather, about images of God in the human psyche. Jung, as psychologist, limited his work to considering those things which can be grasped by ego and then verbalized. He expressed these from the ego's side. Buddhism, on the other hand, passed through such an area at once and reached the level of Emptiness or conscious non-discrimination. Thus it describes the consciousness from that side, not from the ego's side. In order to accomplish such a descent in level of consciousness, Buddhism developed various methods of meditation and chanting, practices which maintain full awareness of concentration and observation. The results of such effort are described in many sutras. During such practice as zazen (Zen meditation), for example, Zen refuses to attend to the 'middle zone' of ego consciousness, reaching instead toward Emptiness consciousness. Jungian psychology, it seems to me, focuses on images in that middle zone which Zen practitioners pass through, and interprets them in relation to the ego.

With this key difference in mind, I would like to discuss how I think about and practice psychotherapy. Since I was trained as a Jungian analyst, I believe that, generally speaking, I follow Jung's ideas. I also want to make it clear that I have never had an experience such as what is called Emptiness consciousness. Yet I also, at this point, don't think that I should practice Zen in order to have such an experience. Despite that, I could not help but pay attention to Buddhism because my ego started to change, getting closer to Buddhist views. Even though I thought I was practicing psychotherapy according to Jung's ideas, probably I still have a different kind of ego from that of Westerners. Compared to the Western ego, the Japanese ego is living far more 'in everything,' much as I have described in presenting Hua-yen ideas. Before asserting my ego's independence and integration, I think of myself as an existence living in the world of Interdependent Origination. Frankly, when I meet those Jungian analysts who 'analyze' and 'interpret' everything, I feel like saying to them, 'Everything is Emptiness,' although I really don't comprehend what that statement means. One consequence of having such an ambiguous way of life is that I have obtained a good number of excellent results through psychotherapy in Japan. But what I am doing need not be limited only to Japan. I hope that it also will be helpful to some degree in other cultural regions. Because this contemporary period is a time of cultural collision, I think that no one can live comfortably in their indigenous, traditional culture.

References

Bettelheim, B. (1983) *Freud and Man's Soul*, New York: Freeman Press.

Freud, S. (1964) *New Introductory Lectures on Psychoanalysis*, trans. and ed. J. Strachey, London: Hogarth Press.

Guggenbuhl-Craig, A. (1971) *Power in the Helping Professions*, New York: Spring Publications.

Izutsu, T. (1980) 'The nexus of ontological events: a Buddhist view of reality', in *Eranos Yearbook* 49 (Frankfurt am Main: Insel Verlag, 1981).

Izutsu, T. (1989) 'Cosmos to anticosmos' [Cosmos and anticosmos], Tokyo: Iwanami Shoten.

Jung, C. G. (1963) *Memories, Dreams, Reflections*, ed. Aniela Jaffé, London: Collins, and Routledge & Kegan Paul.

Jung, C. G. (1960) 'On the nature of the psyche', in *The Collected Works of C. G. Jung*, vol. 8, trans. R. F. C. Hull, Princeton: Princeton University Press.

La Fleur, W. R. (1983) *The Karma of words: Buddhism and literary arts in medieval Japan*, Berkeley, CA: University of California Press.

Takakura, T. (1929) *Indo dowa Shu* [*Fairy Tales of India*], Tokyo: Ars Book Company.

Yamada, T. et al. (eds) (1951a) *Konjaku Monogatari* [*Tales, Ancient and Modern*], 5 vols, Tokyo: Iwanami Shoten.

Yamada, T. et al. (eds) (1951b) 'Nishinokyo ni taka o tsukau mono yume o mite shukke suru koto' ['A hunter with falcons taking tonsure by a dream'], in *Konjaku Monogatari* [*Tales, Ancient and Modern*], 19, no. 8, Tokyo: Iwanami Shoten, 77–80.

Yamada, T. et al. (eds) (1951c) 'Shinanono kuni no Wato Kannon shukke suro koto' ['Wato kannon in Shinano, taking the tonsure'], in *Konjaku Monogatari* [*Tales, Ancient and Modern*], 19, no. 11, Tokyo: Iwanami Shoten, 87–9.

10

AMERICAN ZEN AND PSYCHOTHERAPY

An ongoing dialogue

Katherine V. Masís

Introduction

Zen made its way into the United States in the second half of the nineteenth century. In the 1860s, an early wave of Chinese immigrants came to California to work in the gold mines and on the Central Pacific Railroad (Fields 1992; Prebish 1999). Chinese, Taoist, Confucian, and some Buddhist temples were soon established on the Pacific coastline, some of these possibly housing Zen priests. Several schools of Buddhism, including Zen, were represented at the World Parliament of Religions, which took place at the Chicago World's Fair in 1893. Present at that Parliament were several key figures in the teaching, dissemination, and development of Zen in the United States: Shaku Soen, Nyogen Senzaki, and Shaku Sokatsu, who were ordained Zen priests and teachers, as well as the scholar and author D. T. Suzuki (Fields 1992; Prebish 1999).

In the early 1900s, D. T. Suzuki traveled throughout the United States with Shaku Soen, translating his lectures. In the 1950s, Suzuki taught courses on Zen philosophy at Columbia University. A prolific writer, his books did much to disseminate Zen teachings in academia and throughout the Beat generation. In 1960, he co-authored the well-known *Zen Buddhism and Psychoanalysis* with Erich Fromm and Richard DeMartino (Suzuki et al. 1960). Shaku Soen, Shaku Sokatsu and Nyogen Senzaki established meditation halls and taught Zen meditation to some Americans, mostly in California and New York, and left successors to carry on their work.

The 1960s, however, was the decade that spawned the establishment of several practice-oriented Zen centers, mostly in California and New York. The majority of Zen meditation practitioners were baby-boomers in their young adulthood who no doubt felt attracted to the progressive counter-culture and cosmopolitan environments in these locations. These centers multiplied in the1970s and 1980s and bred American successors. By the 1970s and 1980s, the number of Zen centers throughout the United States had increased dramatically.

Who practices Zen meditation?

In the United States, who are the people who practice Zen meditation and at the same time provide or engage in psychotherapy? Zazen, or Zen meditation, is only one part of Zen Buddhist practice. Taken as a whole, Zen Buddhist practice involves cognitive, practical, and interactive work, manifested through sitting meditation, listening to talks by and holding interviews with a teacher, the reading of canonical texts, liturgical rites and rituals, chanting, retreats, and relationships with members of a Buddhist community (Dubs 1987; Preston 1988). Zen Buddhist practice is socially organized in such a way as to facilitate the experience of a shared sense of reality (Preston 1988). The longer an individual practices any given meditation technique, the more difficult it is to keep from identifying with that particular technique's contextual tradition (Shapiro 1994). There may certainly be individuals who practice zazen or Zen meditation solely for the purpose of improving psychological and physical health, but Zen Buddhist practitioners are likely to belong to a spiritual community.

Despite the increasing visibility of Buddhism in the media, Buddhists in the United States make up fewer than two million people, that is, less than 1 per cent of the population (Nattier 1998). The larger Buddhist community in the United States has been typologized according to ethnicity and purpose of participation. Prebish (1993, 1999), for example, coined the phrase 'the two Buddhisms,' referring to a Buddhism of Asian American descent and one of mostly, but not exclusively, European American descent. Fields (1992; 1998) coined the terms 'white Buddhism' and 'ethnic Buddhism,' a distinction acknowledged as problematic by Fields himself and by Nattier (1998) and Prebish (1993; 1999). The category white Buddhism is largely made up of white, middle-class, educated Americans who are organized around Asian or American teachers, and is mainly contemplative and lay practice, albeit based on monastic models (Finn and Rubin 1999). White Buddhism is often self-conscious, and mostly monogenerational, with baby-boomers vastly outnumbering practitioners of other generations within a community (Fields 1998).

In contrast, ethnic Buddhism is mostly made up of Asians and Asian Americans, is part of the culture of the country of origin, inseparable from community, non-self-conscious, and intergenerational. In white Buddhism, it is common for an individual to be the only family member who practices. In (white, contemplative, lay) Zen Buddhist communities, it is unusual for both spouses to practice (Preston 1988). Children of white Buddhist practitioners are only occasionally and marginally included in festivities and social activities of their parent's practice communities. In ethnic Buddhism, on the other hand, entire families practice together.

Nattier (1998) proposes three categories of American Buddhism: Elite Buddhism, Evangelical Buddhism and Ethnic Buddhism. Defined by its class background, Elite Buddhism is made up of individuals that are usually, but not exclusively, of European ancestry, but have had the time, inclination, and educational and economic opportunities to learn about and dedicate themselves to meditation training. Evangelical Buddhists are attracted to Buddhism through proselytizing and tend to proselytize themselves as part of their ongoing practice. The Soka Gakkai group, a devotional Buddhist sect born in the 1930s and whose practice is based on the recitation of a simple canonical chant, is typical of Evangelical Buddhism (Nattier 1998). Defined by its ethnicity, Ethnic Buddhism is the cultural legacy of Asian immigrants who traveled to the United States in search of new opportunities, such as jobs and better educational and economic opportunities for their children. These immigrants simply brought their religion along with them and continued to practice it in communal fashion (Nattier 1998).

Old-line Asian American Buddhists, native-born converts, and new-wave Asian immigrant Buddhists with a large gulf between them make up yet another three-category typology of American Buddhists (Seager 1999). Old-line Asian American Buddhists are descendants of the first wave of Asian immigrants who sought better futures in the United States. Native-born converts tend to be educated, and to have characteristics similar to those described for white, Euro-American, and Elite Buddhists. Due to war and political upheaval in their countries of birth, many new-wave Asian immigrant Buddhists have come to the United States as refugees (Seager 1999).

In the United States, the most likely psychotherapists and clients in therapy who also practice Zen meditation will be white, middle-class, educated, of European descent, and will belong to a group that is organized around a non-proselytizing Asian or American Zen teacher (Finn and Rubin 1999; Imamura 1998). Lacking solid, trusting community and extended family ties, these clients and/or therapists will most likely have joined the Zen group as isolated individuals attempting to create an artificial community (Imamura 1998), and will have a commitment to Zen Buddhist practice that goes far beyond intellectual curiosity or leisure pursuit.

Lay, contemplative, Euro-American or Elite Zen Buddhists tend to be far more interested in the connections between Western psychology and Buddhism than Ethnic Buddhists (Imamura 1998). At the same time, as clients, they may view their need for psychotherapy as a failure of their meditation practice, and therefore feel a 'specifically Buddhist shame around seeking psychotherapeutic help' (Finn and Rubin 1999: 328).

Need-based motives for coming to meditation practice do not seem to differ from the motives of non-meditators who seek psychotherapy. Loneliness, alienation, existential *angst*, the yearning to belong, death of loved ones, separation and abandonment issues are among the most common motives to join Buddhist meditation practice (Gopfert 1999; Imamura 1998; Finn and Rubin 1999; Kapleau 1989; Kornfield 1993b; Muzika 1990; Welwood 2000).

Also present are the desire to overcome early emotional losses, restore a fragile sense of self, and heal addictions; the presence of self-hatred, disturbing thoughts and feelings; and the tendency to provide a rationale for self-punishment and for submissiveness to authority (Finn and Rubin 1999). Many meditation practitioners seek freedom from behavioral, cognitive, or affective confinement and wish to enhance their potential and discover a larger meaning in their life (Watson 1996). Suffering from feelings of inner emptiness, some meditation practitioners may misunderstand and likewise be attracted to the Buddhist notion of 'no-self,' and mistakenly seek doctrinal validation for their feelings of emptiness (Rubin 1996).

Benefits of Zen meditation in the therapy process

Stress and anxiety reduction

Several studies suggest that Buddhist concentration and mindfulness meditation practices such as zazen and Vipassana reduce stress and anxiety (Kabat-Zinn 1988; Kabat-Zinn et al. 1992; Shapiro 1976; 1978; Shapiro and Zifferblatt 1976; Shapiro and Giber 1978). The less stress and anxiety in clients and therapists, the greater the likelihood for cognitive and emotional receptivity and presence in the therapy session (Kutz et al. 1985), and for adaptive responses to future stressors (Goleman 1976). Buddhist concentration and mindfulness meditation may facilitate the occurrence of relaxation through focusing the mind on the breath and through non-judgmental witnessing of thoughts and emotions. As thoughts arise and subside, attention shifts away from distressing or unhealthy thought patterns and emotions, and, consequently, involvement and identification with them drops away (Deikman 1982; Rubin 1996; Shapiro and Giber 1978).

On the other hand, Buddhist concentration and mindfulness meditation may not decrease anxiety except after several years of sustained practice, and in fact may bring about temporary phases of anxiety, agitation, and despair as the meditator's usual perception of reality is challenged (Brown and Engler 1980; Compton and Becker 1983; Dubs 1987; Kapleau 1989). Self-regulation strategies such as stress and anxiety reduction may be considered side-effects or by-products of meditation, and may not necessarily be the reason, or at least the main reason, why practitioners turn to meditation in the first place (Brown and Engler 1980; Compton and Becker 1983; Dubs 1987; Shapiro 1994; Walsh 1982). For example, clients who are engaged in zazen for the purpose of calming the mind and improving psychological and physical health are the clients most likely interested in the potential relaxation effects of Zen meditation (Kapleau 1989). Clients engaged in Zen Buddhist practice as a whole do not reject the potential relaxation benefits of Zen meditation, but are not likely to practice it for those effects alone (Kapleau 1989). Therapists would do well to be attentive to the reasons their clients practice Zen meditation and to note to what extent full Zen Buddhist practice is a part of their world and world view (Brazier 1995).

Tolerance of mental processes

Concentration and mindfulness meditation practices such as Zen and Vipassana foster tolerance of diverse mental processes, which in turn fosters tolerance of distressing cognitions and emotions. From a Buddhist point of view, bare, non-judgmental awareness and witnessing of thoughts and emotions as they arise and subside is, in itself, healing (Epstein 1995; Salzburg 1995). As the meditation practitioner brings awareness to his or her own mental processes, disidentification with them takes place (Deikman 1982; Kapleau 1989). In other words, the practitioner gains awareness that those distressing thoughts, images, and emotions 'are not me' (Brazier 1995: 73). The goal in meditation is not to exorcise the psyche of disturbing thoughts and emotions, nor to suppress them, but to hold them in non-reactive, friendly awareness. They may not necessarily disappear from the practitioner's psyche, but through consistent observing and witnessing of them, they cease to trouble him or her (Brazier 1995; Epstein 1995; Kapleau 1989; Muzika 1990; Salzburg 1995; Watson 1996; Welwood 2000). Paradoxically, when it does not matter anymore whether disturbing cognitions or emotions visit the practitioner, they cease to be actively unwanted. When they cease to be actively unwanted, they cease to intrude (Brazier 1995; Epstein 1995; Kapleau 1989; Muzika 1990; Salzburg 1995; Watson 1996; Welwood 2000).

The non-reactive, non-judgmental attention with which cognitions and emotions are treated fosters greater affect tolerance in the meditation practitioner. When a wide variety of mental processes are treated with bare, non-judgmental attention, they are held in an open, spacious container. This enables the meditation practitioner to befriend his or her thoughts and emotions, no matter what they are, and reduces the likelihood of being tyrannized by an inordinately demanding superego (Rubin 1996).

In the course of zazen, mental phenomena such as visual, auditory, olfatory, gustatory, tactile, or propriocentric hallucinations, as well as euphoric or depressed states may occur (Kapleau 1989). These phenomena are known as *makyo* and may range from mild to intense, from short-term to long-lasting, from pleasant or elating to unpleasant or disturbing. Usually, the more experienced an individual is in meditation, the better able he or she will be to handle these states. When strong, vivid *makyo* emerge from consciousness, this may indicate a significant intermediate point in a Zen meditator's practice; neither is the practitioner a rank beginner, nor has he or she seen through the layers of self (Kapleau 1989).

Unusual or unfamiliar mental states may also take the form of either pathological or adaptive regressions (Engler 1984; Epstein and Lieff 1981; Fauteux 1987). Adaptive regressive states are transitory, easily reversible, and tend to increase self-esteem (Epstein and Lieff 1981). Such states are reminiscent of Winnicottian 'good enough mothering' and 'transitional phenomena' that the individual never had, thus helping to ease the anxiety of separation, and to recreate early feelings of Eriksonian 'basic trust' that are conducive to psychological growth (Fauteux 1987).

Interception of unhealthy habit patterns

When practicing basic zazen, thoughts are allowed to repeatedly arise and vanish in a non-judgmental way. Thoughts and other mental processes are witnessed and held in friendly awareness. This witnessing leads to a gradual disidentification with ever-changing thoughts and concepts that make up the sense of self (Deikman 1982; Epstein and Lieff 1981). When the hold on these self-concepts is loosened, they are seen for what they are: impermanent components of reactions to experience. When seen for what they are, choice and transformation may take place (Watson 1996).

Due to inertia in the human mind, both positive and negative impulses may set up entire sequences of the same (Brazier 1995). Compulsions, mental habits, and stereotyped reactive patterns are carefully observed and seen through as changing, impermanent phenomena that do not make up the self. With sustained meditation practice, over time they can be intercepted early in the mental chain of events, before mental processes become final products, such as thoughts and images (Brazier 1995; Mikulas 1990; Watson 1996).

When long-standing mental habits and self-identifications are seen through in this way, a greater freedom, openness, expansiveness, and inclusiveness of self-structures takes place (Rubin 1996). Because self-centric preoccupations give way to a more engaged relationship to life, a greater affect tolerance, a more flexible relatedness to self and others, and hence a decrease in self-recrimination ensues (Rubin 1996). By bringing formerly unconscious material to the fore and developing enhanced receptivity to subtle mental and bodily phenomena, meditation fosters self-introspection, and formerly disowned experience may be more easily integrated (Rubin 1996). The Winnicottian 'capacity to be alone' is enhanced by disidentifying with internalized objects and letting go of memories from the past and preoccupation with the future (Brazier 1995; Miller 2001).

Rather than doing away with complexes, for example, Zen meditation enables clients to stop being vexed by them and to stop identifying with them as though they were the real self (Brazier 1995; Odajnyk 1998). In this way, automatic reactive patterns may be seen through instead of acted out (Watson 1996). Zen meditation is a way of 'creating stops' whereby practitioners can take a non-judgmental, witnessing, or observing stance, which facilitates deconditioning from unhealthy, learned mind states (Brazier 1995: 130). From a Jungian point of view, sitting still in zazen and focusing the mind may also have the effect of withdrawing psychic energy from drives, instincts and complexes, including the ego complex, which in turn tends to create conditions of well-being (Odajnyk 1998).

Therapists who meditate

Many Western Buddhist psychotherapists consider it far more relevant for the therapy process that the therapist rather than the client practice meditation. Therapists who practice meditation tend to be more comfortable with and befriending of gaps and silences in the therapy dialogue (Welwood 2000). Meditation provides a context for the therapist to relax into his or her own as well as the client's open spaces between their attempts to grasp onto something. The problem is not entering a void, but knowing how to relate to it without panicking about it. Meditation is valuable for the therapist because it offers him or her experience in entering the void, acquiescing in it, and working with his or her own vulnerability (Welwood 2000).

Through consistent practice of quieting the mental chatter and focusing attention, the groundwork is laid for developing the attentional precision for true listening: the 'evenly hovering attention' that Freud spoke of (Freud 1912/1964: 111–12). By experiencing his or her own deeper, True Nature and opening more fully to the client, the therapist's capacity for empathy is enhanced (Fleischman 1999; Lesh 1970; Miller 2001; Rubin 1996; Schuster 1979; Speeth 1982). Fully present listening, in and of itself, is a form of compassion and unconditional acceptance (Brazier 1995; Rubin 1996; Watson 1996; Welwood 2000). The concentration and mindfulness methods of Buddhist meditation foster both one-pointed and panoramic attention, an indispensable skill for therapists (Speeth 1982).

By sitting with his or her own changing mental processes, observing and witnessing whatever arises and vanishes without identification or judgment, the therapist learns to sit in a similar way with the client (Watson 1996). Rather than obeying subtle, learned commitments to particular theories by listening for confirmation of them, the therapist is enabled to listen to the client's own idiographic material (Rubin 1996). Trusting the client's innate wisdom, True Nature, or the Rogerian 'actualizing tendency,' the therapist is freer of intellectual constraints, theoretical allegiances and personal agendas (Brazier 1995; Rubin 1996; Watson 1996). Committed to the treatment but with no attachments to final results or outcomes, the therapist is more comfortable with the unknown, more open to being surprised, more open to complexity and ambiguity, and more likely to relate to clients in creative rather than habitual, stereotyped ways, more likely to tolerate and respect a diversity of interpersonal and intrapsychic phenomena (Brazier 1995; Rubin 1996; Watson 1996).

By creating and amplifying his or her own inner spaciousness through meditation, the therapist is more capable of creating a similar spaciousness in the therapy room where he or she can better flow with the client (Brazier 1995; Rubin 1996; Watson 1996). Such a therapist is engaging in 'unconditional presence' or the capacity to be fully present with a client, without trying to influence or maneuver what the client or therapist is feeling (Welwood 2000: 118). This capacity to be fully involved moment by moment in the therapy session is much more important than theoretical allegiances or employment of techniques (Christensen and Rudnick 1999; Watson 1996). Such a therapist is less likely to react to articulated content, rush to solutions, offer premature interpretations or react to clients' provocations for projective identification (Brazier 1995; Welwood 2000). Comfortable with gaps, voids, and silences, such a therapist is better able to resonate with the client's pre-articulate, Gendlinian 'felt sense,' to sit with a wide range of emotions, and to notice and acquiesce in his or her countertransference (Welwood 2000). In this way, the therapist will be better able to extend that sense of comfort and affect tolerance to his or her clients (Brazier 1995; Rubin 1996; Watson 1996; Welwood 2000). Zen-inspired psychotherapy would emphasize a fresh way to be with or relate to experience as it arises moment by moment (Brazier 1995; Cooper 1999; Watson 1996; Welwood 2000).

Pitfalls of Zen meditation practice

Contraindications for Zen meditation practice

Not everybody benefits from concentrative and/or mindfulness-oriented meditation practices. A minimum of mental health is required to sustain the discipline of mind training (Tart and Deikman 1991). Failures in early attachment, self-differentiation, self and object integration, autism, and personality disorders may not be amenable to meditation practices (Engler 1984). Attempts to see through the illusion of self may exacerbate self-pathology in those individuals with diagnoses of serious mental disorders. Individuals with addictions, disorganizing mental states, self-harming tendencies, addictive disorders, or disorders that require medication, or that incite suspicion, oppositionalism, or apathy, would do well to abstain from meditation retreats (Fleischman 1999). Even those individuals who may be free of the more serious mental disorders may be overwhelmed with changing states of mind, which may be of varying degrees of intensity and may include elation, excitement, rage, distrust, depression, and panic (Fleischman 1999). Individuals with a history of trauma may be at risk of being flooded when experiencing meditative states (Finn and Rubin 1999). Pathological regression, fear of sexual feelings, and fear of emotional intimacy may also be present (Deikman 1982; Fauteux 1987; Watson 1996). Pressured by a society that overvalues autonomy and volition, certain individuals may feel anxious about their ability to assert, take responsibility for, and share that individuality (Fauteux 1987).

Zen teachers may not recognize severe pathology in students who come to meditation practice. For students coming to meditation practice with faulty ego functioning, the enlightenment ideal may mistakenly represent 'a purified state of complete and invulnerable self-sufficiency from which all badness has been expelled, the aim of all narcissistic strivings' (Engler 1984: 37).

On the other hand, concentration and/or mindfulness meditation practices have been included as a useful adjunct to psychotherapy, even in severe narcissistic and borderline personality disorders (Kutz et al. 1985). Mindfulness meditation techniques may be introduced in therapy programs for clients suffering from trauma, depression, anxiety, and various neurotic symptoms, but not for clients suffering from hallucinations, delusions, thought disorders, and severe withdrawal (Deatherage 1975; Urbanowski and Miller 1996).

Teachers' and therapists' ignorance

Western therapists with little or no knowledge of meditation practice may either pathologize the clients' meditation experiences and/or fail to probe deeply enough into their clients' relationship with their spiritual teacher (Welwood 2000; Finn and Rubin 1999). Asian-born teachers have little knowledge or interest in psychotherapy and, traditionally, have not encouraged their students to seek treatment for their developmental deficiencies (Finn and Rubin 1999; Gopfert 1999). American Buddhist teachers have become more educated and sophisticated in the realm of psychotherapy and more willing to work with professionals in the mental health realm (VanderKooi 1997).

Some Buddhist communities may see personality as a pathology in itself to be corrected, rather than a defensive strategy that contains hidden intelligence and resources. In this case, individuals with personalities that do not fit a prescribed or perceived spiritual ideal will be robbed of those very strengths which will allow them to see through the veil of self (Rubin 1996; Welwood 2000).

Some Zen teachers, Asian or American, may see the self as 'the enemy' to be abolished at all costs and, in pursuit of its annihilation, wittingly or unwittingly engage in abusive or exploitative behaviors toward their students (Gopfert 1999). In the last fifteen years or so, there have been incidents of sexual misconduct and financial exploitation in many white, Elite or

Euro-American Buddhist centers, which have resulted in a form of spiritual incest in the larger American Buddhist community (Boucher 1988; Finn and Rubin 1999).

The Zen teacher–student relationship itself may give way to abusive behavior patterns (Gopfert 1999). Psychological abuse which may take the form of betrayal, shaming, blaming, and constant invalidation on the part of the teacher toward the student may lead to symptoms in Zen students similar to Post Traumatic Stress Disorder: depression, loss of self-esteem, anxiety, and constricted affect (Gopfert 1999). Exploited, abused students present with symptoms similar to those of adults who were sexually abused as children: shame, self-distrust, rage, fear, guilt, and self-inhibition (Rubin 1996). Unfortunately, Zen Buddhist practitioners who are clients in therapy may feel that it is disloyal to talk about the difficult aspects of their relationship with their teacher or spiritual community, and may therefore be reluctant to do so (Finn and Rubin 1999; Gopfert 1999).

Transference between Zen teachers and students

The teacher–student relationship in the Zen setting is one of the cornerstones of Zen practice (Kapleau 1989). Western therapists should take special care to inquire into their clients' relationship with their Zen teacher. Clients who practice zazen only, without the other components of Zen Buddhist practice, are not likely to be involved in a transference relationship with their teacher. Such clients may not necessarily identify with the Buddhist world view or participate actively in the activities of a Zen community. Most importantly, such clients do not tend to perceive their Zen teachers as parental figures, nor to re-enact or elicit problematic familial behavioral patterns from their childhood with them. But for those clients who initially come to Zen practice in deep pain, isolation and confusion, who identify with the Buddhist world view, and who are active participants in their Zen community, intense, sensitive transferences with the teacher may ensue prior to and in addition to the transference they may or may not develop with their therapist.

The Zen teacher–student transference is especially intense and problematic (Gopfert 1999; Young-Eisendrath forthcoming). This particular kind of transference carries a projection of the fully developed True Nature or enlightened mind that the student potentially harbors but as yet cannot access or manifest. Authentic Buddhist teachers may only qualify as such if: (a) they have undergone long and arduous training and testing, often over periods of ten to twenty years or more; and (b) they have been formally authorized to teach by their own teachers (Kapleau 1989; Welwood 2000; Young-Eisendrath forthcoming). Appreciating and perhaps awed by the extensive training that their teachers have undergone, and perceiving the quality of fully developed True Nature or enlightened mind in their teacher, students want to attain it themselves (Young-Eisendrath forth-coming).

Extremely negative transference relationships may occur in the teacher–student relationship (Engler 1984; Gopfert 1999; Rubin 1996; Young-Eisendrath forthcoming). Traditionally, the Zen teacher–student relationship does not encourage the student to express overwhelming or negative emotional states. Zen teachers often have little or no understanding of the nature of transference relationships or they choose to ignore their importance (Engler 1984; Gopfert 1999). Because the student lacks the benefit of interpretation of his or her negative emotional states, and because they are never reflected on in the teacher–student relationship, transference, countertransference, and relational re-enactments tend to remain relatively unconscious (Rubin 1996; Young-Eisendrath forthcoming). At best, these negative transferences may result in a shallow relationship with the teacher; at worst, they may threaten regression (Engler 1984). In any case, this may hinder reflection in the therapeutic setting as well.

Buddhist teachers inevitably become repositories for projections of perfection from their students (Epstein 1990; Gopfert 1999; Rubin 1996; Young-Eisendrath forthcoming). Many Zen students fantasize about their teachers and communities in terms of 'super-parents' and the 'super-family' (Tart and Deikman 1991: 46). The most common transferences in teacher–student relationships are of the Kohutian mirroring and idealizing types; that is, many Zen Buddhist students may invest hope that their teachers will mirror them by providing a source of acceptance and confirmation, or will perceive them as a source of idealized strength with which to merge (Engler 1984; Rubin 1996). These hopes may be fulfilled or thwarted, depending on the Zen teacher's personality and teaching style. Unfortunately, it is often the case that Buddhist teachers are presented as being beyond self-deceit (Rubin 1996). As parental surrogates, some Zen teachers will engage in projective identification; that is, they will unconsciously be induced to act as if they were indeed their students' parent(s) (Rubin 1996).

In addition to the Kohutian mirroring and idealizing transferences, there is a third, more chaotic kind of transference between Buddhist teachers and students, which oscillates between extreme omnipotence and extreme devaluation of the teacher on the part of the student (Engler 1984). When the need for idealization is coupled with debasing of self and others, extreme virtues are attributed to the teacher. But when the teacher is unable or refuses to meet the student's high expectations, very negative reactions may occur which may take the form of extreme vilification (Engler 1984).

A certain degree of idealization of the teacher on the part of the student is healthy and useful in awakening the longing to see through the false sense of self and access his or her True Nature and in spurring the student to practice (Gopfert 1999; Young-Eisendrath forthcoming). But over-idealization of spiritual teachers may arrest development and set the stage for

KATHERINE V. MASÍS

unhealthy patterns of relatedness learned from the past (Gopfert 1999; Rubin 1996; Tart and Deikman 1991). If a student's over-idealization of a teacher, and his or her self-submissiveness, self-devaluation, and deferentiality remain unexamined and unresolved, this may play itself out in other relationships (Rubin 1996). This is especially true if the student, after long years of training with an over-idealized teacher, goes on to become a teacher himself or herself (Young-Eisendrath forthcoming). In dealing with Buddhist clients, perhaps this very intense transference that they have with their teachers may well compete with any transference that may develop between the therapist and the client. The feelings of disloyalty when revealing difficulties in the teacher–student relationship may further inhibit effective understanding of and working through of negative emotions in therapy. This may result in a lukewarm, marginally effective relationship with a therapist.

Unfamiliar meditative experiences

Ranging from rage and depression on the one hand to bliss and euphoria on the other, meditative states facilitate the upsurge of primitive drives and affects (Engler 1984; Epstein and Lieff 1981; Rubin 1996). In traditional Zen Buddhist contexts, meditation students are instructed to ignore the content of these states and focus on the object (such as the breath, or koan) or on the mental process itself, which leaves meditation practitioners with little opportunity to understand or resolve various mental states.

Extreme oscillations in unfamiliar mental states, such as may occur during the emergence of *makyo*, may further weaken a faulty functioning ego, and the practitioner will tend to resort to disavowal of negative states and splitting mechanisms to keep the good and bad apart (Engler 1984). *Makyo* may take the form of regressive reactivations of childhood or primordial states, including unresolved 'bad' internalized object-relations which appear as primary-process type images or hallucinations (Krynicki 1980). The 'observing self' (Deikman 1982) may be unable to sit with what emerges in consciousness (Epstein 1990). Both in individuals with and without a family history of psychosis, psychotic breaks have been known to occur after weeklong Zen retreats, and have traditionally been linked to overexertion in meditation practice (VanderKooi 1997).

Through deepened concentration, the practitioner's mind may be significantly calmed during meditation, but negative emotional states may return after meditating because they were suppressed rather than examined and worked through (Cooper 1999). While thoughts, feelings, and fantasies may be made more available for scrutiny, non-judgmental attentiveness to their emergence while ignoring their meaning may not be enough (Rubin 1996). Therapists working with advanced meditators who are experiencing unusual mental states might consider working with senior meditation teachers (Finn and Rubin 1999).

160

Ignoring personal wounds

Consciously or unconsciously, Western meditation practitioners may use their meditation practice to avoid facing developmental tasks or old psychic wounds that would be better dealt with in psychotherapy. Quite a few meditation teachers convey the message that enlightenment or seeing through the false self gets to the root of human suffering, and thereby eradicates personal emotional difficulties. Unfortunately, this is not the case. Enlightenment is seeing through the illusion of self, but is not necessarily a way to heal a wounded self. In fact, wounds may continue to be there, hidden from consciousness, and operating in much the same way as they did before enlightenment (Engler 1984; Kornfield 1993a; 1993b; Muzika 1990; Odajnyk 1998; Rubin 1996; Welwood 2000; Young-Eisendrath forthcoming). Mistaken, glamorized notions of enlightenment present it as a discrete, unchanging, once-and-for-all life-changing event that will eradicate all kinds of suffering and human shortcomings (Brown and Engler 1980; Epstein 1990; Kapleau 1989; Kornfield 1993a; 1993b; Muzika 1990; Rubin 1996; Young-Eisendrath forthcoming). Enlightenment experiences may be shallow or deep, short- or long-lasting, but in any case, they are capable of endless development and are part of a continuum (Epstein 1990; Kapleau 1989). Enlightenment experiences may be temporarily healing, but if old wounds are still operating, the practitioner will be unable to integrate those experiences into his or her daily life and may be using spirituality to avoid dealing with those very wounds (Kornfield 1993a; 1993b).

Engler coined the well-known phrase, 'you have to be somebody before you can be nobody' (Engler 1984: 31). Many students who are attracted to meditation practice may mistakenly attempt to bypass or prematurely transcend important developmental tasks by annihilating the self at all costs (Engler 1984). From a developmental perspective, it is necessary to integrate a differentiated, cohesive self-structure before undertaking rigorous meditation practice to see through the self (Engler 1984; Welwood 2000). This minimum of cohesiveness is presupposed in Buddhist thought: if Zen Buddhism emphasizes seeing through the self, it is because it implicitly acknowledges its centrality in human development (Engler 1984; Suler 1995; Welwood 2000). Initially, Engler argued that this basic, intact self-structure must precede the perception of ultimate illusoriness of the self. More recently, Engler has modified his views and has stated that this process need not be linear (Engler as cited in Cohen 2000) but, because spiritual life and psychological life are interwoven, work in both realms may proceed synergistically.

Epstein (1990; 1995) takes issue with Engler's dictum of 'you have to be somebody before you can be nobody,' but nevertheless describes a similar process of disownment of negative mind states. Some meditators may observe their thoughts and feelings during meditation in a detached manner as a means to intellectualize, to dissociate from libidinal drives, rationality or aggression, or to produce the opposite of their drives in order to fit into a spiritual ideal (Epstein 1995; Epstein and Lieff 1981). As Epstein aptly puts it, any realization in a meditative state is 'vulnerable to narcissistic recruitment' (Epstein 1990: 18). Blissful, rapturous states may deceive practitioners into evading certain aspects of their experience; self-abasement may masquerade for spiritual asceticism (Rubin 1996). Emptiness may be confused with incompleteness; 'no-self' with absence of healthy ego functioning (Epstein 1990: 22).

Misunderstandings of the Buddhist view of self-nullification may entail similar pitfalls (Rubin 1996). The doctrine of 'no-self' may appeal to students who feel empty, hollow, or unreal, or who are seeking to avoid autonomy, responsibility, or intimacy. It is possible to cultivate blissful, quiet states of mind and at the same time neglect personal needs and disavow negative and shadow aspects of the personality that, because they are not worked through, are eventually acted out. This may explain, at least in part, the recent eruption of scandals involving sexual misconduct and financial exploitation in many American Buddhist centers (Rubin 1996).

Welwood coined the equally well-known phrase of 'spiritual bypassing,' or 'the tendency to try to avoid or prematurely transcend basic human needs, feelings and developmental tasks' (Welwood 2000: 64). Traditional Eastern parenting practices in infancy and early childhood may be much more conducive to solid object-relations constancy than modern Western parenting practices (Roland 1988; Welwood 2000). This may in part explain why Buddhist meditation traditions presuppose a solid self-structure in the students who initially come to practice (Engler 1984). Given the loss of supportive social networks such as close-knit communities and extended family ties, the neurosis of the nuclear family (in which most American Zen Buddhists have been raised) is inevitably magnified (Welwood 2000). Contemporary Western society does not facilitate the achievement of ordinary developmental tasks, such as obtaining stable, meaningful work, engaging in significant long-term relationships, and belonging to a supportive community (Welwood 2000). It is only understandable that some, if not many, meditation practitioners are tempted to use spiritual practice as a way of avoiding the need to face and work through their personal wounds or distress.

Integrating Zen meditation and psychotherapy

The need for integration

As Buddhism spreads throughout the United States, perhaps its most visible adaptation to Western culture will be through psychology (Kornfield 1993b). Whether Buddhist principles will inform psychotherapy or Western psychotherapy will inform the way Buddhist meditation is practiced in the West and, in this way, become a form of therapy in itself, remains to be seen (Brazier 2000). Much of the current debate on integrating Buddhist meditation and Western psychotherapy emphasizes the importance of Buddhist teachers becoming aware of psychological principles and, conversely, Western therapists becoming cognizant of Buddhist-inspired meditation techniques.

In the last ten or fifteen years, several pleas have been made for an integration between Buddhist meditation and psychotherapy. The more forceful pleas have come from Western Buddhist psychotherapists who are long-standing practitioners of concentration and mindfulness meditation, such as Zen, Vipassana, and Dzogchen-Mahamudra, some of who are meditation instructors as well. Their writings are visible in both Buddhist and psychotherapy journals. Concerned about the tendency in Western teachers and students of Buddhist meditation to ignore their personal wounds, their cry is for Western Buddhist practitioners of meditation to incorporate psychotherapy into their lives (Engler 1984; Kornfield 1993a; 1993b; Rubin 1996; Welwood 2000). If not integration, at least Western Buddhist teachers and students of meditation would do well to take emotional deficiencies that are common in Western society into account (Kornfield as cited in Tworkov 2000). The milder pleas for integration have come from therapists in the West who also practice Buddhist meditation and whose writings are more visible in psychotherapy journals than in Buddhist journals. Convinced of its overall contribution to psychological health, these therapists enthusiastically urge their colleagues and clients to explore meditation and consider using it as an adjunct in therapy (Cooper 1999; Deatherage 1975; Dubin 1991; 1994; Kelly 1996; Kutz et al. 1985; Mikulas 1981; Muzika 1990; Urbanowski and Miller 1996). There is a third group of therapists in the West who feel that the best way of integrating Zen Buddhist and mindfulness meditation into psychotherapy is for therapists to practice meditation themselves and to bring their full presence and attention to the therapy session (Brazier 1995; Epstein 1995; Watson 1996).

From a psychodynamic perspective, the key to integration may lie in revising and giving equal value to the views of the self that psychoanalysis and Buddhism offer respectively (Rubin 1996). Western psychodynamic psychotherapy views the self as a historical, embodied, substantial agent capable of perception, choice, and action. Buddhism views the self as a fluid, changing, moment-by-moment unfolding process.

Traditionally, Western psychodynamic psychotherapy does not acknowledge the influence on consciousness and behavior of episodic, transient, mental states that arise in the present, moment by moment. Nor does it acknowledge non-self-centric modes of human subjectivity, nor transcendent mind states, as conducive to psychological growth (Rubin 1996). Buddhism, on the other hand, lacks a developmental perspective on the formation of the self. Buddhism disregards the role of early childhood events in the shaping of the personality (Engler 1984; Krynicki 1980; Muzika 1990; Rubin 1996). Due to mistaken notions of emptiness and no-self, Buddhism may foster pathological self-denial, which may also lead to another form of self-centeredness. By denying the subject, the Freudian 'return of the repressed' resurfaces in acting out disowned aspects of the self that have not been worked through because, as contents of the mind, they have not been examined (Rubin 1996: 67).

Western psychotherapy can shed light on Buddhism regarding transference, countertransference, and unconscious phenomena. Buddhism can go beyond the limitations of an excessively egocentric concept of self and offer a psychology of non-egocentric modes of being and adaptive, transcendent mind-states (Rubin 1996). While Western psychotherapy explains early human development and the formation of psychopathology, Buddhism describes advanced stages of development and well-being once the basic developmental tasks have been taken care of (Engler 1984; Rubin 1996).

Lacking the cultural supports found in Asian cultures, and because unresolved conflicts and developmental deficiencies often hinder the full integration of spiritual practice into daily life, Westerners might have to engage in psychological work as a preliminary or supplementary practice to spiritual work (Engler 1984; Engler as cited in Cohen 2000; Kornfield 1993a, 1993b; Miller 2001; Rubin 1996; Tart and Deikman 1991; Welwood 2000). Psychotherapy in a spiritual context, practiced by a meditating therapist, may constitute an intermediate step between conventional Western psychotherapy and meditation practice for the client (Welwood 2000). For those who wish to do so, clients and therapists may engage in conventional Western psychotherapy, alongside meditation practice to enhance their synergystic effects (Brazier 1995; Engler as cited in Cohen 2000; Cooper 1999; Kornfield 1993a; 1993b; Miller 2001; Tart and Deikman 1991; Urbanowski and Miller 1996; Watson 1996; Welwood 2000).

Should therapists teach clients Zen meditation?

Supposing the client is interested in and willing to undertake zazen practice, the question arises, who should teach zazen? Because most schools of Buddhism, and especially Zen Buddhism, are traditionally non-proselytist, it is likely that those psychotherapists who engage in zazen as part of their spiritual practice and who embrace the Zen Buddhist world view might feel reluctant to teach zazen to their clients (Brazier 2000). This, however, may not necessarily be the case for those therapists who practice zazen solely to improve their mental and physical health.

Zen meditation can be, and indeed has been, taught as a psychological technique. Finn and Rubin (1999) pose the question whether in doing so the therapist is merely offering a useful behavioral or coping strategy or is engaging in spiritual direction to some degree. In keeping with tradition, Buddhist teachers may not instruct without having undergone extensive training and testing themselves, and without having received formal authorization to teach (Kapleau 1989; Welwood 2000). And yet, procedural packages involving formal zazen instructions for clinical and research purposes have been put together since the 1970s (Shapiro 1976; 1978; Shapiro and Zifferblatt 1976). Today, meditation instructions are available to the public in books, tapes, and interactive media (Finn and Rubin 1999).

Without claiming to be meditation masters, some therapists recommend meditation-derived awareness-developing techniques for their clients. For example, Zen-derived listening meditation (the client 'just listens' to sounds) and breathing meditation (the client follows or counts the breath) are recommended for use both in session and as homework (Wortz 1982). Therapists may prescribe body awareness exercises, and observing the contents of the mind in mindfulness meditation (Mikulas 1981; Muzika 1990; Urbanowski and Miller 1996).

Based on the client's developmental characteristics, detailed models for therapists who wish to teach meditative techniques in psychotherapy have been devised (Kelly 1996). Such techniques may include relaxation, body awareness and slow breathing, imagery and metaphors for internal phenomena, imaging pain, sensing reactions in body areas, finding the inner child and opening to emotional expression, acquiring a better sense of limits and personal space, accepting intuitions and letting go of old perceptions and judgments that have outlived their usefulness (Kelly 1996).

Some Western Buddhist therapists emphasize that psychotherapists should not pretend to be spiritual authorities. By teaching formal meditation practice to their clients, the roles of psychotherapist and meditation teacher may be confused (Watson 1996). Clients may be coached to be mindful in action and daily life, but if they wish formal meditation instruction, therapists should recommend they seek it elsewhere (Kutz et al. 1985; Watson 1996). Some Western Buddhist therapists avoid teaching formal meditation practice, and limit their recommendations in session to coaching clients in watching their symptoms without trying to change their course, and suggesting that they engage in activities that promote groundedness, such as gardening, mindful walking, body awareness exercises, and observation of their surroundings (Brazier 1995).

To teach clients to meditate during a therapy session may well contaminate the transference, in which case assigning meditation as homework might be preferable (Kutz et al. 1985). Introducing meditation procedures to clients in therapy, regardless of its potential efficacy, may reflect transference and countertransference issues that have not been explored and worked through by the therapist (Cooper 1999, Deikman 1982). Such practices may be introduced prematurely and may not necessarily be what the client needs from the therapist at that particular time (Cooper 1999, Deikman 1982).

Other Western Buddhist therapists neither hide nor flaunt the fact that they are meditation practitioners, abstain from prescribing meditation to their clients, yet are open to offering information so they may seek it elsewhere if they are so inclined. Yet other therapists do not even bring up the subject of concentration and mindfulness in session, to the point where their clients are surprised when they find out that their therapist is a meditation practitioner (Coltart as cited in Molino 1998). This raises the Buddhist ethical question of withholding the Dharma. Unless clients know what their therapists' theoretical affiliations are and what influences their clinical approach, how can they make informed choices about their own treatment?

Instead of teaching meditation techniques to clients, some Western Buddhist therapists advocate teaching therapists only. Using centering exercises, focusing on symptoms rather than getting rid of them, and observing symptoms as they arise, are common techniques (Dubin 1991; 1994). In workshops for psychotherapists, meditation teacher Shinzen Young (as cited in Tart 1990) advises therapists to teach meditation only to some, but not all, clients who are ready for meditation and to work in session in meditative states.

Convinced that a Buddhist-informed psychotherapy is implicit in the way the therapist works rather than in the application of techniques, some therapists claim that there is no need for clients to be aware of the Buddhist inspiration behind the psychotherapy or for clients or therapists to embrace Buddhist beliefs (Watson 1996). Other therapists argue that, in order to benefit from them, clients do not need to know they are practicing meditation-derived techniques introduced by the therapist, and advocate adapting and even disguising meditation techniques before prescribing them to clients as part of their treatment (Deatherage 1975). This raises serious ethical questions about the client's right to know what his or her treatment is. Some clients may be wary of practices that are not derived from their own cultural traditions (Kelly 1996), although there seems to be some awareness about introducing only those practices the client feels are compatible with their own belief systems (Muzika 1990; Urbanowski and Miller 1996).

A recent, intense debate has sprouted over the fact that some (usually white, Elite, or Euro-American) Buddhist psychotherapists who are also teachers of meditation engage in dual relationships with their client–students (Simpkinson 2000). Right or wrong, perhaps this recent state of affairs reflects the welding of the meditation teacher to the therapist-as-archetype in Western, and especially American culture (Tart 1990).

Whether therapists decide for or against teaching their clients meditation techniques, psychotherapists whose lifestyle encompasses a long-standing practice of meditation and decide to introduce it into the therapy setting will have sufficient personal experience of its benefits and pitfalls and will be in a better position to determine which clients may or may not benefit from meditation than those therapists who at best have obtained meditation instruction from a weekend seminar and who rarely practice it themselves (Deatherage 1975; Urbanowski and Miller 1996).

Technique or tradition?

Should the client wish to engage in Zen meditation, and should the therapist decide to introduce meditation techniques as part of the therapy process, instruction would best be limited to the basic form of zazen, which is counting the breaths. Zen Buddhist teachers strongly emphasize that more advanced forms of Zen practice such as working on a koan should be undertaken only under the guidance and supervision of a qualified Zen teacher (Kapleau 1989). Nevertheless, there are therapists who are in favor of reading contemporary literary adaptations of koans as a cognitive adjunct to Rational Emotive Behavior Therapy (Kwee and Ellis 1998). This falls short of an aberration of Zen practice and is an instance of carrying the reductionist model too far by divorcing meditation practices from their naturalistic, spiritual context (Shapiro 1994; Walsh 1982).

It is far easier to isolate Zen meditation from its Buddhist context and consider it a technique rather than a component of an integrated practice (Dubs 1987; Preston 1988). Reintroducing the spiritual context of meditation with knowledge of its rich tradition may provide a healthy challenge to the generally unexamined belief systems, values, and cultural assumptions of the scientific community and larger society (Shapiro 1994). Meditation instruction provided by a qualified teacher of meditation may well yield more favorable or at least more genuine results than that provided by a laboratory researcher who, in true reductionist fashion, has isolated the bare bones technique in order to measure, confirm, refute, or predict outcomes.

References

Boucher, S. (1988) *Turning the Wheel: American Women Creating the New Buddhism*, San Francisco: Harper & Row.

Brazier, D. (1995) *Zen Therapy: Transcending the Sorrows of the Human Mind*, New York: John Wiley.

Brazier, D. (2000) 'Buddhist psychotherapy or Buddhism as psychotherapy?', in G. Watson, S. Batchelor and G. Claxton (eds), *The Psychology of Awakening: Buddhism, Science and Our Everyday Lives*, York Beach, ME: Samuel Weiser, 215–24.

Brown, D., and Engler, J. (1980) 'The states of mindfulness meditation: a validation study', *Journal of Transpersonal Psychology* 12: 143–92.

Christensen, A., and Rudnick, S. (1999) 'A glimpse of Zen practice within the realm of countertransference', *The American Journal of Psychoanalysis* 59: 59–69.

Cohen, A. (2000) 'The 1001 forms of self-grasping: an interview with Jack Engler', *What is Enlightenment?* (Spring/Summer): 94–101, 169–71.

Compton, W., and Becker, G. (1983) 'Self-actualization and experience with Zen meditation: is a learning period necessary for meditation?', *Journal of Clinical Psychology* 39: 925–9.

Cooper, P. A. (1999) Buddhist meditation and countertransference: a case study', *The American Journal of Psychoanalysis* 59: 71–85.

Deatherage, G. (1975) 'The clinical use of "mindfulness" meditation techniques in short-term psychotherapy', *Journal of Transpersonal Psychology* 7: 133–43.

Deikman, A. J. (1982) *The Observing Self: Mysticism and Psychotherapy*, Boston: Beacon Press.

Dubin, W. (1991) 'The use of meditative techniques in psychotherapy supervision', *Journal of Transpersonal Psychology* 23: 65–80.

Dubin, W. (1994) 'The use of meditative techniques for teaching dynamic psychology', *Journal of Transpersonal Psychology* 26: 19–36.

Dubs, G. (1987) 'Psycho-spiritual development in Zen Buddhism: a study of resistance in meditation', *Journal of Transpersonal Psychology* 19: 19–86.

Engler, J. (1984) 'Therapeutic aims in psychotherapy and meditation: Developmental stages in the representation of self', *Journal of Transpersonal Psychology* 16: 25–61.

Epstein, M. (1990) 'Psychodynamics of meditation: pitfalls on the spiritual path', *Journal of Transpersonal Psychology* 22: 17–34.

Epstein, M. (1995) *Thoughts Without a Thinker: Psychotherapy from a Buddhist Perspective*, New York: Basic Books.

Epstein, M., and Lieff, J. D. (1981) 'Psychiatric complications of meditation practice', *Journal of Transpersonal Psychology* 13: 137–147.

Fauteux, K. (1987) 'Seeking enlightenment in the East: self-fulfillment or regressive longing?', *Journal of the American Academy of Psychoanalysis* 15: 223–46.

Fields, R. (1992) *How the Swans Came to the Lake: A Narrative History of Buddhism in America*, 3rd edn, Boston: Shambhala.

Fields, R. (1998) 'Divided Dharma: white Buddhists, ethnic Buddhists, and racism', in C. S. Prebish and K. K. Tanaka (eds), *The Faces of Buddhism in America*, Berkeley/Los Angeles: University of California Press, 196–206.

Finn, M., and Rubin, J. (1999) 'Psychotherapy with Buddhists', in P. S. Richards and A. E. Bergin (eds), *Handbook of Psychotherapy and Religious Diversity*, Washington, D.C.: American Psychological Association, 317–40.

Fleischman, P. R. (1999) *Karma and Chaos: New and Collected Essays on Vipassana Meditation*, Seattle, WA: Vipassana Research Publications.

Freud, S. (1912/1964) 'Recommendations to physicians practicing psycho-analysis', in J. Strachey (ed. and trans.), *The Standard Edition of the Complete Psychological Works of Sigmund Freud*, vol. 12, London: Hogarth Press, 111–20.

Goleman, D. (1976) 'Meditation and consciousness: an Asian approach to mental health', *American Journal of Psychotherapy* 1: 41–54.

Gopfert, C. R. (1999) 'Student experiences of betrayal in the Zen Buddhist teacher/student relationship', doctoral dissertation, Palo Alto, CA: Institute of Transpersonal Psychology.

Imamura, R. (1998) 'Buddhist and Western psychotherapies: an Asian American perspective', in C. S. Prebish and K. K. Tanaka (eds), *The Faces of Buddhism in America*, Berkeley/Los Angeles: University of California Press, 228–37.

Kabat-Zinn, J. (1988) 'Compliance with an outpatient stress reduction program: rates and predictors of program completion', *Journal of Behavioral Medicine* 11: 333–52.

Kabat-Zinn, J., Massion, A. O., Kristeller, J., Peterson, G. L., Fletcher, K. E., Pbert, L., Linderking, W. R., and Santorelli, S. F. (1992) 'Effectiveness of a meditation-based stress reduction program in the treatment of anxiety disorder', *American Journal of Psychiatry* 149: 936–43.

Kapleau, P. (1989) *The Three Pillars of Zen*, New York: Doubleday/Anchor.

Kelly, G. (1996) 'Using meditative techniques in psychotherapy', *Journal of Humanistic Psychology* 36: 49–66.

Kornfield, J. (1993a) 'Even experienced meditators have old wounds to heal: combining meditation and psychotherapy', in R. Walsh and F. Vaughan, *Paths beyond Ego: The Transpersonal Vision*, Los Angeles, CA: Tarcher/Perigree, 67–9.

Kornfield, J. (1993b) *A Path with Heart: A Guide through the Perils and Promises of Spiritual Life*, New York: Bantam.

Krynicki, V. E. (1980) 'The double orientation of the ego in the practice of Zen', *The American Journal of Psychoanalysis* 40: 239–48.

Kutz, I., Borysenko, J., and Benson, H. (1985) 'Meditation and psychotherapy: a rationale for the integration of dynamic psychotherapy, the relaxation response, and mindfulness meditation', *American Journal of Psychiatry* 142: 1–8.

Kutz, I., Leserman, J., Dorrington, C., Morrison, C., Borysenko, J., and Benson, H. (1985) 'Meditation as an adjunct to psychotherapy', *Psychotherapy and Psychosomatics* 43: 209–18.

Kwee, M. G. T., and Ellis, A. (1998) 'The interface between rational emotive behavior therapy (REBT) and Zen', *Journal of Rational-Emotive and Cognitive-Behavior Therapy* 16: 5–43.

Lesh, T. V. (1970) 'Zen meditation and the development of empathy in counselors', *Journal of Humanistic Psychology* 10: 39–74.

Mikulas, W. (1981) 'Buddhism and behavior modification', *Psychological Record* 31: 331–42.

Mikulas, W. (1990) 'Mindfulness, self-control, and personal growth', in M. G. T. Kwee (ed.), *Psychotherapy, Meditation and Health*, The Hague: East/West Publications, 154–61.

Miller, M. (2001) 'Zen and psychotherapy: from neutrality, through relationship, to the emptying place', in P. Young-Eisendrath and S. Muramoto (eds), *Awakening and Insight: Buddhism and Psychotherapy East and West*, New York: Routledge.

Molino, A. (1998) 'Slouching towards Buddhism: a conversation with Nina Coltart', in A. Molino (ed.), *The Couch and the Tree: Dialogues in Psychoanalysis and Buddhism*, New York: North Point Press, 170–9.

Muzika, E. (1990) 'Evolution, emptiness and the fantasy of self', *Journal of Humanistic Psychology* 30: 89–108.

Nattier, J. (1998) 'Who is a Buddhist?', in C. S. Prebish and K. K. Tanaka (eds), *The Faces of Buddhism in America*, Berkeley/Los Angeles: University of California Press, 183–95.

Odajnyk, V. W. (1998) 'Zen meditation as a way of individuation and healing', in A. Molino (ed.), *The Couch and the Tree: Dialogues in Psychoanalysis and Buddhism*, New York: North Point Press, 131–41.

Prebish, C. S. (1993) 'Two Buddhisms reconsidered', *Buddhist Studies Review* 10: 187–206.

Prebish, C. S. (1999) *Luminous Passage: The Practice and Study of Buddhism in America*, Berkeley/Los Angeles: University of California Press.

Preston, D. L. (1988) *The Social Organization of Zen Practice: Constructing Transcultural Reality*, New York: Cambridge University Press.

Roland, A. (1988) *In Search of Self in India and Japan: Toward a Cross-Cultural Psychology*, Princeton: Princeton University Press.

Rubin, J. B. (1996) *Psychotherapy and Buddhism: Toward an Integration*, New York: Plenum Press.

Salzburg, S. (1995) *Loving-Kindness: The Revolutionary Art of Happiness*, Boston: Shambhala.

Schuster, R. (1979) 'Empathy and mindfulness', *Journal of Humanistic Psychology* 19: 71–7.

Seager, R. H. (1999) *Buddhism in America*, New York: Columbia University Press.

Shapiro, D. H., Jr. (1976) 'Zen meditation and behavioral self-control strategies applied to a case of generalized anxiety', *Psychologia* 19: 134–8.

Shapiro, D. H., Jr. (1978) 'Instructions for a training package combining formal and informal Zen meditation with behavioral self-control strategies', *Psychologia* 21: 70–6.

Shapiro, D. H., Jr. (1994) 'Examining the content and context of meditation: a challenge for psychology in the areas of stress management, psychotherapy, and religion/values', *Journal of Humanistic Psychology* 34: 101–35.

Shapiro, D. H., Jr. and Giber, D. (1978) 'Meditation and psychotherapeutic effects: self-regulation strategy and altered states of consciousness', *Archives of General Psychiatry* 35: 294–302.

Shapiro, D. H., Jr. and Zifferblatt, S. M. (1976) 'Zen meditation and behavioral self-control: similarities, differences and clinical applications', *American Psychologist* 31: 519–32.

Simpkinson, A. A. (2000) 'Riding two horses', *Tricycle: The Buddhist Review*: 59–61: 112–17.

Speeth, K. R. (1982) 'On psychotherapeutic attention', *Journal of Transpersonal Psychology* 14: 141–60.

Suler, J. (1995) 'In search of the self: Zen Buddhism and psychoanalysis', *Psychoanalytic Review* 82: 407–26.

Suzuki, D. T., Fromm, E., and DeMartino, R. (1960) *Zen Buddhism and Psychoanalysis*, New York: Grove Press.

Tart, C. T. (1990) 'Adapting Eastern spiritual techniques to Western culture: a discussion with Shinzen Young', *Journal of Transpersonal Psychology* 22: 149–65.

Tart, C. T., and Deikman, A. J. (1991) 'Mindfulness, spiritual seeking and psychotherapy', *Journal of Transpersonal Psychology* 23: 29–52.

Tworkov, H. (2000) 'The sure heart's release: an interview with Jack Kornfield', *Tricycle: The Buddhist Review* 9: 37–44.

Urbanowski, F. B., and Miller, J. J. (1996) 'Trauma, psychotherapy, and meditation', *Journal of Transpersonal Psychology* 28: 31–48.

VanderKooi, L. (1997) Buddhist teachers' experience with extreme mental states in western meditators, *Journal of Transpersonal Psychology*, 29: 31–46.

Walsh, R. (1982) 'A model for viewing meditation research', *Journal of Transpersonal Psychology* 14: 69–84.

Watson, G. (1996) *The Resonance of Emptiness: A Buddhist Inspiration for a Contemporary Psychotherapy*, Richmond: Curzon.

Welwood, J. (2000) *The Psychology of Awakening: Buddhism, Psychotherapy, and the Path of Personal and Spiritual Transformation*, Boston: Shambhala.

Wortz, E. (1982) 'Application of awareness methods in psychotherapy', *Journal of Transpersonal Psychology* 14: 61–8.

Young-Eisendrath, P. (forthcoming) 'Transference and transformation in Buddhism and psychoanalysis', in J. D. Safran (ed.), *Buddhism and Psychoanalysis: A Creative Dialogue*, Washington, D.C.: APA.

11

LOCATING BUDDHISM, LOCATING PSYCHOLOGY

Richard K. Payne

Introduction

Just as it is important to understand the cultural assumptions – psychological and religious – of our own society and historical period, it is important to inform our discussion of Buddhism and psychology with a sensitivity to the social, cultural and historical origins of the practices and teachings which are being appropriated, lest our own concerns and preconceptions distort the tradition so greatly that it loses its ability to effect change in us. As I understand it, the Buddhist tradition itself holds that everything that exists, exists as the result of causes and conditions. Throughout this essay, whenever I speak of what Buddhism or the Buddhist tradition holds, the reader is to understand that this is simply shorthand for what I myself understand Buddhism to be. I am not attempting to cloak my own views in the authority of the tradition, but rather simply avoid cluttering up the essay with repeated qualifications.

Existing as the result of causes and conditions, as Buddhism teaches, entails viewing every existing thing in terms of its particular location. This includes self-referentially applying this view to the teachings and practices of Buddhism itself. In my own experience there are three more specific reasons for giving special attention to the social, cultural, and historical location of a religious teaching or practice. As indicated by Geertz's often-quoted definition of religion, both religion and culture have the effect of presenting a particular world view as simply given, natural, just 'the way it is,' and therefore unquestionable. Yet, after having lived in Japan for almost a year and a half, it seems obvious to me that much of what is taken for granted as simply natural is actually conventional, an agreement reached implicitly and without discussion. The amount of culture shock I and my family experienced upon our return to the United States was in fact far greater than when we went to Japan. While we had expected the unfamiliarity of Japan, our sense of alienation when we returned to what was supposed to be home was disconcerting. Attitudes, behavior, dress, everything that we had taken so much for granted now seemed strange and arbitrary.

Second, I have seen how Buddhist teachings can be unintentionally distorted by those who fail to recognize their own assumptions about the character of religion. Assuming, for example, that like Protestantism all religions give primacy to the authority of a text, they give primacy to the texts of Buddhism, even to the extent of compiling for Buddhism a 'Buddhist Bible.' As a textualized tradition, mastery of Buddhism became mastery of the texts which were relocated from Asia to Europe and treated as authoritative sources of doctrine (Trainor 1997: 9–11; Lopez 1995: 283). And third, I feel very strongly that understanding the variety of religious cultures within which Buddhism has existed – India and the other cultures of South and South-east Asia, Tibet, Mongolia, and other Central Asian cultures, and in East Asia the religious cultures of China, Korea, and Japan – is essential to understanding the teachings and practices of Buddhism. A meditative practice such as visualizing the syllable 'A' taught in the Shingon tradition of esoteric Buddhism in Japan only makes sense when understood in the context of Indic conceptions regarding the nature of Sanskrit (Payne 1998).

From my own perspective then to assert without qualification that 'Buddhism is psychology' would simply be anachronistic. This is even true of the school within Buddhism that was most explicitly concerned with developing theories of how the mind works, the Yogacara school. What the Yogacarins were doing is only analogous to what we call psychology. Psychology is our category, not theirs. Given the centrality of understanding how the mind works for the entire Buddhist tradition, there is a significant conceptual overlap between Buddhism and psychology. Thus, it may look to us like it is psychology, but it is important to remember that the similarity arises from the way in which elements are selectively highlighted for comparison. Such selective highlighting necessarily throws the balance of the tradition into shadow, obscuring aspects which may not be conducive to the cozy sense of familiarity created by fitting Buddhism into our own psychological world view.

The inescapable importance of understanding social, cultural, and historical location is clearly exemplified in the terminology used to describe various forms of Buddhism to Western audiences. As is commonly the case for most Americans, I grew up thinking in terms of meditation and ritual as two completely separate categories of activity. The fundamentally Protestant religious culture of America generally dismisses ritual as empty and meaningless. Meditation, however, is positively valued, being found in various contemplative practices of Protestantism. This dichotomy in American religious culture between meditation and ritual, together with the relative valuation of each, goes back to the conflicts of the Reformation, when Protestants called into question the sacramental practices of Catholicism. As such, it is a deep and pervasive assumption in American society, even among those who are not particularly religious. It also explains, at least in part, why Zen, which is described in the West almost exclusively in terms of meditation, has been one of the most successful forms of Buddhism in the West.

That the dichotomy between and the relative values placed on meditation and ritual is a cultural assumption, rather than a universally applicable set of categories, was made clear to me in my work in Japan. In the early 1980s I went to Mount Koya, the main center of study and practice of the Shingon tradition of Vajrayana, or tantric Buddhism. While there I both completed the training and received dharma transmission as a Shingon priest (Japanese: *ajari*; Sanskrit: *acarya*), and conducted research for a doctoral dissertation on Shingon practice (Payne 1991). Like other forms of Vajrayana, Shingon practice is generally described as ritual. However, just as Zen meditation and monastic practices are highly ritualized, so is Shingon ritual deeply meditative. Outside of the Western context, with its cultural assumptions, the dichotomy between meditation and ritual cannot be applied uncritically, i.e. without considering the nuances and values that the terms carry in our own culture. Failing to do so deeply distorts the way in which Buddhism is understood.

It has long been held within Buddhism that the teachings themselves are not timeless, eternal absolutes. The idea that with the passage of time the dharma will decay in three identifiable stages is very widespread. This can be seen as acknowledging that the teachings exist in particular social, cultural, and historical locations, and changes in those locations, even subtle ones, can change the meanings of the teachings. As Faure succinctly puts it, 'Similar teachings and behavior or institutions can acquire a radically different meaning when their intellectual or social context is modified in sometimes hardly visible ways' (Faure 1991: 16).

There is a difficult balance to be achieved between adopting the entirety of a tradition uncritically, and recreating the tradition so completely that it only reflects one's own preconceptions. At the same time that the various forms of Buddhism are informed by the religious cultures of their origin, psychology is also deeply informed by the social norms and values of Western culture (Cushman 1995: 2). It also is not context-free and neutral in the ways in which it structures the discourse by asking the questions that it does.

This last issue is central to the concerns I wish to raise about the discourse. It was noted many years ago in relation to the introduction of Buddhism into China that while the central issues of Indian religious culture are epistemological, the central issues of Chinese religious culture are ontological. The Chinese, therefore, asked ontological questions of the Buddhist tradition, and produced thereby a different form of Buddhism. It is important that there be critical self-reflection on the way in which we ask questions of the tradition. 'The spiritual' and 'the psychological' are not universal categories existing in some metaphysical realm of absolutes. Rather, they are part of the contestations making up the history of Western culture, and therefore entail a large number of implicit assumptions.

For these reasons, my tendency is to strongly highlight the distance between the social, cultural, and historical origins of Buddhist teachings and practices and their present interpretation in the context of our own highly psychologized social and cultural location. However, at the same time I think that there are important ways in which interaction between Buddhism and psychology can be mutually beneficial. The discourse to date can be organized into three different areas: the hermeneutics of understanding Buddhism as psychology, the appropriation of meditation practices, and the problematics of understanding emptiness of the self.

Is Buddhism psychology?: hermeneutic issues

Several authors have described the basic teachings of Buddhism as having psychotherapeutic value. Frequently, the teaching of suffering (*dukkha*), as the result of mistaken expectations of permanent satisfaction, is cited in this regard (Young-Eisendrath 1996: 2, and this collection; Brazier 1995: 19). Another teaching that could be interpreted as psychotherapeutic is the three characteristics. Realizing that all of existence is unsatisfactory, impermanent, and lacking in any essential nature to which one can cling (*dukkha, anitya, anātmaka*) may help those who hold themselves responsible for the failure of their own particular situation to be perfect (Lamotte 1988: 27).

It would seem that being able to engage the teachings and practices of Buddhism, or perhaps of any religion, in such a fashion as to benefit both self and others requires a healthy ego, one that is both strong and flexible. Young-Eisendrath has stated in connection with her approach to psychotherapy, 'The first step in personality development . . . is to come fully into possession of the experience of being an individual subject – the ego complex' (Young-Eisendrath 2000: 433). What is meant by a healthy ego is in need of definition, however. Welwood has pointed out that in general 'Western psychotherapy emphasizes the need for a strong ego, defined in terms of impulse control, self-esteem, and competence in worldly functioning' (Welwood 2000: 35). As a more appropriate definition, however, he suggests that 'we define ego strength as the capacity to function effectively in the world, without being debilitated by inner conflict' (Welwood 2000: 38). As I am using the concept of a strong ego, it also implies a flexibility which allows for change without fragmentation or dissolution.

In some cases, however, the assertion that the Buddhist teachings are therapeutic seems to overlook the need for relatively strong and healthy ego structure that can integrate the teachings and practices. Imamura, for example, dismisses the diagnostic categories of contemporary psychotherapy as simply an instance of Western psychotherapy's tendency to be 'highly judgmental' (Imamura 1998: 231). In place of such diagnostic categories and theoretical understandings of causes and treatments, he seems to be claiming that learning the doctrine of suffering, or simple mindfulness practice alone, will solve all problems. The likelihood that there are those whose psychopathologies are so profound as to make them incapable of benefiting from hearing the teachings or engaging in any kind of meditative practice is not considered.

Although Buddhism claims to address the suffering which is universally true of all human beings, this is not the same as saying that Buddhist practices are all equally appropriate for each and every person. An extreme instance of this is the Indian Buddhist concept of the *icchantika*, those whose actions (karma) have cut them off from any affinity with the Buddhadharma, and who therefore can never achieve full awakening. This idea was rejected in later Mahayana and East Asian Buddhism, being replaced by a teaching of the universality of the potential for full Buddhahood, i.e. the Buddha nature inherent in all living beings (Shih 1990: 159). In the hands of some East Asian Buddhists, such as Shinran and Dogen, this idea was extended to the entirety of the natural world, including the ultimate awakening of trees and grasses. Even the teaching of a universal Buddha nature does not assert, however, that awakening can be attained in any particular lifetime.

The Buddhist tradition can itself be understood to suggest that while the dharma is universal, it may not be equally accessible by all, nor should it be made equally accessible to all. There are no panaceas, and the judgment of a wise physician is needed for the prescription of appropriate remedies. What is medicine for one person may be poison for another. Speaking of esoteric Buddhist practice, Tajima has said that

> It works like medicine, extracting beneficial remedies from the most violent poisons. Just as it is dangerous to give a sharp sword to a small child as a plaything, giving esoteric teachings to those who cannot comprehend will lead them into error, and ultimately injure them. All forms of esotericism condemn individual study by non-initiates and insist on the importance of oral transmission from master to disciple.
>
> (Tajima 1959: 10; my translation)

Another instance of this understanding is found in Buddhaghosa's masterpiece, *The Path of Purification*. In the section on meditation (samadhi) he describes at great length a system for assigning meditation subjects to different practitioners and guiding them in their practice (Buddhaghosa 1975: 104–368). This system can be understood as a diagnostic-prescriptive system employing psychological categories (Payne 2000: 2). It is based on diagnosing which of the three poisons – greed, hatred, and delusion – is predominant in the personality of a practitioner. With this knowledge, the meditation teacher can then prescribe one of the forty different meditation subjects described by Buddhaghosa which will be appropriate for that particular practitioner. Understanding Buddhist teachings and practices as psychotherapeutic requires understanding the Buddhist system within which these exist, not removing them from the contexts within which they originated. Otherwise it is like removing a statue from an altar inside a temple, and placing it on display in a museum or selling it as an exotic piece of artwork.

In addition to interpretations of Buddhism as psychotherapeutic, comparisons between Buddhist conceptions of the mind and psychological theories have been made. Making such comparisons not only necessitates sensitivity to cultural, social, and historical location, but also requires some sense of why the comparison is being made. It is not enough to simply identify similarities and differences. The question also has to be asked, What do the similarities and differences mean? For example, what does it mean that depth psychology and Buddhist thought both have an idea of the unconscious? The foundational consciousness (*ālayavijñāna*) the Yogacara school of Indian Buddhism appears to be very similar to the unconscious. While the Yogacara school developed in medieval Indian Mahayana Buddhism, it influenced both Indo-Tibetan Buddhism and East Asian Buddhism very deeply. Existing Buddhist conceptions of the working of the mind as a structured and structuring sequence of moments of conscious awareness (dharmas) found in what is known as the *abhidharma* were extended by the Yogacara thinkers in order to explain the experienced continuity of consciousness and the workings of karma.

Waldron has made a detailed comparison of the concept of the unconscious found in depth psychology and the idea of the foundational consciousness (Waldron 1988). He both identifies three significant similarities and identifies the specific differences between the two concepts. Waldron's study is a model of principled comparison. By focusing on the classic period of Indian Yogacara (fourth to fifth centuries), his study is limited enough to be able to draw meaningful conclusions. At least equally importantly, he articulates his theoretical basis, i.e. the reason why making such a comparison is meaningful. The point of the comparison for Waldron is that the similarities between the two suggest that both the classic Yogacara thinkers and analytical psychologists are working to explain fundamentally identical aspects of human consciousness, or in Waldron's terminology, they share a common problematic.

In addition to understanding the contextual background, and providing a theoretical basis for making a comparison, it is also necessary to establish that the comparison is being made between two terms that are actually comparable. For example, comparisons between Zen and Jung's psychology, several of which exist in the literature, in most cases serve no useful purpose because the two terms of the comparison are not in fact comparable. Where Jung is one early twentieth-century European psychologist, Zen is a major East Asian Buddhist tradition, extending from early medieval China to contemporary New Jersey. Found in China, Korea, Japan, and today in the West, in feudal and industrialized societies, in a variety of lineages and sub-lineages that in their turn become lineages, Zen is a very diverse whole. Since such a comparison can draw on all kinds of different sources to represent Zen, by picking and choosing, the comparison can be constructed so as to demonstrate entirely opposite conclusions: either Zen and Jung are saying the same thing, or they are saying completely different things. As Ruegg has observed about similar comparisons in the philosophic study of Buddhism, the majority of such studies prove 'to be of rather restricted heuristic value, and methodologically it often turns out to be more problematical and constraining than illuminating' (Ruegg 1995: 154).

Interpreting Buddhism as psychotherapy and comparing the two systems of thought require adequate attention to the social, cultural, and historical origins of both Buddhism and psychology. If comparisons are made between truly comparable items, and the purpose for making a comparison is explicit, then we can expect to learn more about how the mind has been understood to work, and contribute to the further development of both Buddhism and psychology.

Appropriating meditative practices

Although some authors see psychotherapy as a useful preliminary to meditative practice, necessary for some individuals before they can begin 'the true work,' others embrace a view of psychotherapy and meditation as simultaneously complementary to one another. Epstein is one of those who views the relation as a complementary one. Holding that meditation and psychotherapy are distinct, he sees the two as working in a mutually supportive fashion. For Epstein,

> Psychoanalytic psychotherapy tends to lead to experiences that reenact earlier and more formative emotional relationships so that the person's history can be, in effect, *reconstructed*. Buddhist meditation tends to intensify certain ego functions so that the sense of self is at once magnified and deconstructed.
>
> (Epstein 1995: 129)

Another conception of the relation between Buddhism and psychotherapy is to view the two as engaging different aspects of the person. Buddhism is viewed as dealing with the universal aspects of the human condition, while psychotherapy is viewed as dealing with the personal. A difficulty with this view is that the distinction between personal and universal seems obvious and straightforward only in the context of Western thought, heir as it is to Aristotle. Upon examination, however, the distinction is itself based on a number of problematic implicit assumptions. First, Buddhism rejects any essence or universal characteristic as having any existence other than in the particular actually existing entity or person, and therefore the distinction is arbitrary. More subtle, and therefore potentially more distorting, is the uncritical acceptance of the Buddhist tradition's description of the human condition as in fact universal. This fails to acknowledge the constructive role of religion in defining a person's conception of what the human condition is and, therefore, the way in which that person then conceives of his/her own situation. The universality of suffering and its cause is itself a claim made by Buddhism that creates a particular view of one's own situation, and at the same time offers a solution to that situation.

Addressing the genre of apocalyptic writing, Thompson has pointed out that

> People discover the crisis dimensions of their existence by reading an apocalypse. An apocalypse thus functions in a social situation not only to bring comfort, hope, perseverance, and the like but also to cause people to see their situation as one in which such functions are needed and appropriate. An apocalypse can create the perception that a situation is one of crisis and then offer hope, assurance, and support for faithful behavior in dealing with the crisis.
>
> (Thompson 1990: 28)

In the same way, the teachings of Buddhism are not simply a universally applicable description of the human condition, despite their own claim to be that. They are, rather, a view of the human condition as problematic in a particular fashion, while at the same time offering solutions to the particular form that the problems take when understood in the terms established by the view itself. This shift in self-concept is, however, exactly what makes the Buddhist teachings and practices psychotherapeutically effective. It is exactly this shift – conceptually, emotionally, experientially – which is the goal.

Moving even beyond the view of meditation and psychotherapy as complementing one another is Miyuki's approach which smoothly integrates the two into a psychotherapeutic whole that makes no distinction between the personal and universal. Miyuki's case vignette concerns a middle-aged, male client from Japan, who sought assistance with his depression. In addition to being culturally Japanese, the client was also a Judo practitioner and, so, already familiar with some of the teachings of Buddhism and receptive to Buddhist practice. The client claimed never to dream, yet to his own surprise remembered a dream image and brought it to the therapy (Miyuki 1977: 156). Thus, the situation with this particular client allowed Miyuki to combine seated meditation, dream analysis, free association, and amplification of the cultural symbolism.

With this client, who did not remember dreams, it seems that the meditation was essential to opening up a relation between the ego and the Self. Here there was no distinction between personal and universal. The universal – suffering and its resolution – are exactly the personal. They have no other existence. Having already established meditation as part of the therapeutic process, Miyuki suggested to the client to meditate on the dream image as one would a koan.

Psychologically speaking, by focussing on a *koan* one can create a vacuity in the consciousness, thus the consciousness is wide open to the emergence of the contents of the unconscious, and this results in the activation of what can be called an altered state of consciousness. . . . Zen sitting can, therefore, be understood as a form of the transcendent function as it facilitates the transition from one psychological condition to another.

(Miyuki 1977: 160–1)

Miyuki's psychological interpretation of koan practice is reminiscent of the idea that one does not need to depend upon the traditions of koan practice codified in the koan collections, and institutionalized in Zen monasteries. Rather, it is life itself that presents each person with their own koan. However, according to Foulk, the 'idea that "anything can serve as a koan" . . . is a modern development; there is scarcely any precedent for it in the classical literature of Ch'an, Sŏn, and Zen' (Foulk 2000: 26). Not only is Miyuki's interpretation of the koan psychological, but it is also based on the interpretation of koan practice promoted by Suzuki and his followers. Suzuki represented Zen to the West in a version that was deeply imbued with Romanticism. In this interpretation of koans they are paradoxes that force the mind beyond the constraints of reason. Because Suzuki was so widely influential in molding the Western conception of Zen, this interpretation of the koan is commonly accepted as the only one. However, the image of Zen, and of koan practice, presented by Suzuki and the other members of the Kyoto School, including Abe, must be understood against the background of their own historical situation. Attempting to defend Zen from attacks by the modernizing and Westernizing forces of Meiji Japan, they constructed an interpretation of Zen that made it congruent with the then-modern Western religious philosophies of James and Otto (Sharf 1993; 1994; 1995).

Even with these reservations and considerations regarding Miyuki's use of the concept of the koan, we need also to note that his integrated approach combining meditation and psychotherapy appears, upon his report, to have been successful. His client moved through the impasse in his life that was causing the depression, and was able to develop a new life for himself, one that was more satisfying because it was more his own, rather than the fulfillment of social and familial expectations.

In addition to using meditation practice for the benefit of clients, several authors have discussed meditation as a useful mental training for psychotherapists. In order to do their work, psychotherapists need the ability to attend closely to what the client both says and doesn't say, and also to their own reactions without being reactionary. Epstein has traced this conception of the mental state of the psychotherapist back to Freud, who recommends an 'evenly suspended attention.' From this mental stance, the analyst suspends critical judgments, while attending impartially to all of the psychic content of dreams, fantasies, and free associations. Epstein sees this as a type of 'beginning meditation' (Epstein 1995: 114). Similarly, Rosenbaum recommends bringing meditative practices into the daily routines of a psychotherapy practice. Breathing, relaxing mind and body, allows the psychotherapist to 'focus on the immediate experience of the moment,' setting aside thoughts of previous sessions and the psychotherapist's own personal concerns (Rosenbaum 1999: 12).

In this collection of essays Young-Eisendrath discusses the need for the psychotherapist to hold to this kind of non-judgmental attention in terms of the transference. The psychotherapist is the recipient of 'sexual, aggressive, or other frightening feelings' which need to be explored rather than rejected or defended against (Young-Eisendrath this collection). Also in this collection, Heynekamp discusses how the practice of Zen meditation has improved her skills as a psychotherapist (Heynekamp this collection).

However, one of the possible dangers of appropriating meditative practices, either as psychotherapeutic techniques or as practices supportive of the psychotherapist, is removing meditation from its intellectual and religious context, and treating it simply as a kind of psycho-technology. It is characteristic of American society to treat technologies as value neutral and context free. This allows for the export of not only such concrete technologies as telecommunications and computers, but also such things as accounting procedures and standards of taxation, without considering or taking any responsibility for the societal and cultural impacts that such technologies will have.

In the context of such a cultural attitude about technology, it may be all too easy to think that one can treat the meditative practices of Buddhism as kinds of technologies which can be divorced from the belief systems that support the practices. It is not the goal of Buddhism to control pain or psoriasis (de Silva 1997: 68). This may be an effect of mindfulness or other meditation practices, a kind of coincidental consequence. But this and other admittedly beneficial consequences may also result from the practice of Transcendental Meditation or Christian contemplation. If mindfulness practice is divorced from the goal of nirvana, is it still Buddhism? Similarly, one may ask: If seated meditation is practiced in the context of a belief in an immortal soul, rather than in the context of the teaching of the emptiness of the self, is it still Zen?

Problematics of the empty self

Central to Buddhism as I understand it is the concept of emptiness and the assertion that the self is empty. In this usage, both 'emptiness' and 'self' are technical terms with very specific meanings. Unlike its use in psychology, 'self' here refers to the idea of an essence – something eternal, absolute, unchanging, permanent – which gives existing things their identity as some particular kind of thing. Familiar to us in the West from the works of Plato, as well as the even more influential though less well known Neoplatonists, this concept is also foundational to much of Indian thought. It is in its rejection of essences that Buddhism makes a radical break from the rest of the religious culture of India, and continues to offer a radical challenge to our own conceptions of the world. Despite much confusion about the matter, emptiness of the self does not refer to non-existence of the personality, but rather to the absence of any essence from each and every thing that exists. In other words, it means exactly the same thing as the teachings of impermanence and interdependence. As Nagarjuna, founder of the Madhyamika school, says

> Whatever is dependently co-arisen
> That is explained to be emptiness.
> That, being a dependent designation,
> Is itself the middle way.
>
> Something that is not dependently arisen,
> Such a thing does not exist.
> Therefore a nonempty thing
> Does not exist.
> (24.18, 19; Garfield 1995: 69)

Despite Nagarjuna's clarity, some authors in the area of Buddhism and psychology speak of 'the experience of emptiness,' by which they mean the feelings of loss or sorrow that arise when something that one loves or identifies with proves to be impermanent. For example, Gunn opens his study of Dogen, Merton, and Jung by saying:

> Whether it is an experience of loss of things outside oneself, as depicted in the story of Job, or an inner experience of having no purpose, or even self, or of life lacking any meaning of satisfaction, the experience of emptiness most commonly thought of is an experience of being without, of not having: not having answers, not having property, not having love or power or hope.
> (Gunn 2000: 1)

Such feelings may be short, light, and easily forgotten, or they may lead to profound depression, ennui, or an *abaissement du niveau mental* (Jung 1971: 451, 765). But while all of these result from the fact of impermanence or emptiness, they are emotional responses which are being experienced. This is different from the meaning of emptiness as it is used in Buddhist philosophy, the absence of any permanent, eternal, absolute, or unchanging essence in either things or people. There is no such thing as emptiness which may itself

be experienced. One cannot experience an absence of something. (It is important to note that in some forms of Buddhism there is discussion of direct,
intuitive comprehension of emptiness, but that this is said to occur only in
very advanced, subtle meditative states, and is something very different from
the emotional experiences Gunn identifies.) Speaking of the 'experience of
emptiness' creates the danger of reifying emptiness as something that can be
experienced. It is in order to avoid just this reification of emptiness that
Madhyamika asserts the emptiness of emptiness.

Related to Gunn's use of the idea of experiencing emptiness is the very difficult issue of the epistemological status of experience (Pickering 1997: xii;
Varela et al. 1991: 15–33; Petitot et al. 1999: 1). Certainly one of the ideas
widely held in religious studies and now becoming increasingly an issue in
psychology is the assertion that experience is irreducible and, therefore, an
unquestionable source of valid knowledge. Sometimes this argument is limited to what is called religious experience, which is defined as experience of
the transcendent absolute, but this simply creates a circular argument.

This way of thinking about particular kinds of experience as inherently
self-validating enters contemporary American religious studies from the
Romantic emphasis on the irreducible character of experience as a defense of
religion (McCutcheon 1997: 60). By analogy with biblical fundamentalism,
this might be called 'experience fundamentalism'. Recent philosophy of religion has given this view a renewed vitality as an epistemological proof for the
existence of God. Not only is this doctrinally problematic for Buddhism,
which is atheistic, but there are philosophical problems with the notion of an
epistemology based on irreducible experiences. The teaching of interdependence asserts that everything that exists is the result of causes and conditions,
and that when those causes and conditions change, then existing things will
change as well. Therefore, neither experience nor valid knowledge can be
irreducible, i.e. they are empty of any permanent, eternal, absolute, unchanging essence. The value of experience in Buddhist practice and philosophy, and
in the interaction with psychology, cannot simply depend upon a kind of
experience fundamentalism, any more than it can depend upon a belief in
substantive essences or materialism. As Young-Eisendrath and Hall have
expressed it:

> the phenomenal experience of an emotion-laden image depends on
> the context in which it arises, just as other images depend on the
> intersubjective world in which they arise. From a Buddhist point of
> view, images that arise in core emotional states are 'real' as much as
> the phenomenal world is real. Buddhists do not privilege the mater-
> ial world as the generator of phenomena. They take the position
> that all phenomena are dependent on a context for their substantia-
> tion and leave it at that.
>
> (Young-Eisendrath and Hall 1991: 167)

Conclusion

In my work, including preparing future Buddhist ministers to provide counseling to their sangha members, I have seen how Buddhist teachings and practices are not simply antique curiosities. Rather, they are psychologically relevant for individuals struggling with their own present difficulties. As a living intellectual tradition, Buddhist thought needs to both be accurate in interpreting its teachings and practices in psychological terms, and reflect on the value of psychological theories and psychotherapeutic practices. For its part, psychology can also expand the range of human experience it considers, and test its theories against the question of whether they can be applied cross-culturally. We cannot predict, nor should we prejudge the possible outcomes of this interaction.

However, we can know that the value of the interaction will be limited by whether or not adequate attention is paid to the social, cultural, and historical locations of both Buddhism and psychology. The discourse on the relation between Buddhism and psychology is basically an interpretive project, and all interpretation references the cultural, social, and historical concerns and preconceptions of the interpreter. For contemporary Westerners, the question of Buddhism and psychology is an attempt to establish a relation between our own present concerns and preconceptions and the teachings and practices of the tradition. We need to understand the tradition in ways that are relevant to ourselves, and at the same time avoid simply seeing ourselves in the mirror image of the exotic other. In this fashion we can find our own middle path.

References

Brazier, David (1995) *Zen Therapy: Transcending the Sorrows of the Human Mind*, New York: Wiley.

Buddhaghosa (1975, reprint 1999) *The Path of Purification* (Visuddhimagga), Seattle: BPS Pariyatti Editions.

Campbell, Donald T (1996) 'Can we overcome worldview incommensurability/relativity in trying to understand the other?', in Richard Jessor, Anne Colby, and Richard Shweder (eds), *Ethnography and Human Development: Context and Meaning in Social Inquiry*, Chicago: University of Chicago Press.

Corbett, Lionel (1996) *The Religious Function of the Psyche*, London and New York: Routledge.

Cushman, Philip (1995) *Constructing the Self, Constructing America: A Cultural History of Psychotherapy*, Reading, MA: Addison Wesley.

de Silva, Padmal (1997) 'Buddhist psychology: some basic concepts and applications', in John Pickering (ed.), *The Authority of Experience: Essays on Buddhism and Psychology*, Richmond: Curzon Press.

Epstein, Mark (1995) *Thoughts without a Thinker*, New York: Basic Books.

Faure, Bernard (1991) *The Rhetoric of Immediacy: A Cultural Critique of Chan/Zen Buddhism*, Princeton: Princeton University Press.

Foulk, T. Griffith (2000) 'The form and function of koan literature: a historical overview', in Steven Heine and Dale S. Wright (eds), *The Kōan: Texts and Contexts in Zen Buddhism*, New York and Oxford: Oxford University Press.

Garfield, Jay L. (trans.) (1995) *The Fundamental Wisdom of the Middle Way: Nāgārjuna's Mūlamadhyamakārikā*, Oxford: Oxford University Press.

Gunn, Robert Jingen (2000) *Journeys into Emptiness: Dogen, Merton, Jung and the Quest for Transformation*, New York: Paulist Press.

Imamura, Ryo (1998) 'Buddhist and Western psychologies: An Asian American perspective', in Charles S. Prebish and Kenneth K. Tanaka (eds), *The Faces of Buddhism in America*, Berkeley, Los Angeles and London: University of California Press.

Jung, C. G. (1971) *Psychological Types*, Princeton: Princeton University Press.

Lamotte, Étienne (1988) *History of Indian Buddhism from the Origins to the Śaka Era*, Louvain-la-Neuve: Institut Orientaliste, Université Catholique de Louvain.

Lopez, Donald S., Jr. (1995) 'Foreigner at the lama's feet', in Donald S. Lopez, Jr. (ed.), *Curators of the Buddha: The Study of Buddhism under Colonialism*, Chicago and London: University of Chicago Press.

McCutcheon, Russell T. (1997) *Manufacturing Religion: The Discourse on Sui Generis Religion and the Politics of Nostalgia*, New York and Oxford: Oxford University Press.

Miyuki, Mokusen (1977) 'The psychodynamics of Buddhist meditation: a Jungian perspective', *The Eastern Buddhist*.

Patton, Kimerley C. and Benjamin C. Ray (eds) (2000) *A Magic Still Dwells: Comparative Religion in the Postmodern Age*, Berkeley: University of California Press.

Payne, Richard K. (1991) *Tantric Ritual of Japan: Feeding the Gods, The Shingon Fire Ritual*, New Delhi: International Academy of Indian Culture and Aditya Prakashan.

Payne, Richard K. (1998) 'Ajikan: ritual and meditation in the Shingon tradition', in Richard K. Payne (ed.), *Re-Visioning 'Kamakura' Buddhism*, Honolulu: University of Hawaii Press.

Payne, Richard K. (2000) 'Meditation as therapeutic intervention in Buddhaghosa's *Vissudhimagga*', lecture given at the Institute of Buddhist Studies, Berkeley, 13 September.

Petitot, Jean, Francisco J. Varela, Bernard Pachoud, and Jean-Michel Roy (eds) (1999) *Naturalizing Phenomenology: Issues in Contemporary Phenomenology and Cognitive Science*, Stanford: Stanford University Press.

Pickering, John (1997) 'Foreword', in John Pickering (ed.), *The Authority of Experience: Essays on Buddhism and Psychology*, Richmond, Surrey: Curzon Press.

Rosenbaum, Robert (1999) *Zen and the Heart of Psychotherapy*, Philadelphia: Brunner/Mazel.

Ruegg, D. Seyfort (1995) 'Some reflections on the place of philosophy in the study of Buddhism', *Journal of the International Association of Buddhist Studies*.

Sharf, Robert H. (1993) 'The Zen of Japanese nationalism', *History of Religions*, reprinted with postscript in Donald S. Lopez, Jr. (ed.) (1995) *Curators of the Buddha: The Study of Buddhism under Colonialism*, Chicago: University of Chicago Press.

Sharf, Robert H. (1994) 'Whose Zen? Zen nationalism revisited', in James W. Heisig and John C. Maraldo (eds), *Rude Awakenings: Zen, the Kyoto School, and the Question of Nationalism*, Honolulu: University of Hawaii Press.

Sharf, Robert H. (1995) 'Buddhist modernism and the rhetoric of meditative experience', *Numen*.

Shih, Heng-ching (1990) 'T'ien-T'ai Chih-I's theory of Buddha nature: a realistic and humanistic understanding of the Buddha', in Paul J. Griffiths and John P. Keenan (eds), *Buddha Nature: A Festschrift in Honor of Minoru Kiyota*, Reno, NV: Buddhist Books International.

Tajima, Ryūjun (1959) *Les Deux Grands Maṇḍalas et la Doctrine de l'Esoterisme Shingon*, Tokyo: Maison Franco-Japonaise; and Paris: Presses Universitaires de France.

Thompson, Leonard L. (1990) *The Book of Revelation: Apocalypse and Empire*, New York and Oxford: Oxford University Press.

Trainor, Kevin (1997) *Relics, Ritual, and Representation in Buddhism: Rematerializing the Sri Lankan Theravada Tradition*, Cambridge: Cambridge University Press.

Varela, Francisco J., Evan Thompson, and Eleanor Rosch (1991) *The Embodied Mind: Cognitive Science and Human Experience*, Cambridge, MA, and London: MIT Press.

Waldron, William S. (1988) 'A comparison of the Ālayavijñāna with Freud's and Jung's theories of the unconscious', *Shin Buddhist Comprehensive Research Institute Annual Memoirs*.

Welwood, John (2000) *Toward a Psychology of Awakening: Buddhism, Psychotherapy, and the Path of Personal and Spiritual Transformation*, Boston and London: Shambhala.

Young-Eisendrath, Polly (1996) *The Resilient Spirit: Transforming Suffering into Insight and Renewal*, Reading, MA: Perseus Books.

Young-Eisendrath, Polly (2000) 'Self and transcendence: a postmodern approach to analytical psychology in practice', *Psychoanalytic Dialogues*.

Young-Eisendrath, Polly, and James A. Hall (1991) *Jung's Self-Psychology: A Constructivist Approach*, New York and London: Guilford Press.

12

BUDDHISM AND PSYCHOTHERAPY IN THE WEST

Nishitani and Dialectical Behavior Therapy

Christa W. Anbeek and Peter A. de Groot

The question with which this paper deals is as follows: How can we compare different world views which originate in different contexts? Our reason for trying to clarify this question is the growing amount of literature in which Buddhism and psychotherapy are placed alongside each other. In these studies different contexts and historical backgrounds are not always or only superficially taken into consideration. This results in unclear treatments. Terms and concepts from originally very different backgrounds and meanings are taken as referring to similar phenomena, without making clear if (and how) they do refer to the same matter.[1] In this paper we focus especially on differences between Buddhism and psychotherapy or, more generally, religion and psychotherapy. Once the difference has been made clear, we will discuss which similarities exist and on which points we can work towards fruitful integration.

We will start by giving some definitions. Then we will introduce the metaphor of 'path' as a helpful metaphor in comparing Buddhism and psychotherapy. Next, we will show how this metaphor of 'a pathway' is very effective in analyzing and clarifying the Buddhist path as found in the work of the Kyoto School philosopher Nishitani (1900–91). Nishitani throws light on the modern human condition by means of insights from Zen Buddhism. He is convinced that in this way a source can be indicated that might be of crucial importance to finding new meaning within modern life. Nishitani can be seen as a modern voice that tries to reformulate Buddhist wisdom about the meaning of human life.

Next we will use the metaphor of 'path' to analyze the therapeutic path of dialectical behavior developed by Marsha Linehan. This therapy is a result of an integration of her expertise in behavioral therapy and her experience as a Zen student. Buddhist mindfulness exercises are used as techniques in this form of therapy. Thus, parts of the Buddhist path are integrated into this therapeutic path.[2] Finally, we will try to show differences and similarities between a Buddhist path and a psychotherapeutic path and draw some conclusions.

187

Some definitions

We will now provide some definitions and thus try to clarify our subject of research. Our first thesis is that Buddhism and psychotherapy are representative of two systems of a different order; if we do not realize this, all comparisons will end up in a confusing chaos. Buddhism belongs to the field of *religious–philosophical meaning systems*, whereas psychotherapy belongs to the field of *psychological–medical treatment* of distressing symptoms.

A *religious or philosophical meaning system* helps people give meaning to the different experiences they go through during their lives. At its most fundamental level, a meaning system deals with questions like: Why am I here? Where do I come from? What is life for? What is good? What is evil? How do I live a good life? Why do I have to die?[3] A religious or philosophical meaning system gives perspectives on the fundamental questions of human existence. These perspectives are not only (and not in the first place) presented on an intellectual level but also, and even more importantly, on an experiential and practical level. They teach people not only how to *see* but also how to *live* life properly.

One of the problems of the contemporary era is that there is no longer any religious meaning system that is commonly accepted. More than ever, people have to find their own way in dealing with the fundamental questions of life and death. On the one hand, this is an inspiring situation which opens up new possibilities – thus, for example, many people in the West feel inspired by traditionally Eastern answers to fundamental questions. On the other hand, in many cases it is too immense a task for an individual to perform. People are dependent upon others in giving meaning to their lives. We do not create meaning by ourselves but commit ourselves to a meaning system which is presented by a surrounding community or a tradition (Van Baal 1981). In modern society many complain of the lack of meaning that they experience, resulting in feelings like alienation, fear, isolation, lack of moral guiding principles, and increase in violence.[4]

Psychotherapy belongs to the field of *psychological–medical treatment*. It is a relatively young branch of scientific research and the application of this research to human illness. Psychotherapy is the systematic use of human relationships for the therapeutic purposes of alleviating emotional distress by effecting enduring changes in a patient's thinking, feeling, and behavior. 'Psychotherapy' is a general term covering the entire spectrum of psychological treatment methods. Although there are many different types of psychotherapy, the mutual engagement of the patient and the psychotherapist both cognitively and emotionally is the foundation for effective psychotherapy (Strupp 1986).

If we compare the description of a religious–philosophical meaning system and psychotherapy we can already see a striking difference. The starting point of a religious meaning system is the fundamental questions of life and death.

The starting point of psychotherapy is psychological distress which hinders an individual or a relational system from functioning well in social or personal life. A second difference is also apparent. Psychotherapy, as a result of modern scientific development, is bound to live up to scientific standards (basing its methods on evidence). The results should be in accordance with an objective standard. Religious meaning systems are not products of scientific research. Although some insights of religions and science do converge, it is not necessarily expected that they will or must converge.

The metaphor of the path

In order to compare religious meaning systems and psychotherapy we will introduce the metaphor of 'path.' In the introduction to *Paths to Liberation*, Buswell and Gimello point to the clarifying potential of the concept *marga* or 'path' with respect to cross-cultural studies of religions (1992: 2). They mention various advantages. Using the path metaphor makes clear that religion is seen as a system of practice and performance, as opposed to a system of concepts and ideas. Religion is not a collection of concepts and beliefs but the existential embodiment of truth, which can be realized by walking the path. This metaphor also directs attention to a general pattern of discipline encompassing both the whole of life of the individual adherent and the corporate life of the community, rather than to the isolated effects of specific religious practices (Buswell and Gimello 1992: 3–4).

As a summary of an existential embodiment of truth, the 'path' has several characteristics. The path has a *starting point*. A certain situation is described and will be transformed in the end. The path has a *goal*: the ultimate transformation of the starting point. Compared to the starting point this goal is a situation of well-being. The path is characterized by a *process* of movement along the way. It is dynamic, not static. In this movement *different phases* are described. The movement along the path is stimulated by *guiding rules and techniques*. The path is supported by an *underlying principle*.

We are going to apply the metaphor of the path to both a Buddhist world view and a psychotherapy. By doing this we hope to gain insight into differences and similarities.

The Buddhist path

If we try to make a kind of general summary of the Buddhist path, we end up with something like the following.

Starting point. In the traditional canonical descriptions of the Four Truths, the first truth is *dukkha* (usually translated as suffering). It encompasses all human negative experiences – everything that hinders happiness. Three different forms of *dukkha* are mentioned: first, physical pain, i.e. being born, illness, death; second, emotional pain, i.e. being united with things that one dislikes and separated from what one likes; third, existential pain, i.e. trying to grasp something which is transient and impermanent creates suffering (First Sermon of Benares, *Mahavagga* I.6.17–22).

Goal. The goal of the path is the cessation of *dukkha* – the extinction of suffering. For the most part, the goal is described as beyond reason and beyond description – the highest bliss, the opposite of *dukkha*.

Guiding rules and techniques. As guiding rules, techniques, and different phases on the way, many things can be mentioned. One of the earliest and simplest statements concerns the so-called three trainings. The practitioner is instructed to begin the pursuit of liberation by cultivating *sila*, the practice of basic moral rules. This practice aims at purifying mental, psychological, and somatic impulses that initiate action. The second training is the growth of *samadhi*, concentration. Mindfulness is the anticipation of wise insight, *prajna*, the third training. This insight is the result of a thorough investigation of the world and the self. In the Noble Eightfold Path we find a description of the three trainings. One important aspect of guiding rules and techniques is the master–student relationship. The student is taught by the master how not to become stuck at one spot on the way.

Underlying principle. The underlying principle which supports the whole path as a crucial pillar is *faith*, i.e. faith in the Buddha Way, faith that the Buddha announced a way to the end of suffering, which he himself traveled and which others can travel as well.[5]

The psychotherapeutic path

A rough sketch of a psychotherapeutic path would look like this:

Starting point. The starting point of psychotherapy is suffering, emotional or psychological distress. This suffering creates unhappiness and hinders a person from functioning well in private, social, and/or professional life.

Goal. The goal of psychotherapy is decrease of suffering or to make suffering manageable. The goal is not explicitly the end of suffering. In this context Freud's expression has become famous: 'But you will be able to convince yourself that much will be gained if we succeed in transforming your hysterical misery into common unhappiness. With a mental life that has been restored to health you will be better armed against unhappiness' (Freud 1986: 305). Sometimes a distinction is made between neurotic suffering and existential suffering. Neurotic suffering is characterized by abnormalities of emotions, behavior, and thought that all originate in unconscious psychological conflicts.[6] Existential suffering is suffering from the conditions of life: old age, illness, and death. The goal of psychotherapy is to expose neurotic suffering until it becomes existential suffering.

Guiding rules and techniques. Many different techniques are used, depending on the kind of therapy. A common factor that appears in every psychotherapy is the relationship between client and therapist. The therapist has to accept the client's subjective experience of emotional pain and conflict.

Underlying principle. The underlying principle depends on the therapy which is used. Often this principle consists of a theory in which the core idea of the therapy is expressed. A fundamental insight about human life, human nature, or human behavior is expressed. This insight determines the direction in which healing is sought. It also has an influence on the techniques that are used.

Most contemporary psychotherapeutic systems utilize some of Freud's fundamental principles, though they affix their own labels to them. The underlying principle for all psychotherapies is a *meaningful relationship* between the therapist as helper and the client as being helped. This aspect of the relationship has been called the *therapeutic or working alliance* (Zetzel 1956; Greenson 1967). Another contextual underlying principle behind all therapeutic paths is that the results have to be evident.

In the next two paragraphs we will describe in more detail a Buddhist path, as found in the work of Nishitani, and a psychotherapeutic path, as found in Dialectical Behavior therapy for borderline personality disorders. In describing the work of Nishitani and Linehan (the founder of the therapy), we will keep to the structure of the path. We will thus describe the following aspects: starting point, different phases, goal, guiding rules and techniques, and underlying principles.

The Buddhist path in Nishitani

Starting point

The starting point of the path in Nishitani can be indicated in his description of how life, which is experienced as meaningful, can be shattered and broken into a meaningless, fearful, doubting mass of existence. In his work *Religion and Nothingness*, Nishitani shows in different ways how in modern life nihility can loom up, draining everything of meaning. One way Nishitani elaborates on how this crisis works is by analyzing the way people ordinarily live their lives:

> Ordinarily people see their lives as more or less ordered – organized according to usefulness and functionality of things. We want to

know what everything is for, something to be eaten, something to drink, etc. This division of life on the basis of the function of things happens constantly and most of human life is limited to this level of existence.

(Nishitani 1982: 1)

In this process the person sees herself or himself as the center and aim of all things. The objects outside ourselves are held as real, but in fact we have no real contact with objects and people. In that sphere of consciousness where we normally dwell we are separated from things. There is an interior world (I) and an exterior world (objects). This separation is functional and enables the person to act but at the same time places the person in opposition to things and prevents real contact. Experienced as most real is the *I* in the center of the world. Each *I* is experienced as independent, but at the same time it is imprisoned in itself – isolated and endlessly mirroring itself (Nishitani 1982: 14).

Nishitani indicates that the position of self-consciousness is the position with *I* as the middle point, and looking from this position it cannot be seen that our existence coincides with non-existence. Death and nothingness are fundamental problems for the person living in the ordinarily meaningful world, because, viewed from the position of *I*, death and nothingness do not exist.

But death and nothingness are realities and by their reality the meaningful world with the absolute *I* in the center can be turned upside-down and lose its matter-of-factness. If a person is existentially confronted by the inevitability of death, his whole meaningful world falls apart, all things lose their certainty and importance and become unreal (Nishitani 1982: 7).[7]

Questions such as 'Why was I ever born?' and 'Where have I come from and where am I going?' play a role. These questions are not intellectual questions which can be answered with speculative thinking. They open an emptiness in our being which is not so easily reasoned away (Nishitani 1982: 3). We become aware of the limits of our existence (an awareness which was absent from the meaningful world where each *I* was without limitation). The awareness of limitation shatters that self-consciousness which never doubts the existence of the self. The being of the self is challenged and becomes one huge question; existence turns into a problem (Nishitani 1982: 16).

Continuing on the way; different phases

The starting point of the path by Nishitani is the confrontation with death and nihility, which shatters the central position of the *I* in the middle of the meaningful world. The possibility of not-I creates a doubt which undermines every certainty. The next phase which Nishitani describes is a doubt that increases to the point where the whole person collapses.

DOUBT, GREAT DOUBT

Nishitani describes how in this process nihility becomes apparent as the hidden reality in everything, both in the person and in all things. This casts everything into doubt. No answers can be found. Finally, the doubt grows to the point where there is nothing at all that is not doubted. Everything becomes subject to doubt. The person becomes doubt through and through. This doubt emerges out of the ground of self-being and of all things. When this doubt appears it is unavoidable and the person is at a loss as to what to do about it.

Nishitani indicates that Zen Buddhism speaks of this radical doubt and calls it the *Great Death*:

> Zen refers to radical doubt as the Great Death. The Great Doubt comes to light from the ground of our existence only when we press our doubts (What am I? Why do I exist?) to their limits as conscious acts of the doubting self. The Great Doubt represents not only the apex of the doubting self but also the point of its 'passing away' and ceasing to be 'self'.
>
> (Nishitani 1982: 21)

A result of this profound experience of doubt is the fading away of the 'person-centered' way of being in the world. The person-centered way of being is challenged by the exposure of the nothingness behind the person. This causes an existential reversal; existence as it was is turned upside-down. The self as middle point and the way of being and knowing which depends on this self fall away (Nishitani 1982: 122).

> In this process we lose our grip on things and our knowledge of reality. The unity of things (being of things) falls apart and what remains is a bottomless nihility which is reflected in everything around us. A world collapses. It does not matter at all how gigantic the mountain was or how healthy the man or how stable the personality: the whole of existence is challenged.
>
> (Nishitani 1982: 122)

Nothing is clear anymore. Everything becomes uncertain and unknown. The other, too, with whom we have become friends and whom we trust, disappears out of sight. We no more know whence our closest friend comes and whither he is going than we know where we ourselves come from and where we are headed. At this home-ground, a friend remains originally and essentially a stranger, an 'unknown' (Nishitani 1982: 100). The experience of nothingness places the person in an impossible, unbearable position.

Nishitani begins to describe the next phase by recommending the phase of doubt. Confusion and doubt, resulting from the confrontation with death and nihility, are experienced as painful and fearful, but in fact the doubt is a sign of growing clarity. Confusion is placed in the context of insight, insight into life which is not separated from death.

GROWING INSIGHT

Nishitani emphasizes that in the experience of doubt a light begins to glimmer for the first time. The certainty of life is challenged. This is excellent because life is not only life but life and death. The two cannot be seen apart from each other.

> This kind of double exposure is the true vision of reality. In the same sense, the aspect of life and the aspect of death are equally real, and reality is that which appears now as life and now as death. It is both life and death, and at the same time it is neither life nor death. It is what we have to call the non-duality of life and death.
>
> (Nishitani 1982: 52)

This seeing together of life and death has enormous consequences for the 'self' because it is outside the self itself. With the coming together of life and death Nishitani does not suppose a mixture wherein life and death mingle with each other, and life is not life and death is not death. On the contrary, life is life and death is death and (they) are both present in everything which exists (Nishitani 1982: 93).

Nishitani uses a specific expression to indicate this simultaneous vision of life and death: existence is life-*sive*-death. The essence of this term is in *sive*.[8] Life-*sive*-death must not be taken to mean that 'life is sometimes life and sometimes death.' *Sive* has to be regarded as the middle point. Existence is at once life and death – life-*sive*-death – and each being is being-*sive*-not-being. This is the reality of things: the true view of reality. Seeing things as being and not-being is seeing things as they truly are. For seeing being-*sive*-not-being or life-*sive*-death, Nishitani uses the expression 'seeing things from the field of emptiness.'

The non-duality of being and non-being has great consequences for the person. Characteristic of the person was the central place occupied by the subject in the experiential world. This central place was disputed by the confrontation of death and nihility and the resulting experience of doubt. Even the process of doubt can be seen as a form of consciousness which is still in the context of the *I* grasping itself. This is why the process of doubt has to be carried through to its very end. When we go through the doubt to the Great Doubt, which is the Great Death, we reach the ultimate phase of transformation, the goal of the way.

THE GOAL

True insight demands a personal existential conversion. Not only is the nihility behind the person then apparent, but the person himself is being-*sive*-not-being. That being wherein the person safely dreamed was blasted by nihility, but this nihility is not the only reality. One has to let go of this nothingness and only then can true subjectivity be attained. Truly being oneself is being oneself without an *I* center. The *I* is surrendered, the middle-point forgotten. The person is there, but is no longer person-oriented anymore (Nishitani 1982: 71).

From this perspective there is no distinction between the person and all other things in the world. As being-*sive*-not-being the person is thoroughly himself or herself. This being truly oneself rests not only in being but also in not-being. The coming together of being and not-being establishes another way for us of self-identity. The way of self-identity is overcome. The person is just as the person truly is in the midst of things as they truly are.

That self which truly is not-self rests completely in the present moment. Our life and our actions are without any 'why'.

> They are without aim or reason outside of themselves and become truly autotelic and without cause or reason, a veritable *Leben ohne Warum*. At bottom, at the point of their original, elemental source, our existence, behaviour and life are not a means for anything else.
>
> (Nishitani 1982: 252)

Nishitani describes how in Buddhism the transcendence of the cycle of life and death (*samsara*) ends in *nirvana*. This means overcoming the burden of life; nirvana is 'rebirth to true life' (Nishitani 1982: 177). True life must not be sought outside the cycle of birth and death; the cycle of birth and death itself is the place where 'the bliss of nirvana' is truly present (Nishitani 1982: 180). The cycle of life and death is nirvana; samsara is nirvana and nirvana is nothing else than samsara. The coming and going of each instant in their 'thusness' is the true life. Each moment is truly absolute, bottomless reality; each moment is as it is. The liberation from life is not beyond life but is life itself.

Guiding rules and techniques

How can the way of existence which Nishitani describes with such terms as death-*sive*-life, self-*sive*-not-self, etc. be realized in daily life? Are there any techniques? Are there any instructions on how to travel along the path?

Nishitani does not answer this question directly in *Religion and Nothingness,* although his many references to Dogen can be seen as an answer.[9] In his article 'The significance of Zen in modern society' (1975) Nishitani refers to sitting in zazen as a way. According to Nishitani, zazen is a process of abandoning or cutting off that duality which is preventing one's true self from manifesting itself (Nishitani 1975: 20). He mentions different aspects of zazen. Thus, he says that the practice is not merely sitting but also practice within movement. He also points to non-reliance on language and writing in the search for knowledge and truth. Zazen is not an intellectual endeavour – it is being aware of one's total being in the mode of direct experience.

From other writings as well we can conclude that Nishitani sees zazen as a way to realize the transformation from doubt, to Wondrous Being. Although he sees zazen as a way, he also emphasizes that zazen is not the only way.

> Although we speak of 'practising' Zen and 'observing' the Way of the Buddha, this is not to suggest that showing the original countenance of existence in observance is a matter for Buddhism alone. It is implied in all true religious life.
>
> (Nishitani 1982: 261)

Underlying principles

One of the underlying principles for Nishitani can be expressed as *faith*: the faith or trust that it is possible to travel the path, to go from doubt through great doubt and the Great Death to Wondrous Being. Although even this faith disappears in travelling the path, one can still say that it is one of the major pillars. Nishitani discusses this faith in many interviews and articles (cf. Nishitani 1975; 1984; 1985; 1985/86). Another underlying principle, which is not made explicit in the work of Nishitani but could (and should) be stressed, is the relationship with someone else who has already travelled the path – the relationship with a mentor or a teacher.[10]

We will now leave the description of the Buddhist path as found in Nishitani and turn our attention to the therapeutic path as developed in Dialectical Behavior Therapy.

The cognitive-behavioral therapeutic path as described by Linehan[11]

Starting point

The starting point of this path is the borderline personality disorder. The formal concept of borderline personality disorder (BPD) is relatively new in the field of psychopathology and different behavioral syndromes and etiological theories are associated with the term. The disorder is characterized by disturbed emotional, behavioral, and thinking patterns which cause enormous suffering and pain and often danger to one's life. Linehan describes a number of difficulties associated with this personality disorder.

First, borderline individuals generally experience emotional dysregulation. Emotional responses are highly reactive and individuals have difficulties with episodic depression, anxiety, irritability, and problems with anger and expression of anger. Linehan sees this emotional dysregulation as the core disorder. Second, borderline individuals often experience interpersonal dysregulation. Relationships often are chaotic, intense, and marked by difficulties. Third, borderline individuals have patterns of behavioral dysregulations, as evidenced by extreme problematic impulsive behaviors, such as attempts to injure and mutilate themselves, as well as suicidal behaviors. Fourth, borderline individuals are at times cognitively dysregulated. Brief, non-psychotic forms of thought dysregulation, including depersonalization, dissociation, and delusions, are at times brought on by stressful situations and usually clear up when the stress is ameliorated. Finally, dysregulation of the sense of self is common. It is not unusual for a borderline individual to report that she has no sense of a self at all, feels empty, and does not know who she is (Linehan 1993a: 11).

Linehan stresses that unpredictable emotional lability leads to unpredictable behavior and cognitive inconsistency, which interfaces with identity development. The disorder often contributes to an absence of a strong sense of identity. The numbness associated with inhibited affect is often experienced as emptiness, further contributing to an inadequate and at times completely absent sense of self (Linehan 1993b: 4).

Linehan sees a biosocial cause to the disorder. The disorder results from genetically based irregularities combined with certain dysfunctional environments. Emotional vulnerability is a biological disposition which, when combined with an invalidating environment, can result in BPD. A main characteristic of an invalidating environment is the tendency of caregivers or others to respond erratically and inappropriately to various experiences of private or social meanings.

Goal

The goal of the path is described in the following terms. The general goal is to learn and refine skills in changing behavioral, emotional, and thinking patterns associated with problems in one's life that cause misery and distress. The aim is decreasing suicidal behaviors, and decreasing behaviors that interfere with the quality of life. Another aim is the increase of behavioral skills, which is specified as increase in interpersonal skills, emotion regulation skills, distress tolerance skills, and core mindfulness skills (Linehan 1993a: 144). This goal could be summarized in the following way: decreasing crises and the danger to life and increasing the quality of life, so that there is less suffering and less pain.

Underlying principle

Before we can explain the techniques and guiding rules of the therapy we have to look at the underlying principle, because the underlying world view is determinant for some of the important techniques.

Dialectical Behavior Therapy (DBT) is based on a specific world view which Linehan calls a *dialectical world view*. She points to three important components. First, dialectics stresses the interrelatedness or wholeness of reality. The self or person is defined as 'in relation' and viewed as part of a network. Dialectics directs one's attention to the immediate and larger context. A second characteristic of a dialectical world view is that reality is seen as dynamic, comprised of internal opposing forces, out of whose synthesis evolves a new set of opposing forces. Within each thing, no matter how small, there is polarity, and all propositions contain within them their own oppositions. Applied to clinical practice, this principle has a profound impact. For example, it means that dysfunction also encompasses function, distortion accuracy, destruction construction. One of the first polarities treated in DBT is the polarity of acceptance and change. Linehan stresses the dialectic between the need for the client to accept herself as she is at the moment and the need for change on her part. Finally, the dialectical world view sees reality as a wholeness continually in the process of change. Change, rather than structure or content, is the essential nature of life. Life is in a constant process of transformation.

Two important concepts arise out of this dialectical world view. The first was mentioned already and consists of the emphasis on the balance of acceptance and change. The focus is not only on change: acceptance is as important to clients as change. A technology of encouraging acceptance is as important as a technology of change. Linehan refers to her experience with Zen meditation as a main source for her insight into this balance. To be able to work towards this acceptance, she uses some techniques named *core mindfulness skills.* We will look at these skills more closely in the next paragraph.

A second important concept or underlying principle is the idea of *Wise Mind.* Wise Mind is a focus on the inherent wisdom of clients. DBT assumes that each individual is capable of wisdom with respect to his or her own life, although this ability is not always obvious or accessible. The DBT therapist trusts that the client has within himself or herself the potential necessary for change. The essential elements for growth are already present in the current situation. The therapist searches for the grain of wisdom or truth inherent in each of the client's responses and communicates that wisdom to the client. A belief in the client's essential desire to grow and progress as well as a belief in his or her inherent capability for change underpins the treatment (Linehan 1993a: 33).

Techniques and guiding rules

Progress on the path is stimulated by the following components: individual psychotherapy, skills training, telephone consultation, and consultation meetings for therapists. All these components and how they should be used are described extensively in Linehan's book. A core element of the therapy is the training in mindfulness skills, which is the first and basic module of skills training. The other modules are: emotion regulation skills, interpersonal effectiveness skills, and distress tolerance skills. In these last three modules the mindfulness skills recur and are applied to special problems. These skills are psychological and behavioral versions of meditation skills found in Eastern spiritual practices. There are three 'what' skills and three 'how' skills.

The first 'what' skill is observing: attending to events, emotions, and other behavioral responses, without necessarily trying to terminate them when painful or prolong them when pleasant. What a person learns here is to allow herself to experience with awareness whatever is happening at the moment, rather than leaving a situation or trying to terminate an emotion. A person learns surrender to the given moment, acceptance without resistance. The second mindfulness 'what' skill is that of describing events and personal responses in words. The ability to apply verbal labels to behavioral and environmental events is essential for both communication and self-control. It prevents one from being blindly driven by emotions and events. The third mindfulness 'what' skill is the ability to participate without self-consciousness. It means entering completely into the activities of the current moment, without separating oneself from ongoing events and interactions. The quality of action is spontaneous: the interaction between the individual and the environment is smooth and partly based on habit.

The other three mindfulness skills have to do with *how* one attends, describes, and participates; they include taking a non-judgmental stance, focusing on one thing at the moment, and being effective. Taking a non-judgmental stance means taking a non-evaluative approach, judging something as neither good nor bad. The second 'how' is learning to focus the mind and awareness in the current moment's activity, rather than splitting attention among several activities or between a current activity and thinking about something else. The third 'how', being effective, is directed at reducing the client's tendency to be more concerned at times with what is 'right' than with doing what is actually needed or called for in a particular situation (Linehan 1993b: 63).

In many techniques used in all the modules of the skills training we see the previously explained dialectics at work. Radical acceptance of one's own situation, of pain, anger, being in the moment as it is, without judging, inevitably brings about change.

Nishitani and Linehan

In this paragraph we will compare Nishitani's Buddhist and Linehan's psychotherapeutic paths.

Starting points

If we look closely at both starting points, a couple of differences come to light. Nishitani describes how the person sees himself or herself as the center of all things. The *I* takes the middle position and experiences itself as most real and without limitations. It sees itself as independent and a large separation between the person and the rest of the world exists. This central position of the *I* is shattered by the confrontation of death and nihility – by the confrontation with *not-I*. This confrontation shakes the whole meaningful world of a person. A great doubt arises in which fundamntal questions play a role: What is the purpose of life? Where do I come from?

Linehan describes the starting point of borderline personality disorder in which a lack of sensed self is experienced. There is no *I* in the center, no middle out of which life is organized and no sharp distance between inner and outer world. There is no central *I* position and no strong sense of identity. It is this lack of sense of self, this lack of sense of identity, that is the main source of the problem and creates a great deal of suffering.

By *continuing on the path* Nishitani encourages the process of doubt which began through the shattering of the central position of the *I*. The person should not try to go back to the earlier safe position but should pass through this doubt to the very end. Feelings of despair and alienation do not mean that the person is on the wrong track. Although a person feels that he or she may disappear, in reality a process of birth is taking place.

In Linehan's method we see a different approach. Many techniques are used to try to develop a kind of stability and a sense of self. Through many exercises the patient is encouraged to recognize a center, an anchor. The concept of Wise Mind is used to find this central point. Feelings of competence, self-confidence, being in control, and being capable of mastering things and situations are encouraged throughout the whole therapy.

In *continuing further* along the path, Nishitani emphasizes again and again that the process of doubt, which is experienced as a crisis, has to be carried through to its very end – to where great doubt ends in the Great Death. The Great Death represents a radical transformation, an existential conversion. Here the fundamental questions are left behind. Existence shows itself as it really is, a coming and going of everything without any reason. The *I* is decentered.

In Linehan's therapeutic path such a point of radical transformation cannot be found. By steadily practicing the various exercises, the person will gradually learn to change destructive behavioral patterns and be capable of organizing life and relationships more adequately and peacefully.

Conclusions

Differences

It is helpful to analyze Nishitani's life view and Linehan's therapy by the metaphor of a path, which clarifies the different approaches of a spiritual and a therapeutic path. The suffering of the two starting points is different. Nishitani describes a suffering that results from a normal life being confronted by the fundamental questions of life and death. We could say that Nishitani is writing about *existential suffering*. Linehan describes a suffering that results from not being able to organize life. Because of biological and environmental factors, a person did not develop a healthy self-identity. Although all kinds of fundamental questions play a role in this situation, Linehan does not explicitly focus on these existential questions in her therapy, because there are more urgent questions to be treated.

Nishitani describes a path in which life is transformed by taking up the unanswerable fundamental questions. The crisis is encouraged in order to reach a point of radical transformation. Linehan describes a way in which life is transformed from chaos and crisis to organized well-being. Patients are trained to prevent crises and to deal with difficult situations in such a way that a crisis can be avoided. One could conclude that these paths have different starting points and different goals – the paths are of different orders. Nishitani's path is a spiritual one where the core of existence is transformed. The roots of I-consciousness are cut off. Linehan's path is one of psychological–medical treatment where behavior and psychical reactions are transformed and I-consciousness is given the opportunity to develop itself in a healthier way.

Similarities

It is truly remarkable that on these two different paths some of the same insights and techniques are used. Observing what is happening, just being there, not judging and accepting where one is now (surrendering to the moment) and at the same time seeing that in the following moment nothing will be the same any more (non-attachment to a state of mind, a thought, or an emotion) are crucial insights on both paths. Nishitani uses these insights to make clear that the central I-position is based on illusion. Linehan, who took these insights from the Zen path, uses them to train her patients to handle situations without fear and in a realistic way.

The element of faith in Nishitani, trust that it is possible to go the way, and the Wise Mind in Linehan, trust that the seed of healing is already present in the person, closely resemble each other. The role of a mentor (another person who has traveled along the path) and the role of the therapist have similarities, although this role is made much more explicit in the work of Linehan.

Both mentor and therapist represent the 'faith' or 'awareness of the grain of wisdom already present' which is sometimes not seen by the student or client. The mentor or therapist has to be able to endure the tension (to stand in the middle) of a paradox – being-*sive*-not-being, life-*sive*-death, acceptance-*sive*-change – until the other can see through this paradox by him- or herself.

Another shared insight on both paths is the interrelatedness of reality. The self, person or thing, is seen as part of a network. Independent objects or persons do not exist – everything participates in an interdependent wholeness.

General conclusion

If we draw a general conclusion, we could state that, although the Buddhist path as found in the work of Nishitani and the psychotherapeutic path as found in Linehan are of different orders, a comparison is very worthwhile. Further research may focus on working out more deeply the similarities and/or differences that can be located. Concerning the similarities we could ask questions such as: Could more Zen elements be integrated in a therapeutic path? How do the role of the therapist and the religious teacher resemble each other? What exactly is the meaning of *trust* on both paths?

Concerning the differences, issues that need to be tackled are: Should questions about the meaning of life be left out in therapy? Is mental stability needed before being able to travel along a spiritual path? Is the Zen path advisable for all people or do some people benefit more from other religious paths in which the disintegration of the *I* is less emphasized?

This case study on the Buddhist path of Nishitani and the psychotherapeutic path of Linehan cannot be broadened to general conclusions on Buddhist paths and psychotherapy. Nevertheless, we could conclude that working with the metaphor of a path is helpful in analyzing Buddhism and psychotherapy and throws light on differences and similarities. Applying the metaphor of a path to other case studies could be a help in further clarifying the discussion.

Notes

1 Cf. the many publications in which no account is taken of the very different historical and contextual backgrounds of Buddhist and psychological concepts. Cf., for example, Epstein (1995), Kopf (1998), and Brazier (1995).
2 The choice for Nishitani and Linehan has also an experiental basis. A few years ago Anbeek wrote her dissertation (Anbeek 1994) on a comparative study of Buddhism and Christianity in relation to death. At this time she is working as a counselor in a psychiatric hospital, where she participates as a co-therapist in a group that works with Linehan's Dialectical Behavioral therapy.
3 Hick (1989) makes a distinction between physical, ethical, and religious meaning. For an elaboration of meaning in religion and philosophy see pp. 129–72.
4 See, for example, the introduction to Rubin 1996, pp. 1–2.
5 This faith has received many different expressions in the Buddhist tradition, e.g.

Buddhahood, innate enlightenment, etc. See, for example, Abe, who emphasizes the importance of faith for Dogen (1992b: 189).

6 Cf. Young-Eisendrath 1996: 140: 'Neurosis is a barrier to encountering fully the meaning in our pain.'

7 Nishitani describes various ways in which this confrontation with death and nihility can happen. Many times it is through the loss of another person or through the confrontation with one's own sickness. See for example Nishitani 1985/86. This is an autobiographical essay.

8 *Sive* is Latin, meaning *either* or *or*. With this term Nishitani identifies life and death, being and non-being. Nishitani takes this expression from the *Heart Sutra*, where *form* and *emptiness* are identified. Abe (1992a: 54) suggested using the term *qua* instead of *sive*, since it expresses the identification more clearly.

9 Cf. the following citations from Dogen: 'The practice of Zen is the dropping off of body-and-mind: it is just sitting' and 'dropping off of body-and-mind means sitting in Zen meditation' (Nishitani 1982: 185); 'Through working out a resolution in just sitting, body and mind comes to drop off. This is the technique for release from the five desires, the five hindrances and so on' (Nishitani 1982: 186).

10 Cf. the comment by Ueda, one of Nishitani's students, on Nishitani's relationship to Nishida (Ueda1992: 1): 'Writing thirty years after his own teacher Nishida Kitaro passed away, he said, "Even now I tremble when I think of him". We can see from this that he was in a sense always face to face with his former mentor.'

11 Linehan describes the therapy in Linehan 1993a and 1993b.

References

Abe, Masao (1992a) 'What is Religion', *The Eastern Buddhist* 25: 51–69.

Abe, Masao (1992b) *A Study of Dogen: His Philosophy and Religion,* New York: SUNY.

Anbeek, Christa W. (1994) *Denken over de dood. De boeddhist K. Nishitani en de christen W. Pannenberg vergeleken,* Kampen: Kok.

Brazier, D. (1995) *Zentherapy,* London: Constable.

Buswell, R. E., Jr. and R. M. Gimello (1992) *Paths to Liberation: The Marga and its Transformations in Buddhist Thought,* Honolulu: University of Hawaii Press.

Epstein, M. (1995) *Thoughts without a Thinker: Psychotherapy from a Buddhist Perspective,* New York: Basic Books.

Freud, S. (1986) 'Studies on hysteria (1893–1895)', in *The Standard Edition,* vol. 2, London: Hogarth Press and The Institute of Psycho-analysis.

Greenson, R. R. (1967) *The Technique and Practice of Psychoanalysis,* New York: International Universities Press.

Hick, John (1989) *An Interpretation of Religion: Human Responses to the Transcendent,* London: Macmillan.

Kopf, G. (1998) 'In the face of the Other', in A. Molino (ed.), *The Couch and the Tree: Dialogues in Psychoanalysis and Buddhism,* New York, 276–89.

Linehan, M. (1993a) *Cognitive-Behavioral Treatment of Borderline Personality Disorder,* New York.

Linehan, M. (1993b) *Skills Training Manual for Treating Borderline Personality Disorder,* New York.

Nishitani, K. (1975) 'The significance of Zen in modern society', *Japanese Religions* 8: 18–24.

Nishitani, K. (1982) *Religion and Nothingness*. Berkeley: University of California Press.

Nishitani, K. (1984) 'The standpoint of Zen', *The Eastern Buddhist* 17: 1–26.

Nishitani, K. (1985) 'An interview with Keiji Nishitani', *FAS Society Journal* (Summer): 3–9.

Nishitani, K. (1985/86) 'The days of my youth: an autobiographical sketch', *FAS Society Journal* (Winter): 25–30.

Rubin, J. B. (1996) *Buddhism and Psychotherapy: Toward an Integration*, New York: Plenum Press.

Strupp, H. H. (1986) 'The nonspecific hypothesis of therapeutic effectiveness: a current assessment', *American Journal for Orthopsychiatry* 56: 513–52.

Ueda, Shizuteru (1992) 'My teacher', *The Eastern Buddhist* 25: 1–8.

Van Baal, J. (1981) *Man's Quest for Partnership: The Anthropological Foundations of Ethics and Religion*. Assen.

Young-Eisendrath, P. (1996) *The Gifts of Suffering: Finding Insight, Compassion and Renewal*, New York: Addison-Wesley.

Zetzel, E. R. (1956) 'Current concepts of transference', *International Journal for Psychoanalysis* 37: 369–76.

Part III

TRADITIONAL IDEAS IN A NEW LIGHT

13

KARMA AND INDIVIDUATION
The boy with no face

Dale Mathers

Karma is a traditional Eastern concept, mirrored in Western analytical psychology as 'individuation'. These notions about how meaning is made are concepts near the top of the hierarchy of ideas in their respective traditions: both are theories about connections between a time-bound part of the mind which analytical psychologists call ego and a time-free, transcendent experience which they call Self. The concept 'complex' describes both a structure and a process: repetitive patterns of thought and behaviour create suffering. From stillness and clarity, Self unfolds into unresolvable oscillations; its developmental spiral is arrested, forming instead a 'strange attractor', ever circling and never reaching its archetypal core in the psyche (Lonie 1991).

Jung saw individuation as a task involving working through complexes, a project for the second half of life, requiring a stable identity and persona. His 'classical' view, emphasizing the role of archetypes and the collective unconscious in the individuation process, contrasts with that of Michael Fordham and 'the developmental school'. The latter are close to Eastern ideas – both see Self as a gradual unfolding from potential to actual throughout the whole of a life.

This paper explores karma and individuation, through the psychotherapeutic work I did with a young Japanese man born with severe bilateral cleft palate. Overwhelmed by shame, he believed himself beyond help due to 'bad karma.' Repeated emotional traumas hindered identity formation, producing deep problems in forming symbols and relating to others. Born with a malformed face, he felt fated continually to 'lose face.' As a new sense of identity emerged, with it came the courage to have a new face. The enactment, 'gaining face' by plastic surgery, was a counterpoint to our work.

Introduction

What is 'losing face'? It is shame. Outcast from family, social group, and culture, wounded at the core of our being, in pain more than we can bear, we lose belief in our value, we feel of no value to others. Suffering mounts. Identity becomes a trap. We question life. Can this suffering have any meaning or purpose? We may seek answers in religious experience, therapy, or analysis; escape into spirals of co-dependence; remain stuck in paranoid or depressive mind-sets, unable to reach, maintain, or tolerate ambivalence.

Let's take karma and individuation as narrations on the meaning of suffering – the first from a tradition of moral philosophy, the second from a tradition of depth psychology. A religion, Buddhism, is also an Eastern depth psychology. Analytical psychology, a Western response to psychic suffering, is not a religion. Both treat 'religion' as a natural, human instinct expressing patterns vital to survival. Exploring how meaning contributes to individuation is the purpose of this chapter. I'll define karma, individuation, and complex, and look at these concepts in analysis – principally through dream interpretation, which, with active imagination, allowed a mute part of my patient's psyche to talk, to find new meaning.

Karma and individuation

How we are given meaning by external systems in the collective pre-empts how we give meaning in our own inner systems, and this determines the strength and shape of our ego–Self axis (Edinger 1962). My patient, Yukio, born with a bilateral cleft palate, was abandoned by his parents to be raised by their traditional Buddhist rural extended family. His ugliness led to exclusion and abuse. Stigmatization, in social psychology (Gregory 1987: 721–2), is a negative myth. Yukio, as a small child, internalized a religious myth, the myth of karma. He thought it meant that ugliness results from bad acts in a past life: 'I am ugly, so I am bad, so I deserve all the bad things that happen to me.'

'Religion' derives from Latin: 're-ligare' – 'to bind back to' (Cassell 1963) back to mother, to another individual, or to society. Transference and countertransference are also forms of 'binding back to'. As we become aware of movements of feeling in these experiences, there can be moments when we feel aware of 'something bigger than us'; a consciousness of Self, which is a prerequisite for individuation. Unfolding of 'Self-as-purpose' (will, or volition), parallels a Buddhist concept, karma, the unfolding of cause and effect through our intentions and actions.

Karma means, in Buddhist terms, 'Self in action' – or, in Zen, 'Not-Self in action' – a paradox (Watson 1999: 172). Gordon calls 'Big Self', 'a metapsychological construct or concept . . . which refers to the wholeness of the psyche and includes the conscious as well as unconscious areas . . . it lies behind phenomena such as those symbols that convey wholeness and the eternal, as well as behind all those drives that seek fusion and union . . . it is the object of individuation' (Gordon 1993: 143–60).

Buddhism has no belief in 'God' in a Western sense. It seeks direct experience of numinous mind, here and now. This can happen through the simple practice of watching the breath in meditation. Watching thoughts wander creates and strengthens reality-testing, builds what Westerners define as 'ego strength'. The gain is clarity.

> Buddhism is a religion which puts wisdom to the fore rather than faith. Intelligent and honest inquiry are not only welcomed, but encouraged. Part of this inquiry requires a good background under-standing of the way cause and effect function on the personal level. This is the domain of ethics or morality, and the specific domain of karma.
>
> (Payutto 1996: vi)

The Buddha taught 'Four Noble Truths': suffering exists, has a cause, can cease, and cessation comes by cultivating awareness:

> Buddhism's great innovation was the ethicisation of the pan-Indian doctrine of karma, the law of cause and effect, by reinterpreting it in terms of intention . . . Buddhist teachings are centrally concerned with the functioning of the mind, how willing comes about.
>
> (Watson 1999: 69)

Prior to the Buddha, karma meant just 'the law of cause and effect'. Traditionally, it explains how actions in previous lives affect experience in this life. Whether or not we accept reincarnation, there are in all lives patterns in the mind which become habitual, that is, 'unmindful', unintentional, outside of volition, arising from unconscious complexes. These patterns arise from conditions in our early development.

Jung demonstrated their reality with the word association test, described in the Clark Lectures (1909). Subjects respond with free associations to a list of words. Both content (words) and form (time delay between stimulus and response) give information. Time delay results from awareness being given subliminally to repressing associated painful feelings. Actions without mind-fulness give rise to anguish and suffering, creating negative karma. Understanding karma as intention emphasizes the concept of human beings as free agents with choices to make.

However, for Yukio, karma meant simply 'past actions have inevitable present consequences'. He believed that he deserved his bad karma from pre-vious lives. Though choice depends on personality (Wood 1977: 53), circumstances reinforced Yukio's negative belief and entrenched his com-plex. After giving clinical details, which we both fictionalized to preserve confidentiality (Tuckett 1993), I'll use them to examine the concept of com-plex.

The boy with no face

Yukio was born in rural Japan into a traditional Buddhist extended family. His mother left him within days of his birth, to live abroad with his father. He was raised by a nanny. In his early years he had needed many operations, yet the centre of his face sank inwards, speech was impaired, he looked and felt ugly. Soon his behaviour fitted his 'bad' face. He joined a rough gang of older boys, truanted, stole, and ran away which drove his uncles to distraction. His escapades often ended with a whipping and him being locked in his room.

Negative attention reinforced his personal myth that 'attachment means abandonment'. Being 'exiled', sent to live with his unknown parents at the age of ten, confirmed it. Abroad, at an international school, he found Western children didn't notice his odd looks. He joked, 'to you, we all look the same anyway'. A gifted child, Yukio achieved highly at his studies, in sports, and in music. He worked hard to get to university, have a 'student life' and escape from his closed family. Yet, when he got there, he could not cope. A few weeks into his course he became suicidal.

When I met Yukio, as he was then, he wore shapeless grey clothes. He hid his squashed face behind thick pebble glasses and lank greasy hair. He hardly made eye contact. Eighteen, he knew he looked, felt, and behaved like a scared ten-year-old. I suggested he join a therapy group and, bravely, he did. A year later, he came again. He wanted to talk about incest with his elder sister, and felt too ashamed to tell the group.

Trust was extremely hard to create. Gradually he told me about several serious suicide attempts during his teens, and his 'loss of face' at lacking the courage to kill himself. Eventually, he told the group, learning others had survived similar experiences. The therapy group were like the gang that supported him during childhood – his confession was an initiating ritual, and, as he began to feel he 'belonged' he began to change. He started dressing like a student, studying, and playing music again. He graduated and returned to Japan. A few months later he wrote saying he wanted to come back to England to study music. He'd begun thinking about having plastic surgery and could he see me? He began analysis using the couch, three times a week. We've now worked together for seven years.

In the transference, I quickly became an idealized 'good father he'd never had'. He longed for advice, was furious when I didn't give it; then, terrified I'd retaliate, withdrew. He'd lie silent for long periods, facing the wall, hiding his face. He'd make sobbing movements, but never cried. I asked if he did the same when being whipped. Yes, crying meant giving in. Together we valued the stubborn courage of the 'boy with no face'.

Yukio talked of his desperate longing for 'a father', and his envy of the boys in 'the gang' who'd had one. Alas, when he met his real father, he was physically and sexually abused. Yukio had powerful, distressing, repetitive, ritualized sado-masochistic memories and sexual fantasies, and despaired of ever having any intimate relationships.

The effect of early experiences of rejection, physical pain, and abuse (in his first sexual experience) was that he couldn't imagine sex any other way, nor see himself as anything but grotesque, ugly, and unlovable. Suffering, and making others suffer, equalled 'intimacy'. No experience of others could be symbolic, that is, a bridge between the known (himself) and the unknown (the other). Psychoanalysts call this a 'core complex' (Glasser 1986). The complex held unbearable murderous wishes toward his father for abuse and his mother for abandonment. Her inadequacy as father's partner and as Yukio's protector meant he gave her role to his sister.

Using active imagination, we created together the idea that he could become a 'good father' to the 'boy nobody wants' in himself. He'd imagine what it might be like to 'be different', with a new face. I'd encourage him to visualize this and to talk to the 'new face'. As his confidence improved, the 'new face' was able to talk with the child he had been.

Dreams

After three years came an important dream sequence. First, he saw himself naked on a beach on a Polynesian island, at puberty, being held down whilst the men of the tribe tattooed on a new, adult, face. Second, lying naked on my couch, whilst I buggered him. Third, on a hot summer afternoon, naked, on a London pavement with his closest male friend, having sex.

The dreams explore his complex. The first dream is the past, his constant wish for a new face and, with it, proper initiation into the world of men. The second is his 'here and now' fear: if he's attached to me, an 'idealized father' analyst, then I'll sodomize him. The karmic pattern will repeat. The third is his 'current relationship', his hope/fear that he is gay. Nakedness he associated to being a baby, to innocence and vulnerability, to being stripped before being beaten, as well as to sex.

Yukio was scared by strong homosexual feelings towards me and his friends. A homoerotic phase is a normal part of development. Being able to love another has to start with loving oneself (and one's Self), exploring one's own body . . . and bodies like one's own. In traditional cultures, as in Polynesia, rites of passage humanize these feelings. This is a 'group event'.

Maleness (the animus) is a 'group' experience and it often appears in dreams as a group or crowd (Emma Jung 1978: 1–43). All men group and need secure identification with other men before seeking partners of the opposite sex. Yukio's next dream was of being part of a 'tribe of eco-warrior lads' young, colourful, environmental protestors fighting to save a forest. In waking life, he increasingly shared these values, ones opposed to either capitalist or collective social order. He 'hung out' with such lads, and restarted martial arts – enacting his dream.

In his early twenties, he was reaching adolescence. Gradually, he could imagine himself having good sex on his own without sadistic fantasies. Encouraged by the Polynesian dream, he took steps towards surgery. The new face given by the 'group of men' is an image for a new persona, as well as for the face itself. He realized he'd never go through all the pain involved until he knew he 'was worth it', yet to accept he might be 'worth it' felt like betraying his karma.

At this point came a powerful dream. His sister tried to seduce him, but he didn't want sex with her anymore. While telling me this, he rocked to and fro like a baby. I felt, for the first time, intensely maternal and said, 'You're rocking like an abandoned infant.' I said his sister stood for mother, and suddenly found myself suggesting he tell me how he felt in his 'mother tongue'.

Yukio said, 'But you don't speak Japanese.' 'No, but you do,' I agreed, 'and maybe you need to tell *you* what you feel like.' The whole atmosphere changed. Time stopped. Then he took a huge breath, and began. His voice was like a frightened little boy. He started to cry, then he choked. I gave him a glass of water. As he recovered, he told me (still in Japanese) about being ten, sent alone on a long-haul flight to parents he didn't know in a country he'd never visited, with a culture and language he didn't understand.

As he wept, I gently said, 'now you are crying like a baby, like a baby who chokes on his mother's milk, like the boy nobody wants.'

He said, 'I want him.'

I said, 'Yes, you do. That's new, you didn't want him before.'

Complex

Complexes are neural networks through which sensations change first to feelings, then to thoughts. Jung's definition is 'recollections, composed of a large number of component ideas . . . The cement that holds the complex together is the feeling tone common to all the individual ideas' (Jung 1973). Samuels et al. (1986) say: 'collections of images and ideas, clustered round a core derived from one or more Archetypes, and characterised by a common emotional tone. When they come into play (become "constellated") they contribute to behaviour and are marked by affect, whether a person is conscious of them or not.'

Complexes shape unconscious habits, unfold from birth, through sexual differentiation, initiation, courtship, parenting, ageing and gaining wisdom, to death with its attending rituals. The archetypal core is humanized by *rites de passage*. Often, religious ceremonies mark developmental stages (Sullivan 1987: 27–51) with religious signifiers to orient us in our social group.

A well functioning ego complex relates to Self through less conscious complexes in a way similar to a Self relating to the collective through the cultural unconscious. Henderson (1988: 72–81) suggests information moves in both systems by a transcendent function capable of mediating between opposites, say, dependence and independence.

Religious ideas, by definition, 'bind things back', from a part to a whole. Ego moves towards Self: Self moves from its own uniqueness to universality. Religious attitudes create myths, shape perceptions, give meaning and purpose to suffering. 'True compassion is a powerful antidote to our own suffering because it counteracts alienation' (Young-Eisendrath 1996: 59).

Jung viewed 'religion' as a psychological system. He defined Self as 'the whole range of psychic phenomena in man.' Appearing in time, developing its archetypal patterns a bit at a time, Self is an ocean, finite yet uncountable. Ego recognizes psychic wholeness, maintains identity, personality, and temporal continuity (Jung 1971a). It appears as 'me' in dreams and active imagination. The dream ego is not the 'me' of the waking world, rather, the 'me' Self sees, or wishes 'me' to see (Whitmont and Pereira 1989: 18–22). Ego is a complex which tests reality.

Nakae Toju, a Japanese Taoist philosopher from the seventeenth century, who used *Ri* as a name for world soul (collective), *Ki* as a name for world stuff (ego), and *Ryochi* as a name for 'Self'. Tao argues about 'darkness, water, the "uncarved block", emptiness, energy, anti-action, transformation and self-likeness' (McNaughton 1971). Like Buddhism and analytical psychology, Taoist philosophy takes the view that psychic structure provides our route to the phenomenal world, to inner and outer worlds, and to the collective. It says we know through our sense perceptions.

Jung borrowed similar epistemological ideas from the philosophy of Kant (Nagy 1991: 49–63) and Plato's (Jung 1974: 316–22) ideal types. Jung (1971b) described 'the irrational third', 'the existence of two mutually antagonistic tendencies, both striving to drag man into extreme attitudes and entangle him in the world, whether on the material or spiritual level, sets him at variance with himself and accordingly demands the existence of a counterweight.'

Buddhism and analytical psychology agree that part of the mind is concerned with *episteme*, that is, with objects of knowledge: analysts call this ego, Buddhists call it self. Knowledge arises from perception, when 'not-doing' interacts with 'being with'. In analysis, this knowledge of not-doing is called Self (*Ryochi*).

Bridging functions in the ego complex bring together parts of the psyche. This mediation is essential for individuation (Fordham 1985: 34–9); yet in that the ego inevitably experiences defeat by the Self. Contemporary Jungians stress that ego provides continuity of personal history, and maintains 'persona' (Hall and Young-Eisendrath 1991: 6–7). In individuation, ego derives and develops from Self. It is defended against the outside world and the Self by persona and shadow. Persona is the face we show the world. The word derives from Ancient Greek theatre; 'personae' were the masks worn by actors to represent different characters, just as in the traditional Japanese Noh theatre.

Jung uses persona as a concept within his theory of object relations. 'The persona is a functional complex existing for adaptation, but it is not identical with individuality. The persona is exclusively concerned with the relation to objects. The relation of the individual to the object must be sharply distinguished from the relation to the subject' (Jung 1971c).

Shadow – the 'thing a person has no wish to be' (Jung 1954a) is the unlived good in a bad person, the unlived bad in a good one. Karma and individuation are negotiations between ego and collective, *Ki* and *Ri*; but which has control? For developmental theories of analysis, ego is primary.

> The ego, according to Freud, is the organised part of the self, constantly influenced by instinctual impulses but keeping them under control by repression; furthermore it directs all activities and establishes and maintains the relation to the external world. The self is used to cover the whole of the personality, which includes not only the ego, but the instinctual life which Freud called the id.
>
> (Klein 1975: 249)

In analytical psychology, Self is primary. It appears in dreams as a ruler or wise being, a mandala figure, or, commonly, a crowd – or an ocean.

> The ego stands to the Self as the moved to the mover, as object to subject, because the determining factors which radiate out from the Self surround the ego on all sides and are therefore supra-ordinate to it. The Self, like the unconscious, is an a priori existent out of which the ego evolves. It is, so to speak, the unconscious prefiguration of the ego. It is not I who create myself, rather, I happen to myself.
>
> (Jung 1958)

Self and ego are not *things*, they are concepts, imprecisely linked to anatomical or neurophysiological correlates. They name two sides of one boundary, the border between time-bound and time-free experience. Self relates to time-free modes of perception and experience, ego relates to time-bound modes. They attribute value to percepts through our feeling function. Feelings become thoughts as we learn names for them through cultural rituals. Reification of either concept leads to premature closures in the systems (individual–collective) and (ego–Self).

Closure and non-closure: opening and failing to shut

Theory is a heuristic, explanatory device, an explanation of a system, an aid to and part of helping a person retell their story. In Systems Theory, 'theory' is closure round an *episteme*, a 'bit' of knowledge. To illustrate – Yukio and I have a 'bit of knowledge' – 'having a cleft palate means you cannot suck.'

Systems theory examines movements of information within structures. The 'byte' is a unit of information. When I understand Yukio's difficulties using a theory, I am moving a 'byte of information' – for instance, amplifying its informational content, by using active imagination with dream material, or 'asking for associations'.

Analysis is a 'theory of system' – the system being the psyche and its structures. A structure is a model of operations that allows for subsequent transformations while still conforming to the structure's rules. A structure may be open or closed, opening or closing. I'll show you what this means by using this clinical example.

> If I link 'having cleft palate' with 'maternal deprivation' to get 'severe narcissistic injury' I am using a form, 'if . . . then . . .' to make meaning. 'If you couldn't suck, then you couldn't attach to mother: if you couldn't attach to mother then you can't attach to me' . . . This is a closure.

The same 'byte' can be 'spun' in a narrative about 'archetype'. 'An archetype is a pattern of imprinted behaviour, like suckling. If you could not suckle, the developmental failure prevented archetypal installation.' This is also a closure. Theories are predictions and, systemically, a subset of (myth). Any analytic language – 'classical' ('Self-ish') or 'developmental' (ego-ic) – is a member of the set (myth).

Theories are myths designed to convey meaning and define a range within which meaning may be made. When we are 'in a complex' it is as if we can't read the script of the psyche. We live our story the same way every time:

closure. Structuring meaning is formally called gestural praxis. Greimas (1987: 27) says that meaning can be referential or directional. In a referential meaning an expression (a word or gesture) refers back to a content (an associated set of ideas): the words 'This boy is ugly' refer to a code about facial appearances. In a directional meaning, there is intention. 'This boy is bad because he is ugly' – the ugliness developed because of the badness.

Developmental theory is directional, archetypal theory is referential. A developmental metaphor says, 'Yukio suffered severe narcissistic injury as a result of failure of early attachment.' An archetypal theory says, 'An archetype could not express itself, could not "unpack", could not "install and run" properly.' Developmental theory is about the directed expression of archetype, archetypal theory refers to the ordered expression of development. Developmental theory views structures from the point of view of ego, and archetypal theory from that of Self. Both are true, each is true separately, and, in my view, neither is true alone.

Using both developmental and archetypal viewpoints was essential to help Yukio understand an experience of congenital difference, a premature closure. In archetypal metaphor I might say, 'Yukio, look. You could not embark on your hero's journey for deliverance from the terrible great mother because you didn't have a real mother.' Or, developmentally, 'Yukio, you can't take in what I say, just like you couldn't take in the milk your mother had to give you.' I said something like both at the 'crux', the centre of the clinical material, when Yukio spoke Japanese. I could not translate his words. Yet, at that moment and for the first time, I understood his pain, he knew I understood and we both knew we had changed. We 'made a word', an analytic signifier out of his experience. A closure opened.

Problems in analysis arise from linguistic failure, which amplifies intrin-sic failures of trust. For example, we are genetically programmed to bond to mother through suckling. If this is difficult, later tasks involving bond-ing will also be difficult (Bowlby 1958: 119–36). In the gestural praxis of attachment theory we recognize 'I' exist, then we discover 'I' am separate from 'mother', and 'm/other' has things I need to survive. In the negative form, this is called envy; in the positive form, it is 'awareness of twoness'. The theory predicts that if early attachment is 'no attachment' then we form the myth 'no attachment' means 'attachment'. We can't manage twoness, tolerate difference, or recognize envy – particularly the envy of ego for Self.

In the gestural praxis of alchemical theory 'the gold of the Self' exists; it can be separated from *prima materia* through condensation, distillation, and so on. 'Matter' gives us the things we need to survive. Mother is earth mother (Gaia) material world, a Self which can supply every need of the ego. Theory predicts that if we deny the existence of 'the gold of the Self', then we never learn to meet our basic developmental needs. We remain for-ever greedy.

But, and this is crucial, there is no reason to suppose developmental fail-ure or inadequate humanization of archetypal patterns together or separately 'cause' complexes. Our analytic language shapes our theories about meaning and its disorders. Some things can be said in one language and not another, for languages are themselves relatively closed systems. Analytic communication is a relatively open system: we are not objective, only intersubjective (Stolorow et al. 1987: 88–99). If we concretize cause and effect I believe we create more 'bad karma'. We become prisoners of our interpretation.

Discussion

Individuation means 'a person becoming himself, whole, indivisible and dis-tinct from other or collective' (Samuels et al. 1986). It is archetypal, inevitable, and happens when Self has cultural freedom and ego has a persona, capable of meeting its age-appropriate responsibilities. Jung defines individuation as individual, rather than collective, psychology.

> Levelling down to the collective stunts an individual, a society of such individuals is not healthy. Social cohesion and collective values exist only when an individual has sense of their own value, and therefore, of their value to, and the value of, society. Individuation involves opposition to the collective, not antagonistically, but due to different orientation.
>
> (Jung 1971d)

Fordham (1976: 36 – 40) saw individuation as 'differentiation of the individual personality.' Primary identity, the experience of fusion between an infant and mother, yields to experience of part objects (like the breast or penis) then whole objects (like mother or father). Individuation presupposes, includes, and depends on collective relationships. This is why it cannot happen if parts of the psyche, objects in the psyche, can't enter relationships. Yukio's complex was an eternally repeating scene of abuse, a karmic trap. The part trapped could be called 'autistic' – the boy crying alone.

I understand 'autistic' to mean a part of the Self is encapsulated, unable to participate in what Hillman (1983: 26) calls 'soul making'. The hallmark of soul making is imagination: not 'what would I be if?' rather a 'releasing of events from their literal understanding into a mythical appreciation'. This requires imagining our own personal myths over and over again until envy, an experience of twoness, and an 'I do not have that, I wish to become it' opens us to a change in our personality. As it does, we learn to live with our own 'twoness', with being both a Self and an ego.

Yukio learnt to re-imagine good boyhood experiences as well as bad ones, and future experiences. Using a chair and the couch, he could move – and become 'the boy with the new face', who is envied by 'the boy nobody wants'. He could sit in different places, talk as, to and between these 'subpersonalities' (Redfearn 1985: 88–100). This technique comes from Psychosynthesis, a humanistic therapy originating with the Italian psychiatrist Dr Roberto Assagioli (1975), who worked with Jung at the Burgholzli Hospital in Zurich.

Now, autistic parts of the psyche can't re-imagine, or put value to percepts. (Fordham 1976: 36–40; Tustin 1981: 35–43; Hobson 1993). Autistic people profoundly lack imagination, can't see how their acts affect others, or do so in highly specified ways; complexes have us, we don't have them. Yukio's sado-masochistic complex counteracted deep inner emptiness. In it, as his first three dreams showed, shame-filled sexual fantasies recurred excluding other forms of relating. This prevented individuation. There was profound turning inwards of psychic and sexual energy. Using one theory, this complex arose from a fundamental failure in the mother–infant relationship, for he literally could not 'take in good things' without risking choking to death.

> In psychoanalysis, one does encounter individuals who have been so traumatised that they cannot take in anything from others that they have not already thought of themselves. If in order to preserve the coherence of the self one must exclude other versions of reality, one's ability to learn from others will be impaired.
>
> (Modell 1993: 179)

Yukio found it extremely hard to learn in the therapy group. Until his trauma repeated in the analytic space, with a different outcome, he could neither 'put out' how he felt or 'take in' interpretations. What went in came straight out. This was repeated many times, during which I often felt severely nauseated. He 'made me feel sick' by projecting sensations.

As we amplified his dream about incest and he spoke to me, his 'analytic mother', in his 'mother tongue', then a body-memory, an encapsulated experience, came back, overwhelming and terrifying. As Winnicott (1990: 140–53) says, 'the original experience of primitive agony cannot get into the past tense unless the ego can first gather it into its own present time experience.'

Yukio couldn't suck. And it was as though his emerging ego kept on seeing his Self as a mother who contains all good things but who deliberately chokes him when he expresses his most basic needs. A physically embodied complex formed, centred round feelings of rejection and starvation. In any relationship, he expected always to 'lose face' and be punished. He relived this, having a severe choking fit on my couch. Time stood still, what happened before happened again.

Beverley Zabriskie (1997) calls this the 'thawing of a frozen moment'. Ajahn Sumedho (1984: 109–15), Abbott of Chithurst Monastery in Hampshire, says karma is a memory pattern, a habit which only ceases through recognition; neither striving to change it, nor not striving, will ultimately work. Or, as my first analyst once told me, 'its being able to say, "there I go again", and accept it'. It is being able to survive shame.

As recognition of his complex increased, his attacks on himself diminished. The most powerful of these was an intense persecuting belief in his ugliness, denying the possibility of intimacy or ordinary sexuality. Also, he'd always known he'd need more surgery. However, the surgery also felt like betraying the tough kid who'd struggled so hard with the face he'd got from his 'bad karma'.

As the complex changed his energy became available – for martial arts, for music, for friends, for concern about social and environmental issues. Attacks by his ego on his Self (and on me) moved into the background. Exchanges

218

between psyche and physicality became easier. A few months after the choking incident, Yukio turned up with his eyebrow pierced. He did it, he explained, to show himself he owned his face. It fitted him in with his new 'gang' (the eco-warrior lads). He felt he needed to do this to remind himself of who he'd been after surgery.

The body is 'the physical materiality of the psyche' (Jung 1959). Yukio's inner transformation was paralleled by the surgical enactment of his 'Polynesian' dream. The operation was long, painful, and successful. Afterwards, he brought a dream: 'I'm a naked child standing on the shore of the Pacific, beside a Tori (a Japanese Shinto ceremonial gate). The sea stretches away. I feel its timeless . . . its everything'.

We both felt awe at his numinous experience. He felt at one with himself and completely bewildered, as if he'd died and been reborn. There was a mirroring of a mother and a newborn in the awe present between us; he saw in my face the 'sparkle in mother's eye' he'd been born expecting, but which, because of his deformity, he'd missed. And, with joy, he brought a dream in which he'd met a 'girl with a face like me'; a shy, wild anima figure, who, he dreamed, was actively seeking him out for love making. He had undergone his *rite de passage* and felt able to be a man.

Conclusion

Analysis means 'resolving a thing into its parts,' opening and closing. For Yukio, his face was taken apart and resolved. He no longer believed it his karma to be ugly. His ego opened prematurely due to difficult conditions in infancy. He was too soon cut off from Self, the oceanic source of being; from mother, who represents Self as a 'flow of wholeness'. Jung describes Self thus:

> The undiscovered vein within us is a living part of the psyche; classical Chinese philosophy names this interior way 'Tao' and likens it to a flow of water that moves irresistibly towards its goal. To rest in Tao means fulfilment, wholeness, one's destination reached, one's mission done; the beginning, end and perfect realisation of the meaning of existence innate in all things. Personality is Tao.
>
> (Jung 1954b)

Yukio felt this with his new persona and new face. This meant first recognizing, then accepting his shadow, as it appeared in his sado-masochistic complex. As he did so, its hold relaxed, leaving an ego capable of letting Self have many relationships. For, like 'society', Self is a collective noun. It contains infinite possible 'subpersonalities', – 'father', 'mother', 'child', 'hero', 'shadow', 'boy nobody wants'. As the health of society depends on harmony between members, so, in individuals, psychological health depends on harmony between different personae in the psyche. Active imagination helped Yukio integrate his subpersonalities.

Jung (1960) emphasizes that integration is not individuation, nor is it simply ego emerging into consciousness. It is the unfolding of Self . . . finding the face we had before we were born . . . having choices about how we appear. Underlying this is a purpose. At its simplest, it is relationship to others in order to survive (Fairbairn 1952: 34–5).

Individuation is relationship. Its processes are both causal and final. They occur simultaneously in the timeless Self and the time-bound ego (Wiener 1996). The *Tibetan Book of the Dead* (Fremantle and Chogyam Trungpa Rimpoche 1987: xvii) describes this process. In his introduction, Chogyam Trungpa makes clear that whilst the text describes experience 'between lives', it is also a metaphor for the unfolding of Self through the ego. The parallels to the process described above are strong:

> there is a primitive 'self' aware of an external world. Now as soon as this happens, the self reacts to its surroundings: this is . . . feeling. It is not yet fully developed emotion – just an instinctive liking, dislike or indifference, but immediately it grows more complicated as the centralised entity asserts itself by reacting not only passively but actively. This is . . . perception, in its fullest sense, when the self is aware of stimulus and automatically responds to it. The . . . concept, covering the intellectual and emotional activity of interpretation . . . follows perception. It is what puts things together, and builds up the patterns of personality and karma. Finally there is consciousness which combines all the sense perceptions and the mind. The self has not become a complete universe of its own; instead of directly perceiving the world as it really is, it projects its own images all around it.

Whether Self forms ego, or ego forms Self, is irrelevant. Holding firm to the first is 'classical Jungian theory', and the second, 'developmental theory'. Both can become attempts to freeze a fluent process, which Michael Fordham called deintegration and re-integration – opening and closing (1976: 27–8). Deintegration is the opening of Self to experiences, and re-integration the closure of ego around the experience which can then be taken into Self – where it forms a stable internal object. We cannot say where Self begins or ends. Self is, by its nature, a paradox. It holds and contains opposites, so statements about it are often both assertions and denials, as in these few lines taken from *The Thunder: Perfect Mind* (Robinson 1988: 295–404):

> For I am knowledge and ignorance
> I am shame and boldness
> I am shameless, I am also ashamed.

The nature of Self is to raise religious and mystical questions. As it is similar to a God Image, there can be unfortunate confusions between analytical psychology and religion (Noll 1996). One way to understand the Jungian notion of individuation is to use the Buddhist notion of karma, and the way to understand Self is the Buddhist notion: No-Self. A Buddhist could have written, 'The Self is not only the centre but also the circumference which embraces both conscious and unconscious; it is the centre of this totality just as the ego is the centre of the conscious mind.' But this was Jung, in 1953. Ego can never hope to accommodate Self in all its aspects. No more than a naked child with a new face can hope to accommodate the Ocean.

Acknowledgements

I am most grateful to Yukio for kind permission to use this fictionalised account of his life story. He read it, I include his suggestions and those of my tutor, Andrew Samuels (SAP) my colleagues Christopher Perry (SAP), David Freeman (AJA) and Polly Young-Eisendrath (New York) and especially those of my wife, Carola (SAP).

References

Assagioli, Roberto (1975) *Psychosynthesis*, London: Turnstone.
Bowlby, John (1958) *A Secure Base: The Role of Attachment in Personality Development*, London: Tavistock.
Cassell (1963) *Latin-English Dictionary*, London: Cassell.
Edinger, Edward (1962) 'The ego Self axis', *Journal of Analytical Psychology* 5: 3–18.
Fairbairn, Ronald (1952) *Psychoanalytic Studies of the Personality*, London: Routledge.
Fordham, Michael (1976) *The Self and Autism*, London: Heinemann, Library of Analytical Psychology, vol. 3.
Fordham, Michael (1985) *Explorations into the Self*, London: Heinemann, Library of Analytical Psychology, vol. 7.
Fremantle, Francesca, and Chogyam Trungpa Rimpoche (trans. with commentary) (1987) *The Tibetan Book of the Dead*, Boston and London: Shambhala.
Glasser, Mervyn (1986) 'Identification and its vicissitudes as observed in the perversions', *International Journal of Psycho-Analysis* 67: 9–17.
Gordon, Rosemary (1993) *Bridges: Metaphor for Psychic Processes*, London: Karnak.
Gregory, Richard (ed.) (1987) *The Oxford Companion to the Mind*, Oxford: Oxford University Press.
Greimas, Algericas Julien (1987) *On Meaning*, London: Frances Pinter.
Hall, James, and Young-Eisendrath, Polly (1991) *Jung's Self Psychology*, New York: Guilford Press.
Henderson, Joseph (1988) *Cultural Attitudes in Psychological Perspective*, Toronto: Inner City Books.
Hillman, James (1983) *Archetypal Psychology*, Dallas: Spring.
Hobson, Peter (1993) *Autism and the Development of Mind*, Hillsdale, NJ: Erlbaum.

Jung, C. G. (1909) The Clark Lectures appear in the *CW* as follows: *CW* 2: 939–98 'The association method'; 2: 999–1014 'Family constellations'; and 17: 1–79 'Psychic conflicts in a child'.
——(1953) *CW* 12: 44 'Psychology and alchemy'.
——(1954a) *CW* 16: 470 'The psychology of the transference'.
——(1954b) *CW* 17: 323 'The development of the personality'.
——(1958) *CW* 11: 391 'Transformation symbolism in the mass'.
——(1959) *CW* 9/1: 392 'The phenomenology of the spirit in fairytales'.
——(1960) *CW* 8: 432 'On the nature of the psyche'.
——(1971a) *CW* 6: 789–91 'Psychological types: definitions'.
——(1971b) *CW* 6: 369–460 'The type problem in poetry'.
——(1971c) *CW* 6: 465 'Psychological types: definitions'.
——(1971d) *CW* 6: 757–62 'Psychological types: definitions'.
——(1973) *CW* 2: 733 'Studies in word association'.
Jung, Emma (1978) *Animus and Anima*, Dallas: Spring.
Klein, Melanie (1975) *Envy and Gratitude*, London: Hogarth Press.
Lonie, Isla (1991) 'Chaos theory, a new paradigm for psychotherapy', *Australian and New Zealand Journal of Psychiatry* 25: 548–60.
McNaughton, William (1971) *The Taoist Vision*, Ann Arbor: University of Michigan Press.
Modell, Arnold (1993) *The Private Self*, Harvard, MA: Harvard University Press.
Nagy, Marilyn (1991) *Philosophical Issues in the Psychology of C. G. Jung*, Albany: SUNY Press.
Noll, Richard (1996) *The Jung Cult*, London: Fontana.
Payutto, Ven. P. A. (1996) *Good, Evil and Beyond: Karma in the Buddha's Teaching*, Bangkok: Buddhadhamma Foundation.
Plato (1974) 'The simile of the cave', in *The Republic*, London: Penguin.
Rabjam, Longchen (1998) *The Precious Treasury of the Way of Abiding*, Junction City, CA: Padma.
Redfearn, Joseph (1985) *My Self, My Many Selves*, London: Academic Press, Library of Analytical Psychology, vol. 6.
Robinson, James M. (ed.) (1988) *The Thunder, Perfect Mind*, in *The Nag Hammadi Library in English*, 3rd edn, Leiden: Brill.
Samuels, Andrew, Shorter, Bani, and Plaut, Fred (1986) *A Critical Dictionary of Jungian Analysis*, London: Routledge.
Stolorow, Robert, Brandchaft, Bernard, and Atwood, George (1987) *Psychoanalytic Treatment: An Intersubjective Approach*, Hillsdale, NJ: Analytic Press.
Sullivan, Barbara (1987) 'The archetypal foundation of the therapeutic process', in Nathan Schwartz–Salant and Murray Stein (eds), *Archetypal Processes in Psychotherapy*, Wilmette, IL: Chiron Clinical Series.
Sumedho, Ajahn (1984) *Cittaviveka: Teachings from the Silent Mind*, Hemel Hempstead: Amaravati.
Tuckett, David (1993) 'Fictions about patients', *International Journal of Psycho-Analysis* 74(6): 1181–93.
Tustin, Frances (1981) *Autistic States in Children*, London: Routledge.
Watson, Gay (1999) *The Resonance of Emptiness*, London: Curzon.
Whitmont, Edward, and Pereira, Sylvia (1989) *Dreams a Portal to the Source*, London: Routledge.

Wiener, Yvette (1996) 'Chronos and Kairos, two dimensions of time in the psychotherapeutic process', *Journal of the British Association of Psychotherapists* 30(1): 65–85.

Winnicott, Donald (1990) 'Ego distortion in terms of true and false self', in *The Maturational Process and the Facilitating Environment*, London: Karnac.

Wood, Ernest (1977) *Zen Dictionary*, London: Pelican.

Young-Eisendrath, Polly (1996) *The Gifts of Suffering*, Reading, MA: Addison Wesley.

Zabriskie, Beverley (1997) 'Thawing the "frozen accidents": the archetypal view in counter transference', *Journal of Analytical Psychology* 42(1): 25–41.

14

THE CONSCIOUSNESS-ONLY SCHOOL

An introduction and a brief comparison with Jung's psychology

Moriya Okano

Since the early 1970s I have worked for the synthesis of Buddhism, especially Zen and Consciousness-only, and Western psychology. I am now the director of Sangraha Institute for Psychological and Spiritual Studies, whose purpose is to deepen our studies in this direction, sharing results with many people. While there have been many comparative studies between Zen and psychology, I believe the Consciousness-only School is the most psychologically refined of all Buddhist teachings, offering a penetrating and efficient understanding of human beings. First, I present its outline, and then, I suggest succinctly how it is possible to synthesize it with Jungian psychology.

The founders of the Consciousness-only School

Consciousness-only (*vijñapti-mātratā*) is the doctrine of the Yogacara School, a stream of Mahayana Buddhism that first developed in the second to fourth century of the Common Era. Indian Mahayana Buddhism reached the peak with this school as well as with the Madhyamika School.

The expression 'Consciousness-only' derives from the basic ideas of the Yogacara School that the appearance of all things depends upon the mind, and further that all things appear as the mind depicts. The outlook of this school is so filled with psychological insights that resonate with modern Western psychodynamic psychology that I call it the Mahayana-Buddhist version of depth psychology. The oldest existing text of the Yogacara School is *Saṃdhinirmocana-sūtra*. As is the case with many other Buddhist texts, the author is unknown. Opinions differ widely with regard to the date when it was written, ranging from *c*.150 to *c*.300.

Yogacara psychology is not the creation of a single individual but was gradually systematized, especially by three philosophers: Maitreya, Asanga, and Vasubandhu. It is not clear whether Maitreya (?–430 or 270–350) was a mythical or a historical figure. Those scholars who assume his historical reality ascribe to him the encyclopedic work of *Yogacara-bhumi*. Asanga (?–470 or 320–400) was born in Purusapura of Ghandara in North India, and at first belonged to Theravadin Buddhism. Later studying with Maitreya and realizing Emptiness (*śūnyata*), he was converted to Mahayana. The most representative of his writings is *Mahāyāna-saṃgraha*, which is a systematic presentation of Mahayana Buddhism from the viewpoint of the Yogacara School. Vasubandhu (–480 or 320–400), Asanga's brother, became a priest of Theravadin Buddhism, and then was converted to Mahayana under his brother's influence, and completed the system of the Consciousness-only School. He wrote *Abhidharma-kośa-śastra*, *Viṃsatike-kārikā*, *Triṃśika-kārikā*, and *Mahāyāna-saṃgrahabhāsya*.

Basic tenets of Buddhism

The Yogacara School shares with other schools of Buddhism the idea of a 'dharma seal' which means the sign of truth by which Buddhism explicitly distinguishes itself from non-Buddhist schools. Three dharma seals that distinguish the Buddhist perspective are: (1) all conditioned things are impermanent; (2) phenomenal things are in existence only by condition and so have no substance, and (3) the mind becomes calm by extinguishing the forces of craving or attachment to things and states of being.

From the viewpoint of Buddhism, ordinary people are restless and discontent because they lack insight into impermanence and non-substantiality, and attach themselves to various things and persons. That is why Buddhists speak of four dharma seals by adding to the three above the reality that events of life inevitably go against one's will and thus lead to distress and anguish.

The goal of Buddhism is to resolve these sufferings and attain a lasting peace of the mind by realizing that all things, including humans, are limited and have no essence in themselves, and therefore excessive attachment is both impossible and unnecessary. In this sense, Buddhism has originally a therapeutic character.

In Japan as in the West, the concepts of impermanence, non-self, suffering, and nirvana tend to be misunderstood in the direction of negativism and life-denial. Even within Buddhism there seems to have been the tendency to advise people to go into nirvana in the sense of death as soon as possible because life leads to desires which in turn result in sufferings. More exactly speaking, Buddhism inherited the ancient Indian outlook that teaches that human life does not end with death but repeats itself. In the history of Indian Buddhism, there was a phase after the Buddha's death in which the dominant school sought individual liberation and equated it with the complete liberation from reincarnation or rebirth in any form.

Emptiness and nirvana with no fixed abode in
Mahayana Buddhism

At about the start of the Christian era, there emerged a group of Buddhists who criticized this pessimistic tendency as *hinayana* or 'lesser vehicle', meaning that one is content with escaping alone from this world of suffering into the world of calmness. Mahayana, namely a 'bigger vehicle,' was developed as a means of saving all sentient beings from the world of suffering. The core concept in Mahayana was Emptiness (*śūnyata*) and nirvana with no fixed abode (*apratishita-nirvāna*).

Śūnyata literally means zero. This word was, and is still, often misunderstood as mere nothingness. However, it seems to be a concept that synthesized, condensed, and deepened meditative experiences that had been expressed by words such as 'arising causation' (*pratītya-samutpāda*), impermanence (*anitya*) and non-self (*anātman*). Mahayana Buddhism explains the Emptiness of all beings from various angles.

First, it is pointed out that all things are empty because they arise from causation. Everything comes into being only through its causal connection (*pratyaya*) with other beings. There is nobody that was born without parents and can live alone without any care from others. Emptiness, therefore, has the connotation that there is nothing that could exist by itself.

Then, it is said that all beings are empty because they have no self-nature. The quality of anything is determined by and varies with its relation to other beings. For example, the hot water in the bathtub brings relaxation to humans, but death to fish. Emptiness, therefore, suggests that there is nothing in the nature of a thing that does not change in accordance with the situation.

It is also noted that all things are empty because they are impermanent. Everything changes. Our whole universe itself has been changing since its beginning. Emptiness also means that there is nothing that does not change.

It is also stressed that all things are empty because they have no self. There is no essence that exists eternally by itself without any change. The term Atman from Sanskrit means not so much ego but entity, and so 'non-self' refers to non-entity. Emptiness also includes this concept of non-self.

Further, Emptiness also suggests that all beings are related to each other, forming one unity. Therefore, Emptiness overlaps with the notion of indivisibility and absolute unity (*tathatā*). This is close to a concept of cosmic consciousness, in the sense that all beings including one's self constitute a universe.

One more important thing to note is that Emptiness is not so much a concept but a verbalization of ineffable experiences during meditation. In Buddhism it is believed it is possible for humans to enter the state of absolute freedom, nirvana with no fixed abode, when they realize the oneness of all beings and become aware of the identity of all beings with the True Self. Thus, we are perhaps right in thinking that the goal of Mahayana Buddhism is to reach the state beyond boundaries of individuality, the absolute free personality. Based upon this understanding and upon Buddhist practice of meditation, the Yogacara School made a further step toward a more systematic and refined theory of the mind.

The three kinds of perceptual patterns

In the view of the Yogacara School, because humans grow up by learning to see the world through the lens of language, every being, be it a thing or a person, looks to be individual and separate in a way that is expressed by a word, especially a noun. If we look at a tree, making use of the noun 'tree' in our mind, for example, we tend to become almost unconscious of its connection with innumerable things without which it cannot exist: the ancestor tree which brought forth seeds for the tree, the water it must absorb for its growth, the earth on which it grows, the air it needs for photosynthesis, the sunlight, the galactic system which includes the solar system, etc. We are usually living with this perceptual pattern that prevents us from seeing how beings are related to each other. The Yogacara School calls this perceptual pattern that is produced from imagination or fallacious discrimination *parikalpita-svabhāva*.

When we see reality more closely, however, we find that every being only exists through its connection with others. There is nothing that is isolated and exists by itself. That is what is expressed by 'arising from causation' (*pratītya-samutpāda*), to use the pre-Yogacara terminology. Remember the example of the tree. Everything only exists in relationship to other things. This constitutes a perceptual pattern in which one is aware of the relatedness of all beings to each other (*paratantra-svabhāva*).

When we further look into reality, we understand that all beings have been connected with each other from the beginning as far as we know. If all beings are connected with each other, then they should be called one; if they are one, they are individually empty in the sense that there is no separate being. *Pariniṣpanna-svabhāva* refers to the perceptual pattern in which one is aware of the fact that all beings are one and empty.

By connecting two of these three perceptual patterns (*trayaḥ-svabhāva*), the Yogacara School epistemologically explains how vexing passions and Enlightenment happen. We are caught in delusions when we assume that each being is a separate entity that has become an element of the world by connecting with other beings. We are enlightened when we realize that all beings are originally connected with each other. The Yogacara School teaches that it is the mind that decides through which of these perspectives we see the world and ourselves.

Primary and secondary vexing passions

This theory of three kinds of perceptual pattern, when isolated, might seem philosophical, having nothing to do with our concrete psychology. The perceptual patterns, however, constitute the foundations of our daily feelings, needs, and behaviors. Failing to see the connection of all beings as the basis of their separateness results in the attachment to the ego that is wrongly perceived as existing alone without any connection with other beings. Each ordinary person is, more or less, egocentric, believing that the world and others should exist for him or her.

Because this substantiation and centralization of the ego does not fit with reality, it produces various sufferings and conflicts. These are called vexing passions (*kleśa*). The Yogacara School distinguishes minor or secondary vexing passions (*upakleśa*) from primary vexing passions and enumerates twenty such *upakleśas*: fury (*krodha*), enmity (*upanāha*), concealment or hypocrisy (*mrakṣa*), vexation (*pradāśa*), envy (*īrṣyr*), parsimony (*matsarya*), deception (*sāṭhya*), flattery (*māyā*), harmfulness (*vihiṃsā*), pride (*made*), shamelessness (*āhrīkya*), non-integrity (*anapatrāpya*), agitation or restlessness (*auddhatya*), torpid-mindedness or low-spiritedness (*styāna*), unbelief (*āśraddha*), indolence or sloth (*kausīdya*), negligence (*pramāda*), forgetfulness (*musita smrtih*), distraction (*vikṣepa*), and non-discernment (*asaṃprajanya*).

Most of these secondary vexing passions come from seeing the self and others as separate and different. By contrast, it also enumerates eleven virtues (*kuśala*) as states of the mind that lead to Enlightenment: belief (*śraddhā*), sense of shame (*hrī*), sense of integrity (*apatrapā*), non-covetousness (*alobha*), non-anger (*adversā*), non-delusion (*amoha*), zeal of diligence (*virya*), composure of mind (*prasrabdhi*), vigilance (*apramāda*), equanimity (*upekṣā*), and harmlessness or non-injury (*ahiṃsa*).

These virtues express that the mind is functioning, realizing its connection with itself and others. Non-foolishness in particular means the wisdom that begins with connection and moves toward unity.

Unlike modern psychology, the Yogacara School had no intention to describe human mental phenomena in general; it is primarily concerned with Enlightenment as the liberation from vexing passions. Therefore, in my view, it compensates for depth that is lacking in modern psychology.

The Yogacara School's dealing with vexing passions is not content with the description of minor vexing passions but penetrates into the primary vexing passions (*mūla-kleśa*), and further divides them into six superficial fundamental vexing passions: covetousness (*rāga*), anger (*pratigha*), delusion (*moha*), conceit (*māna*), doubt (*vicikitsā*) and false views (*kudṛṣṭi*), and four deeper fundamental vexing passions: self-delusion (*atmamoha*), self-belief (*ātmadṛṣṭi*), self-conceit (*ātmanana*), and self-love (*ātmasneha*).

The theories of eight consciousnesses and the four wisdoms

The Yogacara School discovered the unconscious more than a thousand years earlier than Freud with the theory of eight consciousnesses in which the human mind is divided into eight spheres. First, the five consciousnesses refer to the spheres of five senses: eyes, ears, nose, tongue and body. Beyond these five is consciousness (*mano-vijñāna*), considered as a sense whose function is to perceive outer objects. Until the Yogacara School the human mind was identified only with the six functions. The Yogacara School assumes that behind these six is a seventh, the manas-consciousness (*manas-vijñāna*) which substantiates and centralizes the ego and attaches to it. *Manas* is a Sanskrit word that denotes calculation or conjecture. The manas-consciousness refers to the sphere of the mind that calculates the ego as an entity.

The four deeper primary vexing passions mentioned earlier are the functions of the manas-consciousness. It is this consciousness that makes us ignore non-self and Emptiness (Japanese: *gachi*), believe in the self (*gaken*), be proud of and dependent upon it (*gaman*) and attach ourselves to it (*gaai*). So, in the view of the Yogacara School, this manas-consciousness is manifest as ignorance of the fact that the ego only exists in connection with others and therefore is empty in itself, and as the assumption that the ego is an entity and the center of the world. The manas-consciousness is the mind that divides self and non-self and excessively adheres to the former.

Yogacara psychology further posits the alaya-consciousness (*ālaya-vijñāna*) as the eighth consciousness that is the deepest sphere of the mind. Alaya is a Sanskrit word that means storehouse. So the alaya-consciousness refers to the sphere where seeds (*bīja*) of all beings and all lives are stored. With the ancient Indian *Weltanschauung*, Buddhism shares the idea of rebirth or samsara, the belief that a life does not end with death but repeats life and death. The alaya-consciousness is the agent of samsara; every deed leaves behind a consequence that has a power or influence over later events. Karma (literally, 'action') involves both a deed and its influence. The alaya-consciousness is the storehouse for seeds of karma. Owing to the functioning of this consciousness, we humans both maintain and attach to our life. It is the mind that discriminates life and non-life and excessively sticks to the former.

The manas- and alaya-consciousnesses and their interaction result in excessive attachment to the self and life. The alaya-consciousness produces the manas-consciousness, which clings to the self, and the manas-consciousness sees the alaya-consciousness through its attachment to the ego, and so it seems to us that life is in the ego's possession and therefore at its disposal. The vicious circle of the interaction between the manas-consciousness and the alaya-consciousness is the source of all other vexing passions.

However, the alaya-consciousness is in itself neither good nor bad, but neutral. Indeed, ordinary humans repeat the vicious circle that the seeds stored there, going through the manas-consciousness, are transformed into vexing passions, leaving behind seeds of karma that are, in turn, stored in the alaya-consciousness. Seeds of Enlightenment are also sown in the alaya-consciousness, to bloom sometime in the future.

The Consciousness-only School does not believe in a sudden leap from vexing passions to freedom through Enlightenment, but rather holds that this transition takes a long time. In this view, only the discipline of many years makes possible the transformation of the eight consciousnesses from vexing passions into wisdom.

The Alaya-consciousness is then transformed into the great mirror wisdom (*mahadarśanajñāna*), which reflects the world as it is in which all beings are connected with each other, forming a unity. Correspondingly, the manas-consciousness becomes equality wisdom (*samatājnana*), which makes us realize that the self and others are essentially equal and one. Consciousness turns into the profound contemplation wisdom (*pratyavekṣaṇa-jñāna*) that observes this wonderful state of the world. Finally, the five consciousnesses change to the perfect achievement wisdom (*kṛtyānusthāna-jñāna*), and thus, the eight consciousnesses are transformed into the four types of wisdom (*catvari-jñānāni*).

As is clear from these explanations, then, the psychological transformation from vexing passions to Enlightenment is in the Yogacara School reformulated in a far more refined way. In this respect, the Consciousness-only School seems similar to Ken Wilber's psychological system in which human development does not end with the establishment of the ego, but may include stages of self-realization and even self-transcendence. From this perspective, we may regard Yogacara psychology as a therapy with the goal of self-transcendence.

The theory of the five stages

According to the Consciousness-only School, the transformation from vexing passions to Enlightenment does not take place through a single leap but through several phases. Though each phase involves some leap, this leap is not so much sudden, as is often imagined in Rinzai Zen, but gradual.

The Yogacara School offers stages of transformation from the eight consciousnesses into the four types of wisdom and the ten stages of developing the Buddha-wisdom (*daśa bhūmayaḥ*) and the five groups (Japanese: *goi*). For purposes of brevity, the present essay only details the latter. This corresponds to the theory of consciousness development in modern psychology.

In the first stage, the stage of moral provisioning (*saṃbhāravasthā*), the student arranges money and food for a trip, and he or she finds a teacher and comrades, and study the philosophy of the Consciousness-only School.

In the second phase, the stage of intensified effort (*prayōgavasthā*), the student becomes involved in the practice. The classical Consciousness-only approach prescribes not only meditations, like zazen, for getting rid of thoughts and images, but also meditation that makes use of images and deepening thoughts as well as the six practices.

In the third stage, the stage of unimpeded penetrating insight (*prativedhavasthā*), the student attains the first Enlightenment, and understands the meaning of Emptiness, Oneness or Suchness (*tathatā*), not only intellectually but also through the transformation of the manas-consciousness and the alaya-consciousness. This stage is only an entrance into Enlightenment and the student must pass further through two stages for the eight consciousnesses to be transformed into the four types of wisdom. A transitory spiritual experience never amounts to the transformation of personality as a whole.

In the fourth stage, the stage of exercising cultivation (*bāvanāvasthā*), the student assimilates the experiences through further practices and makes them habitual. In the fifth stage, the stage of ultimate realization (*niṣṭhāvasthā*), the eight consciousnesses have been completely transformed into the four wisdoms, and all vexing passions have been overcome.

Much time is certainly needed to finish this course of discipline. It is believed to take a *kalpa* (a single kalpa is eons of time) to go from the stage of moral provisioning to the stage of intensified effort, and another two kalpas from the stage of unimpeded penetrating understanding through the stage of exercising cultivation to the stage of ultimate realization.

The Consciousness-only School takes very seriously the negative aspects of human beings in pointing out how long a discipline one needs to attain the ultimate Awakening. Rather than denying the possibility of Enlightenment, this approach suggests that Enlightenment is possible when we devote ourselves to discipline as long a time as three kalpas. Humans seem without hope in the possibility of spiritual salvation, but the Consciousness-only School teaches us that it is possible if we devote enough time and follow certain procedures. In this sense, it seems to provide us with a promising outlook concerning human growth.

The six kinds of practice

If the Consciousness-only School is regarded as a psychology that facilitates human growth and self-transcendence, the theory of the six kinds of practice (*sat pāramitāḥ*) would be the practical part of the psychology.

Pāramitāḥ (often translated as the 'perfections') is the practice of accomplishment or of going beyond ordinary suffering. Vexing passions and Enlightenment are respectively compared with this shore and that shore of the river. So paramita means to cross to from the shore of vexing passions to the shore of Enlightenment. The six perfections are stressed not only in the Yogacara School but also in Buddhism in general.

The first of these, generosity (*dānā-pāramitā*) must be fundamentally distinguished from donation in the ordinary sense in which the donor and the donated are separate from each other. In the Buddhist outlook, the self and others are originally one and only different aspects of the same reality. Donation as a paramitah is practiced so that the student may realize this truth. Just as water that happens to be in different places tends to be one when it flows from high to low, so donation in the Buddhist sense takes place like a natural phenomenon. It is training for developing the wisdom of equality.

The second practice, ethical discipline (*śīla-pāramitā*), does not mean to passively observe imposed injunctions but to strive for the goal of Enlightenment that the student spontaneously chose. It involves doing what is necessary and not doing what is not necessary in regard to the ethical training. It presupposes some autonomy before heteronomy.

The third practice, patience (*kṣānti-pāramitā*), refers to the acceptance and equanimity that allow one to be present with all of one's feelings moment to moment. It is also fundamentally different from patience in the ordinary sense that presupposes the separation of the self from the outer world. It is the attitude in living that develops from the deep recognition that the world is not at the individual's disposal, therefore full of disappointments.

The fourth practice, diligence (*vīrya-pāramitā*), is understood in our everyday language as making effort, but should more deeply mean a basic posture in human life in which one spends every day as discipline without being idle, knowing that our life is limited, on the one hand, and that it offers us the possibility of developing deep concentration and mindfulness, on the other.

The fifth practice, meditation (*dhyāna-pāramitā*), is especially indispensable for attaining Enlightenment or Emptiness. It must be stressed here that merely intellectual knowledge of Buddhist concepts alone never amounts to the experience of what is meant by them.

The sixth practice, wisdom (*prajñā-pāramitā*) is both the means and the goal of discipline. It involves the transformation of the deep structure through the discipline that begins with the intellectual study and understanding of Buddhist basic concepts and the other five practices.

Like other schools of Mahayana Buddhism, the Yogacara School has the goal of reaching the state of Nirvana with no fixed abode, the final stage of human development, beyond suffering and conflict, in which one lives in the real happiness of both the self and others.

The dual meaning of non-self

The Consciousness-only School, like Western depth psychology, differentiates the psyche into the surface and the depth, but is very different from the latter in that it focuses upon awakening in humans.

The teaching of 'no-self' (*anatman*) in Indian Buddhism originally referred to the fact that not only self, but also all beings and things have no essence apart from anything else. The person who is fully aware knows this non-substantiality of all things. Briefly, there is no self as a substance; the excessive attachment to the self, imagined as a substance, must be renounced and in the higher and more developed state of consciousness, the error of imagining the self as a substance has been overcome.

If the self is understood as a function that organizes sensations, feelings, thoughts, and volitions, but has no essences, then it is naturally observed among the Buddhas as well as the Bodhisattvas. This is a flexible and mature self that is free from any illusion and open to others. From the standpoint of the Yogacara School, Enlightenment is not the elimination of self, but the transformation of the whole mind from the state of eight consciousnesses to the four wisdoms. The conception of non-self in this sense would lead us not so much to the opposition of self and non-self but to the continuous and integrative vision of transformation in three stages: the pre-self stage, the provisional self stage, and the higher self stage.

Jung and the Consciousness-only school

Finally, I would like to explore the possibility of a productive synthesis of the psychology of the Yogacara School and Jungian depth psychology.

Jung's psychological theory and the scheme of the human mind corresponds closely to the Consciousness-only School. With the concept of the collective unconscious Jung seems to suggest that there is a sphere of the human mind that goes beyond individuality, and includes all human races, all living species, and even non-living being, extending to the whole universe. What he calls self in distinction from ego, which is individual, is the core of the whole psyche that includes both consciousness and the unconscious, personal and collective. The collective unconscious or the self seems to cover the same area as the alaya-consciousness, though from a different angle.

Lacking in the Consciousness-only School is the insight into the functioning of archetypes in the collective unconscious such as mother, father, and shadow. Therefore, insight into various processes of human life, resulting from the relationship between consciousness and the unconscious, is unexplored. The Jungian perspective on human life as the process of individuation, involving the integration of consciousness and the unconscious, or ego and self, will be a great addition to the development of the Consciousness-only School.

However, the self in Jung, despite its cosmological character, seems to be still conceived as an entity, and thus refers to a stage before the Formless Self or the True Self that is Emptiness in Mahayana Buddhism. Individuation, or self-realization, remains, therefore, incomplete in comparison with the Buddhist transformational scheme that begins with the ordinary, is transposed into the Bodhisattva, and ends with the Buddha. That is, I think, why the Jung–Hisamatsu conversation gives us the impression that the two men were arguing on different planes.

Lacking in Jung's analytic psychology, as in other depth psychology, is the insight into the vicious circle between human existence as a living being and the self-consciousness that conceives itself as a permanent entity. That is what Buddhism, especially the Yogacara School, most clearly grasps through the concepts of the manas-consciousness and the alaya-consciousness, showing how it is possible to grow beyond the structure of eight consciousnesses to become a Buddha who has cultivated the four wisdoms.

15

THE PROBLEMATIC OF MIND IN GOTAMA BUDDHA

Haya Tatsuo

What is Buddha?

Around the fifth century BCE in India, a series of factors, including increased levels of agricultural production, improvement of trade, population concentration, and general monetary and economic development, led to the founding and flourishing of cities. This was also a time when the economic and cultural focus changed from rural communities to growing cities. A progressive royalty and an affluent merchant class attained prominence and power. These open-minded people were innovative in many ways and demolished the basic, controlling superstructure of rural society: the religion of the Bhramans.

I am a scholar of Early Buddhism, especially researching the original thought of Gotama Buddha, and teach undergraduate university students the religious and philosophical theories of Buddhism. In this essay, I introduce the broad aspects of a Buddhist philosophy of mind and show how it alleviates the *suffering* (here the term means subjective anguish or discontent) of self-attachment. The changes in ancient India eventually introduced a whole new psychology of the individual.

These social changes also influenced the fields of philosophy and religion, where freethinkers who had refused the Bhramanical tradition, dominant since the times of the Vedas, began to assert themselves. The early Buddhist scriptures offer examples of moralistic critical thought, and skeptical, deterministic, and materialistic doctrines. Similar movements occurred in Greece with the Sophists, and in China with the so-called Hundred Philosophers. It can be argued that within the context of Indian history, freedom of thought had rarely been granted. Gotama Buddha, the founder of Buddhism, was among the freethinkers of this period.

Gotama Buddha is said to have been born in 463 BCE and passed away in 383 BCE. He was a prince and led a life of comfort. However, after much contemplation on the transitory nature of life (the fact that one is born, ages, gets ill and finally dies), he finally left home and dedicated himself to deep meditation and asceticism. After having mastered and transcended these practices, he attained enlightenment and became a Buddha, an Awakened One. These two words, 'enlightenment' and 'Buddha,' express the essence of Buddhism. In Pali, as well as in Sanskrit, both words have their linguistic origin in a single verbal root, '*budh*' which means 'awakening' or 'enlightenment' when used as a name, and 'awakened' in its adjectival and past participle forms. The name originating from this radical is translated into English as the word 'awakening,' while its past participle, translated as Buddha, is used in its original form and means, as is well known, 'awakened.' Buddha also means Awakened One. Hence, expressions such as 'to gain enlightenment' or 'to become a Buddha' carry exactly the same significance, and should be understood as a natural designation of one and the only fact: the act of awakening.

Taken in its literal sense, 'awaken' means to stop sleeping or make somebody stop sleeping. According to this definition it is not absurd to say that every morning when one wakes up, he or she becomes a Buddha, that is, an Awakened person. Nevertheless, in a Buddhist context, this expression acquires a completely different meaning. For Buddhism considers that what we normally call 'awake' is in reality nothing but a state of (deep) sleep. In our everyday lives we accept without questioning as self-evident the concept of a world that revolves around us, and leads a completely antagonistic and independent existence from us. Also, whether conscious or unconscious – it does not matter – we think of ourselves as something solid and stable and separate from others, even though we may feel emotionally connected. From this self-centered point of view, our existence appears to be something that has sprung from the depths of darkness. Based on this perception, we become extremely attached to the idea of an immutable and supposedly immortal self. In reality, however, we all know that we are going to die. Between us and this self that we suppose we are and to which we ordinarily cling, a gap develops. This gap leads to the so-called existential *sufferings* of coming into being, aging, getting sick and finally dying. 'Why am I going to die?' 'Isn't this a mistaken idea?' we ask ourselves. And not being able to come to terms with reality, we go on asking questions like 'What happens after death?' Such questions turn up new and insoluble torments. In all probability too, such a situation eventually becomes the target of nihilistic questioning about its own meaning. This process is referred to in Buddhism by the expression 'to be asleep,' which describes the state from which our *sufferings* are derived, a state, I think, all of us are familiar with.

If we realize that there is no immutable separate self and that such an egocentric point of view is not in any way something absolute, but rather and simply a fictitious assumption, then there is also the possibility that an entirely new world can unfold before us. We begin to feel that all things are connected and form a whole and that they are all intimately related to each other. Then we are able to realize that we are nothing but a part of the whole, and also that this whole leads its own life as a whole and realizes itself as the life of each and all of its parts. To experience this is enlightenment in which the self and the world are perceived as existing in a state of union; furthermore, each world is seen – for all the intimate and meaningful connections it contains – as something based on what one could describe by the term 'correlativity.' It is like being touched by an extreme feeling of inevitability and necessity, as if everything that is taking place has always been there from the very beginning of the universe.

Yet it should be emphasized – due to very frequent misapprehension on this point – that an experience of enlightenment developing exactly in the specific way described above is not an essential demand of Buddhism. Regardless of the contents of this experience, the key point is that we can overcome our ordinary way of perceiving things that is characterized by profound self-attachment. Even an experience of enlightenment, wrongly assimilated, can be used to increase self-attachment because certain delusive ideas can arise from grasping onto the experience. For instance, one might interpret such an experience as something exclusive and then feel exceptional and superior. This is a very easy trap to fall into, especially when the experience of enlightenment is taken to be a goal in itself. Nevertheless, enlightenment should not be seen in this way. The real goal is to ally enlightenment with an after-insight-state that can enable us to understand the separate self as a fictitious assumption. Thus, by means of this understanding, we are able to dispense with self-attachment, and thus the existential *sufferings* of coming into being, aging, getting sick and dying. This is what is meant in Buddhism by 'awakening,' a state where our distresses have been eliminated; a state – I dare say – we are not very familiar with. In Buddhism, to stop sleeping and to awaken is considered equal to attaining enlightenment. Both awakening and enlightenment mean to free oneself from the woes and *sufferings* one has created for oneself.

Concerning the word 'Buddha' itself, it is not a proper noun making special reference to a specific individual. As a common noun or adjective it can be used in reference to anyone. Any awakened being is a Buddha. Gotama Buddha is only one among an immense number of others who have awakened in this way. Consequently, we too, if we awaken, are said to be Buddhas. By stressing this point, it becomes clear that Buddhism's main concern is to teach people that anyone can become a Buddha, rather than to demand faith and worship of Gotama Buddha as though he were a god.

This was certainly the case in early Buddhism, when Gotama Buddha was not taken to be an absolute being towards which religious worship was due. Gotama, as the result of a spiritual process of growth, became a Buddha. That is why his followers dedicate themselves to practices that, in all likelihood, could bring them similar results.

Emancipation from *suffering*

Gotama Buddha's basic way of thinking about the problematic of life and death can be characterized as being an inquiry on the causes of *suffering* and whether or not they originate from the fact that someone considers himself or herself to be a sufferer. Therefore, his main concern is subjective, rather than objective suffering. From this it can be said that Gotama Buddha's teaching has little to offer to someone who does not have the consciousness of being in distress. Anyone who does not perceive himself as sick is, in all likelihood, beyond the reach of medicine.

Gotama Buddha's first attempt to instruct others on the nature of *suffering* can be found in the so-called 'Four Noble Truths': 1. There is *suffering*; 2. *Suffering* has a cause; 3. *Suffering* can be extinguished; and 4. There is a method to extinguish *suffering*. Considering that his personal *suffering* was the expression of something more universal, related not only to him as an individual, but inherent in all human beings, it can therefore be said to have been Gotama Buddha's motivation to start preaching.

Furthermore it is said that Gotama Buddha, after much consideration, at the time he gained enlightenment, came to the realization of what is usually designated in Buddhism as 'The twelve-linked chain of causes and effects as related to *suffering*.' Here we can find a more elaborate and methodical explanation of the Four Noble Truths. This realization of 'dependent co-origination' or interdependence can be taken as an elucidation on how non-awareness causes *suffering*, and how it is possible to awaken. For further discussion on this point, let us refer to the sutras.

Without being able to realize the source where it springs from (*avijjā*, ignorance), but employing all available resources (*saṃkhāra*, the factors of forming a self), a fixed, substantialized self that conceives of itself as existing separately, comes into being. Without questioning – as though it was a commonplace everyday fact – an egocentric way of perceiving the world (*viññāṇa-nāmarūpa-saḷāyatana-phassa*/consciousness, external objective world, the six kinds of consciousness, the connection between the perception organs, the object of perception, as consciousness) comes to be formed on the assumption that the self and the world are opposite, antagonistic entities. Thus, the self and the world are taken as existing in isolation, without any inherent interconnection. An experience of the self emerges in which the self judges the world (*vedanā*, value), according to criteria established by itself. This, in the form of self-centered passion(*taṇhā*, desires), becomes an unconscious habit without revealing its true character as an enigmatic drive inciting us from the depths of darkness. The self clings (*upadana*) more and more to itself as something fixed and substantialized, giving rise to the various distresses (*dukkha*, *suffering*) associated to our existence (*bhava*), i.e. coming-into being (*jāti*), aging (*jarā*), getting sick and dying (*maraṇa*). Fear and insecurity arise which cannot be helped, because the basic cause of our *suffering* is to be found in this point of self-clinging.

By means of something ordinary in one's daily experience, the practice of meditation, a crevice can be opened in the carapace of this refractory self so that a breakthrough and transformation happens. The belief and experience that there is a separation between the self and what is not the self, on which basis these elements are supposed to exist without any interconnection, in a complete state of isolation, becomes the basis for judging the world. Only when these factors are shattered and perceived as fictitious can one realize that it is not the case and that all things at all times are necessarily interwoven and interconnected (*paṭiccasamuppāda*, interdependence). This is the experience of enlightenment which, together with a balanced insight, enables one to understand that a separate self is a fiction, and that *suffering* is extinguished when one no longer clings to this fiction.[1]

Although acquainted with many examples of mystical experience, I must confess that cases like Gotama Buddha's – where this experience is related to our existential *sufferings*, the basic cause of these *sufferings* is clarified, and even a method to eliminate them is provided – is rare, I believe. Yet, Gotama Buddha's attempts are not concerned with objective – or external – causality. The objective facts that we come into existence, age, and get sick and die are not in themselves – he argues – causes of *suffering*. 'It is Mine' coming into being, aging, and getting sick and dying that is the cause of *suffering*. When Gotama Buddha's teachings are linked to our *sufferings*, for the first time, they have real personal significance.

Gotama Buddha himself became aware of his *suffering*; this realization made the elimination of *suffering* his pursuit. In the course of his quest he came to realize that the basic cause of *suffering* derives from ourselves. We bring about *suffering* by constructing a fictitious image of ourselves as fixed, stable, and separate. And, from this image, clinging radically to fabrication in a way that makes us perceive all things in a self-centered manner, we act according to this perception.

Even though by acquiring knowledge of the causes of *suffering* one is presumably capable of getting rid of them, reality shows that the way to this accomplishment is far from easy. Gotama Buddha set forth a clear method for eliminating the basic causes of *suffering*, and it must be noted that the most direct means to achieve this goal is meditation. Through the practice of meditation we can ease the extreme, unconscious attachment to self.

From a psychological point of view

Yet, if we pay close attention to it, what Gotama Buddha is pointing out as the basic cause of *suffering* is something that we take as a matter of course. As part of the process of growing up, we find ourselves needing to develop a stable identity in order to function interpersonally and socially with others. Thus, the process toward the formation of a self is taken as a positive aspect of life while its lack, on the other hand, is seen as problematic. And yet Gotama Buddha insists that the fundamental cause of all our distress concerning life and death has its origin in the formation of such a self. To realize that something that is necessary for ordinary life is also deeply problematic requires painstaking efforts. And perhaps this is the reason why many find it so difficult to understand the core of Buddhism.

Another reason why Gotama Buddha's doctrine is usually considered difficult to understand is because it gives us the impression of denying our
ordinary, commonplace way of looking at things. But, as a matter of fact, his
doctrine should be regarded as overcoming the ordinary, by transcending it.
Even the enlightened Gotama Buddha himself did not lose a great part of
what we call the commonplace view . . . for, if one called his name he was sure
to respond. He continued to have a separate identity after his supreme enlightenment.

The simple existence of the self does not constitute the cause of *suffering*,
because the self is transcended. What is being criticized is not the formation of
the self (understood as a basic step in the genesis of a fully developed person) –
for this is not something that should be criticized; what is being said is that this
process alone is not the final aim or goal of living a human life. 'The establishment of oneself,' or 'the realization of oneself,' is ordinarily considered the
mature stage of adulthood, but according to Buddhism this is still unfulfillment.
By not perceiving the incompleteness and non-fulfillment of what we suppose
to be our mature state, *suffering* finds its origin. Gotama Buddha shows, however, that there is more beyond this state, and, what is more, that it is exactly
because these possibilities exist that *suffering* can be brought to an end.

To become a Buddha does not mean to become something superhuman.
Rather, it means a step in the whole dynamic of changing one's way of perceiving the world. The change is illustrated in Buddhism by the process of
awakening, extinguishing *suffering*, getting out of a state of illusion and
acquiring enlightenment, and eventually becoming a Buddha. Attainment of
status as a Buddha can be interpreted as a step in the process of growth and
transformation of the human mind (psyche) itself.

Buddhism is concerned with nothing but the above-mentioned process.
Because the elimination of *suffering* is not an easy goal to achieve, *suffering* is
sometimes overemphasized in Buddhism. One could almost get the impression
that the stage beyond attachment to self is not connected to *suffering* at all.

Psychologically, though, we can say the human mind's growth process
includes both a state previous to identity formation, as well as a posterior one
(Pre-Ego (self) – Ego (self) – Trans-Ego (self)), and trace a parallel with what
in Buddhism is expressed in stages: pre-sleep / sleep / awakening; pre-*suffering*
/ *suffering* / extinction of *suffering*. Then we are aware of the stages which
involve *suffering* as a pertinent part of the growth process, to be seen in a positive way. Thus, it is not that there is a complete denial of our ordinary
individual identity, but rather that, while recognizing its pertinent points, one
should go on and transcend the ordinary as part of what can be seen as a consistent step in the overall development of the human mind.

The truth discerned by Gotama Buddha is something that transcends the
boundaries of Buddhism itself; it is a truth concerning all humans. As far as
we can all be said to be in a state of mental distress, Buddhism can undoubt-
edly be understood as a kind of practical psychology. Buddhism is not simply

a matter of believing, or not, in something existing outside us which we do not understand. It is not a matter of following a practice without understanding its meaning. Buddhism represents, instead, a unique and far-reaching opportunity to examine the very essence of human life, something each individual can ponder. It is not a question of faith or obedience, but of restless self-inquiry and doubt.

Note

1 P. Steinthal (ed.), *Udāna*, London: Oxford University Press, 1948, pp. 1–2. This is the translation including the author's original interpretation.

16

THE DEVELOPMENT OF BUDDHIST PSYCHOLOGY IN MODERN JAPAN

Akira Onda

Introduction

My career as a psychologist began with the study of creativity. I was mainly inspired by Gardiner Murphy's works on the subject which made me realize that it is only approached through the combination of conceptual thinking and emotional intelligence. This field of creativity seemed to suggest that it was necessary to go beyond confinements and compartmentalization in psychology.

Creativity was then connected with Zen in my study when I participated in the 1961–2 project on 'Medical and Psychological Studies of Zen' financially supported by *Monbusho,* the Ministry of Education (Onda 1962). At that time I also began to practice Zen, dealing with koan and *Shikan-taza* practices. The comparative studies I was involved in at the time showed that other forms of meditation or methods like hypnosis, autogenic training, yoga, nen-butsu, mantra, and ajikan are also relevant to creativity and healing (Onda 1965; 1967). Since the 1970s, during which arose the interest in Eastern meditation among Western psychiatrists and psychologists, I have also been involved in international projects on the subject (Onda 1974/75; 1986; 1992; 1993).

Dhampada, one of the oldest Buddhist texts, begins with the words: 'We are what we think. All that we are arises with our thoughts. With our thoughts we make the world.' This suggests how Buddhism is itself a psychology, though the word 'psychology' here may not be spoken in the Western sense. About a hundred years ago William James recognized the uniquely psychological character of Buddhism when he invited Dharmapala, a young Buddhist from Sri Lanka and a leader of an international Buddhist movement, to give a lecture before his students. After the lecture he told them, 'This [Buddhism] is the psychology everybody will be studying twenty-years from now.' But with a few exceptions like C. G. Jung, most psychoanalysts, under the influence of

242

Freud's reductive characterization of Eastern thought as 'oceanic feeling' in *Civilization and Its Discontents* (1930), until recently tended to regard Buddhism as a regressive state to primary narcissism, or, at best, a form of mysticism. It is only since the 1990s that more and more psychoanalysts have come to see in this representative Eastern religion a refined system of psychological insights (Molino 1998).

Most Western people first came to know Zen in particular and Buddhism in general through Daisetsu T. Suzuki's writings in English. Though he held with Erich Fromm a symposium on psychoanalysis and Zen in 1957, he, mainly leaning upon the Prajna thought, mystified Zen in a sense and made it something beyond Western psychology. Zen was later introduced to the West also through translated writings by Japanese Zen masters like Zenkei Shibayama (1974) as well as by Japanese religious philosophers of the Kyoto School such as Keiji Nishitani (1980). They all emphasized on the whole a less psychological than religious character of Zen. In this respect we must not overlook what King critically remarks in his foreword to Nishitani's book: 'Yet this relationship [between Buddhism and psychoanalysis] or lack of it is of some consequence because part of the . . . interest in Zen has been attributed to the strength of the psychological–psychiatric "tradition" in America' (quoted in Molino 1998: xii).

In this chapter I would like to present studies by a number of Japanese Buddhist psychologists who were antecedent to or contemporary with Suzuki but have been much less known in the West than he. I taught psychology for many years at Toyo University, a key agency in the development of Buddhist psychology in Japan. Western psychologists today who are pursuing the integration of Western psychology and Buddhism will find in them both pioneering works possibly relevant to the trend in psychology today and works specifically relevant to the Japanese development of Buddhist psychology so far. I hope my historical presentations will fill a gap between the West and Japan in the understanding of Buddhism.

Stances of early modern Japanese psychologists

In the Meiji Reformation (1868), early modern Japan, not long after the opening to the West in the middle of the nineteenth century, adopted for its survival in the rapidly changing world, seemingly opposing stances toward its own cultural tradition and modern Western civilization. In order to strengthen and modernize the country so as not to be colonized by the West, on the one hand, it had to absorb Western science and technology as much and as soon as possible. In order to maintain and reinforce its national identity, facing the threat of being assimilated to the Western civilization, on the other, it had to defend and assert its cultural traditions distinct from the latter. The result was the combination of Western science and technology with Japanese mind.

This seems to be also true of the development of psychology in Japan.

During the initial phase Western books in psychology, mostly academic and professional psychology, were translated into Japanese. In one of these translations Amane Nishi coined *shin-rigaku*, the knowledge of principles governing mental phenomena, as a Japanese word for 'psychology,' and it was to be used thereafter. Then, Yujiro Motora (1858–1912) and Matataro Matsumoto (1865–1943) imported Western experimental psychology to Japan by studying respectively with Stanley Hall (1844–1924) in America and Wilhelm Wundt (1832–1920) in Germany. As early as in 1903 Motora established, in collaboration with Matsumoto, the first psychological laboratory in Japan. So they were the founders of Japanese scientific psychology.

There were, on the other hand, endeavors to develop psychology in a way that fits the Japanese cultural, especially Buddhist, tradition, as we shall see. They involved expositions and theoretical developments of Buddhist psychology, empirical studies of Buddhist meditation, and the application of Buddhism to psychotherapy.

Another feature of early modern Japanese Buddhist psychologists, to be mentioned, is their universalism. They were not involved in any particular tradition within Zen or Buddhism in general. They were not interested in the difference between Rinzai Zen and Soto Zen or between Zen Buddhism and Shin Buddhism or Shingon Buddhism in Japan. Further, they wanted to find something common among Buddhism, Hinduism, and Christianity, and between religion and non-religious creative activities such as arts. For their primary concern was universal human experience. And this universalism was shared by early modern Japanese intellectuals in other disciplines as well. For philosophers of the Kyoto School initiated by Kitaro Nishida, for example, Zen was not Zen of the Zen sect but simply Zen, or Zen of what could be called Zen spirit.

Enryō Inoue

Enryō Inoue (1858–1919) played an important role in initiating both philosophy and psychology in early modern Japan. As early as in 1884, as a student he founded the first Japanese philosophical association, and in 1887 he published his first book *The Outline of Psychology*, and started a philosophical journal, founded Tetsugakukan, the antecedent to Toyo University, and lectured on applied psychology there.

Inoue saw in Buddhism an advantage that could not be expected from Christianity. While Christianity refused the Copernican theory and Darwinism, Buddhism seemed to have an affinity with modern rationalism. Unlike other cultural traditions such as Shintoism, Confucianism, and Taoism, Buddhism was for him, therefore, a promising cultural heritage for assimilating modern Western civilization. In other words, he thought it would be compatible with Western science. That is the point where Inoue and his followers differ from Suzuki and other Zen philosophers.

Two seemingly opposing stances are clearly evidenced in Inoue: on the one hand, he tried to dispel irrational elements in his cultural traditions, including Buddhism, with the aid of the Western rational mind. Writing books and articles in the discipline that he called *Yōkai-gaku*, which literally means phantom studies, he studied seemingly mysterious phenomena, and believed most of them were merely superstitions to be explained away by science, especially psychology.

On the other hand, he systematically presented Buddhist psychology in his books, *Eastern Psychology* (maybe 1894), *Buddhist Psychology* (1897), and *Zen Psychology* (1902). Inoue was not only the first Japanese psychologist in general but also the first psychologist in particular that combined the Buddhist psychological tradition with modern Western psychology. Other Japanese Buddhist psychologists were indebted to him in one way or other.

Expositions of Buddhist psychology

Inoue grasped the nature of Buddhist psychology in distinction from Western psychology. In his view, the former is not, like the latter, as a science, based upon experimental study and therefore exact in the scientific sense, but pursues a religious purpose of helping people relieve themselves from delusions, with the goal of Awakening. It is therefore expected to serve as a path to nirvana. Inoue's insistence that Buddhist insights should be able to be experimentally demonstrated was to materialize only more than half a century later. Buddhism and Western psychology, however, were considered to share the view that mental phenomena are ruled by psychological laws, and therefore can be studied psychologically.

Inoue's expositions of Buddhist psychology are based upon Abhidharma, Yogacara, and Zen. Abhidharma is a psychology of Theravada Buddhism that systematically classifies and analyzes mental phenomena without positing the mind substance. According to this psychology, a person is nothing but a composite of five aggregates (*pañca skandhāḥ*): forms of matter (*rūpa*), perceptions (*vedanā*), conceptions (*saṃjñā*), volition (*saṃskāra*), and consciousness (*vijñāna*). Suffering (*dukkha*) comes about due to ignorance (*avidyā*), and ceases through the realization of the truth that there is nothing like a substantial separate self. Nirvana seemed to Inoue, however, to be emphasized less in Theravada Buddhism than in later Mahayana Buddhism, and he was clearly on the side of the latter.

Yogacara is a psychology in Mahayana Buddhism that divides the mind into eight consciousnesses: the five consciousnesses as five senses, the sixth consciousness as imagination and thinking, the manas-consciousness as the mind attaching to itself, and the store-consciousness (*ālaya-vijñāna*) as the mind in which impressions of earlier experiences are stored, and from which all mental phenomena develop. The manas-consciousness is the very source of all delusions, but only functions by receiving their material called seeds (*bīja*) from the alaya-consciousness. (See Okano's paper in this volume for a complete account.)

Yogacara psychology is considered to be a Buddhist version of depth psychology. The alaya-consciousness is, therefore, sometimes compared with the collective unconscious in Jung's analytical psychology. Yogacara psychology was, however, elaborated in India more than fifteen centuries earlier than psychoanalysis in the West. Further, Freud and his colleagues had only begun to develop their depth psychologies when Inoue, without knowing them, presented the system of Yogacara psychology.

Yogacara psychology's primary concern is to introspectively understand how we fall into delusions and are liberated from them. No wonder that contemporary psychotherapists now look to Yogacara psychology for helpful insights into the mechanism of falling mentally ill, and being healed. Yogacara psychology explains it with a theory of three kinds of existence (*tri-svabhāva*): *paratantra-svabhāva*, *parikalpita-svabhāva*, and *parispanna-svabhāva*. *Paratantra-svabhāva* means the ontological fact that all things occur through dependent origination, *parikalpita* is the psychological fact that suffering comes about through attachment to the view that things are substantial, and *parispanna-svabhāva* refers to the state of kind of being free from *parikalpita-svabhāva* and able to realize *paratantra-svabhāva*.

In *Zen Psychology,* Inoue, going beyond the initial monistic position, adopts an apparently dualistic one, though not in the Western sense. Zen is for him the realization of the true nature of the mind through the arrangement of both mind and body, and calls the true nature of the mind, the Mind Essence (*Shintai*), which is identical with the True Self. This coinage of the Mind Essence seems to derive from the three universals of essence (*ti*), forms (*xiang*), and functions (*yang*) elaborated in a Chinese Buddhist text, *Ta-ch'êng-ch'i-hsin-lun.* Forms and functions are not separate from but aspects of essence.

The relationship of mental phenomena to the Mind Essence is metaphorically expressed by that of waves to water. Just as waves appear on the surface of water agitated by the wind, so do mental phenomena from the Mind Essence stimulated by the outer world. Waves referring to mental phenomena are relative, whereas water referring to the Mind Essence is absolute. So Inoue formulates Zen psychology in a dualistic and metaphysical way. The relationship of mental phenomena to the Mind Essence is, however, for him not abstractly speculated. On the contrary, it is only known at the critical moment at which the mind experiences its death and renewal.

Inoue's system of psychotherapy

In *Psychotherapy* (1904) Inoue coined the word *shinri-ryōhō*, which literally means therapy from the psyche, the original Japanese title of the book, which was to be also the term currently used as the Japanese translation of 'psychotherapy.' His concept of psychotherapy is, however, somewhat different from psychotherapy in the Western sense. He claims it to be based upon Buddhism.

246

Inoue's basic idea in systematizing various therapy methods at the time is the mind–body correlation. They are either body therapy, an approach from body, or psychotherapy, an approach from mind, but these two categories of therapy are not mutually exclusive. On the contrary, they are complementary to each other.

Psychotherapy in Inoue's system is largely divided into natural therapy relying upon spontaneous cure, and faith therapy expecting healing through religious belief and prayer. Psychotherapy is also divided into autotherapy and heterotherapy such as hypnosis. Autotherapy consists of 'faith method,' and observation method. In faith method, the patient is asked to firmly believe that he will recover health someday in the future, either through self-confidence or through the confidence in the Buddha or some other deity. In the observation method, the patient is asked either to realize, practicing some form of meditation, that there is nothing to worry about in his life, or to remove pathogenic ideas and sufferings by travelling or moving somewhere else and seeing new things there.

There are also two types of self-observation method: artificial and natural. While the goal of artificial self-observation method is self-control through self-reflection and satori, natural self-observation makes the patient realize that basic adversaries like sickness and death are beyond human power and is advised not to fight them but to entrust oneself to nature. Masatake Morita (1874–1938), the founder of Morita therapy, seems to be indebted to Inoue's specifically Eastern ides of the natural self-observation method.

Other theoretical elaborations in Buddhist psychology

Though less systematically than Inoue, other Japanese psychologists also attempted to enrich our psychological knowledge beyond Western psychology by elaborating their traditional spirituality of Buddhism. Characteristically, their emphasis is on the difference in the concept of mind between Buddhism and Western psychology. They generally believe that, while Western psychology is either subjectivism or objectivism, Buddhist psychology is neither this nor that but beyond both. Various authors name differently the basic principle of Buddhism: the True Self, Suchness (*tathatā*), the Buddha-nature (*Buddha-dhātu*), Emptiness (*śūnyatā*) and so on. No matter how it is called, it is neither a merely empirical phenomenon nor a metaphysical entity, but embraces and is beyond both. It cannot be grasped with the discriminating intellect but must be experienced directly when the subject and the object are revealed to be one. That is what Motora, based upon the practice of Zen in a temple, wanted to tell the Western audience in his presentation at the 1905 seventh International Conference of Psychology in Rome: 'The Idea of Ego in Eastern Philosophy'.

With his studies of *Kan* (1933, 1938), Ryo Kuroda may have greatly contributed to the development of Buddhist psychology as well as phenomenological psychology. *Kan* refers to the intuition functioning in religious experiences, artistic creations, and crisis management. In his view, the primary concern of Eastern psychology is the description of *jinaishō*, spontaneous inner verification that is the core of psychological experiences in Zen.

Now Rinzai Zen recognizes four types of outlook (Japanese: *shiryōken*): (1) that there is no subject without object; (2) that the entire world is a mere reflection of one's own consciousness; (3) that there is a state in which the subject–object duality is transcended; (4) that ultimately there is no subject and object (Daito Shuppansha 1991: 319). Kuroda characterizes each of these four types respectively as materialist, idealist, parallelist, and Zen Buddhist.

Kuroda distinguished the phenomenal mind called consciousness (*shiki*) from the essential mind called awareness (*kaku*). Satori in his view is the experience of directly pointing to something in the extremely purified form of the latter that is hard to describe in terms of the former.

Tanenari Chiba (1884–1972) is the first Japanese phychologist who, relying upon Yogacara psychology, elaborated the concept of the unconscious. His unique concept of the original consciousness (*koyū-ishiki*) refers to that consciousness in which everything conscious is embraced, present, and lively functioning, from which it emerges, and to which it returns. It is divided into the relative original consciousness as the basis of personal development and the absolute original consciousness as the collective spirit beyond the personal consciousness. The original consciousness is studied by the method of self-observation that is neither empirical nor inductive as in Western science, but rather intuitive. It is in the late 1910s that Chiba began to speak of the original consciousness, and his concept, which comprises the unconscious as well, seems akin to the collective unconscious in Jung, who was his contemporary psychologist in the West.

Empirical studies of Zen meditation

Empirical studies of Zen were initiated by Chijō Iritani (1887–1957). Making use of questionnaires as well as the traditional texts of dharma talks and Zen sayings, he observed the motives for Zen practice, experiences during Zen meditation, concrete strategies for disposing of diversions occurring to the mind during it, the deepening of respiration and becoming aware of the emptiness of both the subject and the object in the state of *samādhi*, individual differences in the depth of Enlightenment, and increase in the differentiation of perceptions after Enlightenment. He also notes psychological benefits of Zen meditation: mental stabilization, non-attachment, increase in will power, and optimism.

Kanae Sakuma (1888–1970) predicted in 1938 that an electroencephalographic study of Zen meditation would reveal the emergence of alpha wave during *samādhi*. More than twenty years later, stimulated by this prediction, Tomio Hirai experimentally verified this prediction, demonstrating that Zen meditation brings about the change of electroencephalogram, therefore consciousness as well. Sakuma himself organized the 1961–2 project 'Medical Psychological Studies of Zen,' the first scientific study of Zen in the world.

Sakuma coined *kichō-ishiki,* the basic consciousness, to describe the state of consciousness to be pursued in meditation and characterized it as quasi-homogeneous duration or quasi-constant flow. For him it is not restricted to Zen but also observed in various forms of meditations practiced in other Buddhist sects, Christian mystical experiences, and artistic creation or appreciation. It is therefore something universal.

Sakuma further pointed out that the functional significance of meditative experience consists in self-control. This kind of self-control is, however, different from the strengthening of the ego as pursued in psychoanalysis. Becoming aware of the true self, or coming back to the original self, provides the basis for the flash of an insight in the midst of difficulties. Sakuma's studies were succeeded by Yoshiharu Akishige, Shōji Nakamura and others, forming a tradition within Japanese psychology.

Applications of Buddhism to psychotherapy

As mentioned earlier, the purpose of Buddhism is liberation from delusions, and so it is very akin to psychotherapy. Though possibly overlapping each other, Buddhism and psychotherapy are, however, not completely the same in the method of removing one's worries. Buddhism, on the one hand, gets rid of them by making a student aware of the truth that there is basically nothing to worry about. In other words, that there is nothing or nobody else but the person in delusion who is making them. Psychotherapy, on the other hand, resolves psychological problems by making a patient realize how they have been and are being produced according to some psychological law. Therefore, Buddhism is expected to learn from psychotherapy much about empirical matters like what is going on in a person's mind and how to handle a therapeutic relationship with the patient, whereas psychotherapy can learn from Buddhism much about essential things like the nature of human being.

Buddhist counseling advocated by Kiyoshi Fujita (1907–88) is an attempt to integrate Buddhism and psychotherapy. In Fujita's view, the Buddha's sermons were akin to counseling practiced in the West, but their specific Buddhist features were very flexible, varying in accordance with whom he spoke and where he was, and that he revealed the illusory nature of apparent problems by making one aware of the attachment to one's perspective. The goal of Gishō Saikōs Buddhist counseling is the development of spiritual awareness which is realized when the subject and the object are experienced as one. In my view, Buddhism, especially Zen, and psychotherapy share the goal of the development of creativity.

There are two psychotherapies that were developed in Japan and are also now known in the West as well: Morita therapy and Naikan therapy. Masatake Morita, the originator of Morita therapy, claims his therapy to be based upon Western medicine. Given the fact that it advises patients to give up the *attachment* to their ideals and to accept things as they are, it seems to be indebted to Buddhism, especially Zen. It is very likely that he was influenced by Inoue's writings as well.

Naikan in Naikan therapy, meaning introspection, derives from *mishirabe*, a method of self-exploration traditionally practiced in the True Pure Land School of Buddhism. Ishin Yoshimoto, practicing *mishirabe,* got Enlightenment, and developed *Naikan-ho*, a method of self-exploration free from its religious background. He lent this title to the book *The Method of Naikan* (1936) by Yū Fuiikawa, a pious believer of the school who also lectured on educational pathology at Toyo University.

Like psychoanalysis, Naikan therapy uses recollection as the fundamental healing agent. But unlike psychoanalysis, it confines what is to be remembered to definite themes in one's relationship so far to one's significant other, who are mostly one's parents and teachers. They are formulated in three questions: 'What good things have they done for me?'; 'What good things have I done for them?'; and 'What troubles have I given them?' In the course of therapy the patient is forced to confront himself with the extraordinary selfishness in his relationship to them, and is overwhelmed by guilt and remorsefulness. Then his attitude will totally change with deep gratitude, realizing that they still love him despite his unworthiness.

Indeed, Naikan therapy emerged from the Japanese, Buddhist, and Confucian cultures, but seems to be universally valid, as is evident from the fact that not a few Westerners have already experienced it. No matter what external environment we may live in, human happiness depends upon our acceptance of it as it is, feeling happy. That is what Naikan therapy makes possible. The trainee observes himself or herself with another's eyes and becomes aware of distortions in perception; by accepting oneself as one is, one gets peace of mind, which enables one to perceive and realize things anew; one is alive here and now.

Finally, I must mention *Psychologia*, a journal in English started and initially edited by Kōji Satō as a medium for international communication between Eastern and Western psychologies. Many important articles relevant to our subject matter were published in this journal in the late 1950s and the 1960s. Satō arranged a series of special editions entitled 'Psychotherapy: East and West' with the themes of psychology and Zen (1959), the unconscious (1960), and the self (1961).

Conclusion

We have so far sketched the history of the relationship between Buddhism and Western psychology in Japan. In concluding my article, we must be careful not to contrast them too schematically, as early modern Japanese Buddhist psychologists did. Buddhism is also concerned with empirical problems and has its own theory of causality, as we see in Yogacara psychology. Western psychology, too, is full of insights into the nature of human life and death that have been cultivated in the Western traditions and religions. So it would be misleading to simply combine Western science and technology with Eastern spirituality. Rather, what seems to be needed is a combination of spiritual approaches, each of which involves a psychological dimension as well. This may be developing already in transpersonal psychology, as well as Buddhist psychology (psychological Buddhism), as we witness the coming together of the East and the West in understanding their shared interests in psychology and spiritual development.

References and further reading

Chiba, T. (1956) *Muisihiki no Shinrigaku*, Tokyo: Kawade-shobo.

Daito Shuppansha (1991) *Japanese–English Buddhist Dictionary*, revised edition, Tokyo: Daito Shuppansha.

Dampada (1993), trans. Thomas Byron, Shambala.

Fromm, E., Suzuki, D. T. and De Martino, R. (1968) *Zen Buddhism and Psychoanalysis*, New York: Colophon Books.

Fujita, K. (1975) 'Bukkyo Kaunseringu', in *Kōza Bukkyō-Shisō*, Vol. 3: *Rnrigaku Kyōi-kugaku, Risosha*.

Hirai, T. (1960) 'Zazen no Nōhateki Kenkyū, *Seisinn Shikeigaku Zasshi* 62: 76–105.

Iritani, C. (1920) *Zen no Shinriteki Kenkyū*, Shinrigaku Kenkyukai.

Inoue, E. (1887) *Shinri Tekiyō*,' Tetsugaku Shoin.

Inoue, E. (1894) *Tōyō Shinrigaku*, Tokyo: Tetsugaku Shoin.

Inoue, E. (1896) *Yōkaigaku Kōgi*, Tokyo: Tetsugaku-kan.

Inoue, E. (1897) *Bukkyō Shinrigaku*, Tokyo: Tetsugaku-kan.

Inoue, E. (1902) *Zenshū no Shinri*, Tokyo: Tetsugaku-kan.

Inoue, E. (1904) *Shinri-ryoho*, Tokyo: Nanko-do.

Kuroda, R. (1933) *Kan no Kenkyū*, Tokyo: Iwanami-shoten.

Kuroda, R. (1938) *Zoku Kan no Kenkyū*: Tokyo: Iwanami-shoten.

Molino, A (1998) *The Couch and the Tree: Dialogues in Buddhism and Psychoanalysis*, New York: North Point Press.

Motora, Y. (1905) *An Essay on Eastern Philosophy: Idea of Ego in Eastern Philosophy*, Leipzig: Voigtlander.

Nishitani, K. (1980) *Religion and Nothingness*, Eastern Buddhist Society.

Onda, A. (1962) 'Zen and Creativity, *Psychologia* 5: 13–20.

Onda, A. (1965) 'Autogenic Training and Zen', in W. Luthe (ed.), *Autogenic Training*, Stuttgart: Georg Thieme Verlag.

Onda, A. (1967) 'Zen, autogenic training and hypnotism', *Psychologia* 10: 133–6.

Onda, A. (1974/75) 'Zen, hypnosis and creativity, *Interpersonal Development* 5: 156–63.

Onda, A. (1986) 'Trends in creativity research in Japan', *Journal of Creative Behaviour* 20: 134–40.

Onda, A. (1992) 'Zen, satori (enlightenment) and creativity', in M. Blows and S. Srinivadan (eds), *Perspectives on Relaxation and Meditation*, Melbourne: Spectrum.

Onda, A, (1993) 'Meditation and Psychotherapy', in M. Blowe (ed), *Proceedings of the Workshop: Towards the Whole Person: Intergrating Eastern and Western Approaches to Body-Mind Skills*, Kenthurst: Linking Publications.

Saikō, G. (1983) 'Kaunseringu to Bukkyō, *Bukkyo Fukushi* 9.

Sakuma, K. (1948) *Shinpiteki Taiken no Kagaku*, Hikarino-shobo.

Shibayama, Z. (1974) *Zen Comments on the Mumonkan*, New York: Harper & Row.

17

COMING HOME

The difference it makes

Enko Else Heynekamp

Introduction

This chapter deals with extensive Zen training and the impact it can have on the practice of psychotherapy. My starting-point was the feeling I had that such training made me work with clients differently than before and the wish to get a better understanding of the way in which these differences manifested themselves. Briefly I can say that Buddhism involves insights, exercises, and rules of life, which can be important for psychotherapists and which can complete, complement, or correct the theory and practice of Western psychotherapy.

The title of this chapter, 'Coming home: the difference it makes,' refers to a common way of pointing to the spiritual path. It is depicted as an inner journey, as coming home to oneself, in order to return to the world afterwards, when one has been changed, to a world that is then perceived differently. One can make this journey on a large scale by actually retiring to a monastery for a longer or shorter period, or on a smaller scale by drawing one's attention back within oneself and following one's breath a few times.

First I'll say something about my background. Next, using vignettes from psychotherapeutic practice, I'll try to clarify the influence that my training in Buddhist meditation and insights has had on this work. Finally, I will offer a short description of Buddhist ethical guidelines.

Training and experience

When I was ordained as a Zen Buddhist nun in 1995, sold my house, and resigned from my job, I had already been working as a psychotherapist for twenty years, more or less full-time. I treated my first few clients during my graduate internship in psychology, where I learned both psychoanalytic psychotherapy and behavior therapy. Afterwards I became a psychoanalyst and I did a three-year course in body-oriented psychotherapy as well.

I started with Zen in the early 1970s, but after three years this faded into the background. It was not until 1990 that I started Zen again, quite serious by this time. I have been training in India, the United States, Germany, and the Netherlands with several teachers and masters, among them the most significant for me being Zen master Gesshin Prabhasadharma Roshi. She founded the International Zen Institute, a school in the Rinzai line of Zen, in which I was ordained as a nun. She died in 1999. My training was continued with her successor, a Dutch woman named Jiun Hogen Roshi from the International Zen Center in the Netherlands. In addition to Zen meditation, I have had some experience with the Tibetan tradition and with mindful awareness meditation.

An empty nest

During my Zen training, which partly took place in a monastery, I did not see any clients for two years. That was quite an experience, and although my days in the monastery were filled up from five o'clock in the morning until ten o'clock in the evening, it could in the beginning probably be best compared with the empty nest syndrome of mothers whose children have left home. Eventually I felt a freedom of inner space not having to sympathize with that much pain, sadness, and anger in others. This was space to experience myself when not working as a therapist. Who are you when you do office work and you have problems when performing the simplest tasks, while you used to have a secretary for twenty years? Who are you when you're ironing the laundry for hours and hours for the third day in a row on a cold floor, when previously you had help? Simple questions for which you find the simple answers in meditation.

Since my monastery time I'm ironing when I'm ironing and when I'm doing therapy I'm doing therapy. That may have been the case earlier also, but at that time, when ironing I never had the feeling that it was my *real* job, it was just something that had to be done. In Zen one learns to *be* one hundred percent what one *does* at that moment, what you do now, here. Now, here I'm drinking a sip of water.

This moment

In this water here the whole universe manifests itself. Someone drew it off the faucet, poured it out and put it down here. The water that is drawn from our dunes here in the Netherlands arrived there from a river flowing down the mountains where it was snowing from clouds that came floating from the sea. It has been cleaned and transported by people who were eating bread baked of grain on which the sun was shining . . . and so on. It maintains my body, disappears into the sewer, and after being filtered, flows to the sea again, evaporates, forms clouds which float to the mountains again and drop the water as rain or snow . . . and so on. Everything comes together in this one sip of water. Not only in the material aspects, but also in the intentions of all who co-operated in making this moment happen. In space, at this spot, everything is coming together, also in time, now. Sea, sky, and mountains are present in it, and the climate of our green planet as well. The past is present in it, and this moment is already carrying the seeds from which the future will germinate. Your past and mine form this moment and everything that our parents and other people we met did, right or wrong, and the way we reacted to that. This moment will never come back in its present form, and it is gone before one can think about it. My drinking this water is already long ago by now. Many of the people who were involved in it have died. The shortness of the moment, with the consequences for the future of what one is doing now, makes it very precious and important. Precious and important enough to be awake, to have full attention for what one is doing right now, whether one is eating or drinking, housekeeping, watching TV, or talking with a client.

The realization of this makes one grateful for everything that happened in one's life, even for the unpleasant things. I remember how intensely grateful I was – on a particular moment in my first four-day retreat – for the most awful thing that ever happened to me, even to the one who did it, because without that event I would not have been sitting now here on my cushion, so I thought, and I would never have wanted to miss this very moment. Afterwards it surprised me: how is it possible to be grateful to someone for the harm he caused? But it was possible, evidently, and later the surprise disappeared and it became a common experience: to be grateful for everything, good or bad, pleasant or unpleasant which, by the way, does not mean that one shouldn't set limits sometimes or should accept everything.

A new nest

By now I have clients again, although not as many as before, because I cannot work long hours because of health problems, and because I teach courses in Zen meditation as well. I experience the therapeutic work differently now, having been away for two years, although the difference is difficult to describe. In so far as it appealed to motherliness or sometimes to fatherliness previously, I feel more like a grandparent now. Grandparents often enjoy their grandchildren more than they once did their children, because the upbringing of the children required so much of them. It was a duty, being parents they had to do it well, and the children should live up to their expectations. With grandchildren, they don't have to worry about these things, and they can just be with the children, at the same time having enough experience of life to help them when needed. With my new clients I feel a closer bond, which doesn't interfere with the necessary therapeutic distance.

Primarily, I attribute this to my ability to experience directly what is connecting us as people, how we are the same in our deeper layers, besides role, age, and status. We long for esteem and love, we grow up, find friends and lovers, generate something or someone or leave other traces, we lose our loved ones, get old and sick, and die. Our deepest fears and longings are the same. We drink the same water, it is the same sun that gives us warmth. Rain and sun do not discriminate.

Secondarily, the new closeness may result from a different form of trust both in myself and in the other and in the therapeutic process. It is a reliance on that deeper layer I called home, a home we all share and from which the natural life cycle springs. Something arises from it, grows, and develops until a maximum is reached and then decreases and ceases to exist. As the sun is shining behind the clouds always, in the same way I know this deep layer is there all the time, even when hiding behind ever so much resistance.

Finally I attribute the change to having improved my acceptance of any situation as it is here and now, however miserable sometimes. The idea that it should have been different or at least should become different as soon as possible – since the therapist has to settle it, and the client expects that after all – has lost its deluding grip. Everything is exactly the way it is now. It changes continuously, of itself. Do I, as a therapist to myself, dare to admit this fully? That would reduce the resistance to the therapeutic process considerably. If the therapist dares, the client often dares too. If the therapist is defensive about a subject, she gives the client the message that she is afraid herself and that in fact it could be dangerous to confront it. Both can avoid this situation this way.

I don't mean to say that I didn't learn a few important aspects of the things I mentioned before – like having to be attentive, trusting and open – in the psychoanalytic education, or in the behavior therapy course, or in the education for body-oriented psychotherapy. But it was only in Zen that I learned to apply them with real consistency. It was not until the intensive training in the monastery, in particular, for which I had renounced my old life altogether, that my experience went down to the foundation. If I had not given up everything for this, probably I would have used the escape 'that this wasn't my real life, and that I would return.' There was no return. Now I know there is never a return. There is only now. If you're standing on a cold floor for a long time, your feet will get cold. That is all. The lessons were very practical.

Impact on therapeutic practice

As the way I experience the therapeutic relationship has changed, my attitude has changed as well. Now I want to make my point here more specific: Zen training has had the effect of coming to the point soon and being able to keep it, being able to see through transference and countertransference, not sticking to the past unnecessarily. Moreover, I notice a tendency to give more attention than before to what is going well in a client's life and to empathize not only with sadness but with happiness as well.

Happiness

Karlijn begins the session with the statement that she has no money for the treatment of her alcohol problem for which I have referred her. She has a good job and I know her as someone who wastes money and has already skipped some of the few therapy sessions with me for which her insurance company is paying. So I'm not very impressed. 'We have a problem,' she says, emphasizing *we*. I can't help laughing and say: 'We? I've no problem, you have one.' 'I've to manage all by myself,' she tries again. 'I can't help you,' I say. She keeps quiet for a moment, then continues: 'I'm quite well.' She has a new lover, is very happy and isn't drinking more than two glasses of wine a day. It appears to be a new experience for her not to get a good scolding, she's beaming. We find something with which I can help her for the few remaining sessions: she wants to learn to be more assertive towards her ex-husband.

Of course I couldn't foresee the striking break which took place in this session. Suddenly she changed from a complaining, helpless victim of the circumstances into a shining beautiful woman in love. What was happening exactly at that moment? What was it that gave us the space for this surprising change of atmosphere? I want to approach this question by considering the state of concentration of the therapist, which is called 'free floating attention' in psychoanalysis. This is somewhat similar to the mindful awareness training in Zen meditation.

Meditative attention

Meditation is one of the aspects of the Buddhist way, besides insight, or wisdom, and ethical guidelines. There are different forms of meditative practice, but I'll talk about mindful awareness in particular.

Mindful awareness

This is the awareness of whatever happens within and around us. In Zen it involves following the breath, experiencing body posture and movement, registering feelings and thoughts. Handling one's teacup carefully or noticing that someone getting off a train needs help, are forms of mindful awareness too. It's striking that being present mindfully, without judging, without focusing on a specific object, either focusing on oneself or something neutral, is not being taught in psychotherapy education as a skill, as far as I know. Apparently, therapists are assumed to be able to do this already, without training, even in such a complicated situation as a relationship with a fellow human being. Why not first practice it somewhat? Since this mindful awareness may be the most important instrument of the psychotherapist, I want to pay special attention to it. How can we train it and can we find out more about it?

Exercise

By studying how mindful awareness is developed, we might get a clearer picture of what is meant by this concept. When one is starting to learn meditation, watching or counting the breath is one of the first few exercises. In this exercise we continue following the breath scrupulously and we count each time, we breath out, up to ten and then we start again with one. As soon as we notice that our mind is occupied with something else, we resume counting our breath. An untrained mind is unable to follow ten breathings without being distracted. The mind jumps from one subject to another.

One notices: 'Hey, I've strayed off, hey, I'm thinking of something else.' So a part of our consciousness was alert, seeing what happened, neutrally, without any judgment, just 'hey.' Afterwards judgments may appear, such as: 'I'm not doing my exercise well, I have to pay attention.' But at first it's just awareness. When judgments come the moment of 'hey' is gone already. The judgment 'I'm not doing my exercise well' is a thought, which is followed by 'hey,' and then resuming counting the breath.

After much training this 'hey,' this mindfulness, the alertness itself is going to remain present in everything one does, redundant thoughts becoming rarer. In the beginning it is like observing oneself as if there were an observer and an I, but in the long run one discovers that there are not two, and there never were. The sense that there are two, one breathing and one observing the breath, is an artifact of the dualistic mind. There is no 'I' separated from 'my breath.' There is only attention. Attention and breath, these two also seem to be one, streaming, with the center in one's body, most of the time in the belly and sometimes in the stomach or heart region. This experience of not being divided, of oneness, which comes usually only after much practice, we call deep concentration or stillness. This is the spiritual home, the silent spot in each of us, which will not be affected by whatever event or emotion. It is present always. To keep in touch with it, also when I am busy in the outside world, is the object of my training. This creates a different atmosphere in my therapy so that my clients learn to experience and apply a little bit of it too.

After having practiced a lot, one can register what is happening in one's mind and in the environment without losing this basic concentration. You may think, 'I can do this anyhow,' but it's only when you do such a breathing exercise that you notice how many distracting thoughts are developing. And these will be there when practicing psychotherapy as well. 'Am I a good therapist?' 'What would my supervisor think of this?' 'What a pity to be indoors now that the weather is so nice.' 'In fact, I find this a difficult client, I would rather not treat him, but I shouldn't think this way,' and so on.

Back to Karlijn

With this mindful awareness I approach Karlijn's opening of the therapy session and monitor not only what she says, but my own thoughts and feelings as well. I spot the contrast between what she is saying and the feeling she evokes in me. She has no money, she says, for a counseling contact for her use of alcohol. And I think: 'It won't be so bad, if you really should want it, you could do it' and also I'm aware of my feelings, there is some mockery in it, something unkind. I think: 'This is an unkind thought.' And I wait. Karlijn then comes with her: '*We* have a problem' and I laugh: 'I don't have one.' As for the words, they could have been blunt and it could have been a mocking laugh, but it wasn't, it was gentle. Karlijn provokes misery and from my slightly ironic thought I notice she's doing so in the transference now and I stay alert, I don't let myself be distracted or provoked.

Her second and third trials to find out if I intend to provide her with the misery she expects – her 'We have a problem' and 'I've to manage it all by myself' – don't arouse any unkind feelings or ironic thoughts in me anymore. My 'I can't help you' means with the alcohol problem, with money, but maybe also 'I can't take notice of this provocation.' And indirectly this remark also suggests that it is possible that one has to manage something all by oneself, that this need not be avoided. It's a paradox of course: I support you even if I can't help and you have to manage 'all by yourself'. Maybe I sensed that what she tells me in these first few statements isn't an issue for her now on a feeling level. That she's provoking and testing is an interpretation afterwards; at that moment itself I wasn't aware of being busy with it.

Later it turns out that she hadn't been drinking excessively in the past few weeks and that she spent much time with her new lover, who helped her to solve her problems. So at this moment she is not that alone. But I did not know that yet in the situation described and I didn't have to know it either, I just had to be open and attentive, the rest comes of itself. After the third time she tested me, she considers the situation safe enough to come forward with what's on her mind really: she is in love and very happy. That's a possibility also, life doesn't have to be always miserable.

Insight into the interwovenness and variability of all things

Insight, or wisdom, is a second facet of the Buddhist way. Wisdom is insight into the nature of reality itself. Everything in our world is in continuous movement: it arises, changes, flows, and decays. Usually this is called 'impermanence.' I call it variability, which sounds to me more neutral and more precise: everything arises and falls apart. Everything is connected with everything else, is interwoven with everything. I call it interwovenness. I illustrated this earlier with the glass of water. Buddha found out that if we resist this interwovenness and variability and cling to one thing and reject another, then our openness gets lost and we create a fake or delusional world and suffering.

Variability, relationships

Louis comes to ask for therapy because he is not able to have a relationship with a mate after a few disappointments in this area. Exploration of this problem tells us that he doesn't want to run the risk of having to endure that much pain and sorrow again.

Previously I would have been inclined to work from the unspoken viewpoint that the fact that something fails a few times does not necessarily mean that it will fail again, and that in principle, it is possible to engage in a relationship that doesn't break down. I could have said: 'So because you're afraid to lose the other again and you would have to endure that sadness once more, you had rather not start it again,' by which I would implicitly reinforce the illusion that the fairy-tale could end with: 'And they lived happily ever after.' Now I might say the same, but with an occasional remark like: 'It's seldom that partners die at the same time, one of the two will have to miss the other.' Paradoxically this works as a relief, although one affirms the anxiety of the client. The illusion, the fairy-tale, doesn't have to be held true against better judgment. If therapists go along with the illusion of a never-ending relationship, they give the message that the impermanence is unbearable and that you can only engage in a relationship if there is at least a chance that it will last. My statement shows that it is possible to live with the knowledge that this chance is zero, and that the point is rather to use the time given together, that this can be quite liberating.

What I said here is just a basic attitude, which will not resolve neurotic trouble. Adequate therapeutic techniques remain necessary to achieve that.

Variability, emotions

Not only our lives and relationships but also our emotions are variable. An emotion arises, comes to a high, decreases, and disappears. People tend to be afraid of dealing with their stored-up sadness. They're afraid that they'll never stop crying, afraid that the pain never ends. And although it is true that there is sadness that will never heal completely and that some memories remain painful, one can also witness change in one's pain. A crying fit never takes a very long time. Even on the darkest days there may be lighter moments, moments when the sadness is forgotten for a short time. Where is your sadness if you don't think of it? If you don't feel it? Are you a sad person or are you someone who is sometimes sad and sometimes joyful or happy or angry or fearful or glad?

The past

My Zen training taught me not to hold on to the past unnecessarily. Psychoanalysts are very good at producing hypotheses about the origin of symptoms. Sometimes, this may serve to protect us from experiencing existential abysses. After having become familiar with descents into the abysses – there is no bottom, so you can't get hurt, just jump – I reduced the activity of seeking the origin of symptoms; psychotherapy practice was made more efficient by that. In so far as exploration of the origin is necessary to comprehend the trouble in the present, that makes sense. And yet to talk about the past in order to avoid dealing with the insecurities in the here and now, is a defense that it seems better to abandon.

Transference and countertransference

When we do not direct our attention to the past too emphatically, the foundation in the here and now of the real relationship we have with the other becomes firmer and livelier.

> When *Marian* arrives from the waiting room, it occurs to me that there is a reddish glow on her long dark hair and that it is a bit shorter than I thought it was. It's already in the beginning of the interview that I get a special feeling behind my eyes. Questions come up: 'Could it have to do with sadness? If so, where does it come from?' With these questions at the back of my mind I continue listening and waiting to see if the answers will emerge from her story more or less by themselves. I wait, part of my awareness being with my breath in the belly and at the same time I continue talking with her. She feels so insecure, she tells me, and is ashamed of the quarrels between her parents. She cries. She says her father would never say something nice to her mother when she had been to the hairdresser. Immediately the thought pops up that, not yet consciously, she may be disappointed that I didn't say anything about her new hairdo and that this evokes the sadness from her youth again. I continue listening attentively.

Only when her story would become superficial or when she would relapse into repetitions, would it be necessary for the transference to be brought up, but this did not happen. Afterwards this session appeared to have been a turning point in her therapy, until then she was always hiding her insecurity and shame behind quite a lot of verbal aggression, as in the transference. We talked about that in her recent session, when I interpreted the negative transference in order to maintain the therapeutic alliance.

Gaining insight into variability and interwovenness, one learns not to cling to all sorts of concepts and theories. A concept never becomes reality. In a therapy session this means one flows with the stream of developments which occurs in the transference and countertransference constellation. The here and now of the relationship of the therapeutic partners is immediately present in the experience. To be open to this, feeling what happens, staying attentive to it and looking how the feeling develops, are the first tasks at hand. Every attempt to control the situation by trying to discover if it is either transference or countertransference or who's sadness it is after all, would interfere with the openness of the attention and with that the possibility of the client's story unfolding itself. If one is aware and does not cling to concepts, one sees the suchness of the situation directly, without thinking whether it is this or that, mine or yours, good or bad. It is what it is and nothing more. In the example of Marian it was a feeling of wetness behind the eyes. This feeling – generally the most important information – was already there before the story.

Psychoanalytic concepts and theories can be very helpful to understand the therapeutic process, but during the session in particular it is important to insure that thinking doesn't take the place of direct experiencing, functioning as a defense against it.

Ethical guidelines

The main obstacles to realizing such meditative awareness and insights are addressed in a number of rules of life, called Precepts, which someone going the Buddhist way will follow. This is the third important facet of Buddhist training. In brief summary, one vows to treat others, their possessions, and their philosophy of life, with respect. Buddhism sees immoral behavior as revealing a lack of insight which is caused by ignorance, attachment to self, desire, and hatred. These guidelines are not intended as judgment, but as a means to become awakened. When we have to take action against someone, for example in case of transgressing our boundaries, it is not done mainly to protect ourselves, but in particular to protect the other from actions with harmful consequences. It's not good for anyone – oneself or another – to commit harmful deeds.

When I had an unkind thought about Karlijn in the first vignette, I was able to drop it immediately, because of my training in 'coming home.' I do this not so much because these are considered 'bad thoughts,' but rather because they would make me unable to see clearly if I didn't. If I wouldn't have been aware *and* got rid of it, it would have disturbed my attentiveness. If I should have to reproach myself for it, I would have been distracted. Or I could have justified it by ascribing it partly to her, for example when I would have been thinking that she makes me feel this way, implying that this is wrong. She would sense it, having to defend herself and so on. In either case much precious time would have been lost, and unnecessary suffering would have been created. A common third way out, when painful feelings arise in the therapist, is to blame third parties, for example parents. This is a distraction also. The only thing needed is to put it to rest, remaining concentrated, in contact with one's breath, and following the flow of events, not sticking to anything, pleasant or unpleasant, good or bad.

Most clients will sense how the therapist reacts to what they are talking about. So an attitude of respect and attention for all human beings, animals, material things, and the environment, of non-violence, of openness to different religions and living styles, all merge into the therapy practice indirectly. The lack of it also. Fortunately our clients are willing to affirm this sometimes.

Conclusion

Using some therapy vignettes I tried to clarify the impact of my Zen training on the psychotherapeutic work I am doing. Meditation, Buddhist insights and rules of life – all facets of this spiritual way – can give new openness to the psychotherapeutic process.

I have given special focus to mindful awareness for psychotherapists. This undivided attention to what takes place in themselves and their clients appears to be a means of approaching Freud's ideal of an open therapeutic attitude.

Buddhist insights, into the variability and the interwovenness of the reality in which we participate, enhance psychotherapy, because clinging to ideas of invariability and separateness – by the therapist in particular – is often a resistance to an open and flowing therapeutic process.

Summarizing I can say that as a result of my Buddhist training, I would encourage psychotherapists to practice with meditation, particularly with mindful awareness, which will enable them to:

- dare more to rely on the therapeutic process and the direct contact with the client
- come to the point soon and remain there
- recognize one's own feelings at the moment they arise and quickly see through the transference and countertransference
- tend more effectively to give space to and empathize with what goes well and is good.

In short, mindfulness has a healing effect and can become a psychotherapeutic instrument that can be trained very well by meditation and the other facets of the Buddhist Way.

AUTHOR INDEX

Abe, M. 5, 32, 90, 180
Akishige, Y. 249
Alexander the Great 3, 123
Alonso, A. 81, 82
American Institute of Psychoanalysis 84
Anbeek, C. W. 187–204
Aristotle 25, 145, 178
Asanga 224–5
Ashoka 123
Assagioli, R. 217
Atwood, G. E. 86

Balsam, A. 41–2, 43
Basch 89
Basilides 126–7
Batchelor, S. 20
Becker, G. 152
Berger, B. 18
Berger, P. 18
Bergson, H. 59
Bettelheim, B. 137
Bion, W. 101
Boucher, S. 158
Bowlby, J. 216
Brandchaft, B. 86
Brazier, D. 103, 152, 153, 154, 155, 156, 163, 164, 165, 175
Brown, D. 152, 161
Buddha 190, 209, 249, 130–1, 37–8, 72, 96, 235–40
see also Shakyamuni
Buddhaghosa 176
Burtt, E. A. 43
Buswell, R. E. 189

Cassell 208
Charet, F. X. 126
Chiba, T. 248

Chogyam Trungpa Rimpoche 220
Christensen, A. 156
Clarke, J. J. 122, 131
Cohen, A. 161, 164
Coltart 166
Coltart, N. 94, 96–7
Compton, W. 152
Conze, E. 127
Cooper, P. A. 156, 160, 163, 164, 165, 166
Coward, H. 122, 128, 130
Csikszentmihalyi, M. 72

Daito Shuppansha 248
Dalai Lama (Tenzin Gyatso) 96
Darwin, C. 70
Dawson 8
de Groot, P. A. 187–204
de Lube 127
de Silva, P. 181
Deatherage, D. 157, 163, 166, 167
Deikman, A. J. 152, 153, 154, 156, 157, 159, 160, 164, 165, 166
DeMartino 131
DeMartino, R. 36, 149
DeMartino, R. J. 94
Descartes, R. 136, 138
Dharmapala 242
Dharmasiri, G. 73
Dogen 11, 75, 83, 87–8, 94, 182, 196
Dubin, W. 163, 166
Dubs, G. 150, 152, 167

Edinger, E. 208
Eigen, M. 93
Eliade, M. 49
Ellis, A. 167
Engler, J. 152, 153, 156, 157, 159, 160, 161, 162, 163, 164

SUBJECT INDEX

Note: page numbers in *italics* refer to diagrams.

Abhidharma 245
acceptance 198–9, 200, 202
active imagination 211, 217, 220
alaya-consciousness 229–30, 231, 233,
    234, 245–6; *see also* foundational
    consciousness
alone, capacity to be 88–9, 90, 154
alter ego 52
American Buddhism 10, 19–20, 69; *see
    also* American Zen Buddhism
American Zen Buddhism: of Asian
    American descent 150, 151; Elite 151;
    Ethnic 150–1; of European American
    descent 150, 151; Evangelical 151;
    integration with psychotherapy 162–7;
    meditation 151–67; native-born
    converts 151; new-wave Asian 151;
    old-line Asian 151; origins 149–50;
    practitioners 150–2; prevalence 150;
    and psychotherapy 149–67; typologies
    150–1
Americans, Kyoto conference 1, 2, 4, 5, 6
analytical psychology 8–9, 122, 177, 213,
    221; *see also* depth psychology;
    Jungian psychology
anger, keeping in check 97–8
anima/animus 54
anthropocentrism 61
anxiety: reduction 152–3; regarding
    death 115
archetypal theory 215–16
archetypes 53–6, 73–4, 142, 215, 233; *see
    also specific archetypes*
at-one-ness 90
atman 116–17
attachment theory 216

attention: non-judgemental 153, 154,
    155, 181; of the therapist 75, 82, 85,
    155, 180–1, 256–8, 262; wholehearted
    84–6
attitudes, to suffering 115
autism 217
autotherapy 247
awakening 34–41, 43–4, 176, 236–7, 240,
    245; *see also* enlightenment
'awareness of twoness' 216, 217

bare attention 75; *see also* attention; of
    the therapist
behavioural dysregulation 197
being-in-the-soul 26
being-in-the-world 22, 23, 26
being-*sive*-not-being 194, 195, 202
Belgium 1
belief 24–5
Big Self 208
biological determinism 68, 70–1
Bodhisattva 36, 40
borderline personality disorder (BPD)
    196–7, 199
breathing techniques 257
Buddha (as state) 38, 39, 43, 176, 233,
    234, 236, 237, 240
Buddha (Gotama Buddha/Shakyamuni)
    33, 37–8, 40, 43, 72, 96, 130–1, 190,
    209, 235–40, 249, 259
Buddhism: alleviation of suffering
    through 4, 6–7, 9, 17, 67–9, 71–3, 75,
    77–9, 175–6, 225–6, 235, 237–40;
    American 10, 19–20, 69; and
    analytical psychology 122, 213;
    awakening of the self 34, 35, 36,

37–41, 43–4; Chinese 10, 174; and
Christianity 45, 46–50, 56–63, 123;
Consciousness-only School 224–34;
and creativity 242, 249; cultural
specificity of 9–10; differentiation
from psychoanalysis 94–104;
differentiation from psychotherapy
187, 188–9, 200–1, 202–3; *dukkha* 31,
32–3, 34, 38, 40, 42, 43; early 235, 237;
East–West crisis in the study of 20;
fundamental subjectivity 33–4, 35;
and Gnosticism 127; 'I' 135–48;
Indian 9–10, 173, 174, 176, 177,
224–5, 232–3; integration with
dialectical behaviour therapy 187;
integration with psychoanalysis
97–103; introduction to the West 3,
123; and Jung 45, 46–50, 56–63,
122–33; locating 172–84; meaning
systems 188–9; mindfulness 100–2;
no-self 96; origins 18–19; philosophy
of mind 235–41; and psychoanalysis
4, 40, 68, 83–6, 93–104, 111–12,
242–3; and psychology 173, 175–84,
242–51; psychotherapeutic aspects 17,
176–7, 178–81, 249–50; and
psychotherapy 1, 3–4, 6–9, 12, 15–17,
15, 27–8, 41–3, 187–203, 249–50; and
science 244–5; and the self 30–44,
94–5, 96–8, 221; Shingon 174;
similarities to psychoanalysis 93–4;
similarities to psychotherapy 187,
202–3; sociopathological interest of
the West in 19; subjectivity 94, 96;
symbolism 126; Theravada 245;
Tibetan 127, 129; transmission 3, 9;
Vajrayana 174; in the West 19–20;
Western attitudes to 15–16, *15*; and
Western religions 24–5; 'working
through' experiences 98–9; as world
religion 23; world view 60; Yogacara
School 173, 177, 224–5, 227–34,
245–6, 248, 251; *see also* American
Zen Buddhism; Japanese Buddhism;
Mahayana Buddhism; Zen Buddhism
Buddhist counseling 249
Buddhist path 187, 189–90, 191–6, 200–3

'capacity to be alone' 88–9, 90, 154
Catholicism 173
causation 145, 226
change 198–9, 200, 202
Chicago World Fair, 1893 149

child development 88–9
Chinese tradition 10, 129–30, 174
Christianity: and Buddhism 9, 45,
46–50, 56–63, 123; and Jung 45,
46–50, 47, 56–63, 123, 128;
psychoanalysis as substitute for 126;
spiritual failure 11; as world religion
23; world view 60; *see also*
Catholicism; Protestantism
Clark Lectures 209
classical Jungian theory 207, 220
closure 214–16, 220
cognitive dysregulation 197
collective conscious 50–1
collective psychological matrix 88
collective unconscious 50–1, 55–6, 59,
74, 112–13; and the Consciousness-
only School 233; liberation from 116,
132–3; *see also* archetypes
'comparative model' of dialogue 48–9
compassion 77, 79, 125
complexes 72–4, 207–9, 211–19; *see also*
specific complexes
confusion 194
consciousness 51–8, 117; center of 52,
54, 55; collective 50–1; development
113; dissociation from the
unconscious 128; ego-consciousness
52, 53, 57, 58–9, 128, 139, 147;
emptying 143; evolution 60–1; higher
56–8, 59; I-consciousness 113–14;
'lower' 146–7; need for an Eastern
definition 59; original 248; of the self
113–14, 192; and the unconscious 113,
128, 180; *see also* collective
unconscious; 'eight consciousnesses';
unconscious
Consciousness-only School 224–34;
basic tenets 225; eight consciousnesses
and four wisdoms 229–30; founders
224–5; and Jungian psychology 224,
233–4; non-self 232–3; perceptual
patterns 227–8; six kinds of practice
231–2; theory of five stages 230–1;
vexing passions 227, 228, 229–30
construction/reconstruction 100
containment 85–6, 88
conversion, mutual 49
core complexes 211; *see also* complexes
core mindfulness skills 198–200; 'how'
skills 199–200; 'what' skills 199
correlativity 237
cosmos 22–3